D1329933

World Perspectives in Education

SIR GEORGE WILLIAMS UNIVERSITY LIBRARY

WORLD PERSPECTIVES
IN
EDUCATION

Edmund J. King

THE **BOBBS-MERRILL** COMPANY, INC.
A SUBSIDIARY OF HOWARD W. SAMS & CO., INC.
Publishers • INDIANAPOLIS • NEW YORK

First published in 1962
© 1962 by The Bobbs-Merrill Company Inc.
Printed in Great Britain
Library of Congress Catalog Card Number: 69–12191

Contents

PREFACE   *page* 11

Section I: Introductory

1 HOW DO WE UNDERSTAND?   21

An explanation of the approach used in this book. The process of learning as one of synthesizing complementary views. The relevance of this to Comparative Education. Understanding ourselves.

2 FROM CURIOSITY TO COMPLEMENT   32

The need for a cross-cultural examination of educational, social, and technological problems. Examples from Britain, East Africa, the U.S.A., U.S.S.R., &c. of differing approaches to the basic problems of education, and different orders of priority. The need to bear other views than our own in mind when planning progress in the contracting world of the later twentieth century. The relativity of civilizations. The relevance and complementariness of all.

Section II: The Social Context

3 WHO IS EDUCATED?   53

Different answers given to this question. Idiosyncrasies of interpretation, of criteria, and prestige. Different questions as the basis of these divergencies. The need for re-appraisal of the whole concept of education and 'culture'. Our dependence on institutions. The development of subcultures, élites, and cultural ghettoes. The close link between school systems and governmental or industrial needs in the past. New opportunities for shared culture and co-ordinated perceptions. The necessity for these things within countries and internationally.

4 THE PRICE OF PROGRESS   74

Education not a quiet oasis. The cost in terms of children's and teachers' time. Financial expense. Clash with social values (Italy, U.S.A., India, Puerto Rico, Jamaica). Education beyond the state of readiness; out-of-touch or 'corrupting' schooling. Changes in the social context of the teaching profession. Schools as stepping-stones; as investments; as instruments of social change. Links with the status of women and labourers. The craving for industrialization and urbanization. Technical and political advance demand total change and total encouragement. The school as the nucleus of this evolution.

5 CULTURE CONFLICTS   97

Divided loyalties and emotional conflicts. Family tension arising from cultural change. Inconsistencies surviving a revolution or social change (France, U.S.S.R., U.K., continental Europe, U.S.A.). The compensation for upheavals afforded by alternative educational influences in older countries of the West. Deep cultural chasms in Japan, China, Central America, Philippines. The pervasive influence of Western contacts, partly repudiated by impatient new cultures. The anxieties of 'conversion', as in India, Turkey, N. and Central Africa. The suspicion of even peripheral innovations. Reaction. The need for a continual welcome to the modern world, and for a viable future. Failure means demoralization and hostility. Cultural breakdown in a world context.

Section III: The Effect on Schools

6 THE IMPACT OF TECHNOLOGICAL CHANGE   117

Long-standing assumptions about links between vocation, school, and personal qualities. Continental liberal education. The English gentleman. Strata and occupational specialization. 'Automatically ennobling' studies and careers? Devices of exclusion, and the worship of shibboleths. The ambitions of parents and *nouveaux riches*—in conflict with their expanding interests. The interests of businessmen and industrialists demanding and supporting education. (Brazilian S.E.N.A.I. and British 'sandwich' courses. Continental developments.) The demand for technicians. The greatly expanding horizon of industrial training and personal opportunity. What form should extended schooling take? Vocational linkage increasing in many countries. The challenge of this to 'liberal' exclusiveness. The need for continued opportunities to learn and re-appraise throughout adult life. The relative diminution of day-schools' status and of teachers' authority. Difficulties in the last years at school.

7 SELECTION AND DIFFERENTIATION 137

Are some people naturally inferior or superior? Do they find the 'right level', given opportunity? Is selection evil as such? Tests to maintain the *status quo*; tests to permit slow expansion; tests of fitness for new jobs and categories. Testing becomes holy. Testing superseded by different types of 'orientation period'. Examples of this and of comprehensive schools from Sweden, U.S.A., England, Italy. The postponing of selection because of employers' new requirements. The influence of prestige schools and universities on specialization. The advantages and disadvantages of teen-age selection. Examples of U.S.A., U.S.S.R., Japan. Can functional selectivity be reconciled with equality of consideration?

8 FURTHER AND HIGHER EDUCATION 169

Further to what? Adaptation, supplementation, or transformation? Light thrown on juveniles' schooling by experiments and opportunities in further education. Education according to experience and maturity. Social and occupational evolution. 'The hidden persuaders'. Overlap between one country's schools and another's 'further education'. 'Further' or 'higher' education? The need for careful analysis. Examples from U.K., U.S.A., U.S.S.R., Austria, Italy, Denmark. A permanent selection at 'eighteen plus' – or flexible futures? The breakdown of discrimination by social change and by the unpredictable demands of modern states. The topicality and directness of further education. The guardianship of developing institutions during rapid expansion by older and 'respectable' colleges. The increasing participation of all governments in higher education. Technological alternatives to universities. Different patterns of student careers. Adult education.

9 TEACHERS AND THEIR RECRUITMENT 200

Many different ideas of the function and status of teachers. Is no one willing to teach? The links between religion and the teaching profession. Do teachers submit to orthodoxy or do they evoke?

The new-style teacher is not obtainable on the old terms. Do teachers transmit culture? How are they linked with universities, for example? The social origins, schooling, and prospects of teachers in many countries. (Examples given.) Alternative openings for teachers. Teacher-substitutes. The needs of new types of schools and learning relationships. Different strata of teachers. Teaching and marriage. Bridges for teachers. Graduate teachers. The evolution of teacher training in the U.S.S.R. The teaching career as an education in itself.

Section IV: The Study of Education as a Personal and Social Leaven

10 IDEOLOGIES AND SYSTEMS OF CONTROL　　　　231

The concept of ideology in relation to teaching. People 'living in different worlds'. 'World views' and personal commitment. Is indifference possible without disaster? The 'Third Way' of democracy. Education for orthodoxy under religious dispensations and in the U.S.S.R. The Protestant conscience and education. Self-expression and self-determination. The deliberate building of modern school systems: France, Japan. Religion and school in the U.S.A., New Zealand, Canada, Scandinavia, Holland, Britain. Neutralism and secularism. The 'automatic' development of centralization. 'Streamlining' and economy as temptations to under-developed countries. Controls over government interests in education. The pressure of population and of educational demand. Total planning in new countries or in circumstances of rapid change. The social and personal responsibility of the teacher in relation to ideology.

11 PHILOSOPHY, PSYCHOLOGY, AND PROGRAMMES　　　257

Marx's claim that philosophy should change the world. The dependence of philosophy and psychology on context – no complete 'detachment' possible. Thinking in terms of programmes. The need for teachers and administrators to see principles behind practice. Western ideas about personality and philosophy are not universal. The main families of philosophy affecting Western education: (*a*) supernaturalism, rationalism, and paternalism; (*b*) empiricism, pragmatism, humanism, and existentialism; (*c*)

Marxism and Idealism. The embodiment of these theories in practice. The possibility of good programmes with questionable
philosophy, and vice versa. The importance of 'welcoming' programmes to the development of an evolutionary attitude. The role
of the teacher and of adolescents.

Section V: Teachers in a World of Change

12 SOCIAL AND FAMILY CHANGE   287

Is the school's commitment limited? Is school abnegated by what
follows or surrounds it? Problems of being long in school.
'Discipline' and what it means. The youth problem. The breaking
of old norms and the evolution of new. The expanding horizons
of the adolescent. His publicity value and commercial importance.
Do we provide enough opportunities for self-fulfilment, imagination, and co-operation? What is responsibility? The self-organiza-
tion of youth. The blending of personal development and professional education. Courtship, marriage prospects, and their
effects on schooling. Western social influences in India, China, &c.
The problem of the future genius. Can we open up the world to
the creativeness of youth?

13 BARRIERS IN EDUCATION   310

The barriers imposed on our thinking. The complementariness of
views. The risk of believing in 'privileged access'. Natural barriers,
e.g. language. Multilingualism. The links between language and
culture, or religion, or politics, or social class. Problems of dialect.
The problem of scripts and literacy. The notion of national character, and its influence. The consequences of slavery. The impact
of technology on some of these difficulties. The role of the teacher
and the school in breaking down barriers, and in building up
understanding and co-operation.

14 UNDERSTANDING OUR WORLD   337

Public education as a new and still incompletely tried technique.
Some mistakes of our earlier phases, especially in countries with
elaborate educational systems. The need for a world perspective.
The difference between this and communist 'universal ideology'.
The importance of a vastly extended and improved educational
commitment at home and abroad. Everyone's education is to the

advantage of everyone else – and his 'world perspective' is part of total understanding. The atrophy of essential 'world views' in various countries. Are we helped or misled by the way we speak of 'standards'? The importance of comparative study – in context. The practical applicability of Comparative Education. Education for international understanding. The importance of not having the Western way of life written off as irrelevant because of poor understanding and poor communication. Pitfalls in international comparisons. Three distinct levels of Comparative Education as a basis for world-wide understanding. The need for a constant comparison and assaying of views and practices within each country and internationally. The part of the teacher as the sponsor of civilization. The personally educative value of this experience.

APPENDIX: 'THE GENTLEMAN'   360

BIBLIOGRAPHY   369

INDEX   373

Preface

This book is primarily intended for students in colleges and departments of Education, and for teachers; but it is also addressed to all those concerned with the effects on society of today's accelerating transformation of technology and human relationships.

We are on the threshold of the second and more important stage of the Industrial Revolution – the phase of its social implementation. This will obviously be marked by two things: a much more systematic development of all technological skills and resources in all countries; and the application of new abundance and opportunities to improving the condition of most of mankind. Understandably, every country begins this endeavour at home. The degree of alertness and the amount of achievement vary greatly from place to place; but as the pace accelerates so does progress become more nearly universal. It pushes into forgotten places and bursts into inviolate preserves. Institutions, ways of life, and educational precepts are either transformed or left as effete relics. Both to prepare for these changes technologically and to avert disaster which might come from being unprepared socially, all advanced countries are providing for and re-assessing public universal education in a way that would have been unthinkable a lifetime ago.

Consequently, not only teachers and professional educators but statesmen and industrialists too are worried about the supply of suitable personnel, about the impact of all this change on everyday life at home, and about the challenge of competitors abroad. The interests of trade, the public welfare, and the claims of the young are widely recognized as being logically synonymous – instead of being considered competitors, as they were not long ago. There has never been so much public anxiety about education. No previous concern about it has ever seen domestic problems in such a wide international perspective. For that reason it is hoped that this book will also help those public men and women who are for the first time studying education seriously as a political or industrial asset, and looking at it as though from outside.

Modern Japan has been made by education within the lifetime of people still surviving. The Soviet Union's strength is based even more remarkably upon its educational system, and has reached its present level within two generations of scholastic advance. The revolution in China is still too recent to justify prophecy; but without star-gazing we cannot fail to be impressed already (if not alarmed) by the tremendous technological and social upheaval going on there – all intricately bound up with educational reformation. At the end of the Second World War Africa was barely stirring in the sleep of centuries; now she is wide awake, alert with dynamic nationalism; her eager new nations are independently making a powerful future on the basis of education. The 1960s may well be Africa's decade. In any case, they will be the decade of the hitherto underdeveloped countries. The way these turn will decide the future of mankind – of our children – for at least a lifetime.

Therefore educational staff-work is grand strategy. School departments are no longer departments of charity or merely 'spending departments'; they are major ministries of capital investment. We in the older industrialized countries are being overtaken simply because we are so well established. Similarly, the time-honoured methods of static warfare were brought to ridicule in a matter of days by motorized overrunning, and still more by supersonic aircraft, rocketry, and the technology of nuclear fission. It is deplorable that education should ever be thought of in terms of warfare; but from the standpoint of national strength alone it is obvious that security demands the scrapping of our previous half-hearted commitment to education. Not merely security but living standards too are at stake. Consequently, Britain has a Minister of Science; and the United States is ruthlessly analysing the merits and demerits of its colossal experiments with schooling. Schools and educational planning are no longer private possessions but internationally vital lifelines. It is impossible to consider them except in a world perspective.

'Lifelines' was the word used above. That is the positive way in which we must look at schools and school reform; for, if we do not understand 'the world our neighbour' and co-operate in building a new world, we repeat precisely the same mistake abroad which we are at last escaping from at home. Education cannot be partial, rationed, or selfishly enjoyed. Any attempt so to restrict it will deepen the chasm between the 'haves' and the 'have nots'. Our nemesis will be all the more catastrophic when it occurs, as soon it will. The Soviet Union, China, and some emergent new nations regard education as something that will always be on their side. They spend freely not only on themselves but on others. Everyone wants education. They will take it where they can get it, though they may still be uncommitted politically. How can they stay that way unless we also share our views and civilization with them? And how can we do that unless we understand them and can communicate?

This book endeavours not only to make clear the problems and standpoints of others but to assess our own problems and plans in the light of world needs. Since it is usually impossible for people to see themselves as they are, this exercise of getting inside the skin of others may do us a service in return by letting us see ourselves through their eyes. Even if that does not exactly happen, at least we must note that other people's experiments with schools, educational endeavour and technological planning are working over the self-same problems which worry us. The differences in their context may help to highlight both the essence of recurring problems and the powerful influence of individual contexts. Both these aspects are consistently borne in mind throughout the book, and should be constantly appreciated by readers.

World Perspectives in Education may therefore be used in two ways, separately or simultaneously. It is both a book on Comparative Education, with emphasis on the 'problem approach'; and it is a Principles of Education book, picking out the perennial concerns of educators so as to illustrate them with international examples and analyse them by experiments in the world's laboratory. The principles are seen in practice. A third purpose will, I hope, become even clearer as reading proceeds: it is that of helping to make the study of Education a really educative and liberalizing orientation instead of the mere subject-study it all too often is. If people look at themselves and their work in a wider context than usual, they not merely contribute more to their children and their country but will gain even more themselves. Thus, I hope, this book may help to move teacher-training from the plane of expertise and examination-passing to the heights of humane sensitivity – and that without loss of realism. In that respect, therefore, I also hope to serve the interests of international education.

The present book is intended to offer a general survey complete in itself; but for fuller effectiveness, it should be used in close conjunction with my *Other Schools and Ours* or some similar book providing intimate case-studies of cultural systems actually at work. The context of any problem is people's lives; these must be sympathetically understood, to such an extent that we feel at home with them. Only thus can we recognize our common humanity and extend our own humaneness. Some ways of combining the two interests are suggested in the last chapter.

Many of the problems to be analysed are revealed in the list of contents or can be tracked down easily in the index. But some of the most pervasive and difficult of problems can be appreciated only by perspicacity on the reader's part – not, I hope, because I have been slack in my work but because by their very nature they are as pervasive and vital as air and water, which are seldom singled out for 'subject' treatment in books on biology. Our greatest turning inside-out has to occur with the most fundamental influences on our lives – things we may not have noticed or take for granted. These include: the shift of our focal point from Europe; the revolutionary impact of television, radio, and popular press, occupying children for as many hours a week as school; the cultural multiplicity and uncertainty of all Western industrialized nations, as distinct from pre-industrial Europe and highly industrialized Russia and China today; our neglect of creativeness and imagination; our over-intellectual analysis of education and our own problems; our pseudo-distinction between training and educating; the stupendous implications of automation, which is so close upon us that its advent is being deliberately held up until we are socially ready for it; the revolutionary change in consumer expectation, including the universal demand for education beyond the compulsory or bread-and-butter stage. All these factors are such real and penetrating influences in our daily lives that we just do not notice them properly.

In fact, those topics should really be the basis of any book surveying educational change. Yet we are so entangled with them that it is well-nigh impossible to stand back far enough to envisage them comprehensively, let alone cope with them properly. Moreover, a proper study of their interrelated influences would amount to a continuing survey of the whole impact of urbanization and industrialization. Though I have taken in hand such a survey, in a book to be published later, it has seemed more appropriate now to deal with day-to-day evidences of change in the familiar concerns of home and school, work and play. In the practical setting of education teachers and those who train them can do something positive to make themselves and the world's public aware that its outlook is no longer restricted to the perceptions of the parish pump or the village washing-stones. The world is at last our neighbour; and our father and mother may be strangers. So cataclysmic has world change become.

Those changing the world are not outside experts; they are practical people working inside it. Nor are they foreigners in any sense of
the word. They are people like us, working over closely related problems, though perhaps in a different idiom. We must get to know them
and their concerns in three stages. First we need a sympathetic acquaintance with them in their context, which to them is home and living
reality. *Other Schools and Ours* was designed to introduce readers to the
homes, society, and schools of six representatively distinct countries.
The present book follows up by picking out some recurring problems
or universally difficult decisions – not as huge abstractions or vague
'factors', but as living workaday companions. These are not treated
in spurious isolation. From country to country, though in different
garb, recognizable features reappear. Such 'recognition' can be real or
partial or mistaken. There may be only a resemblance to something
with which we are already familiar; or an old friend may have assumed a different role in foreign parts. So we must always be chary of
supposing that we have really 'recognized' anything in any detached
or 'objective' way. We should try to make sure what is actually
going on.

It is only with this proviso that we are justified in a so-called 'problem approach' to the comparative study of cultures, thus reaching the
second stage of our acquaintance with other people's interests (and our
own). So the 'problem approach' depends on a prior and sympathetic
insight into living and working conditions, not forgetting the myths
and time-honoured institutions which affect them. It also requires
careful follow-up at a third level later – that of the interplay of academic insights and researches working on one selected problem or
topic by means of comparative analysis using different disciplines.
Though these three stages interlock, we are justified in dealing with
them one at a time for convenience; and for that reason *World Perspectives in Education* deals with recurring problems and internationally
critical points of decision.

As we have said, however, each point of decision is not an abstract
exercise in logic. It is often as personal a matter as choosing a marriage
partner. It is usually an emotionally linked and socially constrained
climax of many previous encounters. For this reason especially the
people changing the world are far from being isolated experts. They
are caught up in it all – and so are the people whose lives they are
changing. Thus, to be effective at all, teachers and organizers must
always be able to look two ways at once. They must always have

the 'inside view', even when they try to deal with local problems objectively; and they must always have an all-pervading sense of the vast revolution now surging around them and altering their local context. They need commitment and responsibility in the place where they work; yet they are disoriented if they lack an international perspective or an acute sense of their own parochialism. By this combination of insights and endeavours they can know themselves and improve their home circumstances realistically.

That is why this book reviews homes and schools, selection and training, job-getting, tensions, youth problems, problems of class or religion or politics or language, social barriers and all the familiar entanglements of education – but all in the realistic local detail of many countries. Some of the major divisions of our inquiry are indicated by the chapter headings; but no matter how much we cut up the object of our study for convenience in handling, many of the most important concerns transcend the artificial distinctions thus imposed upon it, exactly as they reappear from country to country. We may think of problems of mass education and the sharing of cultural insight, problems of bulk supply and of quality, those of control and responsibility, anxieties about underdevelopment and 'drop-out' or wastage. Each one of these topics and all those mentioned at the beginning of this paragraph recur whether we are talking about vocational education, or teachers, or anything else. Therefore all the familiar topics of the Comparative Education textbook are here, easily discoverable in the chapter headings, the summary, and the index; but rather than present an anatomized catalogue of 'problems' (which must be arbitrary and misleading in its suggestion of 'separate' or workshop treatment) it has seemed preferable to deal with our material realistically in terms of major, recurring aspects or easily recognized phases of education.

For the sake of down-to-earth realism too it has occasionally seemed appropriate to concentrate markedly on the example afforded by a particular country in relation to a problem; but any such temporary concentration of interest is always deliberately broadened by being evaluated in an international perspective. In any case, that preoccupation is compensated for elsewhere. Where concentration has occurred, it has usually been in relation to the examples afforded by the United States, the United Kingdom, and the U.S.S.R., not only for the obvious reason that each of these countries in its special way is politically and strategically important but also for the equally obvious truth that ideologically and institutionally these three countries exemplify char-

acteristic problems or attitudes of world-wide importance. Moreover,
this book is intended primarily for readers in Britain and the U.S.A.,
though the British Commonwealth and the vast English-reading public throughout the world are also addressed throughout. Criticisms
freely handed out here and there are, I hope, distributed equally. All
countries need jerking out of smugness.

A more generalized study of the universal implications of industrialization and urbanization is already well in hand, to analyse the generic
problems mentioned here. For particular illustrations or case-studies,
Other Schools and Ours will round out the local picture. This present
book will serve its purpose if it helps teachers and organizers to see the
total dimensions and perspectives of their work from a local and
everyday on-the-job standpoint. Thus they will be better able to help
others re-orientate themselves responsibly in the making of a new culture to satisfy evolving needs and opportunities. Most directly, however, I hope to contribute to the view that the teacher's task of humanizing others can no longer be just a *job*, no matter how dedicatedly
performed; it must essentially be a humanizing *experience* if it is to be
worth while at all.

EDMUND KING

University of London, King's College
  February, 1962

BIBLIOGRAPHICAL NOTE

Footnotes are provided as required throughout the text. Brief suggestions for reading are made at the end of most chapters to cover the
interests there touched on. A more general bibliography is provided
on page 369.

My sources of information are:

(*a*) first-hand observation in many of the countries discussed;
(*b*) interviews at top executive or ministerial level in several of them;
(*c*) consultations with indigenous educators visiting England, the
     information being corrected against all available evidence;
(*d*) (for the most up-to-date trends) daily reports or special feature
     articles in the London *Times*, the Manchester *Guardian*, and similar
     careful journals;
(*e*) other authors or source books (named) on specific points.

W.P.E.—B

exterior problems or attitudes of world-wide importance. Moreover, this book is intended primarily for readers in Britain and the U.S.A., though the British Commonwealth and the vast English-reading public throughout the world are also addressed throughout. Criticisms freely handed out here and there are, I hope, distributed equally. All countries need jerking out of smugness.

A more generalized study of the universal implications of industrialization and urbanization is already well in hand, to analyse the generic problems mentioned here. For particular illustrations or case-studies, Other Schools and Ours will round out the local picture. This present book will serve its purpose if it helps readers and organizers to see the total dimensions and perspective of their work from a local and everyday on-the-job standpoint. Thus they will be better able to help others re-orientate themselves responsibly in the making of a new culture to satisfy evolving needs and opportunities. Most directly, however, I hope to contribute to the view that the teacher's task of humanizing others can no longer be just a job, no matter how dedicatedly performed; it must essentially be a humanizing experience if it is to be worth while at all.

EDMUND KING

University of London, King's College
February 1962

BIBLIOGRAPHICAL NOTE

Footnotes are provided as required throughout the text. Brief suggestions for reading are made at the end of most chapters to cover the interests there touched on. A more general bibliography is provided on page 369.
My sources of information are:

(a) first-hand observation in many of the countries discussed;
(b) interviews at top executive or ministerial level in several of them;
(c) consultations with indigenous educators visiting England, the information being corrected against all available evidence;
(d) (for the most up-to-date trends) daily reports or special feature articles in the London Times, the Manchester Guardian, and similar careful journals;
(e) other authors or source books (named) on specific points.

W.E.A.—B

SECTION I

Introductory

CHAPTER I

How do we understand?

Why bother to compare the educational experiments of this country with that? Or, if we do, will it not suffice to pick out the best ingredients from here and there? Would it not be better to think out first what we know about the nature of man, and consider afterwards what objectives we are aiming at in the development of that nature? If we are in doubt, why not call in the advice of the great experts, either historical or contemporary, and thus get really clear ideas about the educative process?

Such familiar questions show profound ignorance of how human beings learn and think. It is only in relatively recent years that objective studies have been made of how recognition, learning, and understanding are built up. 'Built up' is the operative phrase, because these things are not simple phenomena that just happen; nor are they 'once and for all' events. They must be continuous in time; they require intimate involvement in society; and all concepts, interests, and endeavours tend to be interrelated. So there is nothing simple about learning – not even about recognition. The 'I' or 'self' that does the recognizing and thinking is marvellous not only in the way each of us usually supposes but in the manifold complexity of the ways in which it becomes and stays a 'recognizing' personality. Even basic activities like seeing objects before our eyes are intensely complicated operations; and from that simple perception onwards we become increasingly involved with other people, other events, and other ideas every time we bring our minds to bear on anything. So each observation, thought, and decision is like the interlocking engagement of some massive apparatus of which we are imperfectly in control.

Let us look at this more simply. Though some animals are able to run about and do all kinds of complicated things very soon after they are born, the human baby lies there almost helpless. The essential movements of breathing and digesting are taken care of; but he cannot find his mother's breast. He has open eyes capable of sight sensations; but he cannot see anything as we understand the term. The bewildering kaleidoscope of light and darkness and colours involved in seeing has not resolved itself into concrete objects. Apart from the great amount of muscular practice that must be indulged in before each eye can focus on and isolate the objects looked at, a time must elapse before repeated familiarity with a recurring object enables the child to distinguish it from its background as a 'thing seen'. The recurring vision of it in different contexts enables the infant observer to form a composite picture of its outline and colour; but such things as its solid shape, its texture, smell, temperature, weight, and so forth are learned only by repeated manipulation, contact, or other associated experiences. As the hands themselves are so slow to develop co-ordination in being extended and grasping, and this control in turn is only slowly co-ordinated with the sensations of the eyes, mouth, and nose, it may be weeks or months before the human infant's experience of things observed gives him as much 'recognition' as some more lowly animals enjoy within hours of birth.

Thus human recognition draws heavily on experience as well as physical apparatus and instinctual skills. The uncertainties involved in building up that experience towards successful recognition also imply great skill in experimentation – one of man's most prized possessions. Experimentation implies coming back to an object or experience again and again from different angles or in different circumstances. All this is true of simple perceptions such as seeing one's mother or a bright spoon. In every return to the experiment of observing, the observer brings back a 'self' that we can describe both as the same self and yet a different and more evolved one – more evolved, that is to say, by having grown older and having had more experiences. These are again fed into each act of observing. They enrich it, of course; but by the same token they make the act of observation less objective. The observer's personality and background enter into it more and more, even in the basic act of seeing and recognizing. When recognition becomes more complicated (e.g. by including an 'understanding' of the object as well as the mere isolation and naming of it), the process becomes distinctly involved. It implies not only the isolated recognition referred to above but the simultaneous recognition of significant resemblances and differences between the object observed and all others apparently like it. Such comparisons are not confined to superficial or descriptive attributes either; they include questions of quality, degree, approval and disapproval, a sense of purpose and fitness, and many other emotional or 'judging' activities on the part of the observer.

These now well-known facts are of great importance in physiology and psychology; but so far too little account is taken of them in the study of how we learn and *understand*. Understanding must surely imply the seeing of things both in their own dimensions and in their proper significance. The words 'significance' and 'proper' involve the observer twice over. 'Significance' arises not only from his powers of co-ordinated perception as described above but from his ability to discern pattern, influences, and cause-and-effect relationships. The use of the word or idea 'proper' implies not only the ability just mentioned but the additional power to judge emotionally and morally. In other words, it entails not only well-organized experience and experimentation within his own personal sphere but also wide acquaintance with external facts, and also social adjustment and education. The further we take this analysis, the more we are compelled to admit that even a supposedly simple description or classification of objects into categories really involves elaborate experiences, education, interests, and the observer's present purposes. Any *value*-judgement that may be indulged in is likely to draw more heavily than ever on his background.[1]

To reduce these remarks to their practical consequences at this point we must conclude that when I use words like 'child', 'parent', 'school', 'education' (let alone 'aims of education'), my meaning cannot be really clear to anyone hearing me unless he knows what sort of a background I have come from and what kind of person I am speaking to. For it is the building up of my experience of 'the child', and 'school', and 'education' in my own peculiar context that has given me notions of what they *are* – not to speak of what they might be. When I think I see a phenomenon in the education of a child, through my eyes there peeps an Englishman or an American or an African as the case may be. Not only that, but my experience as a teacher or parent, as aristocrat or scholarship boy, as Quaker or atheist – all these and many other background connexions make my perceptions as well as my views different from those of my nearest neighbour. We know all about this, of course; but we do not act upon our knowledge practically enough.

Suppose I set out to look at any problem. I not only bring my whole past and my present involvement along with me but I embark on my

---

[1] For a fuller treatment of these influences on observation, thought, and judgement, see Chapter 9: 'Ideologies and systems of control'; see also Whitehead, A. N., *Adventures of Ideas*, chapter XI, for some important philosophical consequences of any observer's involvement in whatever he is contemplating.

studies in a way that is strangely repetitive of the infant's early attempts to see. I pick out points of recognition. There is the recurring phenomenon. Around it are the features often associated with it. They appear and reappear in clusters of impressions. If the clustered impressions always recur together, a definite pattern is presupposed. A rudimentary understanding may crystallize around such recognition. I find myself looking at the data before me as a teacher or parent or researcher. Perhaps I am quite attached to the idea of 'myself as a researcher', partly because of long habituation and also because I like the satisfaction I derive from the role. This in turn will affect my perception. 'The basis of experience is emotional', says Whitehead.[1] My sense of fitness or fairness also impinges on my viewing of the data before me, and still more affects my 'views' upon them. Furthermore, as we shall see at greater length later, my long experience of education as a child, parent, and teacher cannot fail to impart an aura of inevitability or 'naturalness' to some of the practices I observe. Yet these may be no more natural than a Red Indian's warpaint or the latest fashion in women's hats.

This building up of experiences, patterns of observation, and value-systems involves not simply individuals, of course, but also the other people in whose family, social groups, and organized practices they find themselves living. This is not the place to examine at length the consequences of such constellations of experience, interests, and 'ways of life'. Yet we must take note that the blending of habits, satisfactions, values, and theories which we encounter in education (as elsewhere) makes it impossible to suppose that any one of us or any one country can ever be considered to have found educational truth, or to have established 'the best' educational institution of a particular type.

Institutions in particular, like houses and vehicles, have a way of remaining in use long after they fail to accommodate all requirements. They tend to seem part of 'the world around us' instead of temporary expedients. It would be better if we could remind ourselves constantly that they are, so to speak, hypotheses in action. They all make assumptions about the supposedly best way of responding to supposed needs, which are in turn based upon supposedly correct clusters of highly experimental observations. Outsiders can often see flaws of fact. They can still oftener detect false deductions. They can sometimes also detect a fear of non-existent bogies or a worship of equally fictitious idols. But such fictions, when incorporated into anyone's 'way of

[1] Op. cit., p. 205 (Pelican edition).

life', are powerful factors to reckon with. They are therefore, for the purpose of our survey, very important facts to be observed and assessed.

Ideas, cherished fictions, and institutions of all kinds (from public holidays to religions and philosophies) are so much part of our seeing and planning – not to speak of our value-systems – that they must be fully taken account of in any description of education in any one place. For instance, the idea of 'the gentleman' or of 'fair play' is not just an isolated schoolboy or Saturday-afternoon affair but something which turns up again and again in a country's whole way of life. But by the same token, when people from any country peep over into their neighbour's preserve, they must constantly remember that they are not 'seeing' or 'thinking' in any pure, detached way but are peering through all the encumberment of the apparatus with which they have been building their own lives since infancy.

As we shall see later in the book, some internationally revered concepts which are supposed to have universal validity are nevertheless differently envisaged from place to place, and still more differently put into practice. Let us take as an example the phrase 'the Christian attitude to marriage', which is supposed to be so familiar that it needs no description, at any rate. Quite apart from substantial sectarian differences in our own country, we must note much greater differences as between faithful Christians in California and Scotland, Italy and Jamaica – not to mention places further afield. This variation makes it obvious that even those dedicated to a particular concept and taking its factual existence for granted can nevertheless differ markedly in their 'understanding' of a supposedly universal rule, and still more in their application of that 'understanding'. The reason is, of course, that every local 'understanding' (even more than each personal interpretation) brings into play a whole background of data, events, institutions, values, emotions, and opportunities. Thus we see that even alleged certainties supported by unquestionable revelation from outside are in practice widely interpreted and divergently viewed. How much more open to question are those kinds of understanding which do not invoke divine protection but are merely human enterprises!

Schools, institutions, communications, social links, and emotions tend to build up locally patches of similar outlook and activity. This kind of homogeneity does not depend on race or geography, but on local patterns of culture (in the anthropologist's sense). Each one of these is a hypothesis towards total understanding. Each one may well include within itself smaller variants or subcultures. The 'sense' made of the outer world by each subculture includes the results of needs, experiments, communications, and such short-cuts as symbolism or magic. Eventually we get down to individuals, some of whom are stigmatized by their neighbours as being a bit odd in some respects, if not altogether. Yet in the long run, the history of the growth of understanding has shown that the gathering up and comparison of such *complementary* interpretations of the world has been a cumulative process in public just as it is in the private building up of our own personal 'understanding'.

In our private lives we do not concede that any neighbour enjoys infallibility. We recognize that he 'knows a thing or two', perhaps; but any idea that he is always right is rejected as ridiculous. Why should any greater respect be paid to the accumulated views of more and more people, simply because they are accumulated? We do not do this in practice, at any rate in democracies. We test others' views against the 'reality' of our own experience; and though we all individually know best about everything it is still comforting to find that our neighbour agrees with us that a third person is wrong. However, rightness and wrongness are often unprofitable concepts, because we make little practical progress in convincing other people about them. What is more, rightness and wrongness have a way of changing according to circumstances. These truisms are indeed obvious, so much so that we neglect them when it comes to thinking about many of our most important decisions – such as the future of our own children and everyone else's. This is all the more remarkable and selfish because our children's world will certainly not be the world we know – if indeed we do know our world.

Just as it is natural for us to ask someone else to have a look at an object which puzzles us, especially if he can see it from the side or round the back, so it is appropriate for us to seek a second or a third or many views on vitally important matters confronting us. Of all vital concerns, education must stand high on the list of priorities. Yet it is also one of the most intimate concerns in anyone's life; and therefore it is not only critically linked with emotional complexes but crowded about with all the clutter of past experiences and interpretations. It is almost impossible for any one of us alone or any country alone to 'make sense' validly of any one educational problem. And educational problems practically never come singly. Furthermore, they practically never 'stay put'.

For all these reasons it seems impossible to lay down the law about education. Of all constantly changing human activities this is the least static or homogeneous. Yet the great books written on this subject tend to read like the once immutable (but now forgotten) code of Hammurabi. For the same reason they often seem as remote and inconsequential as a now outmoded theology. Yet if anything is down-to-earth and home-based, that surely is education. It is therefore not surprising for those who look abroad to find both a persistent and penetrating working-over of the same family and school concerns and an equally persistent variability. After all, experimentation has gone on throughout the ages and all over the world, with very different resources and for different objectives. Civilizations have risen and fallen, and technologies have waxed and waned; but parents and their children in unimaginable numbers have ingeniously addressed themselves to the problems of growing up to be human and making the most of life. Those are the central themes; and though the variations are endless they all represent contributory views of them.

So we find, as we should expect, that instead of discovering perfection and perpetual truth in any time or place we have to reckon with local and topical systems which at best are *complementary* approaches to problems which concern us all. If once we admit this obvious truth, then it follows that we ourselves must humbly acknowledge our own partiality and incompleteness. What can we say, therefore, about education in our own country that will carry the genuine ring of truth about it for all time? Would it not be better to try to see our problems (if not ourselves) through other people's eyes? If we cannot always do this, at least we may manage it by implication through seeing how they set about comparable problems. Undoubtedly that should be our aim; but the mere selection of genuinely comparable problems is a more delicate exercise than might be supposed at first sight. What appears to be comparable (like a wife or a home) may in some other family circumstances serve a very alien-looking group of purposes. Instead of picking on items, therefore, we must invariably assess the rounded function and purpose of the items or activity reviewed, and we must further envisage the total workability or ecology of the whole system. Any other approach is bound to obscure the relevance, if not the nature, of the item we have chosen to inspect.

Insights of the kind required can be obtained only by the use of comparative techniques both in total surveys and in detailed analysis. We need world perspectives for an *international review* – so that our comparison may then be made between cultures. We must also use a *time-scale*, even within one civilization or country, thus viewing events and institutions in historical context. In our own period of rapid change, institutions and ideas may vary remarkably from section to section of a country's life according to the degree of conservatism or conversion encountered there, thus introducing *culture conflicts*. We cannot overlook the question of *resources*, human and material; so we find that the expedients apparently appropriate to one set of circumstances may be quite inappropriate elsewhere on the ground of economic or social unreadiness. Considerations of this sort at once bring in train many questions of priority; therefore we find ourselves caught up in comparisons of *values and ideas*, i.e. of ideologies and philosophies. If we do not take account of such potent influences on other people's decisions about education and children's whole futures, we are shirking our job as comparative analysts.

But who are we to look at other people's problems and diagnose the crux of their decisions? As we have constantly seen in this chapter, every observation we venture upon is an engagement of our own selves and our background. Blinkered and biased though we may be, however, we may actually be of help to them as friends can help each other everywhere. Yet insight, and certainly communication, can only develop where our study is undertaken *sympathetically* in consonance with the whole life-force of another society's system. We cannot be so arrogant as to assume that like some clinician we have isolated a pathological development and propose some sterile cure. We are not really scientists looking at alien organisms (or problems) from outside. What we are looking at is a variation on ourselves, seen through eyes which have an interest; and whatever expedient we propose will be full of implications for ourselves.

Therefore, though in the interest of academic exactness and universal validity we shall try to bring scientific coldness into our inquiries, we shall vitiate the whole proceeding if we imagine that we can ever actually isolate phenomena and lay them side by side in absolute detachment. Nothing animate can be treated in quite that way, least of all among human kind. Consequently, when we think we have found our comparable items and have started to work on them, we must not only beware of our own personal entanglements as far as possible but also acknowledge that we can never deal with any problem in a 'once for all' snap judgement. It would indeed be remarkable if we could size it up in this way, not to speak of recommending any treatment.

Therefore, just as the child comes back to its problem of 'seeing' again and again, so ought we to return to our study of any one topic time after time, from angle after angle, making tentative comparisons one after the other in relation to different contexts.

In the last analysis we shall discover that some problems can hardly ever be wormed out of their setting, but must be reviewed *in situ* almost by implication. That is to say, we must be content to make progress by glimpses and surmises and by adducing apparently comparable instances, because we cannot really secure either disengaged 'pure' vision in ourselves or convenient laboratory conditions for the study of a deeply entrenched problem. So far from considering this repetitive incompleteness to be the lazy man's woolly way of dealing with such a situation, we ought to recognize that this is the cumulative or peripheral method of the biologist studying any complex ecological problem. Of all ecological complexes, education is the most intricate.

In any case, the recognition of 'truths' about any educational or social activity demands very much more than mere description, categorization, and theorizing. It also requires *empirical* acquaintance with a problem as it works itself out over a period. There is more to our understanding of it than mere cognition. Understanding here demands that inner acquaintance which comes not from outside information but from practical experience. Some truths have to be lived, rather than talked or thought about. Therefore any story we tell will be fiction unless we have the 'inside story' and 'inside feeling', not relying exclusively on the academician's Olympian remoteness. The study of education requires as one of its major ingredients the on-the-spot experimental partiality of the teacher, the parent, and other interested persons. That is why the present book, instead of pretending to quite unreal and futureless compilation of 'comparable' exhibits, sets out to involve teachers and all educators in the continuing evaluation of their own professional purposes through the use of comparative analysis. If only these studies, interests, and practical experiences are surveyed from day to day on the ground with a comparative *attitude*, more will be achieved than by lifetimes of scientism towards other people's educational practices.

Of course, we must all make the fullest use of well-documented and shrewdly assessed insights drawn not merely from different countries but from the differently 'structured' perceptions of many academic disciplines. For instance, psychology, sociology, and anthropology can all provide a different touchstone or analytical apparatus for any topical problem. All of them, and other academic activities, are essential to accurate interpretation. But this is comparison at a loftier level. Consideration of this kind of encounter will be postponed until my concluding chapter.

The contraction of our world and the expansion of our awareness make the international study of all our problems a matter of mounting urgency. Such an interest is however often pursued as though it were a rescue operation only, or even a kind of natural history. Yet in seeing other people's children brought up in what may seem an outlandish fashion we are often looking at our own presuppositions and mannerisms caricatured or taken out of context. Even supposing that is not so, we shall get more out of our exercise if we believe that amidst all the foreignness we are looking for ourselves, if not at ourselves. It is always convenient to profit by others' mistakes and trials – all the more so when we are not merely copying techniques or bright ideas but getting a new slant on a long vexing uncertainty.

Furthermore, as has been said, technology and society are changing so fast that old dispensations are receding like shadows, while ahead of us a world looms up that makes ridicule of any minor *ad hoc* expedients. We need to achieve as long-term a view as possible for our children's sakes. Without saying that no views or theories can be right, we are compelled by ordinary modesty to admit that old certainties are being swept up like old monarchies and principalities. History has already shown us that many of the greatest quarrels of former times have been over issues that now seem minor. International catastrophes have occurred because contestants have fastened on to differences instead of recognizing similarities of purpose. Let us not look for foreignness. It is far better to construct understanding on the basis of complementariness. At least, even if we are 'dead right', the avoidance of antagonisms may make it possible for the rightness of our views to make itself manifest.

A more modest appraisal of our situation should surely indicate that, as in each person's progress from infancy and in each nation's growing up mature understanding has come through reconciliation, order, and synthesis, so a more universally acceptable interpretation of opportunities and responsibilities in education may now be achieved through a similar process. No one person and no one culture is monolithically right or wrong. That could hardly be said with certainty even of any item in any programme, for the reasons given in this chapter. If our decisions are to be sound, therefore, we must acquaint ourselves vividly with the various ties pulling our judgement this way and that (not to speak of our errors).

One of the pleasantest ways of undertaking this salutary exercise is to see our own drama enacted safely elsewhere – writ large, or perhaps on a puppet scale, but still recognizable. That is why the other chapters in this book are illustrated as far as possible with glimpses at other countries. Not only has didacticism been avoided as far as possible in that way but the common interests of human beings everywhere have been presented in homely terms.

BOOKS

Ryle, G., *The Concept of Mind* (London), 1949.
Whitehead, A. N., *Adventures of Ideas* (London), 1933.
Young, K., *A Handbook of Social Psychology* (New York), 1946.

CHAPTER 2

From curiosity to complement

My grandfather's map of Africa showed the familiar coastal outline fringed with a suggestion of land and rivers inside; but a large part of that huge continent was simply left blank. It was unknown. Unknown, that is, except to the people who lived there. To have used such a qualification in my grandfather's time would have marked the speaker as flippant. The whole emphasis in knowing and understanding lay upon the fact that people like my grandfather, in 'civilization', were looking out upon the world from the only point of interest that mattered. The permanent priorities in most human affairs, religious and secular, seemed settled. On a pleasant Sunday afternoon people could read about the recent activities of Dr Livingstone and Mr Stanley among the heathen; they could gaze round-eyed at the steel engravings illustrating the wonders and wildness of far-away places and races. Popular anthropology was a rather satisfying diversion, because it was viewed from the pinnacle of human development in Western Europe – above all, from Britain. Curiosity about other human communities was almost on a par with reading Buckland's *Curiosities of Natural History*, provided the books read were not too heavily larded with information about certain bizarre customs indulged in by the un-civilized pagans. If studied with detachment by male adults, how-ever, such information could reinforce their realization that Western Christendom (Protestant, of course) was the unquestionable criterion of all human aspirations.

At that very time the grandfather of a friend of mine was in the royal compound of the Kabaka of Buganda, waiting eagerly with other courtiers to see the first white man arrive from the unknown world of Europe. The court of Mutesa I had of course heard fact and fiction about the wonders of the far North-West, and knew about the activi-ties of the Europeans along various stretches of the African coast. They had also long had contact with the Arab slave traders from Mombasa. Mutesa himself was a Muslim, and could read the Koran in Swahili – a foreign tongue; but as a cultivated man he was prepared to welcome

32

the pale infidel and learn about his ways. Indeed, he was predisposed towards him, because he had heard that Christians did not believe in slavery, and on that account was beginning to wonder if the white man's faith might be more in keeping with humane ideas than Islam. At any rate, he was prepared to give the outsider a generous hearing. So on the shores of what we now know to be the greatest sheet of fresh water in the world, under the Equatorial sun, the first links were being made to bind two very different aspects of humanity together, and make possible not only contact but sympathy too. My friend's grandfather lived in a land without schools; but he himself, after an education at the University College at Makerere, followed by further studies at London University, is playing a responsible part in the re-interpretation of the ancient aims of education to suit a rapidly developing new country.

Those blank spaces on the map are now full of the highly significant lives of busy people, and the formerly dark regions of Africa are bright with hope. We can travel in little more than a day to the spot where Livingstone was found, though he had long been given up for dead through being completely out of touch with the outside world for more than a year. While we wait at the London airport terminal passengers arrive and depart to and from Rio de Janeiro and Tokyo, Washington and Moscow. They include representatives of races hardly heard of in my grandfather's time; but now they are all people and they all matter. They all have some new dimension to add to the appraisal of human endeavour.

The revolution that has taken place in human perceptions is not limited to the contraction of time and distance, though that is formidable enough. It is nothing to dine in one hemisphere and breakfast in the other. Transatlantic round trips within four or five days are now a common enough experience. A much more important consideration is the interpenetration of all our lives and viewpoints, no matter where we live. Britain's food and clothing, for example, are contributed by the labour and skills of people in every part of the globe. Their lives are part of our daily sustenance. In the long run all such services depend upon an exchange of services, and not simply upon a requital of cash or some other transaction which is finished as soon as it is achieved. Every contact means impact, therefore, and the impact is mutual. The systematic organization of demand and supply to cater for any one person presupposes a corresponding organization somewhere else. This in turn is based upon other people's

economic, social, political, and educational readiness – if not complementariness.

The whole structure of human roles, values, and priorities throughout the world has therefore been transformed through industrialization,
even in countries which do not appear to have yet industrialized in the
usual sense of the word. People's conception of what is possible and
knowable and desirable has exploded beyond the confines of what was
merely imaginary in our grandparents' time. The knowledge and
values of the world are now directly relevant to the understanding
built up in each one of us. No one can pretend to exclusiveness or
isolation in this respect.

New kinds of relationship are everywhere called for by the international need to live in our present interpenetration of cultures and
services, of course. But in each community too new roles are developed,
with new kinds of personality and new kinds of skill. Education in
some altered form has therefore not merely become possible for everyone but is a prime requisite. It is no longer a one-way benefaction to
those who receive it, for the well-being of all demands training and
mutual adjustments in each one. The whole of a country's enterprises
need the fullest possible development of every material and resource
as a contributory and complementary part of the total growth; and
that refers especially to the human beings whose endeavours sustain
those enterprises.

Thus education is removed from the plane of private luxuries or class
embellishments to the level of a universal necessity. At first people
thought of 'mass education' as a basic *foundation* to industrialized
development, as though it were a concrete flatness. Undoubtedly, a
foundation of education serves this utilitarian purpose; but we should
be careful not to err in our analysis of how basic support is achieved.
The more mechanized and precise the organization through which
we live our lives, the *higher the degree* of general education demanded
in the populace – and also the greater the extent of *diversity* beyond
the elementary foundations. In addition, the many semi-skilled operatives, distributors, purveyors, and managers, and all the craftsmen and
middlemen need more training still. Behind the middle rank of skilled
managers just described there stand the so-called 'back room boys' –
researchers in basic science and technology, and in the biological and
social sciences so necessary for the understanding of what it means to
live healthily in our unprecedented modern cities.

So we can see clearly that men and women must be formally educated now at no fewer than three levels: (*a*) that of basic facts and daily 'know how'; (*b*) that of business and professional contacts of all kinds; and (*c*) that of the researcher who is pushing human and factual understanding out beyond the frontiers of the known. Everyone needs very much more of the first level than many so-called 'educated' persons had two or three generations ago; a considerable middle range of workers and citizens will need a great deal of skill at the second level; and the third level will be required not just by a small proportion of the population but by an increasing number – even though that third level is on the rarefied heights of specialization. But even lower down we all tend to be specialists nowadays. The reason is that trained or educated persons often have to spend their lives now on detailed specialization within fields which a generation ago were merely areas of the most distant surmise. That is to say, the total scatter of advanced knowledge has become wider and wider, and at the same time the detail of advanced knowledge has become more and more minutely investigated.

Therefore the activities of the educated person (no matter what his level of attainment) are infinitely more a matter of diligent learning and precise follow-through than our grandfathers could have imagined. That is to say, within a single lifetime there has been a revolution in the quantity of knowledge and the numbers of people involved. Even more striking has been the qualitative change that has made instruction both more a matter of public concern and more consciously purposeful for nearly everyone receiving a formal education. The feeling of purpose is experienced socially, professionally, and personally. Except for a few latter-day oases or ivory towers, there is a very stong feeling abroad of urgency and responsibility in education – the responsibility of the educator, of the educated, and of education itself. 'Learning for learning's sake' is widely suspect as a hobby – a respectable one, and possibly in the public interest, but still a hobby. How can anyone stay out of the total commitment which politicians and teachers endeavour to foster? Both initial specialization and maturing responsibility (if it *is* fostered) demand that our activities and learning become constituent parts of someone else's interests and well-being. Teamwork, with participants in different positions on the field or contributing complementary skills, tends now to replace the older concept of a few doughty captains leading the docile 'masses of the labouring poor'.

The meaning of the very word 'education' can no longer be taken for granted, any more than old-fashioned hierarchies of social position. What is it for? Who gets it? Who educates? What is the public interest? What is to be taught? What is the end product? Is the production line efficient? These and similar questions (though not in such crude terms, perhaps) start up at once now that the answer is made so plain to the much cruder question 'Who pays?' We all pay, and we all gain.

Amid the uncertainties some things are clear. These include preeminently the *different kinds of relationship* already referred to as daily formative experiences in everyone's life. The most obvious revolution in fact (still lacking effective recognition in schools) is the transformation of woman's role. With emancipation, health, and greater equality comes greater expectation by women and from women. Though woman's role is more enjoyable, and more enjoyed by both sexes, it is more complicated and onerous in some respects. All other roles are similarly altered too. Those which seem the same are found in a different ecology or context. The very process of further subdividing labour and producing different kinds of job (with different kinds of job-perspectives) is bound to alter the circumstances of any surviving occupation which may seem to have the same general purpose as in former times. It is obviously surrounded by different kinds of people with different kinds of interest – all contributory to the meaning and responsibility of whatever one human being undertakes.

So much is clear on historical grounds alone because of the evolution of all human societies. But the educational emphasis has shifted also because of alterations within technological operations themselves. As we have already noted, in modern enterprises much of the skill has gone out of the actual processes of production themselves. It has been lavished instead on the preparatory phases: schooling, research, the making of machine tools, the construction of production lines and proper distribution. Without asking the schoolmaster's permission, or even without consulting him at all, so much of his ancient stock-in-trade has thereby been devalued. Different kinds of competence or perfection are aimed at in school, though the pedagogue has not always spotted the change of emphasis. Copper-plate handwriting went out as the typewriter and carbon-paper made the human copy-clerk's laborious diligence an unnecessary toil – a serious misplacement of effort, in fact. Was some great virtue lost thereby? Or is the change only comparable with the emancipation of our mothers and wives from the wash-tub by means of washing machines? Effort is better released for better things; and opportunity makes other roles both possible and necessary. We see these truths clearly in the kitchen, where wives are pitiable and can protest. They are perhaps more cogent in the classroom, where revolutionary questions might be asked about much once-esteemed arithmetical and grammatical prowess and about a great deal of old-fashioned memory-work. Outmoded expertise that does not impart a sense of contributory *significance* to the material learned and to the learner has no more educational virtue than the memorizing of sports league tables – perhaps less!

Resulting from the changes we perceive in the structure of social and occupational roles, we must also note change in the sensitive interplay of human relationships. This comment does not of course refer to the absurdly limited 'human relations' of some of the 'scientific management' people or 'social engineers'. They have tried to reduce 'human relations' to a mere technique – the time-and-motion-and-friction study of our most complicated mechanism. Instead, we must always think essentially of the complementary building up of emotions, 'hunches', perceptions, and aims that is achieved in every kind of human intercourse. Every successful experience of reciprocity enriches something old and builds something new. Together with emotional satisfaction and an intellectual sense of particular 'rightness' we evolve a general awareness of more general 'rightness' and values. In favourable circumstances these develop into whole value-systems, whose complexion must vary according to the opportunities afforded in particular social settings. Altered value-systems sometimes mean revolutionary change; but in any case the normal process of technological and social evolution must cause even persistent values to surround themselves with a different kind of embodiment. That means, simply, that people will prefer or admire the 'perennial' values in a different role. Difference can sometimes be seen along a time-scale, from period to period; sometimes it can be seen simultaneously by looking across from one culture to another. However that may be, a different 'philosophy of education' seems bound to prevail.

For example, a highly industrialized and productive society may prize the bland geniality of the salesman above the plodding fidelity of the scholar. Among scholars themselves, the British greatly prefer the Chaucerian attitude of 'gladly wolde he lern and gladly teche' to the aloof litigiousness of the German academic tradition. Such preference really arises from the recognition of the public need for persuasion, consideration, and 'immediacy' – as distinct from remote authority or a pedantic parade of other academic 'authorities' all set about with footnotes. Some intriguing comparisons might be indulged in even within the framework of this paragraph. We should not make the mistake of supposing any culture (even the micro-culture of a country's academic preserves) to be uniform.

Accordingly, we find that the extrovert salesman or managerial type so much prized in the United States torments himself with critical introspection in his few private moments.[1] Likewise, amidst all the ferment of productivity and promotion so characteristic of American industrial enterprise, the dignified university pursuits of the doctoral course may reveal a meticulous scholiasm not often matched in Britain nowadays outside the ponderous annotations on Classical texts. Indeed, to penetrate further, a strange new blend can arise. The greater the productivity (in mass terms) of an American university, perhaps resulting in uncertainty about the quality of some of its scholars, the more elaborate and conspicuous is the 'window-dressing' indulged in by some ambitious young professors. In some notorious cases, pedantic annotations are widely said to owe as much to research assistants and to the superb bibliographical services of American university libraries as to omnivorous scholarship on the part of the professor himself. To be fair, the better American universities themselves and many American writers ridicule such unworthy self-promotion.[2]

The main point to notice is the simultaneous co-existence of different expressions of a national or international value-system – even in one field of endeavour. Any one of the 'aims of education', or any particular ideal (such as meticulous scholarship), must certainly be examined in all the depth and intricacy of its living context. It is precisely the local and topical forces of that context which make sense or nonsense of so many endeavours. We cannot fully understand what is happening if we pay attention only to abstractions or to professed aims. Thus we may fail to notice that in some instances what passes for meticulous scholarship may be little more than a useful control of students' work devised by a harassed professor, or an ultra-conservative reliance on 'authorities', whose antiquity or status becomes more important than the accuracy of their facts or interpretation. Such a substitute for original thought and inquiry kept the ancient *Herbal* of Dioscurus going as 'the Herbal' for centuries. Nowadays it may be symptomatic of

---

[1] Riesman, D., and others, *The Lonely Crowd* (New Haven, 1950), and Spectorsky, A. C., *The Exurbanites* (New York, 1955), *passim*.

[2] 'We saw your ad., Joe' quoted by W. S. Beck in *Modern Science and the Nature of Life* (New York, 1957), p. 31 of the Pelican edition.

status-seeking in the academic world, and simultaneously be prone to use as a device to exclude new exploration and the evolution of unprecedented but highly significant ideas.[1]

We cannot therefore accept scholarly piety and academic authority alone as untainted guides to the understanding either of physical data or of human relationships. We cannot be content with any one examination of anything. The old fantasy of 'pure' subjects gazing in the most detached way at completely external objects must now be gravely suspect. It is therefore necessary for any inquiry to come back to any problem repeatedly, with complementary insights afforded by other interests and practical activities which have a bearing on it. Some of these interests and activities may logically be in conflict with the first 'one-way' observation, not only because of the involvement of the first observer but because all open and rapidly evolving societies can sustain unreconciled points of view. Not all these will be equally 'right', of course; but they are perhaps all equally worthy of consideration. Thus they are not objects of external curiosity, but may be constituent parts of a growing understanding. Because of this process of matching-up and experimentation, new philosophies of education and new social aims become locally and topically paramount; but that is all we can properly say about them.

These changed aims and perspectives are to some extent attributable to improved *political* opportunities; but we underestimate the integral association of social opportunities with technological change if we overlook the great impact on our roles of our improved economic condition. A remarkable transformation has been brought about by the *enhanced economic authority and consumer demand* of previously depressed classes. We can all be ladies and gentlemen nowadays. Indeed, we must be if society is to achieve its expectations. It would be absurd to say that our social and political expectations are influenced solely by our confidence that we are important customers; but it is easier, for example, to aspire to the graceful ways of being a lady when clothes alone or malnutrition and overwork no longer predestine some to being 'women' instead of 'ladies'. Ask any girl about the evocative influence of a smart new dress. So it goes for all of us in our different ways of being trained and educated for significance. We expect more;

---

[1] For a similar deterioration of real inquiry when 'the scholastic now preferred to quote authorities', see R. Ulich's excellent account of 'The climate of disintegration' at the medieval University of Paris, in *The Education of Nations* (Harvard University Press, 1961), pp. 27 ff.

our demands seem more plausible; and we are all more seriously considered.

Thus within this same society of ours the passing of two generations has meant that a secondary schooling may no longer confer automatically on its beneficiaries a superior status with superior prospects, or that superior *cachet* of supposed sensibility once called 'refinement'. Neither the school nor the subjects, nor indeed the organized exercises of childhood, are in themselves reliably credited with being able to work personal, social, or professional magic. Though people still get many subsequent advantages because of special schooling, that fact usually tells us more about adults' partiality than about the ennobling quality of schools. Sensibility in these days entails the possession of a lot of facts about people, an acquaintance with their daily preoccupations close enough to encourage sympathy, and a well informed balancing-out of all the claims and counterclaims of individuals, groups, and society. From the matter-of-fact point of view of the school time-table itself, it is therefore clear that today's programme cannot be the same as that of 1900. The subjects will be different (we hope); and those titles which remain from an earlier date ought to have a vastly enlarged content, with quite a different orientation.

So much goes without saying; but how can we and how should we make it different? When we examine what the programme of many schools was in many parts of the world in the 1930s, we detect very little difference from the intention and complexion of schooling in progressive schools three centuries before – if we except the now universal use of the mother tongue, a modern language, and perhaps a bit more mathematics and science. Yet the three decades since 1900 alone had transformed most human relationships and prospects more than the three *centuries* before 1900! Since the 1930s the rate, scope, and intensity of change have been much more marked, and the whole world is involved instead of that once comfortable 'civilization'. Yet many schools and teachers still go on almost as though little had happened. Careers are different; the financial situation is different; but the subjects are often the same, and the aims of education are perennial!

Are they, though? Supposing we were to admit that no fault could be found with many of the basic aims of schooling before the Second World War, it is quite clear that now there must be a vastly different emphasis if only because of the impending (if delayed) social upheaval now beginning. In some countries political upheavals have revolutionized societies; but even where these do not take place, there can be no gainsaying the imminent presence of the Industrial Revolution's more important phase already referred to. It is transforming social roles and personal expectations. It makes possible a richer and wider sense of self.

An enlargement of horizons in this way must inevitably be contingent upon a complementary sense of others' status, prospects, and demands. Personal significance does not arise from a full wage packet (though that helps) so much as from a sense of opportunities, roles, and responsibilities. In other words, prowess can never in fairness be quite individualistic; nor can instruction ever be thought of again as a mass commodity, a sectional interest, or a personal treasure. Throughout the world education is seen as the prime instrument of social change and economic advancement; but there is nothing repetitive or unitary or localized about the job it now has to do. It must stress and develop complementary roles and responsibilities (as part of personal status) both at home and internationally.

None but the most parochial and purblind of teachers could really see education in any other terms; yet the purblind contingent is really very large. One reason for this unhappy state of affairs is that the word 'education' is popularly identified with familiar schooling. That is a small and diminishingly powerful part of it. In most countries of the world, schools and teachers are highly characteristic of the societies in which they find themselves. That is to say, they are themselves already 'processed' or 'geared' for certain clearly discernible purposes before they ever set their minds and hands to teaching anything. Moreover, schools handle just as little of the educative process and have just as little influence as pupils, parents, priests, publicists, and politicians are willing to allow.

While schools are engaged on their activities they do not always come realistically to terms with the cultural myths, social and economic expectations, or practical possibilities enveloping the children before, during, and after school. How much (or little) various national school systems can effectively do has been examined at some length in *Other Schools and Ours*, where close attention is also given to the intimate relationship between school on the one hand and many competitive or complementary influences on the other. These include: social, economic, and political institutions; religious organizations and other normative systems; job prospects; consumer opportunities; mobility, both geographical and social; and all the mass media of communication and suggestion. When all is said and done, schools are seldom if ever the main educative influence in the societies within which they operate. These contentious observations have been justified or illustrated in the book referred to, and they will be elaborated in later chapters here.

Another matter which makes it difficult to avoid a hiatus between school and life is the simple fact that the effective life of a teacher is some forty years.[1] In all occupations – often much more than in teaching – some routine patterns of professional behaviour set in. It would be inhuman to expect them to be absent from teachers, at any rate in relation to the subjects taught. Yet routine implies an absence of questioning. Teaching is, as all agree, a worth-while calling and one which can be richly rewarding in terms of human relationships with the pupils. That is the area in which most skill is exercised, and in which strains are likely to be found. With large classes everywhere, dilution of the teaching profession, and many extraneous duties added to teachers, it is no wonder that the job of teaching and all its proper ancillaries (such as marking, visits, and 'reading up') leave even the best teachers exhausted. Therefore, few but the most responsible teachers (in such academic work as we find in the examination forms of selective schools) can fairly be expected to be great scholars or radical inquirers. It is surprising, in fact, that so many of them keep well up to date in their academic fields.

But it is one thing to be a scholar in one's specialism, and quite another to see one's specialism in perspective – especially an altered perspective in a world which is confusing for the most alert of men. This is a civic and personal responsibility, irrespective of professional requirements. Even this feat of standing outside oneself is not enough, however, if it is limited to a re-assessment of the essence of one's subject or a refurbishing of one's methods. What we really require in order to achieve our object is that the teacher should, not occasionally but constantly, re-appraise the whole concept of education. He may have to reshuffle social priorities as well as purely pedagogical values. He needs to be delicately attuned to changing concepts of personality and alert to the different emphases in society's formative opportunities for it.

[1] This expectation is still true of most countries, and everywhere it is the oldest teachers who have most formative influence. Exceptionally, the average working life of American teachers during the 1950s was less than 10 years. In this connexion we should note the preponderance of young women teachers in the U.S.A., the low esteem of the teaching profession there, and the many opportunities open in other professions. A move towards this state of affairs is detectable elsewhere.

All this would require him to be a shrewd social philosopher and a skilled sociologist. These things he cannot really be; and if he could, he would not be on a schoolmaster's salary. Salary and status apart, there are few inducements or opportunities for teachers to venture alone upon this university-type scanning of the educational horizon envisaged here. Such activity is in any case usually possible only after the concerted efforts of several specialists have contributed to such a study as comparative education. Comparative education itself has only in the most recent years been presented in such a way as to be challenging or significant to the mature, practising teacher as distinct from the professional student or administrator. That is one reason for writing such a book as this; but books are not enough. Education is bound to fall into the trap of perpetuating the routine of subjects, methods, and unquestioned assumptions unless universities and ministries everywhere set themselves promptly to the task of turning the whole business upside down. After all, even in schools, nothing is really the same as it used to be a generation ago. Different people are bound to be doing different things for different objectives in a different world. Change is Protean and incessant; but change is useless unless fully informed and well directed.

Experimentation is going on all over the world. Some countries have a patchwork system of educational administration, which permits piecemeal and hit-or-miss attempts at reform. In other countries huge transformations are announced overnight, often to the bewilderment of the teachers. But in no civilized community is education still. It is expanding in scope and ambition; it includes more people for a longer time and takes them further. Much reform might be attributed to an attempt to catch up with technological requirements, so that more people (or a few) might in the end have more material prosperity. But even if that alone were true, those who are given an education are now most unlikely to stay as docile as seven-year-old children. The transformation of social systems begins with teaching ABC or its equivalent. Indeed, it starts before – from the very moment when a peasant or bondman is given a better tool or anything that will improve his relation to toil. At no time has mankind ever been such a seething mass of experiments in education, that is to say, in the altering of perceptions about the facts of life and work and about the proper relationships of one person with another.

One of the most remarkable changes in this world of change has been effected by the contribution of previously despised or underdeveloped countries. In 1900 few people could have taken seriously any suggestion that the U.S.A. and the Tsarist Empire might soon be the two cultural poles towards which the rest of the world might willy-nilly have to gravitate. The countries with rich, ancient cultures like Italy, Austria, or France might have seemed much more likely centres of educational interest, or even such parvenu industrial countries as the British Isles. In fact, European educators tended to look solely to each other for variations on the great educational themes. Being concerned only with a relatively small area of social and pedagogical interest, they tended to magnify their differences (for example, as between Britain, France, and Germany), and overlook the completely different assumptions and arrangements which were already re-shaping the United States in accordance with the unsuspected logic of industrialization.

From our present point in history, however, we can clearly see that by contrast with the U.S.A. all Western European educational systems have very much in common. Moreover, from our present point in geography, we can also see that the educational systems and assumptions of the U.S.A. and the U.S.S.R. have very much more in common than is generally supposed in either of those countries, primarily because (despite obvious ideological and administrative discrepancies) they are both ultimately geared in practice to the possibilities and demands of industrialization. Many educational issues of the utmost consequence can only be diagnosed against a world background which reduces merely local and superficial features to their proper proportions. We can then more easily see basic similarities or the complementariness of interests.

That is one special reason why newcomer countries can contribute something distinctive to the re-interpretation of an educational tradition. As already noted, when each one of us uses a word denoting a social function or need (like 'home', 'family', or 'school') we think of the institutions we know. Therefore, when we approach our survey from different cultural backgrounds we may not mean the same thing at all. It is a commonplace that the family in industrial Britain is not the agricultural and much-ramified family of France, its nearest neighbour. Nor is family life everywhere the same in the U.S.A. Much less does the average American family resemble that of Mexico. So the most elementary examination of school systems in their contexts reveals that the clientèle, activities, and social purposes of the schools differ amazingly. Surprising differences are revealed in the amount of the total business of education that the schools are expected or allowed to do.

Nor is it only the man-made institutions which change their scope and emotional aura from culture to culture, but other and much more fundamental notions too – like 'woman', 'father', and 'friend'.

More obviously, we who live in long settled countries are hampered by time-honoured practices and institutions. What we think of as bold educational and political ventures tend to be cast in an ancient mould. If that is not so, they are nevertheless circumscribed by ancient survivals from the moment of their inception. Even newer countries like the U.S.A. tend to trade in current slogans and organizational campaigns instead, the less tangible influences of which can become equally coercive. A go-ahead and ambitious country like the U.S.A. (or a smaller group of people elsewhere) can actually be entangled even at the height of the greatest venturing, if only because administrators are so well organized that their very skills almost absent-mindedly take over the promotion of whatever project they have in hand. The newest countries of all, however, seldom wish to use their existing institutions for the purposes of modernity; and they often lack the skills and other resources they must use. They then start from scratch or from some revolutionary clean sweep. They are often poor and therefore concerned with human priorities in their crudest form. Our talismans mean nothing to them. They think they see what they want, and go straight for it. Thus they view every human endeavour and claim in the cold light of the morning of their world, with the fresh gaze of children.

Yet even if we suppose that this reduction of the ancient educative purposes of society to their simplest elements in underdeveloped countries is an over-simplification, at least as far as might concern any lessons for us, we have nevertheless much to learn from observing such people's experiments sympathetically in context. After all, the hypothesis behind every social or scholastic experiment is one more variation on the ancient claims and aspirations of man. We can first ascertain just what is being attempted in principle; then we may assess the validity of the principle by observing its evolution in practice. We might find that the same principle has been better approached in a comparable context by a different method. We might on the other hand note that a similar method was used elsewhere for another laudable objective, ostensibly justified by quite a different theory. Thus we may assess the validity of theories or the utility of practices.

We must always, however, be absolutely sure that what we are observing is fairly seen in context. If we do compare we must compare only comparable things. Our ultimate objective is to isolate the various essential elements in all human experimentation with culture and progress. In much the same way a biologist or psychologist or sociologist itemizes and evaluates the constituent factors in a creature's coming to terms with its environment or a community's adaptation to its circumstances; but it is the totality that is his real interest.

The huge difference between our researches and the biologist's is that man largely makes his environment – material, institutional, and symbolic. Therefore the most telling stresses of adjustment and the wonders of progress reflect alike man's conservatism and his creativity. The variations on any one theme must be almost uncountable. This makes it all the more necessary never to feel that *the* answer to any problem is known – least of all in such a problematic and symbolic area as education. From all that has been said so far it is obvious too that not only can no world-wide cure-all be dreamed of, but no old or borrowed prescription can be counted on to work its former wonders in some new circumstance. How strange therefore that so many Education books talk in such universal and timeless terms!

All that we can really hope for is to amass the constituent ingredients of a greater understanding. Though we do not pick up items from here and there as some birds do to embellish their nests, we can greatly gain by piecemeal observation if a provisional world-view or preparatory understanding is taking shape in our minds. Of course, the existence of such a *Gestalt* presupposes careful reading and carefully disciplined insight. So we are not really picking things up or copying, any more than the biologist at work in a field survey. Our approach, if we are very sure of ourselves, may be that of looking for evidence in support of a hypothesis; but it is generally safer to work towards a more global understanding by repeatedly viewing a central interest from the complementary standpoints of experimenters standing on its periphery. Each of their experiments tends to concentrate on one facet of the whole. Thus we are enabled to assess assumptions and methods by others' trial-and-error. It quite often happens that their insights are sharper than ours! Be that as it may, one of the best ways of learning a little parentcraft is to look at our neighbours. At least we think we see what *not* to do; but if we have any humility we are also helped in our treatment of our own children. This experience can also be matched by educators who look abroad; but a much more important result may be success in the endeavour described at the beginning of this paragraph – the approach to rounded understanding of general or recurring problems by the disciplined use of comparative techniques.

Comparative education, like any other comparative discipline, is certainly not just a matter either of compiling data about various educational systems or of describing what we may call the 'natural history' of particular systems. Of course, it needs both elements as raw materials; but the essence of it is the systematic promotion of research into the phenomenon of education *per se*, by trying to penetrate in depth its peripheral manifestations through the use of well-informed and disciplined techniques. Any other endeavour is little more than museum-work or educational tourism – a bland surveying of the curiosities of education in distant parts, usually with the implication that the practice of education at home is true educational 'civilization'. Such an attitude brings us back to the self-congratulation of my grandfather's contemporaries.

An equally naïve attitude is found in those who believe that in educational and social matters they can outdo the lilies of the field in the parable, because 'by taking thought, they can add one cubit to their stature'. Sitting down at home and thinking 'pure thought' in education is useless – indeed impossible. Thoughts obviously involve the whole personality of the thinker, including his past and his envisaged future – to say nothing of his present nexus with institutions and ideas around him. What is true of a single thinker may well be true of a whole committee of thinkers, particularly if they belong to one culture complex such as a headmasters' association or the Académie Française. Nor is ideological involvement limited to 'ideas', somehow leaving 'facts' exempt from impurities. Indeed, the involvement of people in their own perceptions is such that the idea of what constitutes a 'fact' is one of the most difficult of philosophical concepts. How, for instance, are we finally to distinguish a 'fact' from an 'observation' or an 'appearance', particularly in non-scientific matters, when it is difficult enough in physical science? It is particularly irksome to disencumber oneself when emotions, creeds, and 'principles' are implicated.[1]

For example, suppose we try to consider the role of religion or national feeling in education. We note immediately that our state of preparedness for this task of discussing 'religion' is different from what would have been experienced if similar words with a different evocation had been used – like 'churches' or 'The Church'. So it goes with

[1] See Whitehead, A. N., *Adventures of Ideas*, chapters XI–XIV; Mannheim, K., *Ideology and Utopia*, chapter 2; and Chapter 10 of the present book.

'faith' and 'morality' on the one hand, or 'loyalty', 'patriotism', and 'nationalism' on the other. Yet in different parts of the world just such substitutions take place, either by translation of the words themselves or by the transposition of a general idea to the highly idiomatic institution or concern in that region.[1] The same sort of thing happens immediately we touch on some other tender spot, such as language in relation to schools – a very knotty problem in many countries. Similarly questions about parental participation, of 'liberal' versus vocationally linked schooling, or the selection of an élite, and all the other perennial themes of educational debate are heavily loaded, local questions in every context where they occur. Though we must heed the local context, we must also strive for disengagement. We can properly appreciate the local problem itself only by making a wider survey and looking for relevant evidence elsewhere.

We return once more to what has already been said: that a principle for action must be embodied in a programme or policy, and that the programme is executed in a particular context. Each circumstance of a contextual whole is therefore an experimental opportunity for a new insight into the validity of the basic concept or the methods adopted for its attainment. This three-tier form of analysis at the levels of (a) central principle, (b) deductions in detail, (c) practical embodiment is very useful not just in educational matters, of course; it is particularly valuable in social philosophy. So though we may imagine we are undertaking little more than a single case-study in a particular context, we may really be doing more. Each particular case can be appreciated more deeply as the projection of some more universally relevant concept.

Another ingredient of the most profound importance to all educators is also to be found in this kind of comparative analysis. When we see other people sympathetically in their endeavours, we cannot escape seeing them as real people who matter to us. They are no longer objects of study; we are in contact. If we are truly in contact, we make a mutual impact. The old, arrogant subject-object relationship has faded away.

Sometimes we are told by psychologists that sensibility is basically self-identification, and so it may be. We gain in objectivity, person-

---

[1] Some very important social consequences of such 'mistranslation' of ideas on transfer to alien institutions or practices are surveyed at length in Dr H. Arendt's stimulating book *The Human Condition* (University of Chicago), 1958. This is a topic of continuing interest to Professor A. Toynbee too.

ality, and humanity simultaneously, as we rid ourselves of feelings of hostility, condescension, or other people's 'irrelevance'.

In a world of growing mistrust and threats nothing could be more dangerous than ignorance, indifference, and ideological isolationism. These failings already impair our understanding of what matters most in human affairs. Understanding does not necessarily make us love people; but we cannot live with them at all unless we understand them a little. The chances of avoiding friction are greater by far if we increase all kinds of awareness. This awakening is primarily the function of formal education. But teachers cannot awaken world sensibility unless they are continuously alerted to it. So for safety and happiness – nothing less – we cannot afford not to see our educational aims and practice in their true world context. Such a statement would be true even if the world were static, as it certainly is not. With everything changing so fast, and in unprecedented ways, the possessor of the very best current solution to educational problems could never rest on his laurels. That is the best way to be outstripped or superseded.

Technological competition alone demands that we learn all we can from the example of others. But there is much more in the impact of technology than the mere acquisition of data and skills; we must also learn (as we have not yet done) how to come to terms with the social implications of technology as the framework of a better civilization which must now be world-wide. Otherwise we may be left with a scaffold for the older humane values. In our search for a new way of making work and leisure civilizing influences we cannot afford to neglect any possibly relevant interpretation devised by others. So whether other people are deciding simply how much they can afford of formal education, or are deciding in what order to establish their priorities, or are contriving to extend the most luxurious of opportunities to an ever-expanding number of citizens, there may be lessons to be learned from them by all of us.

That is a worth-while exercise in itself; but it must never be forgotten that the whole of this endeavour – ostensibly about schools and the rearing of children – is really an inquiry of profounder significance. We are attempting to understand man (i.e. ourselves) by understanding other men. So education for international understanding, and our own comparative study, are part and parcel of a personal education that is simultaneously liberal and vocational. We do not study far-off things and people; we face the complement to our own self-study.

BOOKS

See the general bibliography on Comparative Education, p. 369.
Cassirer, E., *An Essay on Man* (New Haven), 1944.

SECTION II

The Social Context

CHAPTER 3

Who is educated?

If someone in Britain uses the phrase 'an educated man', both the speaker and the hearer generally think of a rather unusual person. Yet in Russia, one of the best ways of annoying an ordinary man is to suggest that he lacks 'culture'. Indignation can be expected from manual workers to whom such an implication is made in the U.S.S.R., whereas in Britain it is likely that manual workers would merely laugh at the effeminacy of the accuser. An observation like this tells us nothing about the relative merits or availability of schooling in the two countries mentioned; but it does tell us plenty about popular attitudes towards something that schooling is supposed to help to provide. It reveals a good deal too about what we may call 'specialization in culture'.

Many a liberal-minded champion of some self-made working man in France will say of him that he received his *culture* while attending evening classes or by private study. The French word *culture* suggests something rather different from either 'education' or 'culture' in English, being a sort of combination of both with an additional overtone. It implies that only one particular kind of education is likely to impart that special alertness and sensibility which the French most admire. The self-made man's advocate is saying, so to speak, that he has migrated from one community to another. He has joined a rather exclusive club. Exclusive though it is, that circle of men and women with *culture* is generally supposed by French people to represent the mind and ethos of France not just as these things are now manifested but as they have evolved towards their present climax through the glorious past of France. Infidelity to these historic ideals, or *vulgarisation* (i.e. 'popularization') of them, seems to many highly educated Frenchmen to be a special kind of baseness. It quickly arouses hot passions.

There is no wish to patronize our French neighbours in making these observations. Huffish loyalty to criteria indicating class differences is probably more marked in Britain than in France. A glance overseas is mainly intended to let us see how absurd are our own foibles. For example, we say *'standards* of behaviour' (as though there were planes or grades of merit) when we really mean 'idiosyncrasies of behaviour'. These are cherished in some quarters but loathed in others, just like tripe or high game in different parts of the social spectrum. According to our social background and orientation we like or dislike knives and forks used as shovels, affectation in the choice of wines, or a provincial accent. Our extremely elaborate and mainly artificial indices of social status enable the 'insider' or expert to recognize very nicely just what experiences a newcomer has had – within certain limited ranges of experience, of course; and it is also easy to recognize where he has had them. In certain circles in Britain, social intercourse is one long interview, intentional or otherwise. That is what makes Stephen Potter's writing so magnificently funny.[1]

But what is the lifelong interview about? What is its purpose? It is not to make sure that we are good, or sensitive, or well informed, or original, or persevering, or amiable, or charming, or loyal. These highly desirable hallmarks of civilization are assessed in friendship, of course; but before friendship is really practicable with highly educated persons in Britain it is normally necessary for the newcomer either to have been born (or schooled) within a similar group, to have acquired a full set of satisfactory social talismans, or to have crashed in with some latter-day Open Sesame (such as a distinction as a physicist or as a particularly 'angry young man').

Into this limbo of thrust and parry Stephen Potter, Simeon Potter, and Nancy Mitford can be our guides. R. K. Kelsall and others can discern for us the social provenance and economic prospects of those engaged in this proving-ground of shibboleths. What the educator has to notice is that all the fuss is about something *learned.* The items learned, moreover, seldom have any intrinsic merit. They are prized because they identify you with one particular subculture or relegate you to another. If you are welcomed, you can assume that your organized experience (whether in school, or in society, or by self-education) has 'educated' you satisfactorily. Satisfactoriness is a highly idiomatic affair, depending on the standpoint of your judge. The criteria used are somehow identified with an essence to which they are almost entirely superficial. The idioms are taught or unconsciously

[1] See, of course, *How to win at games without actually cheating,* and the whole 'Lifemanship' series. See also the writings of Nancy Mitford. *Pygmalion* and *My Fair Lady* also illustrate the social 'pecking order' very well.

perpetuated by certain traditionally approved kinds of apprenticeship; and the idiom with the strongest forecast of social and economic success in Britain is one associated with particular kinds of schooling. Though Britain is here taken as an example, such devices of exclusion, or of placing in a 'pecking order', are used to a greater or less degree in all countries.

Consequently, because people everywhere tend to be well satisfied with themselves, the assumption prevails that the self-evident virtues of the self-styled torchbearers of human cultivation are attributable to certain familiar exercises, subjects, and institutions. This is 'education'. The more set in its ways a class or a country becomes, the more institutionalized are its pronouncements about civilization, education, and the rest. That is why so many people find themselves trapped into saying 'education' when they really mean 'schooling', and, what is more, the particular type of schooling that is most familiar to them. In the same way people in different parts of the world think about certain moral qualities and promptly say 'Christian', 'Islamic', or 'communist' according to their context. What we must try to do is transcend our familiar formulae or 'gadgets of thinking' so as to examine, if possible, the living realities of education rather than the mere categories into which we have institutionally divided it.

Is education only one formalized part of the characteristic human attribute – the passing on of information, skills, and norms to oncoming generations in various well-organized ways? Or is it more than that – the whole process, in fact? If it is the whole process, how do we make sure of a full rehearsal in all those exercises for which there is no time or scope in the school curriculum? How about those things beyond the ken of school-age children? How about those people who do not go to school, or do not stay long enough, or who do not go to the 'right' school?

We cannot attempt to answer all these questions in this chapter. Nor can we really deal here with the problem of who is to educate, and in what institutions; but we can note what the main questions are. We may profitably take time to look at the different values which different cultures put (by implication) on various aspects of the educative process. We can ask what order of priority has recommended itself when there has had to be a rationing of opportunity. We can see how such an order of priority must often be changed to suit circumstances, such as an alteration in the supply of funds or the availability of teachers or the requirements of technology. A very important facet of educational change already noted is the alteration in the numbers and origins of those at school. Education now includes a larger element of formal schooling, and that formal schooling is specialized in formerly unprecedented ways. In short, we have to come down to some very practical questions. Who is to be educated? And what for? And why? And how? Instead of attempting abstract formulations, we shall try to see a few guiding principles exemplified in practice.

It is a commonplace that the studies of anthropologists have compelled us to re-think the whole concept of education. Our recent ancestors used to describe people in Polynesia and Africa as 'uncivilized', let alone uneducated. Yet civilization surely consists of having organizations which permit people to live together in communities, dividing labour and skills, accumulating material prosperity and knowledge, and generally ameliorating the prospects and perceptions of all participants. Our ancestors looked abroad and (doubtless as we do now) supposed that the absence from other cultures of *familiar* institutions, norms, and objectives proved that those foreigners were also strangers to the essence of humanity, at least at a level of refinement familiar at home. That may or may not have been true; but it was not automatically proved, any more than the absence of American-style plumbing elsewhere means that other people are necessarily less clean than Americans. It is perhaps even more to the point to take a culinary example: the absence of American-style food stores and kitchens in Europe does not automatically prove that Europeans do not like good food, do not know how to make it, or have less discriminating palates. Most Europeans, especially continentals, would be indignant at such a suggestion.

The anthropologists have given us just such a slant on former assumptions about civilization. They have introduced us to a new sense of the word 'culture', which is now used more often in the phrase '*a* culture', implying that well-organized communities elsewhere can enjoy what for them is a rounded and valid perception of what human life really adds up to. They can have a locally and topically justified complex of institutions and values. To say '*a* culture' also implies that there can be no one universal prescription for Culture with a capital C, any more than 'a truth' would enable anyone to know Truth with a capital T. It may be that, as truth has many facets, so culture and education also have many contributory aspects. Just as many 'truths' may need to be aligned before 'the truth' about any matter is established, so many aspects of culture and education may have to be compared before anything very definite or conclusive is said about any one culture or educational pattern. Even then, we may not be entitled to make universal pronouncements about Education or Culture as abstractions, any more than many 'truths' or even 'the truth' would enable us to understand essential Truth itself.

The history of the past few centuries of cultural intercourse is full of examples of misunderstandings in this matter. There is no ground for supposing that, when Marco Polo and later explorers first made contact with the Great Khan and the civilizations of the East, the Asians were less humane than the Europeans in all or many respects, or had established governmental and social systems that were less empirically justified than those prevailing in Europe at the time. In the Western hemisphere the Conquistadores were probably no more refined than their counterparts among the Aztecs, Maya, or Incas. To say so much is not to make out that the American civilizations were such as we should admire now, particularly in terms of cosmogony, social ideas, and technology; but they were great civilizations for all that. Though they were full of cruelties, so was the imported system of the Spaniards. This was indeed more universally invasive because of technological imports: steel, the horse, wheels, navigation, and firearms. These technological devices did not of themselves suddenly civilize the Americas. They had not indeed conferred superior humanity upon the Europeans, as the later war pictures of Goya show only too well. A technological armoury, of itself, tells you nothing about its possessor's degree of civilization, any more than a machine-gun and a gas-chamber prove that their users are more humane than those who use bows and arrows.

In education in particular, however, certain technical devices (e.g. subjects or skills) have been taken as infallible outward signs of inward grace. They have become sacrosanct. Not only have they been holy in themselves; they have been reckoned to be the sole instruments of holiness. To keep them pure, many 'false gods' are unreflectingly cast aside. One of the first lessons of comparative education is to jerk away the false foundation of such smug arrogance. In place of that, we must learn to see surprising devices, even 'idols' and absurd punctilio, as constituent parts of a whole culture. We have to discern the complementary roles of perhaps unfamiliar people, ideas, and institutions in constructing a whole edifice of learning, understanding, and behaviour. Above all, we recognize with the anthropologists that cultures tend to be locally complete and satisfying. The importation of supposedly desirable new ingredients (such as factories, communications, and schools or subjects) may disturb that balance of the whole – and may therefore impair its health or efficiency. The immediate results are not inevitably good. Extremely delicate and useful instruments of human understanding may be destroyed.

We often underestimate the intricacy of fundamentally educative devices in so-called primitive communities. Instances might be the family system or language. Let us take the latter as an example. Many supposedly backward cultures have languages which are much more complicated than our own in all their basic ingredients – which means that everyone using them is alerted to fine distinctions and elaborate relationships of ideas. Basically, the English language is by contrast primitive: in its current, day-to-day use it can be a very unrefined thing with a limited vocabulary and crude in its expression of relationships, even though 'educated' English is a subtle and evocative tongue. That is to say, many 'primitive' populations in other lands may be daily exercised in intricate and elaborate concepts that many of our own people lack. Similarly, sagas and manifold family interests may constantly develop in simpler societies a rich sense of history, society, and literature that urbanized communities have lost.

There is no allegation here that we are backward, while everyone else is splendid. All that is emphasized is that there is nothing automatic about being civilized. Civilization is not something that is possessed or distributed like a consumer commodity. It is at best an artifact whose value lies in the use made of it. Indeed, it cannot be possessed, but must be lived. Studies in cultural anthropology and comparative sociology teach us that civilization, like education (and indeed personality), must be constantly *re-enacted* by all. In different cultural settings, the acting-out must be different. So much we see from our geographical surveys of different parts of the world; but what is equally pertinent is the fact that from epoch to epoch and from phase to phase of technology the whole cultural matrix of our learning and perceptions shifts its emphases. That is to say, our selves and outlooks and capabilities alter. The whole complex concept of what we are, what we are capable of, and in what circumstances we may develop ourselves has undergone a change which is not merely peripheral to us (i.e. outside us like the wind and sunshine), but is part of us in the same way as good and bad habits, or the ability to speak and reason in a particular idiom.

So when we ask questions which sound fairly sensible, like 'who can be educated?', we are really asking either meaningless questions or questions which are really hemmed in with supplementary questions about society. It is obvious that man can learn to see, move about, and develop manual skill only by trial and error. It is also obvious however that this kind of self-education alone will never make a human being of him, but only an efficient animal who happens to be of the human species. To be human as we normally understand the term he must grow up and stay in a human context, learning from the example and precepts of others in institutions (such as families, religions, crafts, and schools). Everyone therefore needs and should get a life-long education, and *recognition*. There are genetic influences at work to differentiate us, of course; and some of these impart the promise of genius or the threat of physical weakness, for example. But most of the differentiation between us is merely one of degree, and of minute graduations at that. The degree to which we develop our potentialities is decided largely by our institutional contacts.

We are not all capable of everything, naturally. Even in the things we are best at, we are not all as capable of the same levels of achievement as some competitors. Yet we are all capable of significance potentially, despite differences in achievement. There are two traps to beware of here. The graduations between us are often slight in quantity, and judged circumstantially – much as a few degrees make a cup of tea a bit too hot or a bit too cool for my taste, but do not stop it being a hot drink rather than a cold one, or even stop it being perfectly right for someone else. The second trap is a result of our being conditioned by industrialization to think primarily in terms of *what* is measurable, and in terms of mutually exclusive categories (e.g. a nut will either fit a particular bolt or it won't; the fact that *other* means of fastening things together would be satisfactory is irrelevant in the context).

So we go on to talk about 'degrees of ability'. Ability, of course, is something that will fit, and can be measured. It is all very well (and indeed justifiable) to talk about educational opportunities appropriate to different types and degrees of ability; but we have first to make sure of three things: (*a*) whether what we recognize as 'ability' really is properly so called, and not just *an* ability of some often arbitrarily chosen type to meet supposed requirements, and leading to the exclusion of other possible types; (*b*) whether our methods of identification and measurement are reliable; and (*c*) whether the treatment we accord to the selected kind and degree of ability is really appropriate to its development and exploitation in our present and future society. We must also consider how restricted our survey of needs and potentialities has been. It is a conservative statement to say that we are not really sure about any of these things. Furthermore, it is open to the gravest doubt whether we would be entitled to draw the social and economic conclusions that we do, even if we were sure. Many of these things will be called into question from time to time throughout this book, not so much by formal argument as by implication, in the examination of what other people do to each other and their children.

But as the term 'ability' has been queried, it seems appropriate to spare a moment here to quieten the misgivings of those shocked by the sacrilege done to established assumptions. Suppose, for the sake of argument, that we know what ability is in the abstract, and can cater for it concretely by manageable examinations and suitable schooling. How are we to compare and generally evaluate such varied manifestations of ability as those of the historian, the Classical scholar, the mathematician, and the musician? How are we to rate these abilities when measured? Why, in the relatively simple matter of reading, the historian surveys a vast canvas of events and personalities as he reads at great speed; whereas the Classical scholar usually reads slowly and meticulously, with an almost fastidious savouring of each word and expression. Surely, though these are both Arts men, they show radically different aspects of ability?

The mathematician and the really advanced physicist on the other hand spend much of their time dealing with the most abstruse abstractions. Their nearest kin – the philosopher, actuary, accountant, or engineer – all show cognate skills which are nevertheless as unlike theirs as any two relatives can be. We usually over-rationalize the connexion between any two disciplines. It is clear that the good engineer has added to the rationality of the mathematician or physicist some indefinable flair of creativity which brings him closer to the fine musician. After all, though music and mathematics are notionally related, what makes a great musician is something other than rationality or an ability to account for his skill in terms of musicology. Can there therefore be one criterion for advanced educability, or must there be many?

What is more, we have been talking about a very restricted range of abilities, i.e. the province of educated people who are much more alike than unlike. To make confusion worse, we have been thinking exclusively about what *we* might want to do for them – not what other people in other circumstances and for different purposes might want to do for them. Still further from our calculations has been the question of what all these able people might have decided about their own future education, or may now think about it as they look back in retrospect from maturity. Least of all have we considered what ideas those other people may have, who are not so far acknowledged to be candidates for more than a limited schooling. Let us take this last omission first, as it so profoundly affects the majority of the world's population.

We shall come to a more just and sympathetic appraisal of their needs if we take a parallel from family experience. Even the most encouraging parent in the most evocative of families (as any reader with children will consider himself) must have noted that a child will sometimes take it for granted that there are some things that elders can do but children not. These may be such matters as keeping clean, or tying bows on shoes, and other petty irritations; but they may also include rather pleasant things, such as making a nesting-box for birds or lighting a fire. We may also have noted that some boys assume that they cannot wash up, make their beds, or cook anything. They are surrounded by opportunities for learning; but such expertise is an alien thing. Yet if they can be induced to learn, boys can become expert cooks, knitters, and all the rest. They can enjoy these things too.

In precisely the same way, some people never learn to swim or dance. It was never expected of them; or if the opportunity did come their way, it was never urged upon them. Anyone who has had much to do with people born before the First World War, particularly if they are now living in modest circumstances, will agree that a large proportion of them have similarly assumed throughout life that only a restricted range of opportunities in learning and living ever lay open to them. If they had been born a generation later, they would without any more effort on their part have grown up with different expectations. We can understand more sympathetically what such an attitude feels like 'from inside' if we ourselves have not come from a family in which the ability to drive cars, ride horses, sail yachts, and hob-nob with the gentry was taken for granted. We may wistfully hanker after such delights; we may even do something about them; but it is (or recently was) statistically probable that we shall assume without more ado that people like us do not do that sort of thing. Similar feelings of 'otherness', often well below the conscious level of reflection, keep many people from attempts to make music or construct things. In other contexts, comparable inhibitions prevent women from speaking their minds to men on anything that matters much. Such self-exclusion is one of the most prevalent and regrettable concomitants of education in many parts of the world. People do not know 'they have it in them'.

In any case, if we are untypical enough to have ideas above our station, our first ventures into an alien subculture may leave us feeling naked and ashamed. The attempt to plunge oneself into such foreignness may in itself require a degree of resolution comparable with that of migrating, or of changing one's religious allegiance. There must not only be the shock and strain of striking out for oneself; there must first be the real surprise of recognizing such a possibility. One consequence may also be a loss of contact with much that is comfortingly familiar, and loved. In any case, why do it? If there is little or no manifest superiority in the alien way, or no material advantage, or little obvious happiness, what is going to induce people to venture upon it – particularly if there has been no invitation to do so? It was, among other things, an appreciation of these psychological barriers that led the United States Supreme Court in 1954 to declare that segregation was of itself inherently unequal treatment, even where 'separate but equal' opportunities were ostensibly afforded. Isolation within ghettoes, whether intentional or merely ideological and purely subjective, must similarly result in the cultural atrophy of the inmates.

In the greater part of the world the 'inmates' of culturally underprivileged compounds are the majority of the population. The same might fairly be said of Britain, even though the nation is committed by law to 'secondary education for all' with 'parity of esteem' and all that. It is always extremely difficult to see oneself; but Britons can see, so to speak, a reflection of their own inhibitions when noting what happens in France and Austria. Britain has not yet reasonable equality at the secondary phase of schooling; but at any rate the idea has prevailed in practice that something better than a lower-grade 'secondary' schooling is within the reach and competence of almost a quarter of the children. The majority of the children now in the prestige-carrying academic grammar school, with its conditional promise of first-class careers, have come from parents who did not themselves have such an opportunity. Popular opinion recognizes this change as not only fair but inevitable.

Yet in France so ardent a champion of reform as M. Roger Gal said in 1956 that the majority of parents 'do not even think of' a *lycée* or *collège* schooling for their children, although access to these is open to all who show ability and there are no tuition fees. The situation has improved somewhat; but it has not radically changed. Likewise, in

Austria there is really no need for any selection examination for secondary school admission – at least in terms of numbers. Pleasant-sounding talk of 'parental choice' disguises the fact that many poor or rural parents do not include the *Gymnasium* and its prospects within their horizon at all. *There is selection according to people level*

We must not make the mistake of supposing that the French or Austrian child thus shut out, perhaps unintentionally, from what is generally considered to be the finest opportunity his country affords is thereby deprived of an education, however we interpret that word. He may receive good general schooling somewhere else, with vocational training in addition if he lives in or near a town. He will certainly become shrewdly informed about local and national politics; he will probably have a good deal of aesthetic education in various media; and he will certainly learn how to enjoy life. Indeed, in some ways it might be said that he is closer to the heart and soul of France (or Austria, as the case may be) than the more cosmopolitan *bourgeois* who wins his way through the rigours of the academic secondary school, or the malcontent who is rejected at one of its many hurdles.

The main lesson for us to draw from our observation of these two countries really concerns the twin concepts of 'readiness' and 'ability'. The majority of the population in those countries and many others may not be 'ready' for formal schooling of the type most esteemed locally, just because it does not inquire about or cater for the things at which they are most able or in which they are most interested. It is streamlined for purposes which largely lie outside their ken or sympathy. It belongs to a different orientation, if not to a 'foreign' sub-culture.

Thus, although in one sense we might say that such children are not 'fit' for the *Gymnasium* or *lycée*, it might be at least equally true to say that those schools were not 'fit' for them. They may really be failing the country too. At least, such a comment would be justifiable if it could be shown that those schools do not provide well-trained people in exactly the numbers and of exactly the variety that France and Austria require to take up positions in industry, learning, and public life. And that appears to be true in each case. In Austria they produce too many people highly skilled in departments of knowledge which Austria cannot properly make use of. In France they produce too few, and in a too restricted range of interests. The integration of very diverse Austrian subcultures into one widely compatible way of life is thereby delayed, as well as Austria's industrialization. In France, the development of a modern, industrialized nation with a stable economy and sound political system is seriously hampered by the tradition-bound rigidities of the secondary school system. A similar statement might be made about Italy.

To come to such conclusions is not to say or imply that our own system is any better than that of France or Austria. Such exercises in self-congratulation miss the whole point. We are really being given a chance to see our own absurdities afresh – by implication or allegory, as it were. Both France and Austria have a history of concern for education that might put us to shame. Their great artists, musicians, thinkers, and indeed scientists are world-famous; but in the rest of the modern world there is a great shaking of heads over both countries, and a widespread belief that they live in the past – a past whose glories may have been more glamorized than real. In exactly the same way the visitor to new and confident countries finds heads shaken over Britain – not least in British dominions. Those who do not believe that this unwelcome solicitude is justified cannot thereby feel exempt from the need, which all nations share, to take stock of their old ideas and routines, to clear out outmoded junk, and also to make sure of a really good bargain basement to widen their scholastic clientèle.

We said earlier in this chapter that everyone needs constant rehearsal in human relationships, reminders of human knowledge, and further evocation – simply to go on being human. Therefore an uninterrupted opportunity for education is a necessary condition for health and sanity, both for individuals and for the manifold groups that make up society. Not all, or even the majority, of these needs will ever be met in schools; but it is obvious that in times of great flux and experiment it becomes more necessary than before to provide formal opportunities for education both inside and outside schools. The most conspicuous changes in the past two hundred years have been the direct consequence of using mechanical processes in industry. People were drawn away from the coercion of tradition in villages and rural enterprises; they were brought to towns which had no precedent, and engaged upon mechanical processes not considered to be educative at all.

Indeed, the situation arose which only a few are now coming to recognize as paradoxical, that daily relationships were considered to contribute nothing to humane perceptions and culture. At best they might be softened or counteracted by culture, as from above. Culture was in fact considered to be something for outside and after work – its very antithesis. So you could not expect the working classes to be cultured at all, *as* working people.[1] Culture was possible only in an oasis provided by the sinews and anxieties of others (as T. S. Eliot explains in *Notes towards a Definition of Culture*), or perhaps in an *escape* from the limbo of working into the (occasional) bliss of leisure. So culture for the worker was placed on a par with Sunday churchgoing, spectator football, hobbies, illicit week-ends and the like. It was a leisure-time extra for some dilettanti among the workers who might happen to go in for it. Like other hobbies, it was for them a matter of choice – especially if, like Bentham, you refused to distinguish between the quality of activities giving equal amounts of happiness. Such culture was therefore extraneous to daily life. Not quite, of course, because there was always an outside criterion for 'culture', namely that of the only people whose views were valid and whose tastes were impeccable – the people who never did the more soiling kind of work, and who were schooled for positions of example and leadership. Their families and social contacts perpetuated their culture, or (if they were parvenus) bought it for them at the Public School.[2] Most such people had, of course, every opportunity to be urbane and cultivated, though in a subculture alienated from the actualities of most of their compatriots' lives; but they also tended to make two pedagogical assumptions: that some people were born to sensibility and distinction as to a profession; and that the proper development of these attributes could be achieved only (or best) by exercises in certain familiar subjects in certain types of school.

It was in many ways fortunate that in some countries (like England) the expanding mercantile class of the nineteenth century had the opportunity to claim access to the prerogatives and mannerisms of the ruling class. In Britain, too, the upper middle class was astonishingly absorptive. Its own expansion, and its acceptance of others, were facilitated by reliance on particular kinds of schooling – such as the Public School and its humbler, local counterpart, the grammar school. In other words, the traditional type of education was provided in greater quantity than before, and to a larger public. There were also

[1] On the theme of proletarian subcultures in industrial Britain, readers are referred to two excellent analyses: R. Hoggart's *The Uses of Literacy*, London (Chatto & Windus), 1957, and R. Williams's *The Long Revolution*, London (Chatto & Windus), 1961.

[2] The English 'Public School' is a prestige-giving and exclusive private school with a high academic standard, a strong emphasis on character-training, and privileged access to the older universities and leading professions. Fuller information is given in the footnote on p. 144.

many reforms and some modernization, especially after Arnold and Thring's widely copied innovations; but none of these in Britain reached the degree of modernity which had characterized the 'dissenting academies' more than fifty years before. Those had offered the sons of the rising *bourgeoisie* not just a general education but modern and scientific studies too of a kind that was logically well suited to the needs of an urbanized, go-ahead community. At least, that is the way it looks now in retrospect; but time and again in human affairs we discover that long-established practices and assumptions invest themselves with an institutional force that can resist both plain common sense and manifest advantage, particularly if some short-term advantage or delight blurs the cleaner outlines ahead.

Thus the 'dissenting academies' and similar schools, which might have put a quite different complexion on the development of education in England, were gradually superseded for prestige reasons. They were doomed by the hang-over of the pre-industrial idea that a 'gentleman' [1] was equipped not just by urbanity but, so to speak, essentially to lead the rest of mankind in all kind of enterprises and discoveries. There can be no doubt that such 'gentlemen', very much as Locke had thought of them at least a century and a quarter before, still had all the social and economic advantages in the 1830s. In Britain they were not cut away by tradition from participation in business, as they were in contemporary Europe on the continent or as they now are in a country like Siam. The very fact that 'gentlemen' could have business connexions, if only at the highest level of administration or at the receiving end of investments, caused a huge expansion of the Public Schools which produced them in the 1840s and later. This expansion was of course favoured by the development of railways and other communications, for these schools were residential, and did not serve a local public. They were highly successful in making pre-industrial or extra-industrial 'gentlemen' out of prosperous manufacturers' and merchants' sons.

About the same time, under the influence of Sidgwick and others, the ancient universities of Oxford and Cambridge built up their standards from the depressed level to which they had fallen by the early nineteenth century, and once again became real centres of learning – but of a restricted kind. They re-established themselves by re-surrecting the time-honoured traditions: the respectable studies, manners, and methods of a former time.

[1] See my essay 'The gentleman: the evolution of an ideal' in the Appendix, p. 360.

A century and a half of scientific discovery had been achieved by 'gentlemen' in their spare time – *after* the university or Public School. Alternatively, improvements were invented by ingenious mechanics of the lower classes who went in for that sort of thing. There seemed no need or reason to bring such concerns into the 'real' universities (for by this time there was, so to say, a para-university development in London and other cities). It was still the alumni of the Public Schools who provided the top administrators and a whole hierarchy of faithful servants for domestic and imperial expansion. So in one sense, in English circumstances at that time, the Public Schools could have been described as providing the finest vocational preparation that could be desired – except that the subjects taught and outlook induced had no real or wide contact with the world around them. An Olympian position was more certain without that.

It is one of the strangest ironies in the history of education that the three distinctive contributions of English education (the Public School, the preoccupation with 'character', and the tutorial system of the older universities) were developed as we know them by playing false to the implied logic of Britain's advance in technology, social ideas, and governmental forms. There is no doubt that some splendid liberal traditions (such as those of responsibility, public service, and team spirit) have not only been perpetuated in consequence but have passed out into many other kinds of schools and institutions. Yet the grudging dispensation of this largesse from above and the hungry snatching from below have diverted attention from many of the real issues. That niggardliness and its attendant jealousy are responsible for very much muddled thinking about education in general and about the various details of British education in particular.

The point that most clearly stands out in the account just given is that Public School education was not Education with a capital E, as many of its advocates and consumers appear to think. It is not and has not been education 'at its best'. It was and is a specialized schooling for a particular kind of future in a particular country or Empire at a particular conjunction of events and institutions. The same might be said about much education in some departments of the older universities, even though new academic subjects are now taught to new kinds of undergraduates who will take up a wide range of careers not always thought quite respectable before the Second World War. It is still widely assumed that residence and instruction in those places do something unparalleled, and almost inevitably so, to students selected by impeccable criteria based on previous schooling and approved experience. So generally unchallenged are these ideas that it is worth emphasizing here that they are severally open to the gravest doubt, and that their amalgamation into one composite attitude is of even more dubious worth. The attitude is dubious, and its social implementation more so.

It is sometimes conceded by the beneficiaries of ancient scholastic prestige that an extension of comparable facilities elsewhere (to similar types of student only, of course) might have comparable results with a perhaps more provincial idiom, if only other universities enjoyed the general amplitude of Oxford and Cambridge's resources – as they do not. But an opposite constellation of views, which some people try to maintain at the same time, could perhaps be expressed as follows:

(a) the English tradition of gentlemanly education in the familiar institutions is not merely partial or topical but general, universally applicable, and of the very essence of Education;

(b) it is something cultivated outside and beyond 'subjects', yet peculiarly associated with particular kinds of subject or exercises;

(c) it is likely to be perceived or appreciated in abstraction and withdrawal, rather than by 'immediacy' and fullness of contact with workaday preoccupations;

(d) it is only dubiously capable of extension to other 'types of person', other sections of society, or clearly vocational interests.

To deal with these arrogant contentions we can reflect on what was said about Austria and France a little earlier. When the French, Italian, or Austrian educator lays down the law about universal values and 'a possession for ever', he seems to us to be caught up in his own history and institutions. His views are local, sectional, and topical in terms of a bygone generation (if that). Our own dominions in the British Commonwealth have moved on faster, further, and more freely than we; and they pass similar judgements on us. A reasonable amount of humility should compel us to see that most of our assumptions about types of schooling are still cast in a mould of outdated institutions, careers, and assumptions. Our vigorous cousins in the Commonwealth – and, indeed, our own social and technological logic – have discarded such antiquities with the hansom cab. We must go on changing or else be superseded or irrelevant.

The foregoing analysis is a good example of how comparisons with other countries, or comparisons between different historical phases within one country, can help to reveal the essentials of an institution or the crux of a problem. They point the way to a truer appraisal of similar problems and aims for the future. Comparisons between any two or more parallel sets of institution at any one place or time may also help us to reach a clearer understanding either of the truth or of a contemporary ideology.

It is particularly important for all of us, at the present conjuncture in world events, to stop talking about education and educational institutions as though our little, local difficulties and little, temporary institutions were the whole panorama of human culture. Books in English, British institutions, and the European or American example are now being considered, with others, as possible blueprints for revolutionary developments of critical importance for the future of the vast majority of the human race. Our judgements and views must therefore be formed with a wide sense of responsibility. Our own children's lives will be shaped by our choice, directly or indirectly.

Some have noted that the American interpretation of democracy, for example, is unpopular in parts of Central and South America; or that American ideas about education are so suspect in Europe that excellent American features are often repudiated along with what is less satisfactory. Not only is this unfair; the development of education everywhere sustains a serious loss. That is mainly because we are sold 'the whole package'. In the most important human decisions there can be no package deal. We too have an immediate obligation to desist from automatically universalizing ourselves (or even our 'better selves'). We must try instead to help other people elsewhere to carry on the great discussions of mankind in their own context. They will thus evolve a new idiom which may enrich the future of all. In human affairs, any unique prescription is probably quackery. There is always the risk that someone else's unique prescription may seem more wholesome than our own, or a sovereign remedy for more people's ills. In the case of communism, both these claims are made and widely believed. Education is energetically canvassed and generously provided in communistic countries, not with reference to 'absolutes', 'human rights', and dignity but in relation to the planned exploitation of all resources on earth, human as well as material.

If only we in the non-communist world had enough sense to see that the systematic development of *all* resources (even human resources) through education is not an infringement of Lockean 'private areas' but the very condition of human dignity! There is no suggestion that everyone or anyone should be *processed* to become part of some supposedly greater process, as the communists and some believers think. To echo Bentham, it is not alleged that we should turn the pig's pleasure into that of Socrates if we could; but at least we should make sure that it is a pig we are leaving behind to enjoy the mud, and not just some poor neglected human being. Almost every single improvement in schooling has been resisted by someone on the ground that it infringed privacy, or that it cheapened culture by attempting to do the impossible to the unwilling. It would be nearer the truth to maintain that smugness is worse than fantasy. It is a perversion of the sense of shared culture which all communities enjoyed until incipient industrialization made 'culture' a sort of craft specialism. It is also a denial of the religious tradition of membership, one with another.

In any case, it is no use attempting to turn back the clock. For all their faults, paternalistic philanthropy and charity have been responsible in all Western countries (especially Britain) for much expansion of schooling among the poorer classes. Such altruism (as often happens) was moving in the same direction as self-interest also demanded. A world survey proves this. As we look around we can see fairly regular patterns of development in education, particularly in relation to technological development. The first development of mechanization requires at least some competence in reading, in following instructions, and in elementary mathematics among the greater part of the population.

It is possible to start industrializing without these things at first, of course; but efficiency stalls until they are provided. Then (as happened in the Mechanics' Institutes between about 1818 and 1845) foremen and the simpler grades of technician feel the need for something more than the crudest rudiments. Soon there is felt a need for minor and major supervisors and managers. These could come from conventional, academic secondary or middle schools. In this category we can lump together the nineteenth-century Public Schools and the modern grammar schools, together with the *lycées* and *Gymnasia* and similar schools on the continent. Alternatively, and usually at a lower social level, they can be recruited from new types of school destined specially to provide them. Such are the *Mittelschulen* of Germany and the various higher elementary schools of many countries. Britain had a number of backroom developments of this kind in the last quarter of the nineteenth century, and revived them in the Central Schools before the Second World War. The main point to note is that the needs of industry alone justified these developments, and indeed required them. Boys and girls with ten to twelve years' enterprising schooling were demanded by technological expansion and trade.

Although in such circumstances ambition and family self-sacrifice are often sufficient to pay for the costs of above-elementary schooling, the financing of institutions and students sooner or later becomes a matter of public concern. Hard-headed business considerations make people in power readier to listen to the champions of the under-privileged, who are eager to help themselves and simultaneously help their masters by becoming more efficient. Pupils in newly expanded school systems come from unfamiliar types of home, and they may be going into jobs and skills without precedent. These matters affect the curriculum, orientation, and relationships of any post-elementary school. Britain first saddled herself with these public responsibilities in 1902; but the questions they raised still perplex people and are unsolved.

Other countries came later to the contest, and were less inhibited. Denmark, Japan, and the United States are notable examples; but the most remarkable is Russia. There was no compulsory education in Soviet Russia until 1930; and then only four years were required. By 1958-9 the secondary schools there, catering for about four times the school population of the United Kingdom, took between thirty and forty times as many children to the immediately pre-university level of attainment. Furthermore, the secondary school period is a purposeful and enriching experience for those not going on to the university.[1] Similarly in India education increased threefold between 1951 and 1960. China's progress is faster still, because it is not a democracy and reforms are pushed ahead ruthlessly. Now these far-away events intimately affect all our thinking about schools at home. The beneficiaries of these changes are our own children's contemporaries. They are not just abstractions in some alien statistics.

A third stage is reached when university training (or something comparable in a college of technology) is required from increasing numbers. The same sort of social and recruitment problems which we previously encountered in secondary schools repeat themselves here. Unprecedented groups of people are trained in unfamiliar ways for new careers. Once again, newer countries realize that higher education is not a luxury but a necessity in the modern world. They therefore provide it in excellent quality, in a wide range of interests, and to a widely recruited body of students. Some older governmental and technological

---

[1] Detailed information about recent developments is given in Chapter 7.

systems too adjust themselves to the actualities of present-day needs. Only Ireland, Turkey, and Norway among the well-developed countries of the world now have university student populations lower than Britain's in proportion to their populations. Austria and Western Germany, for example, exceed Britain's proportion by more than 60 per cent. France, East Germany, and Yugoslavia have considerably more than twice the British ratio.[1] The U.S.S.R. has almost six times as many university students as Britain, and there can be no doubts about their excellent quality. The U.S.A. is in a special position, and American universities will be considered later.

All these changes introduce consequential alterations into the secondary school, and into after-school training of several kinds. We shall have to review these in a special chapter. Just now it is important for us to realize simply that changes are inevitable all along the line – in relation to curriculum, objectives, and the social backgrounds and prospects of the pupils. We shall have to re-interpret the whole purpose of our schools. But one thing that is abundantly clear is often overlooked: the changes made are taking place in a world where parents and teachers are or should be alerted to conditions in other countries. We must not be such simpletons as to suppose that any enlargement of our own opportunities is occasioned only by pure thought or supposedly absolute principles. It is taking place in a world where a great deal is happening, and where everything is getting closer.

Therefore we might well remind ourselves of the dictum contained in the British White Paper of 1943 (Cmd. 6458): 'Education in the future must be a process of gradually widening horizons, from the family to the local community, from the community to the nation, and from the nation to the world.' This sentiment is valid now in ways perhaps unsuspected at the time; but it is particularly valid in a perennial sense – that of the anthropologist's use of 'culture' and 'education'. To be human implies education, not just in having been educated but in being educated all the time. Such continuous re-appraisal of self and purpose must take place not just in school but in a whole matrix of significant occasions. Each one of these, with its nucleus of fact or 'know how', should be made a vehicle of perception for a whole vista of human relationships and humane considerations. If not, our cultural system is failing to live up to the level of the so-called primitives. Our industrialized and urbanized life is indeed well organized – but for different ends than those of real civilization. Its very complication

[1] For figures: B. V. Bowden, *Guardian*, 8 December 1959.

makes it impossible for educative perceptions to develop automatically or haphazard, any more than businesses can develop haphazard. If we are to remain civilized, therefore, it is imperative and inevitable that education shall be increasingly systematized, more minutely and richly provided for, and diversified in such a way that the requirements of working and living can be met and understood in full complementariness.

One thing our comparative survey should have shown us already is that everyone gets an education of some sort. The critical question is whether it is an evocative one or one calculated to depress and blinker him. Civilization and higher living standards alike require the fullest development and refinement of all contributory skills and qualities, no matter how untraditional they may seem to the conservative pedant. With proper education and an effective social welcome, each gift and interest may itself be a medium of refinement. But whether it is or not, we are in no position to blackball it. Our hitherto exclusive enjoyment of 'civilization' was an illusion. We ourselves are also outsiders knocking at the door of a wider understanding. The way to understand our own concerns is to educate all possible participants fully in *their* contribution to humanity.

CHAPTER 4

The price of progress

One of the pleasanter pictures which mankind has painted for itself is that of the teacher sitting in the midst of a small cluster of admiring disciples. This same dreamy picture repeats itself from culture to culture; yet the climate portrayed is always a temperate spring, with warm ground on which to sit, a handy tree to give shade, and an equally convenient absence of any other considerations whatsoever.

The American president James A. Garfield's classic statement is of the same order: 'A university is a student at one end of a log and Mark Hopkins at the other.' Though intended solely as a compliment to Mark Hopkins, of course, this particular piece of admiration has been widely considered to exemplify the whole personal relationship of all good teachers everywhere. The words of wisdom flow; the student imbibes with filial affection; and, apart from the slow infusion of understanding and good resolutions, the good old world slips quietly by, unchanged. In those distant corners of the earth that lack a Mark Hopkins, moreover, an equally edifying picture of education can be found. It is exemplified by the young Abraham Lincoln, poring over his books among the marshes and woods of Indiana. The light shines in the darkness and brings him forth. Though destined for the greatness of the White House, he is still 'good old Abe' – the plain good boy from the log cabin.

All this, of course, is so much nonsense. There is no resemblance to the old-style 'morally improving reader' in the true story of anyone who enjoys a schooling beyond that of his familiar environment. An admiring relative was heard not long ago to say of a working-class girl after her return from a teachers' college: 'She hasn't changed a bit.' If the speaker meant that despite a completely altered view of life the girl was still fully in sympathy with her people, he was paying her a great tribute. But if he meant that she had acquired only knowledge and professional skill, he was unintentionally condemning her. If it comes to that, the mere acquisition of some knowledge should have transformed her. Why should the young perpetuate the past? How can

74

they? Nobody expects today's children to be Edwardians or Victorians. There is still less risk of this when we reveal new horizons to them, whether factually or in terms of their future prospects.

Great though the distance is between the generations in our Western world (for change has never in the history of mankind been so great or rapid as during our lifetime), it is as nothing compared with the huge chasm that gapes between the old way and the new in many parts of the world. Indeed, the majority of the human race are in no timeless oasis where dream-teachers and dream-disciples sit in perpetual Nirvana. They are in an arena where all are foreigners. The prizes may be glittering and abundant; but the exercises and conditions are harsh. The advantage that people enjoy today is that an increasing percentage of them can be prepared for the fray, and that the terms of the contest are more equal. But there is no sentimentality about it. Modern schooling (and wider aspects of education) are not simply enlarged portions of an older dispensation. They do not happen at mother's knee or in the halls of the ancestors. There is little chance of most educated people's returning to the old ways or the old folk. The initial cost of their education was hard enough to come by; the process of education was costly and arduous; and the price of being victorious in the struggle probably includes some form of banishment for someone. Certainly both the educated person and those who provided him with his opportunity have to pay in unexpected ways.

It is with these aspects of the personal and social price that has to be paid for education that we shall deal in the present chapter, rather than with purely financial considerations. For information about those, readers are referred to the many official sources of a statistical kind published by governments and UNESCO.[1] Financial analyses and comparisons are however of little value in themselves. They say little about individual pockets, less about the pang of parting with cash, and still less about the price that individuals, families, and social systems may have to pay in terms of personal self-sacrifice, effort, and upheaval. That is closer to our interest here. We shall also consider by what devices some kinds of schooling or training are 'priced out' of the reach of persons, families, or communities. We shall consider the cost of

[1] *The Year Book of Education* for 1956 (Evans Bros, London) analyses the fiscal and strictly economic problems of education in various national and international contexts. Mr John Vaizey's *The Costs of Education* (Allen & Unwin, London, 1958) surveys the United Kingdom; see also his *The Economics of Education* (Faber, London), 1961; and *Some Economic Aspects of Educational Development in Europe* (with M. Debeauvais) (Paris, International Universities' Bureau), 1961.

certain scholastic assumptions in terms of misplaced resources and of human wastage. When all is said and done, cash considerations are just a reckoning of services and commodities that can be bought (education among them). Even those commodities and services are valuable only in terms of who wants them, whom they will help, or who made them and with what effort. Value and cost are really personal matters.

Of course, the earliest and simplest kind of education is little more than the copying of parental or similar example. But formal education may be a costly commodity. It may seem strange to talk of it as a commodity; but it is worth emphasizing that despite all the talk about education as an investment it is also a commodity that is consumed. We can see this clearly enough if we take a primitive instance of it. Let us suppose we have a child sitting with a teacher in the shade of a tree – nothing else. To make the case more extreme, we shall also suppose that the teacher is some old man or woman fit for little else. What then? The child is consuming time that in many a penurious community can be ill spared. He (for it is unlikely that a girl would be so indulged) is spared from working in the fields or workshop. There he could fetch and carry, weed fields, scare birds, glean crops, herd the animals and do all manner of things from an early age.

In many countries still, children of school age or less work assiduously and skilfully, contributing to the family income something which parents feel cannot be spared. In Italy the period of compulsory schooling officially ends at fourteen; but in many places children of the age of twelve are illegally in paid employment. This happens within a few miles of Rome. Parents are glad of their meagre wages, and employers welcome cheap labour. In some Southern states even of the U.S.A. coloured children similarly work for money alongside their parents from the age of ten or so. (I took photographs of them so engaged in 1959.) In South Africa and India the situation is, of course, much worse. All over the world little girls are kept at home to mind babies and prepare meals. Their absence at school could not (in their parents' view) be afforded.

A little less than a lifetime ago, such practices were common enough in England. 'In 1899 it was computed that at least 144,000 children in full-time attendance at school were working early in the morning or during the evening hours. Of these 40,000 were employed for more than twenty hours a week.'[1] The author quotes (ibid.) the case of

[1] M. W. Thomas, *Young People in Industry* (Nelson, London), 1945, p. 141.

'boys and girls of six years old employed in lace-making, matchbox making, and even in helping to make bricks'. Earlier, it was difficult to keep children at school long enough. The 1874 Factory Act had raised the minimum age of employment in factories from eight years to ten; but it was not easily enforced. Children were not allowed to go *full-time* to the factory until they were fourteen, unless they were *good* enough at school work to pass an attainment test which released them at the age of thirteen. Part-time factory work, however, continued to be allowed at the age of eleven or twelve until after the First World War.

Earlier still, conditions had been much worse. Evidence before the Children's Employment Commission set up in 1861 included such pathetic items as the following: 'My little sister, now five and a half, can stitch a good many little fingers' (on gloves), 'and is very clever, having been at it for two years. She used to stand on a stool so as to be able to see up at the candle on the table. It makes them clever if they begin young' (M. W. Thomas, op. cit., p. 97). This kind of evidence is representative.[1] It goes without saying that none of this work experience was intended to be educative; it meant bread and butter to the parents and gain to the employer.

Of a less reprehensible but equally exhausting kind is employment on the parents' farm or holding. Legislation intended to control the paid engagement of children is almost powerless to prevent a sharing in family enterprises, which can of course be educative – provided that the child is not thereby prevented from profiting by schooling. An abundance of excuses and hindrances hampers the school progress of rural children everywhere, sometimes in relatively advanced countries.

The situation is far worse in such places as the Caribbean, even where there is ostensibly compulsory schooling, as in Puerto Rico. In Jamaica there is still no compulsion to attend, for the simple reason that there are still too few schools. That is honest enough. But a glance at the register of a village school shows that many enrolled children are spasmodic in attendance. Some countries cannot or do not provide schools, and cannot staff them properly where they exist; yet they still pass 'compulsory education laws'. In January 1960, the 17-nation UNESCO conference meeting in Karachi worked out a plan for providing universal compulsory and free primary education for south and

---

[1] For a fuller story of these evils see C. M. Waters, *An Economic History of England* (Oxford University Press), 1925, pp. 333 ff. and pp. 486 ff., and R. Ulich, *The Education of Nations* (Harvard University Press), 1961, pp. 102 ff.

south-east Asian countries, It was calculated that the cost would be $64,000 million (about £22,857 million), spread over twenty years. That is the measure of the shortage, especially when we consider the low salaries of Asian teachers. But the mere provision of schools and teachers is not enough. Schooling may still lie beyond the social resources of the people, or their state of readiness. The bare-footed trudge in all weathers, perhaps along miles of arduous road, is likely to daunt all but the most resolute.

To be so resolute, the pupil needs to be athirst for schooling of the type that is available, and encouraged by home conditions. He must also (as a rule) be encouraged by good teachers whose view of his career is not limited to the end of schooling or the narrow confines of the school premises. But that is not the traditional type of teacher we have so far been considering in this chapter. The simplest elementary school teacher is something much more expensive than the sage, as is the school where the teacher will be housed. We began by considering some older member of the family sitting under a tree. If the child's time is something that a community might feel ill able to afford, the time and salary of a skilled teacher is something still harder to find. Furthermore, even less formally qualified instructors (for example, the *guru* or wise old man of the Indian village) also have a way of demanding support and attention. In many parts of the world they have raised themselves to the status of privileged mendicants living on charity, or indeed to the most revered and expensive positions in the land. Yet they do not contribute much to education as that is usually understood elsewhere. In addition to appeasing the gods and giving instruction in sacred matters, they often hand on great works of literature and may also give some initiation into philosophy; but so far from contributing to scholastic progress of other kinds they may actually be a hindrance. They may be antipathetic to schooling in the European or American sense of that word, and endeavour to counteract its influence when introduced.[1]

So the wise man on his log and the teacher in her school do not suddenly appear in a fresh new world. They take a long time to grow up in a world already full of people whose lives and assumptions are challenged by their activities. The older people and traditional values often claim the greatest prestige. If the old ways do not exactly win people's approval, they often seem inevitable. Formal education of our

[1] An interesting example in 1960-1 was the stress placed on reviving Ayuvedic 'science' (a kind of religious medicine) in Ceylon.

type may look strange, if not dubious. So far we have been considering education as a commodity which some people and some communities may not be able to afford – either in terms of sending their children to a school or in terms of supporting it. Yet these material aspects are far from being the only factors affecting the supply of education. It is difficult for a commodity to be valued if it seems to have little public usefulness.

Formal schooling given in many parts of the world has no manifest relation to the daily preoccupations of the home. These are not merely the concern of the parents but the very activities in which the children themselves are involved from dawn to schooltime, and again from the end of afternoon school until dusk. The week-ends and holidays too may be spent in a world quite alien to the school, particularly when the teacher is a 'foreigner' from a different part of the country or from a subculture out of sympathy with the home. It is not surprising therefore that literacy is often achieved only to be lost within a year or two, simply because nothing is found suitable to read. It is hard to realize how 'remote' books and other school interests can seem in an under-developed country. They may deal in an alien style or idiom with completely alien things.

It is not as though school-going were just a matter of useless literary and factual puzzles, either. It can never be only negative. The bare-footed peasant struggling away behind his heaving ox as he ploughs the stiff soil cannot easily have kind thoughts about the sedentary idleness of young people in school. That is the way it may seem to him when children are actually working at school tasks; but there is also the ques-tion of what they do during breaks, intervals, and other free periods. Many a school system has to have some system of 'rationing' or study periods simply because there is not enough accommodation or a short-age of teachers. In Puerto Rico, for instance, pupils cannot normally have more than four classes a day; but they may be at school all day, without places to study in. They therefore spend much time in the town squares gossiping and learning to be idle.

In other countries, where the children are kept more diligently to their school tasks, the question still arises of the attitudes they learn and the contacts they make with people whose orientation is altogether different from that of the parents. At best, it will be a matter of learning ambitions away from the home and native town; at worst it may seem an occasion for idleness or disaffection. It is not for nothing that 'students' (in English more properly describable as schoolboys, very often) are in so many political disturbances at trouble-spots throughout the world. Even the best-loved parents and homes are challenged by the differently oriented prospects of the schools. When paternalism, family loyalties, and sexual norms are challenged, the school may seem positively undesirable.

Even supposing, however, that the schoolchildren are all exemplary boys and girls undergoing efficient instruction, what are their careers to be afterwards? The prestige attached to a restricted range of administrative positions in many countries makes all too many pupils aspire to governmental service or, in more recent times, to particular openings in commerce. Four out of five people in the greater part of the world still work on the land; so plain arithmetic tells us that about four out of five children are being schooled away from their parents, if such careers are the primary outcome of schooling, and if everyone goes to school. It is no use for us to suppose, on the basis of some untypical schools familiar to us, that children can combine a more advanced schooling with a personal education that keeps them in close touch with their former background. They can; but they seldom do. In any case, the type of vocational-liberal school we are thinking about is probably not there at all. So the price that has to be paid by most parents for their children's education will be some form of alienation. It is not assumed here that this is necessarily a bad thing. The point is simply made that the probability exists, and that the parents and elders know it. It is a harsh price to pay, and we can only be surprised that so many parents are glad for their children's sakes to pay it.

The problem is more acute than might be supposed at first sight, mainly because of the composition and interests of the teaching body. In many villages throughout the world (e.g. in Denmark and Jamaica), the village schoolmaster is still a father-figure of great consequence. He may not merely teach all subjects with marvellous dexterity to children of all ages and aptitudes, but also be a friend and guide to all the neighbours. In Jamaica, for example, he is addressed respectfully as 'Teacher Williams', or simply referred to as 'Teacher'. He reads and writes letters for illiterates, drafts wills, acts as arbiter in disputes, is marriage guidance counsellor, lay preacher, and chairman of nearly all social enterprises. He is hardly ever off duty. In out-of-the-way Danish villages his status may be comparable, except that people are literate and that the pastor shares more of his responsibilities. A similar but less inclusive and rather sterner role was that of the 'dominie' in Scotland.

But in all the countries mentioned, teachers of this type are rapidly dying out. They represent a career which once was the main one likely to be open to the brilliant or diligent child of humble origin – and a career, furthermore, which was not only reasonably well paid by the standards then available for comparison but also highly esteemed for one reason or another. In many countries it was closely associated with the aura of the Church. In republican France it was linked traditionally with the mayor's parlour, for the schoolmaster is still in many things secretary to the small-town mayor. In Italy the village schoolmistress quite often marries the local land-agent or produce factor, who is a man with many advantages. Throughout the world, however, the increase in communication and in the range of occupations open to educated people is profoundly affecting the composition of the teaching profession, especially in out-of-the-way places. Teachers are (like everyone else) also much more conscious of the economic value of their time.

Furthermore, authorities who provide schools throughout the world no longer think in terms of having, so to speak, a resident lay priest living in the midst of a life-long parish community. They think rather in terms of an efficient distribution of educational opportunity, not to mention economy. Therefore school systems nearly everywhere are closing down rural institutions with a small enrolment, and transferring the children by bus or other means to a more centrally sited place with a wider choice of teachers and subjects. All round, there is nothing but gain in this practice for all concerned; but at the first encounter it brings still more alienation. It is also much less likely that the teacher will 'go to earth' in the village or become truly naturalized. Whether he is or is not a civil servant (as he is, for example, in France or Australia) sent perhaps from some distant place to maintain the essential social service of education among the country people, he is almost certain to regard himself much more as a professional specialist and much less as just another villager. The 'consolidation' of school systems, as it is called, is everywhere considered to be necessary at the secondary level. The widening range of subjects and the increasing need for special apparatus both require some concentration; but this process increasingly means that teachers and children alike look away from the remoter outposts towards more urban prospects.[1] Promotion lies that way.

[1] For example, 'England's green and pleasant land' is the third most densely populated territory in the world, with the population mostly packed into cities and large towns. Townward movement is also a feature of the U.S.A. and Canada. Even more remarkable is urban gravitation in Australia. 61 per cent. of South Australia's population live within 20 miles of the centre of the capital, Adelaide. Only Victoria has a greater degree of urban concentration (62 per cent.). Western Australia has 54·5 per cent. urbanization, New South

In addition to the very important fact that a child's whole contact with the school has more often to be oriented away from the parental home, we must also weigh a difference in the quality of the teachers he meets. This difference is likely to be cumulative in the years to come, particularly with the advance of industrialization. In very many countries a special dignity has been attached to the wise man for centuries. This has been partly because the wise men have surrounded themselves with mystery and esoteric symbols, from the insignia of the witch-doctor and the difficult *Kanji* system of writing in Japan to modern graduation requirements; but it has also been a natural result of the low standards of the worker or provincial who judges his teachers. After the dissemination of education, few people will appear educated to an almost supernatural plane. To this day, teachers enjoy much higher esteem in Wales than in England. This situation is not occasioned by a wider prevalence of sound education in England (for it is very doubtful if that exists), but by a more generous offering of lucrative opportunities in business in the cities of England. That is why so many Scots and Welshmen cross their borders to compete for jobs in the more industrialized and urbanized parts of England. As a consequence of this creaming-off process, the teachers are left behind in the upper levels of provincial hierarchies.

Similarly, teachers in India have often enjoyed relatively high status until today. The expansion of industrial and technical opportunities is, however, making it harder to recruit trained, graduate teachers at 75 rupees a month.[1] Of course, such salaries have a higher purchasing power locally than their apparent equivalent in foreign exchange; but a good idea of their real value is obtained from the statement that to have a child in a typical English-language day school in Calcutta costs 30 rupees a month, without lunches. Some schools are a good deal more expensive. In these circumstances it is not surprising that those who can avoid teaching, and above all teaching in small towns and villages, will do so. The fact that there is such a supply of teachers is in part attributable to the extreme conservatism of most schools and nearly all the universities in the world; far too many people are funnelled into courses of study for which there is little ready market except teaching. The huge appetite of industry for well-qualified managers is, however, growing

Wales 54·4 per cent., Queensland 38 per cent., and Tasmania 30·8 per cent. Furthermore, Australia as a whole has a great shortage of small provincial towns, or villages. Thus there is a marked social isolation of the country-dweller, quite apart from huge geographical distances [*Guardian*, 29 May 1961].

[1] A 1960 figure applicable to Bengal, for instance; it is officially worth £5 12s. ($16).

so fast that it now absorbs graduates of unprecedented kinds, including the types who a generation or two ago would have had no alternative but to teach.

So the existing low salaries of teachers, which are already a burden far too great for some poorer communities to bear, are less and less able to secure a supply of people of quality – at any rate of the quality once considered necessary. Yet if children are to go to school, stay at school, and profit by school, they should have better provision made for them, and not worse. Still, in under-developed countries of the type we have been considering, there is widespread awareness that no matter how boring and other-worldly school is, it will nevertheless lead to professional and executive careers. This knowledge induces many children to persevere diligently through the rigours of the curriculum and pass the required examinations. Their relatives too see this as the only way.

But does success mean that they have been well educated? Does it mean that such liberal enlightenment as they possess has come to them through the school? Does it equally help the poor? Will the old curriculum orientation realistically serve those occupational groups which have not so far included the professional-preparatory school in their scheme of life? All these questions should perhaps be answered in the negative. The case of India is one of the best-documented instances of the kind of remoteness we have been talking about. Many Indians firmly believe that the bookish and arid schooling to which they have subjected themselves in recent generations has given them little or no true understanding of their personal or national position. It has resulted in colossal frustrations, much jostling for too few careers (almost all of a white-collar, clerical kind), a neglect of scientific and environmental studies, and an even grosser neglect of the needs and capabilities of the majority of the population.

All these troubles are universal, and not peculiar to India; but many faults of European origin seem to have become specially accentuated by indigenous copying in Asia. The juxtaposition of time-honoured absurdities to the sudden possibilities of technological development has shown up the former in an even more critical light. Yet before there can be much question of remedying faults which everyone everywhere can criticize in teachers and schools, there is an even more urgent problem – the mere provision of enough teachers of any sort. (Schools, as buildings, are not such an urgent problem in a tropical or subtropical country.) 85 per cent of the Indians, for example, live in villages. Of these the great majority are small, and most of the inhabitants live on a subsistence economy. The total *per capita* income of India in 1961 was only £21 ($56) a year.[1] If there were enough teachers to go round (as there are not) how are they to be paid for? At mid-century, roughly half the world's population was asking fundamental questions like this. Also, what sort of people and what sort of things could teachers be expected to teach? And to what end? And in what circumstances? And in what order?

When people are radically taking stock of their needs and resources, these are the questions they ask. It is obvious too that there are needs much more fundamental than schooling. Food is one. In several unfavourable seasons in recent years, India (for example) has just not had enough to go round. Each year there are above 5 million more mouths to feed.[2] There is growing unemployment and under-employment, despite the valiant efforts of the government and others. Even with help from the World Bank, from Britain and the Commonwealth, from Russia, and from other countries, it will require a phenomenal effort to raise the level of India's investment from 9 per cent. of the national income (1960) to the 15 per cent. which economists believe will be the minimum required for her to maintain independent growth. Without some such investment there will be bankruptcy and death.

This is the grim background against which plans for schooling must be assessed. Clearly the cost of education is not just a matter of providing the cash. Ghastly though that embarrassment really is, it looks even more alarming when *any* assigning of capital resources to investment is bound to mean much hardship. The majority of the Indian population (like so many others) live in cruel poverty all the time. Any further saving (supposing that to be possible) must mean going without what we should consider the barest necessities. Therefore by no stretch of any imagination can people play with the idea of education as so much 'refinement'. Poor people see schooling primarily as an opportunity for self-advancement. They want their children to have a far better life than they had; but not even the most ambitious of parents can utterly starve themselves for their children. However, it is second nature for underprivileged populations everywhere to acknowledge that improved

---

[1] *Times* (London) report, 15 May 1961. In measuring liabilities, it should be remembered that only 24 per cent. of the population are literate.

[2] Population is growing even faster than was feared, reaching 438 millions in 1961. In the decade 1950–60, the national income went up by 40 per cent.; but the population increased by 82 millions – an increase of more than 21 per cent. Therefore income significantly increased by only 17 per cent. (ibid).

education may cost much self-sacrifice, and will certainly mean much hard work. Therefore they are willing to see educational improvements as long-term investments, closely related to economic improvements, of which they will never themselves enjoy the rewards. This has long been true of working-class parents in England, Wales, and Scotland; more recently it has been true in the Soviet Union; it is now typical of India and China.

The desperation of poverty has led to desperate cures. China's communist rulers, with totalitarian planning, have made their overpopulated and poverty-stricken country save more than one-fifth of its annual income. Though we like the communist way even less than the Indians, we cannot deny that it is a solution that some people will feel bound to try. The whole population of the biggest nation on earth (between 650 and 700 millions in 1961) has been totally mobilized. It has been put under a system of the tightest rationing of resources and endeavour. With Soviet help, but relying mainly on her own people and economy, China is increasing her productivity three times as fast as India. These achievements are, however, possible only under a kind of martial law, within which education plays the role of grand strategy.

Every single thing is made to subserve the developing industrialization of China, and China's school system is a conscripted part of that process. It has made colossal strides. The already huge population is increasing by 2 per cent. per annum, and the educational arrears were enormous in 1945. Yet there is little more difficulty in supplying teachers of various grades than there is in supplying sergeants, captains, and colonels for the army. People work and study extremely hard, and as a national crusade. In 1950 China still had small and badly equipped schools and universities; by 1965 she expects to have over a million undergraduates.

These young students are in the forefront of China's modernization. They see themselves, as the government does, as crusaders. Let us take the life of a typical undergraduate as an example. The five-year university (or institute) course is carefully co-ordinated to continue indoctrination and to develop skills which will be gladly dedicated to the country's needs. Each year is divided as follows: 33 weeks are spent on study; 5 weeks on examinations; 8 weeks are spent in labour in a factory or a village commune – and at the end of these there is an examination on the student's 'attitude to labour' and 'relations with the masses'. Of the remaining 6 weeks left for holidays, much appears to be given to other labour voluntarily undertaken in the public interest. At any rate, that seems to be borne out by eye-witness accounts, and is in keeping with what may be observed in the U.S.S.R.[1]

Every visitor is impressed by the enthusiasm of China's youth for this total mobilization, and also by the amount of responsibility allowed to youth. High-school teenagers march off singing to voluntary work in the evenings. Hordes of students manhandle heavy freight needed for construction. Thousands of them with picks, shovels, and baskets work long hours on irrigation canals, waterways, railway embankments and the like. The photographs taken of these activities leave no doubt of the infectious enthusiasm universally described. Though the system is undoubtedly one of regimentation, fatigue and occasional boredom with the ever-recurring political sermons seem to be the only unfavourable reactions; and these appear to be heavily counterpoised by the complete conviction that the way to which they are now dedicated is just, satisfying, and certain to be successful. It brings inner satisfaction. To quote the *Times* special article on 11 July 1960, 'The ethic is total: work, devotion, selflessness – it has only one end, a new socialist China under the leadership of Chairman Mao.' All this dedication is reinforced with really worth-while educational provision, and corroborated also with highly tendentious pictures of the decadence of the world outside – all too frequently drawn from our own literature's less admirable elements (as happens throughout the communist world).

The main point for us to consider at this stage is that China's total mobilization in the industrial and technical fields is based upon education which had almost to start from scratch. No effort is spared. This is not merely capital investment; it is the provision of a lifeline by means of a vital supply. The embarrassing 'flowering' of divergent opinions in 1957 has been 'contained' to the satisfaction of the rulers. The reorganization of the commune system on a three-level pattern in 1961 (so as to combine production teams for agriculture into large production brigades below the third and originally planned level of the commune) has been accompanied by satisfactory interpretation in official journals. It is represented as a new aspect of co-operation, even though it obviously means some concession to peasant parochialism and selfishness. This concession is an example of the realism with which the re-education process can fall into lower gear (*Times*, 8 February 1961); but the point

[1] For the details given here I am indebted to a series of articles entitled *China in 1960* which appeared in the London *Times*, beginning on 11 July 1960. Other information about China has been derived from the writings of Dennis Bloodworth and others in *The Observer* from time to time. Some comments are also based on the eye-witness accounts of reliable visitors to China.

to note is that the machinery spreading industrialization even through-out the countryside still has as its mainspring an educational and civic re-orientation. The example of China is of paramount importance in the world of today, not only because she has pulled herself up from the most disadvantageous position on record but also because since 1960 she has clearly been competing with the Soviet Union itself for the posi-tion of world-wide example to underdeveloped and newly emanci-pated countries, particularly in Africa.

India is China's neighbour. In the years which have followed emanci-pation (1947) she has aspired to a similarly exemplary role for the underdeveloped countries in the non-communist world. Between 1951 and 1961 she expanded her educational provision threefold; but it is unimaginable that any free country should wish or be able to con-script its resources in the same way as China. However, *laisser-faire* is equally out of the question. Comparisons with China are made not in order to suggest that India should follow suit (for India's wealth of institutions and democratic habits would make that intolerable) but to show how beholden we in the rest of the world shall be to any non-communist solution that a proudly independent nation may be able to evolve. Any such solution, even so, will be hard to come by and may demand a desperate price – not all in terms of cash but in terms of priorities and postponements. These may include the demolition of many ancient ways of life (as China is doing in the replacement of fam-ily ownership by communes). They will almost certainly mean the abandonment of ancient elegances and some traditional sensibilities – not to speak of age-old craftsmanship and educative relationships. For very life, let alone progress, people must have technological and social transformation of the most radical kind.

What price are people prepared to pay for things? If they are desper-ate, they may consent to pay any price. It may not be a case of willing; they may be compelled. In reaching this conclusion, we in no way support a decision to adopt a communist or fascist régime; it is just that we can understand them as we can understand martial law in war. For the purpose of this chapter it is enough to note that our own comfort-able assumptions about education as a social ladder or an embellish-ment (according to our status) are brought to ridicule by the harsh conditions of other people's struggles. Nor is this the first time that education has been used for the total transformation of societies. From about 1868 until Pearl Harbour, the Japanese systematically brought themselves forward from medieval feudalism to a position in which they could face on equal (and threatening) terms the most industrialized nation on earth. The decision to modernize was forced upon them, initially. It was later reinforced by Japan's spectacular success in transforming its whole outlook and prospects in perhaps the first wholesale educational revolution that the earth has known.[1] Similarly, the Soviet revolution in 1917 was followed by the total overthrow of most previous political and educational assumptions, and by the institution of a communist educational system which within forty years established a rather backward nation in a position of world hegemony.[2]

In these fantastic and almost topsy-turvy examples of radical reconsideration, education has been restored to its earlier position as an integral part of the social process. In communist and fascist states, however, it was no longer *society* that provided a true education in manifold human relationships; it was formal 'education' that more or less abolished existing society (in the sense of an empirically justified structure of human relationships), and established in its place the planned Leviathan *state*. The 'logic' substituted for the ancient dialogues of philosophers and politicians was the mechanical planning of industry and productivity. The needs of mankind were reckoned in accordance with this, as of course any good Marxist would approve; for, to the Marxist, 'technology', 'society', and 'education' are but different aspects of the same process. Furthermore, in 1960, instructors at a Pedagogical Institute in Moscow were heard to say that Marxism, Leninism, and educational theory 'are one and the same thing'. The identification of all these things with technological advance appeals to the hungry populations of the Far East and the long exploited races in other parts of the world, who have no tradition of democracy and humanism behind them. They just want economic success and want it quickly. Their acquaintance with some democratic and 'liberal' countries has not enamoured them of our ways. In their urgent need and dire lack of resources they are understandably willing to expand their minimal opportunities in the most streamlined way.

Fortunately for us, however, the Indians, who are more than a third of the population of the non-communist world, are still an integral part of the Western political tradition, though they are an independent Asian people. If present trends are continued, there is no possibility of China's political example being followed. Certainly no Indian leaders

---

[1] A full account of these changes is given in the 1954 *Year Book of Education*. See Chitoshi Yanaga's article on the Meiji restoration and its consequences.

[2] See my *Other Schools and Ours*, chapter 6.

of any magnitude want to slip into the mere momentum of industrialization. They are prepared to pay a heavy price for scholastic and economic improvements; but they are so far convinced that they can combine
the material and political advantages of the Western way with what
they consider to be the superior sensibilities of their indigenous traditions.

For the well-being of the rest of mankind, no less than of India, it is
to be hoped that they will find some way of producing a viable hybrid.
But there can be no question of their acquiring Western knowledge and
'know how', or even simply importing Western technical instruments,
and still remaining unchanged. What is true of persons educated into
a new situation from previously underprivileged classes is also true of
nations in a similar position. Why, the mere importation of an alarm
clock is itself likely to lead to the destruction of local mores, either in
South Asian or in Irish hamlets! Still, the Indians' order of values will
not permit them to pay just any price so as to obtain teachers and a more
rapidly developing economy. Within the framework of existing democratic institutions they believe that within the next decade or so they can
secure at least five years of universal, compulsory primary education,
and quickly move on from there.

Desirable though it is, the intrusion of literacy and other essentials for
the modern world is bound to alter the whole pattern of working
relationships and formative perceptions in India, Pakistan, and South-
east Asia generally. To take one illustration only, the economy of most
agricultural communities in the world has hitherto been based upon the
extended family in which all the members, even if they do not actually
live together, contribute nevertheless to the general well-being. There
is no such thing as a small, Western family consisting of father, mother,
and unmarried children; there is no single-handed mother coping with
everything; nor is there the opportunity to make one's own career or
marriage without consultation. Strong family links persist even among
city-dwellers, and have their very good aspects as well as their disadvantages. It is no uncommon thing for families to club together so as
to send one or two promising members to secondary school (which is
not free) or even to college or, indeed, to England or the U.S.A. In
these cases the family interest, besides being one of affection, is also
comparable to that of a group of merchant venturers long ago in fitting
out a ship. Although such practices spread education where this would
otherwise be impossible, it does mean that higher education is sometimes heavily mortgaged; the student succeeds or fails on behalf of all,

and has a lot of 'paying back' to do. In countries where family conclaves still plot the marrying-off of young women, the education and careers of boys as well as girls are more than a private matter.

In these circumstances it is impossible to conceive of an expanded educational opportunity for individuals which is not in some respects socially subversive, even if there arises no overt conflict between ancient and modern senses of propriety. The situation is of course grievous when divine or paternalistic interpretations are called into question; but it is also fraught with problems even when change seems primarily economic or administrative. For example, if contact with outside ideas challenges the hardly questioned status of village money-lenders, rent-collectors, or absentee landlords, a snowball development begins which is necessary for the establishment of a modern democracy but which is socially and ideologically revolutionary as well as an economic and political change. The Indians are passionately political, and are not likely to leave any ameliorative possibility undeveloped. Moreover, literacy brings newspapers, magazines, and cheap books. Many of them come from Russia at give-away prices; but it would be much the same if they came from Delhi or London. Radio and films contribute enormously to the change which has inevitably set in. India produces a great amount of film, some of it very good. This is a medium with a profound influence. Much film is actually devoted to the illustration of social change. Examples are Satyajit Ray's *Pather Panchali*, *Aparajito*, and *The World of Apu*; and Aeejay Kardar's *The Day Must Dawn* does the same thing for an East Pakistan village.

The whole status of women, and the whole traditional function of the family, are directly called into question by the long overdue inclusion of girls in school on an equality with boys. Much more radically revolutionary is the official and necessary campaign for birth control, to prevent India from smothering herself to death. Not merely will women be given responsibilities which in previous generations they would never have dreamed of usurping; they will also receive an opportunity to be considered more than mates, mothers, and housekeepers. Indeed, such a change is part and parcel of any success with a campaign of contraception.[1]

India's leaders are not of course blind to these considerations. They have in fact shown remarkable courage in undertaking revolutionary changes in caste legislation, and on similar issues of a nearly ecclesiastical

[1] For further information about these and related aspects of re-education in India, see *Other Schools and Ours*, chapter 7.

kind (e.g. pronouncements on admission to temples, on some matters of diet, and on the unchallenged prerogatives of sacred animals). But even if they had not consciously done anything about these things, industrialization itself would have been bound to make caste punctilio impossible. The restrictive practices of some trade unions are bad enough without that. Moreover, many light factory and office operations (e.g. weaving and secretarial work) are usually assigned to women. Such requirements immediately challenge the traditions of Islam, which about 10 per cent. of the Indians and the great majority of the Pakistanis have so far respected. The non-domestic employment of women is unprecedented enough; but it is worse when women are expected to work with men. When women go to universities, choose their careers, and live where they please (as many already do in the cities), it must seem to many conservatives that Western corruption has already set in for good.[1]

It is naïve to suppose that 'evolution' of an urbanized and industrialized way of life can be effortlessly and successfully allowed to take place. The myth of 'evolution' in relation to industrial progress has been exploded in most parts of the world since the middle of the nineteenth century. Only in Britain and in some age- or social groups in the United States is any credence given to it. Industrialization is planned – either by entrepreneurs, or by syndicates, or by states. Whatever happened under *laisser-faire*, that is the truth now; and it is becoming more completely and more socially true (as well as economically) with every passing day.[2] Those Lockean 'private areas' which still exist for alternative interpretations are often little more than pockets of eccentricity (e.g. among the beatniks). Even these are assailed day in, day out by the would-be regimenters of society to suit production and consumption. Asian peoples as a whole are peculiarly suspicious of Americanization – particularly in so far as this might be equated with 'materialism'. Distaste for the soulless lack of a sense of direction which (rightly or wrongly) many Asians attribute to the 'American way of life' as they see it makes some of them think of the Soviet Union as ultimately a *less* 'materialistic' place. This is truly ironical; but it is an important fact which sways many towards planned economies and so-called 'guided democracies'.

The most determined and progressive leaders of advance in countries undergoing rapid transformation tend therefore to use all means within

---

[1] Contrast such conduct with that recommended in the Koran, iv, 34, and xxiv, 31.
[2] See, for example, W. H. Whyte's *The Organization Man* (New York), 1956.

their power to retain long-standing cultural ingredients and formative relationships. Ancient literatures, for example, and sacred songs and pageants are not merely cherished but revived if they have fallen into disuse. Religious traditions, as being the least likely to submit to change, are re-established; typical and contemporary examples are found in Pakistan, Burma, Indonesia, and Ceylon. The kindliest observer cannot escape serious misgivings when noting some of their consequences in political or communal action.

To avoid a repetition of massacres and less obvious but still more invasive persecution, the government of India has set up a secular republic. The ancient virtues, crafts, and institutions are no less cherished for that – provided that they do not interfere with basic human claims. At the moment, great anxiety is felt lest the innumerable self-employed small craftsmen should lose their livelihood because of industrial advance. Following Gandhi's advice, village and home crafts are being safeguarded by every possible means, not just for economic stability but to be an educative influence. Yet it is hard to see how the advent of power sources (such as electricity) to every village can allow such multiplication of endeavour to persist. Roads and more rational marketing arrangements alone would be likely to break down local and personal links, and supersede cottage industries.

That is one reason why the integration of some elementary school courses with craft activities (as in the 'basic education' schemes recommended by Gandhi and so popular in Bihar) is strongly criticized in larger villages and more urban centres. Despite central government and state encouragement, 'basic education' seems reactionary to many. Moreover, ambitious parents are understandably anxious that their children should have a schooling which seems likely to lead to those occupations which have traditionally had all the advantages, or to modern urban alternatives.

The various complications so far described in this chapter prevent the provision of schooling from ever being a simple matter. The most trivial schooling is sooner or later bound up with total re-education in a wider sense; and that in its turn is bound to affect and be affected by the whole direction of social change. Therefore any government with a comprehensive grasp of its responsibilities must inevitably see its school commitments as bound up with control over many complementary social trends. Much as the nations which industrialized after Britain established a more rational organization of industries, profiting by Britons' mistakes and developing their remarkable 'know how' even more remarkably, so the impecunious nations which have come latest to formal education show more realistic understanding of their task and a more direct purposefulness. They do not imagine that the public provision of schools, for instance, is a pauper supplement to the 'better' schooling of the traditionally privileged groups. Nor are they so foolish as to suppose that the interplay of schools, society, and technological development is a friendly match isolated from international events or from such domestic alternatives as mass communications and business planning. What we might call the 'limited company' attitude of only partial commitment to the task of providing schooling (only so much, and to so many people, and for certain clearly limited purposes) is as logically outdated as the notion of the self-sufficient and unregulated one-man business. The new nations know it. They no more try to potter about in education than modern doctors try to cure one part of the body.

Yet supposing we have a universal provision of schools, all effective, and all potentially developing youngsters to the limit of their powers (as we certainly have not), are we then able to rest on our laurels and let things evolve? We are not. There can be no question of our imagining that the clock suddenly stops. The changes which we have begun will go on faster and more penetratingly. They need to be observed, assessed, and prepared for – in terms of new types of school and teacher and method for newly oriented children – all the time. Is it realistic to suppose that the children will come forward to take up their opportunities? All the evidence shows that, without constant re-education of parents and employers, and without all kinds of ancillary services during and after their school life, they will not.

Economic barriers and the sort of class hierarchy which is found at its most obvious in Britain are not the only handicaps for children coming from hitherto underprivileged sections of society. For example, in Sweden there is one of the most complete social service systems in the world, and every attempt was made to ensure that a full range of opportunities was available to all children of whatever origin. Yet recent surveys[1] showed that although 55 per cent. of the Swedish population were describable as 'working class', only 6 per cent. of the university students belonged to that category. Plain ignorance, self-exclusion, and simple failure to get from somewhere the sort of encouragement

[1] See particularly T. Husén: *The Differentiation Problem and the Comprehensive School* (cyclostyled and distributed by the University of Chicago Comparative Education Center, October 1959).

that every upper-class child gets all the time must be named as deterrents. It is no use supposing, either, that 'counselling' on the American pattern would be enough. The work of Professor Kenneth Clarke and Mr Dan Schreiber with underprivileged children in New York City has shown similar self-exclusion there, and has also shown with what remarkable results it can be mitigated.[1]

It is also futile to imagine that local and empirical 'spotting' of weak patches will suffice. Education in the modern world is not gambling or tinkering. It is part of that total supervision of formative opportunities which societies (in times of simpler economics) and states (in more recent times) have increasingly seen the need to exercise. Too much is happening in too many places under too many influences to allow us to continue in indolent complacency. Education is not a summer afternoon's chatting on a mossy log. Nor is it a perpetual, pleasant Sunday school with a prophet. The slightest innovation is part of total transformation. That needs to be watched, balanced, and provided for.

In the true perspectives of today, progress must be total. There can be no lacunae where ignorance and indifference may fester. Total progress does not of course demand totalitarian progress. It simply means that every possible angle on human perfectibility shall be given due consideration – material, social, and personal. If this means anything at all, it does demand a rejection of the myth that as long as a few people in a few kinds of intellectual pursuit are thoroughly learned and sensitive, they will automatically maintain the advance of civilization. Instead, such people can only tell some of us about some advances made by people before us. Now we all have to make our own advance. To measure our rate of progress we must closely observe the pace of others, some of whom are making giant strides by totalitarian methods in keeping with their ideologies, while we falter a long way behind our own ideals.

Nothing is gained by merely scaring ourselves with others' achieve-

[1] See D. Schreiber's article in the 1959 Proceedings of the College Entrance Examination Board's Colloquium, New York, 1960, published under the title *The Search for Talent*. In relation to other countries, speakers at a conference on 'Ability and Educational Opportunity in a Modern Economy' at Kungälv in Sweden in 1961 gave similar evidence of untapped or thwarted ability. In particular, Professor de Wolff of the Netherlands and Professor Harndquist of Sweden showed that the number of good graduates in their countries could be doubled or trebled without any difficulty, by encouraging girls and poor children generally to use the facilities already available. Mrs Jean Floud showed that in 1946-51 only one in fifty of English working-class boys went to the university, though one in five middle-class boys did so (Report in the *Times Educational Supplement*, 23 June 1961).

ments, or by slavishly emulating alien methods: but the impatience of the world for ever faster progress is making many mark the Soviet Union as the cultural no less than the economic pacemaker. As we have seen, and shall continue to see, economics and politics and education are there seen as integral parts of one process. The rest of the world's knowledge is systematically harvested and consumed in the U.S.S.R. Books, journals, films, radio, and television are most methodically used to make educational opportunity abundant within the communist frame of reference. In one year as many as 15,000 learned journals from almost 100 countries are abstracted. Not merely single copies of such periodicals are made available in a university or other institution of higher education, but as many as twenty or thirty beautifully photographed copies so well done as to deceive all but the practised eye. Countless foreign visiting specialists have been impressed by this abundant academic gleaning in the U.S.S.R. The annual output of such copies (and/or microfilms) amounts to some 318,000. They are regarded as essential tools in the country's economic advance. No money is stinted for such purposes, and librarians are listened to for very practical reasons. Soviet resources are also lavished on other parts of the world.

In the United States too, though not on this vast scale nor with such technologically successful co-ordination, money spent on libraries and comparable resources makes the criteria of the Old World laughable. The old idea that the preserves of learning should be a paradise for pedants or a cultural coterie is rightly seen as a prescription for self-strangulation. Though imperfections arising from other causes make many American research students seem uncritical and omnivorous, criticism must be directed where it is pertinent – towards the failings of the schools and undergraduate courses. The colossal and efficient supply of knowledge available in the United States for those who can profit by it is really the point for others to note. Abstracting, microfilms and bibliographical cross-references make much European scholarship look like dilettantism, and (in some fields) rather shoddy. That is not so much the fault of the European scholars themselves, as the consequence of general complacency, government parsimony, and of stupidly judging the play of progress by the criteria of 'gentlemen versus professionals'.

There is no reason why the professional touch should not embellish even gentlemen. The price of *any* progress today is simply the complete and businesslike cultivation of *all* our potential. Total education is a sort of total mobilization; but this time everyone is eager to move forward.

BOOKS

See the general bibliography on Comparative Education, p. 369.
See also the *Year Book of Education* for 1954 and 1956, London (Evans
　　Bros) and New York (World Book Company).

CHAPTER 5

Culture conflicts

One of the poems of Catullus is thought to be especially poignant. It simply says: 'I hate – and love you. Perhaps you ask why so. I do not know, but feel it happen and am in anguish.'

Ambivalence in the emotions is the central theme of the world's drama. It seems indeed a mercy if dislike can be manifestly felt for what we must reject. It is more excruciating when affection is retained for what we rationally know we should have done with, or when the choice is felt to be one between two goods – both desirable, perhaps both wholly desirable.

The conflict in a single person's emotions is nowadays often magnified in the affairs of a nation. Sometimes, of course, it results in revolution. Though revolutions have their attendant horrors, the fresh start they bring about often gathers up in the zeal of reconstruction the interests and energies of both sides. The worst stresses may occur before the crisis of decision comes. Certainly great heartache or a quieter malaise can develop when a culture still stands undecided at the parting of the ways. In our own time this aspect of social pathology is more prevalent than formerly, and also more acute, for two special reasons. The *pace* of a society's evolution is not everywhere the same, so that parts of it will seem to lag behind other parts in *time*; and the increase of opportunity and social mobility makes many young people move out *spatially*, as it were, into other areas of class outlook or technological venturing.

Yet such culture conflicts are widely discernible not simply in the lack of sympathy between old-fashioned ways and new, or in the alienation of children's technological outlook from the routine of their parents. They are found to some degree everywhere, and (what is more) in one and the same person or institution's internal self-contradictions. The more open and evolutionary a society, the more frequent and deep these differences.

Radical inconsistencies can indeed survive a revolution. Hegel's theory that after an upheaval the thesis and antithesis of the historical dialectic will amalgamate in a compromise is an over-simplification of what we must expect, partly because any state or society in which this is supposed to happen is not simply a unit but an agglomeration of parts which may severally take on a quasi-independent life of their own. We see this more clearly if we regard the constituent parts of a community's way of life as so many acquired habits, which sometimes become nearly autonomous or 'automatic'. So they may persist in an absent-minded sort of way when the need for them has passed. They may even recur when they are an embarrassment, much as nystagmus may persist when there is nothing to be flicked from the eyes.

Thus in the educational world the French have had many scholastic reforms, some of which were intended to be revolutionary; but, as the sociologist Durkheim told his countrymen, their schools in the twentieth century continue the well-organized intellectual system of the Jesuit *collèges* which were given their main characteristics three centuries before. It would be too much to expect that the French, even in times of the most radical reform, would rid themselves of Cartesianism in their school system, with its emphasis on 'the mind' and its derogation of physical and material involvement. So those Frenchmen who introduce remarkable changes in technical training or in adjustment to the actual environment of schools will go out of their way to explain that, although not regular academics, they are still 'Cartesian'.

Similarly, reform in England has to fight hard against certain institutionalized assumptions and practices. It would be hard to imagine reform achieved at the cost of seriously diminishing the remarkable autonomy of individual schools, even of publicly maintained schools. No matter what local education authorities may wish to do in future, the fact that teachers and administrators have grown up under the old system colours their whole judgement of what is appropriate in school relationships. There may be some old stagers ready to repudiate my comment; but that is because parochialism makes them magnify small changes. The first visit of any foreigner to any English school surprises him profoundly, simply because the schools are so independent. He may, for example, ask the headmaster to see the official time-table (on the assumption that it is handed down from above). He will then go on to ask for the schedule which shows the precise amount of work to be done out of officially approved books in each week or month by each teacher responsible for a subject in a particular age-range. He may even ask about recommended methods, and so on. It is a puzzle to him why headmasters and headmistresses cannot arrange for the transfer or re-form of less satisfactory teachers, when they can virtually determine the curriculum and the amount of time to be devoted to each item of it. The idea of self-transferred teachers may be quite startling to our visitor. It is through his surprise that we see best how unthought-of and unthinkable certain reforms might be in Britain.

Those engaged in such self-appraisal sometimes think that funda-mental divergencies of principle are involved. They may be, but usually are not. It is easier to realize that we are reviewing habits, rather than principles, when we note that the decentralized British tradition itself has been profoundly modified in Canada and Australia to produce much greater centralization of control.[1] Nor is it a matter of deciding neatly for or against centralization, or any other matter. In the United States centralization is, on the whole, much more radically resisted than in Britain; yet the administrative units of the much more decentralized American school system sometimes exercise a far tighter control over the engagement and scholastic activities of a teacher, to say nothing of what would seem to a Briton an invasion of his privacy. In short, we can see that people can be willing to accept centralization (or any other feature) in some things while indignantly repudiating it in others. It is often a matter of acquired taste, derived from institutional habits, which are often so unsuspected as to seem 'natural'.

For these and similar reasons we must beware of considering certain cultural features which we may like or dislike as integral parts of the systems in which we now see them at work. For example, everyone knows that the communist political system is an extremely compre-hensive one, supervising and regulating the whole life of its citizens. Therefore, when we see much insistence on uniformity, and intoler-ance of minority opinion, we are inclined to attribute this to Marxism. We reinforce our decision with reference to the Marxian concepts of ideology, class war, and so forth, or to a constitution once officially described as 'the dictatorship of the proletariat'. Yet there is little in communist political methods (apart from the greater application of science to propaganda and enforcement) that was not already there under Tsarism and Orthodoxy. Indeed, historical research shows that from the earliest times the Slav peoples had a tradition of securing or enforcing undeviating unanimity in their public meetings. Thus what we see in modern Russia is far from being a harsh, communist innova-tion; it is the persistence of long-standing habits. Not merely political

[1] Some of these developments are considered more fully in Chapter 10, p. 250.

assumptions persisted, of course, but the police and governmental institutions to go with them.

It is not suggested that schools are necessarily like police arrangements, except in so far as they are both manifestations of human behaviour that may repeat characteristics of human behaviour elsewhere. Of course, a certain amount of bondage is entailed in both government and school – partly because they have a captive public, and also partly because they are inseparably bound up with norms derived from the authority of a previous generation. As we have seen, they can continue to do so after revolutionary change, even when the very things they perpetuate are not supposed to be admired. Bookishness in Indian chooling is often blamed on Macaulay; but he was merely concerned with the provision of literate Indian clerks. Bookishness was mainly derived from the pre-British traditions surrounding the learning of the holy sagas. What Macaulay and his successors might be blamed for (if we allow ourselves to be wise after the event) was for finding no virtue in indigenous literatures and traditions. So Western items were imported; and to these the Indian learned class faithfully transferred their bookish attention. India is now independent, and full of admirable plans for the future; but it will be a very long time before excessive and ancient regard for pedantry wears off.

In fact, the 1958–9 Khrushchev reforms in the Soviet Union itself were mainly caused by an over-production of academically trained seventeen-year-olds there, despite all the careful planning of the Soviet state. The continental tradition of the academic high school (seen particularly in the *lycée* and the *Gymnasium*) had perpetuated in the workers' republic the aspirations and practices of the Tsarist *bourgeoisie*, and thus ran counter to the needs of politics and industry. Similar autonomic disunion of interests was criticized at the first All-Union meeting of scientific workers in Moscow in June 1961. Professor Keldysh, president of the Soviet Academy of Sciences, said that 354,000 scientific workers in 3,800 establishments were 'divided between some 170 Union and republican ministries, *each one of which has been concerned with its own sphere of activities*', resulting in waste or delays (*Times* report, 15 June 1961; italics mine). If this can happen under a strictly co-ordinated State Plan, and despite the vigilant staff-work of the Academy of Sciences, how much more likely it is to occur where overall planning is unthought of!

When such situations arise (as they must do everywhere from time to time) the sectional interests often go on acting as though only their interpretation were permissible. They may act or speak in obvious controversy, until some overriding authority makes a conclusive pronouncement. Yet inner contradictions of the most astonishing kind can also be found where none but the outsider sees them. Let us take the United States as an example. At the heart of the American public schools (i.e. the ordinary schools) is the conscious purpose of welcoming all comers to the American way of life, and of developing in each person not only first-class citizenship but the fullest growth of individual personality. That is what all the books, teachers, and parents say. They firmly believe it, too, and pursue their objectives with edifying energy and enthusiasm.

Yet despite the impressive success with which American schools have spread opportunity widely throughout the land, and notwithstanding the flood of literature examining the quality of school practice in the United States, no particular attention seems to have been drawn to the fact that during an American child's growth from infancy to manhood he will pass through three planes of educational philosophy which are really incompatible with each other. At the level of the primary school (or perhaps even at the stage of school planning before the child actually sets foot in the building) there is the important legend of individualized opportunity. Admission to the school is, so to speak, a ticket towards the fullness of self. It is set in an ideological world whose heroes are the frontiersmen, scouts, and great achievers – those who have vindicated the right of the common man to be great, particularly with the integrity of the Pilgrims. The little red schoolhouse is at once its shrine of initiation and its personal proving-ground. Its scientists are that large body of American psychologists who have done so much for the measurement and study of individual characteristics. Though much of the history of this ideology was written on the moving frontier, its message is not a rip-roaring tale of gun law; it is a story of 'manifest destiny' to civilize a wilderness by inner, personal greatness. It proclaims the virtues of old New England and the graces of Virginia across the continent to be every child's birthright.

Any visitor to an American primary school at once catches the excitement of this offering. The opportunity really is there for all who care to take it, though to be fair we must note that opportunity is much more unequally distributed than most Americans imagine. Still, there are no hatches battened down over anyone's head. By making shift or migrating to another region, or by coming back later, there is always the chance to make the most of oneself. Yet at the very same time the need for Americanization has caused the schools to stress their assimilating responsibilities to a degree that amazes Europeans, who are socialized in their own groups in their own countries by much less obvious processes. In the American school the whole business is engineered not only by the conscious ritual of swearing allegiance every morning before the flag, and the repetitious reminders of nationhood, but by the great stress pedagogically placed on 'sharing', group activities, 'togetherness', popularity, and generally being a regular American.

This socialization, of course, extends far beyond school. It pervades all advertising. It is seen in the great emphasis placed on church membership, not so much for what other nations believe is religious experience, as for fellowship in 'the church of your choice'. True, nobody minds much which church you belong to; but you must belong. There is little concern with what other people think is good religious behaviour or integrity. Outside church and school proper, very great importance is attached to fraternities and sororities among senior pupils and undergraduates. These are not at all like English university clubs, but are instruments of 'togetherness'. The country club cult and social life of suburbia among adults further testify to the universal pressure to be standard within one's group or community. It can be noted also in fashions of dress and behaviour, in the 'supermarket' administration of most American institutions of higher education, and in an almost neurotic dread of being atypical which afflicts many people's most intimate lives. You must never be the odd man out.

Many distinguished sociologists and psychologists have devoted their lives to the study of this major American problem (or is it just a problem of industrialization?); but for convenience we can note a brief self-description by a suburban type in *The Organization Man*: 'Like Russia, only with more money'.[1] In fact, it is a most revealing experiment to interchange American and Soviet educational prescriptions for group work in education; this can usually be done with no more difficulty than the substitution of 'group' for 'collective', or vice versa. The ideology of *The Organization Man* and *The Lonely Crowd* is clearly alien to that of the Pilgrim Fathers and of the little red schoolhouse; yet it is directly fostered by socialization in the school, and particularly by rather unquestioning teachers who worship one aspect of Dewey's work to the exclusion of all else.

The third directly conflicting ideology in the 'American way of life'

---

[1] p. 280, 1956 edition. Similar remarks in this book include references to suburbia as 'a womb with a view', 'a sorority house with kids', and comparisons with Moscow.

as seen by a child passing through school is the intense competitiveness of an acquisitive society, where gain and conspicuous success in material respects have taken the place of older symbols of social status. Little competition in school subjects is allowed to mar the smooth process of socialization; but competition is there in sport, in debating, and in similar contests. Frenzied and elaborate preparations are made to *win* rather than to put up a good performance. Competitiveness is encouraged by all the popularity and other polls, and in many ways that Americans tend to overlook but which promptly strike the stranger. So though the American child is mercifully spared the stresses of selection for secondary education, and though he can confidently look forward to a higher education or at any rate to a well-paid career if he shows the slightest enterprise, nevertheless his school life is also full of reminders of the competitive world surrounding him. At home, both competition and socialization are equally vital forces. But when he leaves school he is at once in what Americans so vividly describe as 'the rat race'.

Now the simultaneous existence of these irreconcilables in the 'American way of life' is a direct consequence of its immense vitality. Exuberant growth is taking place in many directions at once. In these circumstances, institutions are not often reformed from within. Instead of being mended, they are jettisoned like old apparatus or by-passed like dingy towns. At least, that is what many Americans imagine. But the situation is not quite so simple, because institutions and the assumptions they perpetuate persist in teaching everyone dissonant ideas by which to judge present conduct and resolutions for the future. If there is frank incompatibility, or simple bewilderment, it is a human failing to fall into indifference, if not hysteria. Both kinds of disorder are giving great concern in the United States, particularly as the more earnest thinker or the disturbed personality is likely to seek solace in some larger organization that may be inimical to liberal, democratic progress.

That is one reason why Americans show such intense interest in communism, an interest which seems morbid when it extends either to witch-hunts or to the intense despondency of post-sputnik self-criticism. These are symptoms of insecurity and of inner contradictions. Other signs of social pathology include the extravagant cynicism of some 'beatniks', the Zen Buddhism of others, and the general preoccupation with sex, which often seems to be of a distinctive type. The sexuality of young America is on average quite normal, we may be sure, though better publicized than most. It does however frequently seem to lack the gay exuberance of the West Indies or the sophistication attributed to the French. It is often said by Americans themselves to reveal much 'mommism', or need for the forgetful security once felt in mother's arms. American women are slim and boyish by contrast with the women of other countries, as the elegance of their fashions demands; but the dream-figures of the screen more often resemble the Great Mother goddess of ancient times. However that may be, Americans are notably anxious to be loved. All these symptoms are interesting because they show the deep need that is felt for some resolution of an uncertainty caused not only by social mobility and other forms of uprootedness but by the apparent irreconcilability of conflicting American ideologies.

As already suggested, such phenomena may be results of the fragmentation induced by industrialization, rather than attributable to the 'American way of life' itself. If so, they are of universal concern – particularly in those countries which understandably wish to overthrow their present systems in favour of wider emancipation, higher living standards, and richer educational opportunity. The events of the past two centuries have already shown that those countries which have come most suddenly to industrialization have also most often 'gone overboard', with great risks to their humane prospects. By exclusive concentration on the requirements of technology and productivity, they have tended to overlook either the empirically justified social safeguards of the superseded systems or the need for new built-in opportunities for humanizing their workers. Therefore we are all better helped to appreciate our own risks if we can take heed of others' example in a comparable position. The Americans' development of a new civilization (though based upon existing norms) over a vast continent, and its presentation to a 'new' population, are clearly experiments of the utmost significance for those late-comers now attempting to streamline their modernization with even greater haste and risks.

It is, of course, obvious that older cultures (like those of Europe) also have discrepant ingredients in their way of life. But there is one profound difference here from the United States' experience. In European cultures, the various subcultures or sectional points of view have tended to belong to certain classes or to particular levels of education, which have specialized in them as occupations or as prerogatives. This we have already seen; and our observations are reinforced by such books as Professor D. W. Harding's *Social Psychology and Individual Values* (particularly in chapter V). A big difference from the American situation is that each sub-group in a more static society tends to impart to its members (who are to some extent culturally segregated) a whole sectional attitude which may add up to a rounded ideology. They are thus, we might say, specialists in a perception which for them is a 'world view', although it may seem to us to arise from personal advantage or depend upon a partisan interpretation of the complex culture in which they find themselves.[1]

Rapidly developing countries, committed to 'mass' education, may thus inadvertently find themselves presenting to their emerging populations discordant values and unreconciled institutions, particularly if they copy isolated features (such as technical colleges or a selection process); for these may be logically and lastingly incompatible with each other in the form in which they are imported, whereas in the country from which they were borrowed they might have been only temporarily contradictory because education was in transition. Or they might have had some of their contradictions mitigated by correctives co-existing in the other educative opportunities of the old country. This is particularly likely to happen when an older but now widely copied country has hitherto been content (like Britain or the U.S.A.) to rely on the informal self-correction of its traditional *society*. Society is, after all, the somewhat loose and empirically justified associations of unofficial people. Democratic countries have not so far relied nearly as much as newer countries on the co-ordinating mechanisms of the *state* (i.e. the systematic apparatus of government, set up by law and possessing coercive or policy-making powers). The time has long passed when such centuries-consuming self-appraisal and self-correction by *social* forces spontaneously at work could hope to keep up with the extremely purposeful campaigns of industrial development. That is why newly developing countries nearly all envisage their modernization as a process of total (if not totalitarian) overhaul.

Extremely important though the dynamic American example is in revealing unsuspected survivals and the competition of conflicting norms within one generally approved 'way of life', it shows us nothing like the struggles which occur when radically opposed value-systems meet in head-on conflict. This has been the situation in Japan on three occasions since 1868. It has happened several times in China within a lifetime, and especially since the Second World War. It is building up very rapidly not only in Asia and the now independent countries of

[1] For a fuller examination of the terms 'ideology' and 'world view' and their implications, see Chapter 10.

Africa such as Ghana, Nigeria, Mali, Guinea, and Congo, but also in such areas of American influence as Puerto Rico and the Philippines. We can only suppose that countries in the Western hemisphere still waiting to be democratized or industrialized will find themselves in a very similar if not more aggravated position when their time comes. Not even the most sweeping of revolutions starts life afresh from scratch. The old people survive, as do the old aspirations and old institutions even though the whole future seems different. It is with the old social and human material that the new edifice must be constructed. Thus here too the possibility of culture conflict is implied.

It is not simply a question of eliminating an outlook of subjection and backwardness by building up schools and other opportunities. It is not possible to buy a new outlook as one purchases a car or house. A new political status, like a new technology, is a way of life or a 'culture'. It can only be learned in action and by habituation. With sweeping change it sometimes seems that planners can start a new society from a fresh foundation, as though they were building a house on the accumulated rubble of a previous structure. But not even the 'giant strides' of communist China are like that, notwithstanding totalitarian control and ideological conversion. The people involved, and their way of life, approach the most 'novel' of plans with perceptions already made or influenced. To execute their plans they tend to use existing devices or modifications of them. Many a revolution has a shape imposed on it by the very system it is trying to controvert.

In any case, newly emancipated reformers, whether they are totalitarian or parliamentarian, have usually schooled themselves in the ways of Europe. Communism is as European as are parliaments or military dictatorships, and more European (in one sense) than the origins of Christianity. Thus the new leaders in their own persons import into their native lands something that is immediately alien, even if no alien influences have hitherto taken root there. As a matter of fact, very few areas in the world have escaped some large measure of Europeanization – either in the direct contact of teaching and control or at second hand. Some of the countries mentioned in the preceding paragraph have encountered this in well-nigh contradictory phases.

The Philippines, for example, have had superimposed on aboriginal influences the early cultural contacts made with Malaysia; but on top of those there has been a great degree of Hispanization. During the slow centuries this achieved a cultural amalgam with the previous way of life in worldly matters at any rate, though Latin-type Christianity with a local idiom has become the pivot of spiritual activity. During the past three generations, however, the impact of American rule and technology has been enormous. Though this is, of course, another European influence implemented with the uninhibited force of technological logic, it appears to the Filipinos to be astonishingly different from anything they had previously known. As Americanization also seems to offer most of this world's advantages – particularly prosperity, schools, and political viability – it has overwhelmed most of the young town and city dwellers in a sort of dazzled admiration. Understandably, many of them are swept along like corybants. The rational consciences or emotional ties of others will not allow them to surrender; but that does not mean they do not now and then succumb to what Keats called 'quick cat's-paws on the generous stray-away'. They may experience the process as gradual seduction; Americans may see it as piecemeal acculturation; but everyone must recognize it at least as an attrition of the previous way of life. As there is no real resolution of the contradictory influences at work, a cultural schizophrenia develops to cause educational disturbance and perhaps political anxiety. In a now independent country this is a matter of great consequence.

Puerto Rico was similarly annexed in 1898 after the Spanish-American War; but more recently it has come into a not-too-well-defined association with the United States. Many privileges of American citizenship are shared by Puerto Ricans, especially if they migrate to the mainland. (They are only 1,600 miles or a $45 air fare from New York.) Almost every family has some relatives in the United States; and American businesses, roads, and pleasures are manifest everywhere. Undoubtedly, the close dependence of the Puerto Rican economy on American enterprises has brought manifold advantages to the island in material respects, though many of the rapidly expanding population find they cannot achieve the expected standard of living without emigration, and those who stay at home are often cynical or embittered.

Hence there has arisen a real tension between an Hispanic, family-centred and predominantly humanistic way of life on the one hand, and the American alternative which seems to many natives to be harsh and materialistic for all its glamour. The rapid expansion of schools under American encouragement and with American support has not so far been matched by standards that even the friendliest observer could call adequate. This causes much head-shaking among educators who cannot be written off as 'mere reactionaries'. Though the development of large industries, small local industries, welfare services, and the like have all built up in recent decades a prosperity and ambition that would have been unimagined just after the First World War, an increasingly important and vocal section of the population are wondering if the wrong cultural decisions are being taken, that might commit the island's future for centuries.

Embarrassment on this very score may well underlie recent political events in Cuba and elsewhere in Latin America. Educationally the culture conflict is more directly of interest to readers of this book than politically; but we cannot overlook the important truth that economics, politics, and education are integrally associated, especially in underdeveloped countries. As the secretary of the United Nations, Mr Hammarskjöld, declared in March 1960, economic decisions may now be forced on poor countries which will commit them for many years to particular political trends. These in turn will necessarily affect their decisions about schooling; and decisions about schooling are further affected by the emotional or nationalistic consequences of deep cultural cleavages made manifest in international contacts. These may be of marked importance not only in the communities immediately concerned, but in all those areas where the ripple effect may eventually strike. Thus cultural events in Puerto Rico are of prime importance in the whole Caribbean, and indeed throughout Latin America. More than we expect will depend upon the attractiveness or viability of the cultural ingredients imported from one long-established system into those places which must now decide the future of their own brand of civilization for many generations to come.[1]

Perplexing and numerous though Jamaica's problems are for an autonomous and hitherto underprivileged community, they are relatively simple compared with those of their Puerto Rican neighbours, despite the fact that the latter have more obvious material advantages. At least, the Jamaicans know only one major cultural tradition – that of the British Empire. (Whatever there was of Carib culture was wiped out very early, and the brief Spanish period is only of archaeological interest.) Some Jamaicans smart under the memory of past exploitation, and most regret the failure to develop early such obvious local possibilities as cement, bauxite, and other industrial complements to the rich local agriculture. The ever-ready offer of American capital is a constant

[1] For more information about Puerto Rico see Brameld, T., *The Remaking of a Culture* (Harper, New York), 1959, and Friedrich, C. J., *Puerto Rico: Middle Road to Freedom* (Rinehart, New York), 1959.

enticement. So is the generous supply of educational facilities in the United States. These are often made easier because of American scholarships; but even where there is no such assistance, the greater facility afforded by American institutions of higher learning to late starters with only moderate initial schooling makes an American education a welcome stepping-stone for many West Indians.

This seems to be particularly so in the case of teachers with a certificate, rather than a degree. Under the American dispensation such candidates can move on soon to 'graduate' status, which is a potent personal and social factor in the making of choices. There is no doubt that money glitters as brightly in Jamaica as elsewhere, and the United States manufacturers and publishers can also flood the West Indies with their acculturating products. For these reasons it is of tremendous significance that the islands of the Federation of the West Indies have so many British links: passports, language, Commonwealth markets, British advisers, and above all the British parliamentary system and the University College of the West Indies, which is in special relationship with the University of London. However, it is likely that European and British ties will continually weaken if British institutions and regulations appear so much less accommodating to West Indian requirements than American colleges.[1]

The British heritage could only serve to influence West Indian decisions in one of two particular directions. It does not detract from the fact that multiple choices have to be made, and that most of these are essentially social and cultural choices rather than decisions of exclusively political allegiance. There would be little point in taking over the British scholastic tradition – lock, stock, and barrel – any more than there is a question of perpetuating for long the structure of British social hierarchy which is still discernible in the former colonies. Therefore Britons must acknowledge that the West Indians and other communities like them are really asking themselves the manifold educational and social questions which are once again at the heart of their own domestic problems. Newly independent communities can pick and choose between the various cultural legacies left available for selection; but they are also faced with the difficult responsibility of co-ordinating them in a new, local synthesis for long-term development. Being newer at the job than the British they may see needs, appropriate methods,

---

[1] In July 1961 the Prime Minister of Trinidad and Tobago (Dr Eric Williams) announced the decision to found a new-style West Indian University, closer to the American pattern and bearing affinities to Columbia University, New York.

and ultimate ideals more freshly and in a less institution-bound way. The world may have very much to learn from them.

Thus we are reminded that questions asked in schools and education offices are never simple questions. Teachers can never be simple craftsmen; they must inevitably be conspirators in a mammoth plot for long-term social re-orientation. Otherwise they are wasting their time. It would be bad enough if teachers were exclusively Latinists, mathematicians, or any other form of limited specialist; but we have also seen that such blinkered people must inevitably go on to blinker their children too or leave them disheartened as they contemplate the cultural dichotomies which the teachers have sometimes unwittingly helped to accentuate. From A.B.C. onwards, education must surely be an initiation into a world survey; and each item is constructive only when viewed in a world perspective.

Thus the sort of casual hotchpotch of educational practice and administration which we get in the United States and the United Kingdom seems not so much quaint as criminal to most of the newer countries of the world. Supposing other nations do not see their tasks of reorganization with such acute consciences as that, they are nevertheless often driven to rationalize their future progress by the most careful planning. The problems of cultural transmigration are so pressing and complex that nothing else will do. The historic example of totally planned change, of course, is the Westernization of Japan from 1868 onwards, to which reference has been made already. The scholastic ladder was planned from the elementary to the postgraduate level, and the economic development of the country was prepared for in the smallest detail from the very beginning with modern roads, railways, telegraphs, banks, and taxation and land reform. At such an apparently trivial level as styles of haircutting and address – and even of ballroom dancing – the Japanese educational planners seem to have thought of everything. Thus they transformed their country from a quaint oasis in time to one of the most technologically advanced competitors in the whole of the world – all within seventy years!

Needless to say, such agonized conversions can do as much violence to the historical and religious traditions of a country as might be privately the case if a person changed his faith. This comparison is all the more appropriate because educational and social reform often occasions a direct clash with religious institutions or near-religious prejudices. A clear case is the decision of the deeply religious Indian people to make their state secular, as far as all government and institutions are concerned. Thus only, they feel, can religious wrangling of an internecine kind be avoided. Only in this way can they envisage a reform of the caste system, of the industrial structure, and of food habits. Such decisions are never made without heartache and misgiving, and the susceptibilities of the anxious faithful have a way of boiling up disastrously afterwards.

In 1920 Kemal Atatürk shocked many Muslims throughout the world by declaring (in the centre of the Ottoman Empire, of all places!) that henceforward Turkey would be a secular state. Amidst all the turbulence of post-war introspection, Atatürk was able to use his country's national ambitions as the Japanese leaders had done some fifty years before, though in a different way. Islam had not only had considerable strength as a faith; it had also become a whole way of living, expressed in cherished forms and institutions. Yet Atatürk's programme struck at these too. The veil was abolished, and with it the custom of purdah. Men were forbidden to wear the fez, and instructed to adopt the European wide-brimmed hat which prevented them from touching the ground in obeisance at regular intervals for prayer throughout the day. These apparently superficial introductions were considered necessary to ensure the practical acceptance of a non-Islamic way of life – or at any rate of a non-traditional education, social order, and technology.

For doubtlessly similar reasons, President Bourguiba of Tunis forbade his countrymen to observe the holy fast of Ramadhan which should have begun on 28 February 1960 and lasted for thirty days. The President, himself a Muslim, told his people that this protracted dawn-to-sunset fast, aggravated in its effects by the custom of making up by night-time eating (which robs the faithful of their sleep), was something that an underdeveloped economy could simply not afford. Like Atatürk before him, Bourguiba had already abolished polygamy and other customs which impeded the social development of women. Desirable though these reforms may seem to us, the shock they induced (even where Islam was not too scrupulously practised) can be understood only if we contemplate a comparable embargo on religious observances in Spain or Italy. Clearly no leader of a country imposes such a test upon it unless he feels that without it the prospect of educational and political development is remote. Also, it is clear that a head-on clash of this sort may seem preferable to incessant attrition along the borderline between opposing cultures.

Yet we should remember that in 1959 the Prime Minister of Ceylon was assassinated by a Buddhist priest on the ground that he was betraying the faith. Gandhi was earlier assassinated by a pious Hindu in India, ostensibly because of undue tolerance to Muslims. Such religious fanaticism has a way of attacking not only persons and supposedly anti-religious propaganda, but also the unwelcome way of life introduced from the West. That is why many securely westernized Turks look with some anxiety on the post-Atatürk restoration of mosques, the opening of seminaries for imams, and other events which they might otherwise be glad to tolerate. Many broad-minded but not anti-religious people fear that the organized institutions of Islam in Turkey might re-establish its previous fatalistic torpor, or at any rate impede by their suspicions the development of universal schooling. These cultural misgivings accounted for the army *coup d'état* in May 1960.

Wherever such antagonisms arise, as they do when cultural conflict is experienced, the most peripheral innovations may be suspect. Thus, an attempt to provide India with better milch cows has been said by some to entail murder and sacrilege. In other parts of the world (e.g. among the pastoral Africans generally) the self-same attempt is resisted not on religious grounds but because cattle are cash. Lean cattle are hardly more objectionable than soiled paper money elsewhere; they are tokens of wealth, and are particularly important in reckoning a bride-price. Thus agricultural improvement may look like an impairment of the social structure; and this association may in turn remind the aggrieved party that certain other innovations connected with school are also 'subversive'. So the ordinary protests of 'crabbed age' about youth and change develop into bitter reaction.

As we observed at the beginning of this chapter, the cultural crises and conflicts of communities have their counterpart in the silent debates of the heart. Moreover, just as parts of a nation may be advanced while others are backward, so may the constituent parts of a family or personality be. Many Asian students, especially women, find themselves claiming opportunity and emancipation within a year or two of the time when their elder sisters were unprotestingly married off to some unknown business contact of their father's. In Europe or the United States they hold their own and freely mix with men, though at home they might even have had to ask their father's permission to leave the house.

Many thousands of Africans have left their hereditary dwelling-places in search of employment, only to find that the home background of customs, allegiances, and indeed patterns of perception and value had little meaning in a detribalized world, even in African cities. The shock

of being cut off from the old systems and ideologies *can* be the beginning of a new integration with a new society or system of learning; but
there *must* be a warm welcome and a hope of success. Recent studies of
'brain-washing' have shown that this practice is simply an intensified
application of the sort of thing that happens to a person either during
religious conversion or during successful migration from one culture to
another.[1] But it is a condition of success that the neophyte should be
welcomed into a new system which he sees as a sort of 'salvation'.
Otherwise there is mere human wreckage.

This is all specially relevant to plans to extend the provision of education to new nations, new groups within older-established nations, and
indeed to the individuals invited to new opportunities in schooling.
Some culture conflict is inevitably set up in them. If school simply offers
'schooling', and is not seen as an initiation (into either a new social
context or a different 'world view'), all that has happened is that a
young person has been taken out of his familiar matrix and left naked
and alone. Loneliness of such intensity is too great for human nature to
bear. Consequently, the young people may take it upon themselves to
form peer-groups which are alien to home and alien to school – in
much the same way as detribalized Johannesburg Africans have
established peculiar churches and all kinds of bizarre associations, or as
uprooted West Africans have evolved an astonishing near-religion (of
the Hauka sect) characterized by exorcism through a hysterical psycho-
drama.[2]

We should never think of these phenomena as concerned only with
distant lands and alien people. They are universal. In our very midst the
conflict between the old orientation and the new which every increase
of educational opportunity entails can be the gateway to 'salvation' only
if education also includes a *social* welcome for those we have done so
much to uproot. Important though it is to provide opportunities for
newcomers to learn new skills, idioms, and airs and graces, that is never
enough. Whether we plan in a totalitarian way or not, we are obliged
to make sure that the cultural conflicts we set up can reconcile themselves in a continuing cultural evolution which has a viable future.
Along with scholastic reform, this entails the purposeful transformation
of many cultural influences and social institutions that do not always
at first sight seem to have anything to do with 'education'.

In implicit recognition of this need, many newly developing nations

[1] See particularly Sargant, W., *Battle for the Mind*, London (Heinemann), 1957.
[2] See particularly M. Jean Rouch's film of it: *Les Maîtres Fous* (*The mad masters*).

W.P.E.—H

try to ensure total and planned transformation, so as to reduce culture conflict to a controllable size. Those of us who believe in a more liberal approach to our educational problems are not somehow exempted thereby from sensibly recognizing what needs we must liberally cater for. If we do not meet these needs, we may find that the culture conflicts we set up have left our victims with three alternatives: to become cynical or bewildered in a pre-totalitarian frame of mind; to seek a kind of return-to-the-womb comfort of sex, drink, and drugs; or to seek the occasional catharsis of violent activity, seen at its worst in crime and at its mildest in rock-and-roll. All recent studies of mental health force us to some such conclusion.

BOOKS

See the general bibliography on Comparative Education, p. 369.

See also the *Year Book of Education* for 1954, London (Evans Bros) and New York (World Book Company).

Mead, M. (ed.), *Cultural Patterns and Technical Change* (UNESCO), Paris, 1955.

Afrika-Instituut Studiecentrum, *Symposium on Popular Education* (Leiden), 1953.

SECTION III

The Effect on Schools

CHAPTER 6

The impact of technological change

Much more than we generally admit, we tend to assume that certain virtues and attitudes are vocationally linked. 'Like an officer and a gentleman' is a phrase that may make some people smile; but the smile is more often occasioned by the pomposity of the speaker and by his Edwardian views of the social order than by any feeling that officers were not and are not usually expected to develop certain noble attitudes. If we speak of 'professional etiquette', or simply about 'professions' as distinct from 'occupations', we take it for granted that certain standards of poise, behaviour, and perception are associated with doing certain jobs of work.

It is no use for the conservative to protest that it was a man's education rather than his job which induced such excellence in the good old days. Such arguments might hold water in France or Italy, where emphasis is duly placed upon *culture générale* and *studio liberale* for their expected moral and intellectual consequences. It might to some extent have been applicable in Britain, if people had been more honest in speaking rather of 'Etonian excellence' and 'Wykehamist manners'; but the closest Britons ever got to that was in ascribing certain qualities to the *gentleman*, who (as we all know) was characterized by the career of ruling people or by belonging to a certain occupational bracket or by having no occupation at all. Indeed, to make sure of not being misunderstood, Anglo-Saxons have often preferred to specify which occupation virtues are attributed to, and to cut out 'general' (i.e. university) education in favour of some formative life-experience or professional training.

This assumption of vocational linkage in the cultivation of virtues and perceptions is not criticized here. It is simply pointed out, because unreflecting public opinion and the professional advocates of 'liberal education' have combined to deny that the assumption is made. Whether we like to recognize the long-standing nature of this pedagogical theory or not, the important fact for our present chapter is that both this hypothesis and many other tacit assumptions are assailed in no uncertain way by the impact of technology upon all societies and their schools. It should not disturb us too much if we honestly look back and see that, like everyone else, we have taken it for granted that sub-cultures (or 'special' views of the world) tend to be associated with particular groups (see p. 104). It is no surprise that we look for certain qualities in missionaries and nurses, and others in seamen. It is not very different if we expect some skilled people to specialize in research while others are better at personal relations, and others still excel in the minutiae of craftsmanship. No harm is done so far. The harm comes when we overlook the complete re-shuffling of occupational requirements (in terms of human numbers no less than in terms of their distribution or the overall coverage) that is immediately called for by any technological change. Yet this is precisely the error into which most teachers and educational organizers are often trapped.

As we saw earlier (p. 39), industrialists and planners and even the consumer public are daily increasing their demands on the potentialities of industry. More goods are expected; better goods are expected; and a wider and cheaper distribution is demanded. It is to the advantage of both producers and consumers that as many people as possible shall augment these demands, and that they shall have as much leisure and ambition as possible so as to accelerate their consumption. So much we can see in our own Western world with its high standard of living; but the issue is seen even more clearly in the underdeveloped regions where most of mankind lives. At home, and still more abroad, such economic decisions are forcing cultural trends for generations to come (see p. 108). To provide the producers, the executives, and the con-sumers – to say no more – a quite different pattern of schooling is called for from what has been traditional in Europe for centuries. Moreover, we have so far been considering only economic and technical requirements, which are relatively simple. Much more com-plicated readjustments and philosophies are called for when we re-appraise the social and political expectations of the great majority who were once too busily occupied or too subdued for others to bother about. These are now not merely tolerated but required as full partici-pants in the world's business – the business of living, as well as the business of making and carting things.

Finally we come to the considerations advanced at the end of the preceding chapter. Older and more static societies, with pragmatically justifiable roles and attitudes which had evolved in a pre-mechanical age, did at least enjoy built-in forms of apprenticeship for growing up, for acquiring certain skills, and for induction into acceptable roles and attitudes. Many of these have disintegrated with the 'throwing off of shackles', and are not replaced. Clearly, our phase of society resembles all others in needing substitutes for the older formative influences now discarded (perhaps with good reason). We need either the replacement of outworn parts for the tempo of our new context, or improved alternatives to meet new needs and opportunities. We probably need both. As our schools are the major influence in consciously directing the training of young people for the future, they must be minutely scrutinized to show if they are capable of doing all the new jobs that technological and social revolution require of them. Certainly, they cannot be allowed to stay as they are.

The historical development of different strata of schooling to meet differing levels of industrial requirements has already been briefly outlined (pp. 70–72). Industrial demand for successively higher levels of attainment coincided with increasing ambitions below and greater readiness on the part of governments to meet the demand in terms of cash and personnel. But when all is said and done, the logic of these events has still not really been carried to its conclusion. The idea has been allowed to prevail to this day that certain types of person are exclusively suited not only for particular kinds of physical or intellectual activity, but for the kinds of humane perception and sympathy supposed to be associated with them. That is to say, not merely are certain professions 'noble' and 'learned' but the kinds of person who could discharge them are also inherently noble and learned. The kinds of school and schooling previously enjoyed by the restricted field of cadets for the noble and learned professions have also become unquestionably ennobling. And by the same token, because 'lower' types of occupation were supposedly better discharged by 'lower' types of person, the rudiments learned by such persons in youthful preparation for adult livelihood could never be much better than boorish. How deeply ingrained in Western thinking this attitude is can only be realized when we see our neighbours carrying it to absurdity, as when progressive Frenchmen have to explain to their own 'highly educated' rearguard that occupations calling for manual and physical dexterity are also manned by nimble-witted citizens who might in other circumstances have benefited by a different type of advanced schooling. Educated people throughout the world are slow to realize that the liberalizing factor in anyone's upbringing is a responsible and sensitive *attitude*. To be effective, this needs to be met by a corresponding receptivity on the part of others.

It is to be hoped that such truisms are so commonplace with us that they need not be stressed in principle. They certainly need to be stressed in practice. Those of us who have enjoyed extended schooling are quick to allege that the undergraduate masses of today are less industrious, less cultured, and indeed less intellectually fitted than we were. It is often stated that standards of attainment in university degree examinations are being lowered year by year, though those who have taken the trouble to compare both questions and answers scrupulously often tell us that our first impression is mistaken. In Britain at any rate the ingredient of competition in many school and university courses is more marked now.

No one pays much attention to three other considerations which are surely relevant. Even supposing that in certain narrowly specialized fields (e.g. some Classical studies) the quality of attainment is not so scholarly, may that not mean that those learned fields do not claim such a monopoly of first-class minds as a generation ago? Secondly, may it not also be a contributory factor that other kinds of valuable experience and interest now impinge on the intellectual life of the modern undergraduate than penetrated the ivory towers of our forebears, leaving today's youngsters more roundly educated if less donnish? Thirdly, may we not be leading ourselves astray with irrelevant criteria that are more outmoded than we realize? For example, in the Soviet Union teachers tell us that their children are better at handwriting and spelling than ours; whereas nowadays Western educators usually appreciate originality and constructive imagination quite as much as formally perfect copying.

The truth of the matter is that everywhere the beneficiaries of an advanced education that has made them work hard want to extract every atom of satisfaction from their present prestige and their profits. Generous though they imagine themselves towards the young and uncultivated, their obsession with their own concept of academic virtue makes them as sour towards new fashions or forms of activity in education as outmoded prudes surviving from a more grudging age. Moreover, there is a universal tendency in industrialized countries for those occupations which were formerly not in the highest esteem and not well paid to outstrip academic occupations in their financial and social rewards. We see this at its most obvious in the U.S.A., though it is a marked tendency everywhere. Understandably, by-passed professors and schoolmasters become waspish. They are therefore tempted to pick on manifest signs of 'inferiority', such as ignorance of books and the arts, a poor accent, unfamiliarity with fashionable vintages, or even less reputable shibboleths.

Also, just as trade unionists remembering the hard, old days tend to fear any innovation which (though obviously likely to increase the prosperity of the worker himself) they suspect of putting people like themselves out of work, so do those who have struggled to academic and professional success tend to regard as a personal threat anything which looks like some new-fangled 'educational automation' making their distinctive skills unnecessary. Seldom do such crude thoughts come to the surface. They are rationalized, of course; but a truly rational analysis would reveal that with the increasing mechanization of industry many educational skills once considered essential are already as outmoded as were many of the ingredients in an old-time craft apprenticeship. Both educationally and technologically, many of these items appear to outsiders to be little more than an anachronistic clutter – unless they are admitted to be a particularly cumbersome device for restricting admission to certain cherished occupations. This is precisely what many observers think they are. Much school insistence on 'certain minima' is little better than a device of exclusion. — ? perhaps.

Amongst the most gullible consumers of old-fashioned scholastic paraphernalia are those parents who have had little formal education themselves but are eager to provide as much as possible for their children now that they have risen in the world. With the most praise-worthy intentions such parents try to secure for their young hopefuls the very things that have been the despair of better-off children for generations, if not centuries.

From the middle of the nineteenth century the new Public Schools of England catered for such *nouveaux riches* pre-eminently. In deference to the aspirations of their new clientèle, and also out of academic absentmindedness, they neglected the 'useful sciences' and modern studies which had been so promisingly developed generations before in the 'dissenting academies' in Britain, and which were about the same time rising to a bright future in the U.S.A. and Germany. Public Schools which reverted somewhat to the older realistic tradition of the academies were hailed as revolutionary. In our own day, the numerous 'preparatory schools' (in the English sense of those words) usually maintain the romantic backward look of the new rich towards the rich man's prerogatives of yesteryear. With hallowed subjects in privileged types of school, fond parents believe, their children can not merely have a well-proved education but can also 'join the club' – and that is more to the point. Considerable self-sacrifice is found among parents who scrimp and save to give their children private education, not really because they have any assurance that it is better, but because they feel 'it will do more for them'. This ambitious romanticism recurs in many countries thoughout the world.

It would be foolish and unrealistic to be angry with such parents. Anger should rather be directed at a social system which still allows most children to be penalized by the accident of birth, and which fails to recruit or develop for public life and industry suitable talent no matter where it may be found. It is not surprising that ambitious parents pay for advantageous schooling, talismans and all. Yet, paradoxically, the same sort of 'hard cash' outlook which often characterizes the ambitious father investing in private education for his son also now makes businessmen elsewhere pay for such educational advantages for their *firms*. They see that education pays dividends and that they cannot run their own enterprises efficiently with poorly trained personnel. They therefore provide other people's children with privately sponsored education if the state does not rise to its obligations. To get away from the time-honoured example of educational provision in Europe designed to suit the requirements of expanding industry and commerce, we might note the highly successful and imaginative system of general-and-technical schooling provided in Brazil by private enterprises (*S.E.N.A.I.*), and described in the *Year Book of Education* for 1955. Not only is this scheme successful from industry's point of view; it also is an influential factor in social progress, for it initiates an educational opportunity for the underprivileged poor in precisely the Latin-American setting where it might otherwise be awaited in vain. Moreover, it by-passes the obstacles to the evolution of the curriculum raised by Classical traditionalists, which might have been insuperable if reform had been left to the schools and scholars themselves. The very success of such innovations often refutes in the most practical way the theoretical arguments of those who provide reasons in advance why it will be a 'betrayal of culture'.

At a much higher level of instruction, firms in the United States, Britain, and many other countries are now providing either university-level apprenticeships, or scholarships to universities themselves, in order to secure a reasonable supply of technologists. There can be drawbacks to such a scheme, especially if the trainees are given little more than a highly specific induction into the processes of one particular industry and the associated branches of basic science; but in recent years a surprisingly liberal view has been taken of industrial training responsibilities. There are colleges or graduate schools set up within great corporations of the United States which actually award 'degrees' of their own. In Britain it is felt that no matter how highly specialized one's vocation, some general perspective of the related subjects should be afforded along with the training. It is also believed (though not always assured) that a general and personal education must be imparted at the same time. For these reasons vocationally linked higher apprenticeships and sandwich[1] courses are considered by some academic purists to be a 'second best', though many of these vocationally linked courses generously made available at firms' expense are no more technological than many undergraduate courses already are.

On the other hand, a growing body of observers in universities as well as in industry are convinced that, whatever such vocationally linked courses may lose in 'common room atmosphere' and browsing in general libraries, they make up in personal evocation and social realism. These features are particularly encouraging to many students who could not benefit by or even stomach theoretical abstractions. Furthermore, it can hardly be maintained that many such courses of training are any more narrowly specialized than a literary apprenticeship in textual criticism or the rigours of a British medical course – which we must remember are also undergraduate experiences.

Most of us have inherited enough of the Greek disdain for 'industry' to suspect in advance that (quite apart from all questions of exploitation, which may be a risk in certain cases) any education imparted from an industrial standpoint must necessarily be imperfect. We feel we have the truth and the unsullied essence of cultivation, whereas others are tangled up in their worldly involvement. We still have not learned Marx's lesson about ideologies: we are all as 'involved' as anyone else, and just as efficiently blinkered. British undergraduate courses themselves seem to most foreign observers to be unduly specialized and to that extent 'technological', whether they are in sciences or in arts. And why need a detailed approach to learning

---

[1] A sandwich course is one in which technical and 'applied' instruction in a factory or workshop alternates with basic and theoretical instruction in a college or university. Sandwich courses are familiarly referred to as 'thick' or 'thin' sandwiches. In the former, one year in the factory may be followed by three years at a university for a regular undergraduate course and a fifth in the factory. In the latter, periods of up to six months are spent alternately in factory and college until the course is completed.

exclude a humanizing perspective? If it comes to looking around for 'applied' courses, we could hardly find anything more specifically work-oriented than the university courses in the Soviet Union. Yet these are not only technologically efficient but also very successful in building up a broadly based personal and civic education within a Soviet frame of reference.

It is a grave mistake to suppose that there must inevitably be a cleavage between personal and vocational education in practice, although it is customary to make this distinction theoretically. We can see from examples in several countries that children may be readily provided with a vocational form of instruction when either their parents or the education authorities would be unready to afford formal instruction of any other kind. Also, much personal education and liberal re-appraisal can be imparted through an obviously useful form of instruction, although the same suggestions might be repudiated by young people if they were offered in the context of generalities and pious talk.

Thus one of the most remarkable examples of personal training in diligence and integrity (as well as in important aspects of general knowledge) is to be found in the *cours complémentaires industriels*[1] of Paris, educating young glass-cutters, instrument makers, furriers, and the like. They are given an extremely thorough training, which is up to craft standards in all respects and is imparted under the ordinary working conditions of the qualified craftsman for about half the student's time; but both in this activity and in the theoretical studies which absorb the rest of their time these 15- to 18-year-old trainees receive (and give themselves) a very fine kind of general education.

The industrialized world is crying out for technicians. Many countries find it relatively easier to get scientists and engineers effectively trained than to secure a satisfactory supply of middle-rank technicians. This is partly because high-powered commissions have studied and planned for the provision of 'top people'; but it is also because the conventional academic school more readily leads on to non-manual training. Moreover, the technician by his very nature must be concerned with specific techniques, which change with scientific developments and with the evolving structure of enterprises. That is an

[1] Before the rearrangement made by the Law of 6th January 1959 (which cannot reach its full effect before 1969), these *cours complémentaires industriels* recruited able boys and girls about the age of 15 from ordinary *cours complémentaires*. The latter are now called *collèges d'enseignement général*. It seems likely that the features described above will be continued in the new *collèges d'enseignement technique*.

additional reason for regretting that training schemes for technicians are so often rigid and narrowly conceived. They are usually too few in number. In Britain, between 1923 (when a national system of courses was agreed between the Board of Education and industry) and 1960, only fifteen courses[1] had been developed. In France, well over 100 distinct technicians' certificates are trained for; and in the Soviet Union about 1,000 types of training are available. Germany also has excellent training for technicians.

Modern industry needs such expertise in abundance. Modern living can also be prepared for in the same way and at the same time. It has been well pointed out that in a coal-mine approximately 2 per cent. of the employees might be loosely described as managerial; in an atomic plant that figure may rise to 40 per cent. Clearly our technological society requires increasing amounts of professional expertise; but it also demands two parallel kinds of skill which are personal – the possession of a much more intricate perspective of working and living, and the ability to adjust to periodic changes of a more personal kind in our private and public lives.

'Human relations' – in the best sense of those words – are often a question of functional relationships. These, and the moral issues associated with them, are revealed most tellingly to many people in relation to their jobs or the homes which they support with their livelihood. In addition to all the accumulating evidence coming in from the industrial field itself, it must be clear on psychological grounds too that our potential technician or 'middle-ranker' gains in skill and humanity simultaneously by blending, rather than separating, the interests of work and of personality. Therefore the technician and many minor executives or distributors deserve not simply training but a day-by-day and on-the-job perspective which is increasingly important for the well-being of society.

This all necessitates a middle range of educational provision, lying between the old elementary strata on one hand and the traditionally glamorized academic levels which administrators usually think of first when they are considering the extension of scholastic opportunity. Indeed, in time it may seem desirable to let an educational pattern initiated at the middle level, and with a realistic or 'embodied' development of skills, push out more and more into the higher levels of education too. Technological and social development has so far relied heavily on three rather distinct horizontal strata: the planners, the

[1] See a special article in *The Times*, 15 May 1960.

organizers, and the operatives. Industrialization alone demands the interpenetration of insights and experience once isolated in the various strata; social evolution and the growth of consumer demand reinforce this tendency for daily perspectives to win higher esteem and mutual recognition. Something of the old attributes of a 'professional' role may thus accrue to once lowly jobs.[1]

The rapid evolution of higher education itself in areas of enterprise once left to rude mechanics has reduced to ridicule the condescending belief that a vocational linkage for humane perceptions is something for the poor and dull-witted. It is at last becoming clear that many of our familiar school categories and ancient 'principles of education' are fallacious. At least, they are more relevant to a type of diagnosis that is now historically and technologically irrelevant. However, habit dies hard. We go on asking questions that either do not matter any more or will not give us the answer we are really trying to get.

Basically, we should be trying to discover three things: (a) how to discover and develop the potentialities and personalities of young people in such a way that these will continue to be viable in later life; (b) how to pass on such accumulated wisdom or well-proved devices as will be useful to the future progress of our pupils and mankind; and (c) how to ensure a happy blend of skill, character-formation, understanding, and sensibility through the instruction which we impart to them. These are the central questions. The subjects, mannerisms, and institutions ready to our hands may or may not be useful. We must re-examine them radically and constantly to see. We are hampered not merely by our own inertia and involvement but by the self-perpetuation of such institutions as schools. We are also handicapped by the latter-day ambitions of formerly depressed classes. These may unthinkingly want

---

[1] Benjamin Franklin (1749) in his *Proposals Relating to the Education of Youth in Penn-sylvania*; Robert Owen (1813, 1823) in his *A New View of Society* and *On the Importance of Educating the Infant Children of the Poor*; Karl Marx (1867) in *Capital*; and Georg Kerschensteiner (1854–1932) in his practical development of the 'Work school' idea in Munich, have given varied expression to a similar idea. But for historical reasons they could not (apart from Kerschensteiner, perhaps) have envisaged the vast contemporary demand for infinitely varied specialisms which now threaten to crowd out 'general education'. Apart from Marx, they were not considering whole populations either; and he was thinking of a whole society only in terms of a single plane or class. The previous lack of humane and civic elements in vocational instruction did in fact prompt Kerschen-steiner to place great emphasis on self-determination and civic responsibility in his highly successful continuation education programmes; but these too were 'for the poor'. The 'Work school' principle has long been revered in the Soviet Union, and has come to greater prominence since the 1958 'polytechnicization' campaign. This will be described later.

their children (perhaps all children) to have access to those prerogatives which once were 'manifestly' the highest.

Another potent factor in educators' romantic reluctance to change is the relatively low social origin of many teachers. They and their parents have struggled to secure them admission to what Mansbridge called 'the glory of education'. That is a timeless phrase, like 'the glory of Greece' and 'the grandeur of Rome'; whereas education is really topical, not timeless. Hence teachers not merely justify themselves and their deeds like everyone else; they also tend emotionally to retain horizons and perspectives that more favoured social groups began to abandon a generation ago – particularly in relation to careers.

We must however be careful not to attribute to other countries the social characteristics of our own. On p. 62 we have already noted that the majority of French parents 'do not even think of' an academic secondary education for their children; and that is not strictly because the opportunity is not there. Some figures given in 1954 are significant today in showing how social background and parental choice can perpetuate scholastic and economic stratification even in the presence of an emancipating opportunity (e.g. admission to a higher grade of school). The secondary schools of France (including technical schools and *cours complémentaires*) then admitted at the age of about eleven the following groups of children:

85% of the children of parents in 'liberal' professions and of senior administrators in the public service;
68% of the children of industrialists;
55% of the children of junior civil servants, clerks, &c.;
39% of the children of shopkeepers and artisans;
20% of the children of industrial workers;
12% of the children of farmers and peasants.[1]

Though these proportions are generally acknowledged to be under-going change as the result of recent reforms, they are still not radically altered. To understand them fully, we should note that industrial workers, agricultural workers, and shopkeepers and artisans make up the vast bulk of the French population. Therefore the low proportions at the bottom end of the table just given indicate a wholesale rejection of a large part of France's youth. Furthermore, the kinds of secondary school usually frequented by those admitted from the humbler ranks of French society do not carry anything like the same social prestige or

[1] Roger Gal: *Esprit* (June), 1954, pp. 954-5.

career opportunity as the academic schools to which upper-class children tend to go. In contemplating this differentiation, however, we must not miss the point which is most relevant to us at the present juncture: that parents' occupations profoundly influence not merely admission to particular types of school (which we knew already) but also the curriculum and career expectations of those schools.

In France the 'private preserve' attitude of privileged parents corroborates the teachers' attitude, which is one of deeply ingrained reverence for the formal literary curriculum. The humbler, rejected parents regard this as 'bourgeois'.[1] In Britain the 'ever-widening gateway' aspirations of lower-class parents tend on the contrary to make them revere the holy tokens of the preserve to which their children are admitted. Thus, many children may be headed off from industrial, commercial, and technical occupations even though those careers would be more rewarding and appropriate in every sense. Children are often encouraged to concentrate instead on studies and examinations in which they may have only a half-hearted interest and mediocre prospects of success.[2] With more sensible and realistic guidance, they might have devoted their talents to university-level ambitions in other careers or intermediate achievements of a commercial or practical kind. But that might well have necessitated the development of quite

---

[1] In 1957, only 13 per cent. of French agricultural workers' children and 21 per cent. of industrial workers' children requested transfer at about the age of eleven to a secondary course (in a *lycée*, *collège*, or *cours complémentaire*) or to a technical school (*collège technique*). About 4 per cent. of students at the university level in France were from families working on the land, and about 3 per cent. from urban working-class homes. This evidence, secured by the commission preparing for the Billères Bill, clearly reveals a widespread recognition that the secondary schools of France were linked with interests and careers remote from the life of the great majority of the working class. (See also Lizop, E.: *Revue des Deux Mondes*, 15 September 1957.) Moreover, M. Jean Ferrez, deputy director of the French Ministry of Education, showed at an O.E.E.C. conference in 1961 that it was 100 times more likely that a child from some *départements* would reach the university than a child from Eure-et-Loire. Yet, according to the centralized French system, opportunity should be spread evenly. Self-exclusion must be a potent factor here; but that in turn shows the remoteness of university and *lycée* courses from the purview of most people's lives.

[2] In an attempt to diversify the curriculum and prospects of pupils in the less academic type of secondary school, the British Minister of Education in 1961 accepted the proposal of the Beloe Committee that certificates should be made available for sixteen-year-olds on a widely based examination below the level of the General Certificate of Education (G.C.E.). Candidates would be able to offer themselves in single subjects, covering commercial and practical interests as well as formal scholastic attainments. The new Certificate of Secondary Education (C.S.E.) would be administered by serving teachers, under twenty regional examining bodies. These would be assisted in their evolution by a special research and development group.

different kinds of schools and a different complexion of teacher. It would almost certainly call for a reconsideration of which careers are appropriate to a university-level course of study.

In both Britain and France, therefore (and in many countries like France), both the social composition of school populations and their external orientation markedly affect schools' categorization into types or strata – and this differentiation is over and above the formal tripartite division into 'academic', 'technical', and 'general' (or whatever names may be in vogue). Sometimes a quiet revolution is afoot without publicity. For example, in the English academic ('grammar') secondary schools, about 60 per cent. of the pupils now concentrate on the sciences. Though their studies are usually formal and examination-bound rather than practically oriented, we must give credit where it is due. This does not affect the fact that the higher up the social scale we go, the more venturesome the presentation of both subjects and careers is likely to be. '*What kind of* a scientific or technological career?' is a type of question more likely to be asked in a Public School or successful grammar school than in grammar schools less socially favoured or in the 'general education' modern secondary schools. All things being equal, it also seems *less* likely that the brighter alumni of the more spectacular schools will opt for 'straight' academic jobs (like teaching) or relatively undifferentiated 'scientific' careers. More are going in for 'applied' training in the higher levels of industry and commerce.[1]

It might therefore be imagined by observers from other countries that in these circumstances the career choices of the socially most favoured and the socially least favoured would come closer together. This does not follow at all. Far from it. They may be housed in the same factory eventually; but then generals and private soldiers also belong to the same regiment. Simply being in the same enterprise need not bring people any closer together than that. Engineering may be their type of occupation; but their personal style may range from 'mechanics' and craftsmen through 'technicians' to 'technologists' and 'back room boys' (researchers). In societies where life is very simple, enterprising workers of grades corresponding to these can work their way up from one to the other. They are also often enabled to do it in highly complicated societies like those of the U.S.A. and the U.S.S.R., where para-scholastic or work-linked supplementary opportunities are

[1] For comments on an American parallel see: Gordon, R. A., and Howell, J. E., *Higher Education for Business* (Columbia University Press), 1959.

afforded in education. In America and Russia all kinds of effective by-passes to formal obstacles in examination requirements and the like are made available to enterprising students who show late in life what they are capable of. In staid societies like those of Western Europe, formalized even now by the apparatus of pre-industrial social selection, the ordinary selective schools and the universities do not normally provide such opportunities. They do provide them occasionally, but not normally or in significant numbers. Industries are more likely to do so than the school systems themselves.

Therefore in France, Belgium, Germany, Holland, Austria, and Italy some of the most interesting innovations in scholastic curricula and social leavening are taking place where schools either are associated with enterprises outside the public provision of education or are intended to train young people for the middling range of skilled occupations – i.e. between the simple craftsman level and that of the scientist or top manager. This training they can effectively give only where school planners are in closer touch with developing local enterprises than with the universities.

Thus a bridge may be made between the strata representing the lowest types of school and occupation and the socially favoured strata still exemplified by the most academic schools and the universities. In the best instances it would be more appropriate to call this bridge a salient. Through it there can thrust not merely all those trainers and trainees who are destined to man the most vitally expanding levels of industries but also those skills and ideas which are most likely to challenge the ancient formulae of traditional schools.

In Italy, for example, the *istituti professionali* and comparable training centres take children from the *scuola media* (i.e. at about fourteen) and not merely equip them with conspicuous skill to make wonderful designers and craftsmen; they also contribute to their prosperity in an Italy winning world esteem for the excellence of its products. Professional schools rescue able children from the dreary exercises of the university, with its overproduction of intelligentsia foredoomed to spasmodic underemployment. During the period since 1918 especially many countries have developed fast along similar lines. Such institutions are not accurately appraised if they are seen only as forms of 'technical training'. They are that too, of course; but they also often impart a great deal of familiar subject-learning and a well-balanced personal view of life to the young people attending them – all effectively combined with a sense of reality and purpose. They are thus good schools by any criterion. They are also often of sound academic standing because of another fact: the pupils they recruit are not 'dullards' unfit for academic work, but poor children who might have done reasonably well in that area yet do far better now because their interests and sense of practicality are associated with a certain profession in view. Thus, even by conventional standards and criteria, their children are of reasonable academic promise. Such schools, however, are usually despised by the advocates of 'general education' and 'cultural traditions'.

These observations bring us to the consideration of what form extended schooling should take. Although it is perfectly true that the productivity and types of employment associated with modern industry mean that today's employee is an important consumer, a citizen, and a person to reckon with, nevertheless that is no reason why his up-graded schooling and better personal orientation should repeat those of the gentleman a generation or two ago. We might just as well copy the courtly archaisms of the eighteenth century. No one in adult life wants to do this; but we have not altogether stopped doing it in relation to our children's development.

Every teacher knows that children learn best if they are interested; they are more co-operative in every way if they 'see sense in it'. Many social workers even more than teachers themselves are disturbed to discover that the heaviest incidence of juvenile delinquency is always in the last compulsory year at school, *no matter what year that may be*. That is to say, if children can leave school at fifteen, the fourteen-year-olds are the naughtiest inside and outside school. If they can leave at sixteen, then the fifteen-year-olds are the worst delinquents. So it proceeds. The conclusion seems to be that for many children the final stages of school are a climax of frustration, as other indications suggest. They see no future in it all. If boredom does not erupt into anti-social behaviour, a torpor or malaise seems to affect many children. This malaise is peculiarly strong in the U.S.A., where schooling is very lengthy and usually un-vocational.

By contrast, school systems which require plenty of diligent application even to formal subjects often seem to produce happier children; yet those systems which offer plenty of practical ingredients instead (or as well) seem to have the happiest atmosphere of all. Now this happy state of affairs may not be due to the practical aspect (for that is not exactly proved); it may be attributable to concomitant factors in the environment. We can only make guesses about that, so far; but we are bound to note that vocational linkage does not necessarily debase. It may actually induce more gentlemanly and socially desirable behaviour – to say nothing of formal learning! Therefore the old idea that curricula could be sharply divided into the liberal sort and the vocational is being increasingly questioned. The liberalizing factor is a pervading *attitude* rather than a series of items.

Another former axiom that is now under attack (at least in its pristine form) is the belief that it is always desirable to extend formal schooling, e.g. to the age of sixteen or eighteen, depending on your circumstances. With young people who are past the age of physiological maturity, the desire to 'put off childish things' may possibly necessitate a quite different approach to learning. It may require a different place from 'school', as well as a different manner. The universal 'youth problem' is something we shall return to in Chapter 12; but here we have to observe that it may be directly related to school organization and to problems of curriculum.

Familiarity with these uncertainties makes many countries incline towards work-oriented education rather than to the conventional preuniversity type. They suspect it is not only more appropriate to the real future of most children but also more effective in many cases – even if the children will one day find places in higher education. That is certainly a potent factor in the recent Soviet decision (since 1958) to require some working experience in factory and farm of young people during each school week from the age of about fifteen upwards. In the Soviet Union preference is given in higher education (other things being equal) to those candidates who have had a further two years or more of full-time employment after leaving school. Already, it is widely said in schools and universities, the benefits are plainly evident. (This was said in 1960 by persons who did not hesitate to criticize other aspects.)

The Crowther Report in Britain (1959) recommended the raising of the school leaving age to sixteen, and the early adoption of former plans to impose part-time compulsory education up the age of eighteen. This Report, however, disappointed many people acquainted with teenagers because of its assumption that 'general' education must usually be preferable to vocational. Though this is partly a matter of opinion, no doubt, and may be also a matter of different experience, it is certain that much more attention must be paid to the experiments of Denmark, Holland, Germany, and the U.S.S.R. We must not automatically assume with the Americans and British sixth-form masters that more benefit is derived if schooling in the later 'teens is secluded from workaday involvement than when it is part and parcel of it. Indeed, must there necessarily be a choice between two polar extremes? Most of the world's opinion seems to be unconvinced that there must, even if a free choice is allowed. Such a choice does not really exist for many impoverished countries, which must in any case do the best they can to liberalize their peoples through work-linked instruction.

Part of our Western self-deception arises from our belief that only impoverished or underdeveloped countries go in for vocationally linked education in a big way. Or we tell ourselves that nations like the U.S.S.R. favour it mainly for partisan reasons, because it glorifies 'labour'. Perhaps we pretend that a supposed collapse of productivity makes other governments draft children surreptitiously into industry while pretending to the outside word that they are 'at school'. The very countries which we sometimes suspect of these things are most likely to be thoroughly realistic and (what is more) to take a very long-term view indeed. Hard-headed planners are not likely either to forgo good academic results simply to revere some ideological mystique, or to underdevelop the whole potential of their populations.

Among the constellation of reasons for any policy of vocationally associated education, we can pick out at least one central principle and further examine it in four aspects. The central point is this: technological change requires and facilitates the development of far more skills and relationships than were ever envisaged by older social and scholastic systems.

The basic implications of this technological re-orientation of education can be stated as four corollaries:

(a) the modern world requires the training of a much larger proportion of the population than were allowed to rise above elementary schooling by the old selective devices;

(b) modern industrialized society requires people to have a different content to their instruction from that appropriate to older patterns of work and politics;

(c) modern educational experiments suggest that most children, adolescents, and adults will learn and re-learn life's lessons better if these are practically related to some pertinent range of interests (such as jobs and homes);

(d) the whole business of understanding a contracted and yet more complicated world demands more conscious and continuous re-appraisal in *responsible* situations by everyone.

This last-named endeavour demands perspectives and insights which, even if immanent in older 'world views', now need reformulation and re-assessment in all kinds of circumstances throughout life. Understanding cannot therefore be 'learned in advance' at school. Not even 'facts' can be fully appreciated 'in one go'.

For all these reasons, and others attendant on the rapid changes in our way of life, it is obvious that 'continuing education' and 'further education' must ultimately be an extremely significant part of all education. Juvenile schooling depends for its success on adult fulfilment and justification. Less than ever in the history of mankind can there be a question of 'once-for-all' theories of education; nor can there be naïve confidence in the expounding of 'absolute principles', or in 'mental readiness'.

It is significant that despite the imminent prospect of automation (for which, on the practical side, Soviet schools and training centres are already preparing youngsters on a large scale), the U.S.S.R. has since 1958 increasingly emphasized 'work experience'. This modification has taken place at the very time when a progressive reduction of the working day is already in full swing. Not only socialists and communists think along these lines, of course. Several of the French revolutionaries (Diderot and Condorcet, for example) insisted that schooling must be vocationally purposeful. Napoleon believed that the *lycée* itself would have this function. The English Public Schools and military academies everywhere have derived their character-building strength from a sense of solidarity with a particular kind of future. In the widest sense, this kind of identification can only be called vocational. There has been a tendency throughout history for later generations to evaluate in time-less terms institutions which seemed to their founders to have direct topicality and purpose.

In the very countries where such a change is least publicized, the child's focus of interest in learning about life is nevertheless shifting perceptibly. There can no longer be any question of considering school as the permanent source of valid information and guidance. Other people than teachers and professors may know better. Whether they do or not, they are more glamorized and enjoy more popular esteem. Apart from that, there is no real belief nowadays that school is the shrine of knowledge and wisdom which can always be relied on. School leavers take off into the unknown, even into chaos as yet unshaped, far more than they ever did. Therefore, school (to be really helpful) must be only the first (or second) of several stages in a process which takes on shape and significance exactly in proportion as we come to grips with life.

The so-called 'gap between the generations' is increasingly and ever more rapidly one between distinct worlds of experience. Different experiences bring different emotions and a different orientation. The schools have a duty to bridge that gap, instead of allowing it to widen, as technological progress seems to bring about in many countries. There is no need to be despondent, however, if only because piecemeal experiment in many parts of the world is already bringing about considerable readjustments. We shall not despair if we recognize this evolution as respectable.

The change in perspective referred to just now, and the shift in schools' formative emphasis, affects not only the function of the schools themselves but the role and status of teachers too. Teachers are affected not only as persons but in the very function for which they are named – teaching. They do not stand in the same relation as formerly to other sources of information or guidance. They can never be the unquestioned colossi of morality, culture, or knowledge. In relation to the giants of the press, radio, and television, teachers may seem pygmies. They tend increasingly to seem less wise or less well informed factually than parents, employers, or well publicized experts. They may just seem 'out of touch'. If their fate is not to be superseded, then their whole relationship to jobs and adult life and further education (informal as well as formal) must be re-thought and re-enacted.

So in addition to any influence which technological change may have upon curriculum subjects, or upon the various types of person to be recruited for various levels of instruction, it is clear that the most significant consequences of industrialization for teachers are those of an altered orientation. A different attitude is needed towards the requirements of young people – particularly during their later years at school. These readjustments are already being contemplated or attempted in some of our best established and longest tried schools; but they are most likely to be speedily and radically planned for in the newly emerging school systems of countries still underdeveloped.

Fundamentally, then, the role of the school as a dominant influence in culture-building has been internally transformed by a change of logic, even without environmental competitors like the insistent and invasive mass media such as the press, advertising, and broadcasting. The locus of authority has moved, to say nothing of the centre of interest and emotions. In consequence, therefore, the teacher of tomorrow cannot expect to follow in the footsteps of his forebears. He must either work out a new role with a new and realistic orientation, or tag along as an ancillary to increasingly powerful influences outside the school which so often contradict him.

BOOKS

See the general bibliography on Comparative Education, p. 369.

See also the *Year Book of Education* for 1954, London (Evans Bros) and New York (World Book Company).

Mead, M. (ed.), *Cultural Patterns and Technical Change* (UNESCO), Paris, 1955.

CHAPTER 7

Selection and differentiation

Aristotle believed that some men were naturally servile, and fit only to be slaves. He was not of course alone in this; but it is noteworthy that so doughty and fearless a thinker could consider this conclusion axiomatic. When people believe in self-evident stratification, as of nature, they do not bother much about formal selection of youngsters for this career or that. The various orders and occupations man themselves automatically. If perchance some freak or genius appears in the wrong place, his talents display themselves for better or worse, so that before long he sinks or rises to an appropriate level. At any rate, this could happen in many societies where we might not expect it – as in the Muslim world reflected in the *Arabian Nights*, in Tudor England, and to a limited extent under the Tsars. In each of these cases there was a strong sense of 'common birth' (as the Russian word for 'people', *narod*, suggests). The rigid stratification associated with our concept of 'class' or 'caste' (with its corollary of endogamy within restricted parts of society) is then not so familiar as the notion of 'status' only. Status is personal, definite, ephemeral, and provable; whereas 'class' is less tangible, is corporate, persists, and is implied by various kinds of acceptance or rejection.

All societies so far discovered practise various forms of class distinction, though few are so ingenious in doing so as the British. The more open society becomes to the upward and downward migration of individuals, who thus change their *status*, the more is it likely that those who relish their *class* position will apply increasingly subtle criteria to remind themselves and the interloper of his social bastardy. He is never allowed to forget altogether the unfortunate accident of his birth or rearing. The English have become better than almost anyone else at this disgraceful game, perhaps because for several centuries now their upper classes have been astonishingly absorptive of parvenus from below. These are hardly ever completely 'received', though they may be enriched and ennobled, unless their metamorphosis began early enough for them to pass through the educational influences of particular schools or other prestige institutions. Their sons will, however, be acceptable if they go through the appropriate initiation.

Thus, for the English-speaking world and above all in England itself, any consideration of selection for various types of schooling or occupation is bound up with a whole apparatus of multi-faceted scrutiny to decide whether a newcomer is eligible as a friend, a professional associate, a guest, or a suitor. It is inseparable from apparently superficial but actually penetrating observation of the way he talks, walks, eats, drinks, or diverts himself. Hence the paramount importance of that specially Anglo-Saxon device, the interview. Some of these values and prejudices, and the institutions that go with them, have been spread around the world because of the success of the British in colonization and their invention of governmental devices; but it would be a mistake to suppose that other peoples and cultures who use similar devices actually share British foibles in this matter. Still less ought we to suppose that selection *of itself* is a reactionary and wastefully exclusive procedure, even though it may be true that the socially and economically favoured use selection quite largely to exclude others from their private paradise. Some selection faddists actually go to the extent of reviving Pindaric theories of excellence – as though 'the mind' or 'quality' were a single attribute like speed in racehorses, to be sired out of a particular strain and to be safeguarded by training in a particular stable where they have just the knack. It is no wonder that Soviet psychologists smile when they use the alien word 'tests', not because they disbelieve in selection but because they are thinking rather of all the other social considerations that go with much of the defence of testing elsewhere.

Therefore, before we can really consider selection and differentiation objectively, we must empty our minds (as much as we can) of all that we have ever seen these devices used for. To escape from our own ideology is always difficult; but we may be helped when we realize that the *things* we are selecting are probably more real and reasonable than the purposes for which we use selection. For instance, we may decide to select (if we can) future doctors, architects, businessmen, and teachers. This may be fair enough; but we should sober ourselves at the same time with the thought that these are occupations which to Aristotle would have seemed servile, being manned in his day quite largely by slaves. We may actually select and train our businessmen; but whether they manipulate us or do our bidding depends upon our pattern of background values – not on selection and training themselves.

To set our evaluation in its historical perspective, we should remember that selection has been used at different times for recognizably distinct purposes, particularly in relation to educational theory and schools. So much we considered in Chapter 3. Even more important, selection has been and is used to decide applicants' admissibility to particular privileged preserves (such as universities or the army), on the assumption that the *status quo* will be maintained. Thus, in the 1830s, even hairdressers at Oxford University had to 'matriculate', though Cobbett thought at the time that the chief characteristics of the undergraduates themselves were 'folly, emptiness of head, and want of talent'.[1] Such selective procedures are basically devices of *ex*clusion, not of inclusion. They do not envisage expansion or change.

A second function of selection is to pick those of the lower orders who may generally be included in the ranks of a slowly expanding upper class. Examples of persons thus admitted include Cardinal Wolsey under Henry VIII, Ramus at the University of Paris, and George Orwell at Eton. We still see this kind of selection at work preeminently in the Latin countries, as in Spain, Italy, and to a great extent in France. Social evolution is permitted, but under strict control and in obedience to the old rules. In India too the way to the top administrative ranks is still mainly through particular kinds of academic school and the university degree. The passing of examinations in any passable subject is of more concern than what more pragmatically oriented people would call useful knowledge. More people are admitted to success, and from a wider social background; but the idiom and the apparatus do not change much. Indeed, the results may be socially distressing rather than ameliorative, as we can see from the frustrating unemployment of graduates and certificate-holders in Italy, India, and Japan. Education and unemployment are an explosive mixture in any part of the world. It is bad enough if inadaptability to new jobs is the fault of the graduates themselves; but sometimes (as in Japan) population pressure and structural inadaptability in industry or society cause educational bottlenecks and much human wastage.

A third kind of selection is that which becomes fully operative when, in addition to the ruling class proper, an influential lower hierarchy of technicians, clerks, and civil servants is recruited. Reference was made to such requirements on page 70. But inevitably the elaboration of

[1] See a special article in *The Times* (London) on 23 February 1960, quoting the *Oxford University and City Guide* published by Henry Slatter (Oxford) in 1833.

managerial and maintenance jobs, and the increasingly minute division of labour as society changes from a static order to industrialized fluidity, demand the selection and specialized training of more than an insulated 'middle estate' of technicians, mechanics, clerks, or distributors. Modern society requires the ever more responsible participation of people with *different but essential points of view* or distinct items of information. Each one of these is really necessary for the balanced functioning of business and society.

At this point we reach the need for a new orientation such as was described on page 133. We must no longer think so much of hierarchies, or of 'sheep' and 'goats', but of people who are both 'different' and complementary, rather than classified into horizontal strata. So much we are bound to conclude for functional reasons alone, and to preserve efficiency; but we are more strongly reinforced in our utilitarian conclusions when we recognize that, for reasons of social justice and humane considerations, we must now make available to the released children of formerly work-bound classes the opportunities that industrialization has multiplied. Then at last we begin to feel that 'differentiation' may be a better word to use than 'selection', with all its institutional and emotional background.

We saw on page 119 that many of the ancient and less 'scientific' subjects or criteria associated with selection are now thought to be questionable. So too are some of the more recent and 'scientific' devices. Selectors everywhere tend to look for phenomena which register easily and arithmetically on the instruments (or tests) which they use.[1] The more testable a thing is, the more it is tested; and the more important and uniquely valuable it is thought to be. This observation applies quite as much to the elaborate testing now used for top managerial positions in the United States[2] and elsewhere as to the humbler but still influential selection used almost universally to pick children for varied types of school.

Yet even if tests were above criticism, and even if the testers

[1] An astonishing feature of the English academic scene, if only people stopped to think about it, is the number of ex-mathematicians now acknowledged as educational psychologists. It is as though the manipulation of figures and interpretation of statistics were of primary importance for the understanding of those complex phenomena: the mind and behaviour. The social origins and social impact of differentiation may thus be ignored. One might just as well suppose that skilful tailors or undertakers, used to human measurement, might also aspire to be psychologists. Much more sensitivity is required to the whole concept of ecology in relation to many of man's activities and abilities.

[2] See for example Part Four of *The Organization Man* by William H. Whyte, New York (Simon & Schuster), 1956.

themselves were more free from human prejudice than they are, it is evident that all kinds of scholastic testing activity are being gradually robbed of their significance by historical events. It is all very well to pick children for distinct schools and career-strata as long as these things stay distinct; but in fact there has been a gradual fusion of alleged 'types' in all industrial countries. That process is accelerating, too.

Three factors appear to be influential in undermining faith in selective procedures. The first is the multiple range of jobs and forms of training required, instead of two or three neatly distinguishable levels. We have just referred to this phenomenon; but we should now draw the further conclusion that if any testing is to be useful henceforward it must be of kaleidoscopic range and of remarkably penetrating power, to reveal hidden personal qualities in multiplicity as well as depth. The second factor (apart from any question of fallibility in the tests themselves) is the evolution of schools which are neither purely elementary nor purely 'secondary' or 'higher grade', but which comprise the whole spectrum of activity and interests. Such new schools therefore evoke in many children a readiness to learn data and perceptions which might have been spurned if they had been presented in a conventional form and as straitened 'subjects'. There has also arisen a recognition that children's aptitudes and characters show up more reliably in relation to real life opportunities given to them in school and work than in relation to batteries of abstract testing devices – particularly when the 'staggered' development of children at different critical ages is borne in mind. A third factor, more social than strictly instructional, is a growing belief that for reasons of public and private well-being children should not be isolated from each other in personal education even if their intellectual and professional training requires specialist handling. For all these reasons the concept of finally diagnostic tests (whose existence is, of course, queried) seems to be surviving its utility. More and more countries are abandoning this idea.

That is not to say that differentiation must not take place. On the contrary. No matter what adults decided, anyway, children would sort themselves out fairly deftly, if given the opportunity and encouragement. Many countries which are hard-headed about the need to pick out and cultivate their young talent are however coming more and more to offer an extended 'middle' schooling. Though this is considered to be basically an expansion of general education, it is far from being 'higher elementary' in the old sense of those words. It is rather a blend of 'liberal' complement (enriched to suit the children's growing maturity) with a diversified opportunity for talents or needs to show themselves. Thus it affords a period of diagnosis by self-revelation as the world reveals itself to the children. It is a 'middle' school in the sense of being a vestibule to further opportunity.

Of course, no matter what romantic vistas open up to children's vision, there are always jobs to be done and learning to be mastered. These are presented in terms of the adult working world which will soon claim the children. Therefore any choice must, at least by distant implication, be part of a move to or from a group of careers. Thus the school phase between the age of eleven and about thirteen, fourteen, or fifteen years is often called an 'orientation' period. We see it in admirable form in the Scandinavian countries, particularly in the new Danish two-year programme established for all twelve-year-olds in 1959. This was not so much a radical innovation as a nation-wide formalization of what used to happen in many urban middle schools for some years previously. A non-selective secondary school phase has been the rule in Norway for some years. In Sweden it covers half the school population at the time of writing and is becoming universal from 1962 onwards. An orientation phase has been theoretically in force in France since 1959.[1]

A comparable introduction is seen in the new German *Rahmenplan* or 'parallel' school system. The word *Rahmenplan* suggests a framework. In 1959 the Ministers of Education from each of the *Länder* comprising the German Federal Republic agreed to work towards comprehensiveness through school reforms. Very briefly the scheme may be outlined as follows: 6–10 years, *Grundschule* or primary school; 10–12 years, *Förderungsstufe* or orientation phase; above 12 years, the choice of one of the parallel elements of the secondary provision.

The least academic of these is the *Hauptschule* or senior school – a term borrowed from Austria. This replaces the former 7th and 8th classes of the primary school and in future will include a 9th class, later to be supplemented by a 10th class. In 1960, only 3 *Länder* and West Berlin had made the 9th year compulsory. The new *Realschule* is the next alternative in ascending order of esteem. It includes years 7–11 (ages 12 to 17), and will lead to a certificate entitling its holder to take

[1] In France, in fact, such an orientation phase has been repeatedly proposed since 1918, and formed a noteworthy ingredient in the Langevin-Wallon reforms of 1946 and subsequently. (In its original form it was to last for *five* years.) That is why the word 'theoretically' was used in the text. It remains to be seen how far the 1959 reform will be realized in practice.

up certain specified intermediary occupations. Specially bright pupils can transfer to the next alternative after passing entrance examinations. The new *Gymnasium* is definitely an academic secondary school leading to the *Abitur* examination at the age of 19. This gives admission to the universities. Under the older arrangement, a *Gymnasium* usually admitted pupils at the age of 10 for a 9-year course; under the new, the first two years would become the preparatory phase. Furthermore, a radical change is proposed in the nature of later studies in the new *Gymnasium*, by which pupils would concentrate on a few subjects during their last 3 years, instead of the present 9 subjects (of which 5 are main examination subjects in the final year).

In addition to the *Gymnasium*, the plan provides for a *Studienschule* or academic school for children who before the age of 10 have shown 'that they will in all probability be capable of university studies'. They can be admitted after passing special aptitude tests and receiving a favourable report from their primary school teachers. This looks very much like selling the pass. The *Studienschule* differs little from the old *Gymnasium*. Moreover the term 'higher secondary school' (*Höhere Schule*) distinguishes the *Studienschule* and the *Gymnasium* from the other two. The saving grace is that transfer from the latter to the 'higher secondary schools' is facilitated. (*International Yearbook of Education* for 1960, p. 183, Geneva, 1961.)

The famous Leicestershire experiment in England is another example. In fact, many secondary schools in the English midland counties are quietly in the forefront of the self-same development; by postponing rigid differentiation, with its corollary of segregation, they extend opportunities for self-manifestation instead of relying as hitherto on pseudo-selection by fallible tests associated with questionable criteria.[1] In theory, the American junior high school (12–15) serves as a preselection phase; but in present American practice it no longer effectively does so.[2]

Any 'orientation' or pre-vocational phase lasting until fourteen or so presupposes a worth-while follow-up later. There is no point in merely going on and on after that. Objection is sometimes raised against a break at the age of fourteen or fifteen on the ground that it interrupts the traditional pattern of continuous schooling. But that claim is

---

[1] This is in line with proposals made by R. Pedley in *Comprehensive Education* (Gollancz, London, 1956), especially on p. 149.

[2] For authoritative comment on American high schools in transition, readers are referred to J. B. Conant's *The American High School* (1959), and still more his *The Child, the Parent and the State* (1960) (Harvard University Press).

largely fictitious. If we look at England and Wales, for example, it is obvious that until recently more than 80 per cent. of the children left school altogether at about fourteen; of the remainder, the majority continued the work of the middle forms of grammar[1] schools without acquiring any special readiness for life, while the really favoured minority made a distinct move from a 'preparatory school' to a Public School.[1] Public Schools recruit their boys and girls at about the age of thirteen or fourteen. Nobody criticizes them on that score although a lot of fuss has been made about a similar break for a mature phase of junior college in the public system of education. Yet if we look aside from England and Wales, we shall soon note that in Italy and the Soviet Union, for example, transfer to quite different types of school is made for quite different purposes – but about that age. Furthermore, although Americans on the whole prefer to have high school extending from twelve to eighteen (with three years of junior and three years of senior work), almost half of the United States' school systems still adhere to the older pattern of a break at fourteen, with transfer to a four-year high school after eight years of continuous elementary (or 'grade', or 'grammar' [1]) school.

In approaching the study of any scholastic evolution, therefore, it is important to know not only the formal system as it appears on paper, but the actuality of today. Those who really know what goes on in schools (as distinct from what is supposed to go on) will recognize, for example, a growing tendency for boys and girls to leave British grammar schools and Public Schools somewhat prematurely so as to continue with intensive preparation for university and similar examinations, or for jobs, in a technical college. The 'vestibule' or 'general' departments of many different institutions of supposedly 'further' education in many countries are therefore really undertaking a differentiated phase of later secondary education. This period of awakening,

[1] For a full analysis of the terms 'public', 'grammar', and so forth as applied to schools, readers are referred to the chapters on Britain and the United States in *Other Schools and Ours*. Here we must be content to note that in the United States a public school really is public, while a grammar school comprises the first few grades of primary education. In Britain a Public School is a foundation school conducted in accordance with the rules of the autonomous Governing Bodies Association (founded in 1942), or of a similar organization for girls' schools. Many of these schools (often referred to as 'the great Public Schools') are ancient, independent boarding establishments now operated under a trust scheme. In international terminology they are describable as exclusive and expensive private (but non-profit-making) schools with very high academic standards and an enviable reputation both for character-training and as springboards for career success. British 'grammar' schools are selective but free secondary schools offering an academic curriculum which is basically but not exclusively pre-university and pre-professional.

with its purposefulness and general recognition of adolescent needs, effectively reduces the earlier years of secondary experience to the status of 'middle school' experience, no matter what names may be used. In such circumstances the schools may not change; but the children may be making different use of them.

Once more we see that fusion is taking place between the functions and preserves of apparently distinct kinds of institution. This occurs not only where such fusion is formally acknowledged. It may be firmly resisted by the teachers and administrators concerned; but that is not really the point. Three distinct kinds of event can contribute to the evolution of what for convenience we can call a 'middle school' experience: (a) schools may be formally fused; (b) schools may almost unintentionally come closer in content and method; (c) schools, though apparently retaining their pristine form, can be used by their consumers for middle school purposes.

In the last-named circumstance, the central idea at work is that a more meaningful complement should become available for the maturing adolescent after the middle school period is over. This is a matter of increasing concern in many countries where the disturbances of adolescence cause anxiety. It is not the same thing as putting more emphasis merely on the socialization and common experience which children may acquire during a comprehensive middle school phase. Therefore, though the 'middle school' idea and the 'common school' idea may sometimes be served by one and the same comprehensive institution, we should keep the ideas themselves distinct. We have not been thinking about 'comprehensive' institutions as such so far, but about experiments with the middle school period.

To be sure, the 'common school' idea is honoured in the middle school phase to the extent that children are often kept together for as long as possible in the same classes or at any rate in the same school; but few teachers believe that either bright children or backward pupils should suffer thereby, through being refused the differentiated treatment that is appropriate to their performance. Thus, the so-called comprehensive school or *enhetsskola* of Sweden (attended in 1960 by about one-fifth of the children, and intended to include all after 1962) does in fact select children *inside itself* in at least two ways. Firstly, there is no automatic promotion from grade to grade, but 'demotion' of unsuccessful pupils to less difficult courses for the future, or even repetition of the past year's work if necessary. Secondly, selective devices are built into a system of free choices at the age of thirteen (such as the adoption of a second foreign language, and more mathematics and science). But all children in Swedish comprehensive schools attend the same school together until the age of sixteen.[1]

Such selection gradually achieved through some form of middle school is commending itself to educators in many parts of the world. In Sweden, we also find that, after the diagnostic period and the critical choice of subjects at the age of thirteen, children are sorted out by their own indications into several groups before they leave the comprehensive school at sixteen. About half of them are in directly pre-vocational courses during their last year; about one-third follow studies leading to further training or direct employment in technician or minor administrative grades of work; and about one-fifth or less are hoping to enter a university after a further period of study in a *gymnasie*.

Those educators who stress the term 'middle school', and some English speakers using the term 'high school', are really putting their emphasis on such a gradual self-differentiation before the age of about fifteen or sixteen. They are not as a rule exclusively committed to 'comprehensiveness' as a primary purpose. On the other hand, it is increasingly recognized (even in France) that selection or differentiation of pupils is likely to be unjust and ineffectual unless the children have a sense of equal treatment, equal teaching, and a community of everyday background awareness. Champions of an observation or orientation period may thus be in opposition to some of the practices of the English comprehensive schools, for example, which usually differentiate their children into homogeneous 'streams' of supposed ability from the first or second year. Critics of English comprehensive schools also point out that few of them are genuinely comprehensive for another reason. In many areas (for example, in London, because of survivals often beyond the control of the London County Council) academic 'grammar' schools may take off the cream of selected pupils before the comprehensive schools can enrol their numbers. So accuracy forbids us to identify the idea of an orientation 'middle school' with the practice or theory of comprehensive schools as such. The two ideas should be kept quite distinct for other considerations too.

In the United States of America we see what is undoubtedly the most famous example of the comprehensive principle in the non-

---

[1] T. Husén, *The Differentiation Problem and the Comprehensive School* (distributed by The University of Chicago Comparative Education Center, October 1959); and W. James, 'The Comprehensive School in Sweden' in *Progress*, Winter, 1959.

communist world. Very few American children indeed go to schools which are not comprehensive. Even the 15 per cent. of them who go to private or parochial schools are usually in institutions closely resembling the ordinary publicly provided schools in major respects. One feature shared by almost all American schools is that, despite the provision of many 'elective' (optional) subjects, especially from the age of about fifteen upwards, there is seldom conscious or admitted differentiation between children on the grounds of intellectual ability.[1] True, selection is done more often than it is admitted or even realized – if only by pupils' choice, for example, of physics rather than beauty care. It is also done by directly 'counselling' pupils to take this option rather than that. But implied in most schools' organization in the United States is the conviction that all activities and subjects are of potentially the same degree of importance to the school and the child, meriting the same degree of attention – and no more.

An important social principle is at stake here, which we might well give more weight to than we usually do. We do not necessarily know which skills and characters will ultimately be of value. Moreover, people can be equal without being identical. Even if they are demonstrably unequal in certain kinds of efficiency, they may still be entitled to claim equal consideration because of the immeasurable contributions they make to humanity in other respects. Social justice apart, there is also the educational possibility that people who have not yet seemed too promising may belatedly show themselves worthy of continued cultivation in some important respect. No matter how late people come to learning, admission to it should never be a matter of dates only, or of formal experience only, but rather a question of readiness.

All these encouraging considerations are admirably characteristic of the American system of education; but because the otherwise pragmatic and practical Americans tend to lose all logic where schools are concerned, these important sentiments of humanity are sometimes weighted out of all practical proportion. Therefore, to give special attention to special children is usually stigmatized as undemocratic – at any rate when it would result in accelerated courses, 'tougher' subjects, and intellectual differentiation as the rest of the world knows it.

[1] Those American high schools which do carefully distinguish very able or industrious children from the others are well worth study; but they must still be recognized as untypical, despite a growing interest in more arduous school programmes. This is revealed in part by the increasing patronage of private schools by wealthy parents. The 1961 figure of 15 per cent. in private schools shows a rapid trend in their favour.

Yet no one in the United States quarrels with special coaching for athletes or with special adulation for the handsome, the heroic, or the commercially venturesome. Unreflecting and repressive egalitarianism is preached against intellectual eminence as against no other distinction.

It is so much easier for some Americans to go on the rampage against scholastic differentiation while other Americans make full use of it, because of the simultaneous co-existence in the United States of fully independent school systems and institutions. The United States has many thousands of autonomous school districts. Many of these are manifestly better than their neighbours. Thus pupils and their parents may appear in theory to participate in public school systems or careers comparable with those of their compatriots, whereas everyone knows that certain communities, colleges, and scholars get a much better deal. This may be the result of geography, or of social status; or it may ensue merely from having children in different courses. There is, however, little or no finality about such initial advantages. In such a highly fluid society people are socially and educationally mobile to an extent which few others would credit. When Americans speak or write about their system, they take all this background for granted. Outsiders interpreting an American write-up out of context are seldom aware of it.

But despite the existence of snakes-and-ladders opportunities for hidden talent to emerge and fulfil itself in some part or other of the American school system, the fairest and friendliest picture of it must portray the United States (at any rate until some time after Sputnik, Lunik, and the space flights) as a place where the able or diligent child has been neglected to the point of injustice. American scholastic practice often permits talent to rise only through a smokescreen of irrelevancies which serve to apportion to average citizens their ration of general knowledge, a sense of shared American values, and an implicit promise of opportunity which may or may not be explicitly taken up. In providing the American public with these basic essentials for socialization it does more for them than most other school systems do for the majority of their population, of course. The *average* level of attainment in the United States, educationally and socially, is admirable. That overall level has steadily mounted during the past sixty years to be rightly the envy of most countries. But that is not really the point. The question is, whether the present system is fair to all American children. A further question coming more insistently to the fore is whether its pace is consonant with America's future as a progressive nation, especially in view of her world responsibilities and competitors.[1]

Therefore much more attention has been given by Americans in recent years to questions of quality, which do not seem so unpatriotic now that the basic minima are so generously provided – albeit over a protracted period of schooling and often under names which are more magnificent than the achievement justifies. To paraphrase the conclusions of Dr J. B. Conant in his book *The American High School Today*, the concept is fine and the goodwill and endeavour are fine; but what is required is more of the same stuff and a further raising of the average quality of schools to the level of the better examples. This is a move which Americans can well afford – and must. Many foreign observers will consider Dr Conant a particularly benign assessor of his country's schools, as many Americans do; yet he does urge the institution of more systematic study courses, and also the establishment of ability grouping on three levels in some key subjects. Both he and many others are now anxious to have talent recognized, recruited, and rewarded. It seems more appropriate to quote Dr Conant in this context than some other writers, just because he is a fervent admirer of the American public school. There is no question of his having panicked into hasty comparisons with the U.S.S.R., as some strong-arm critics have done. Nor is he associated, like Dr Hutchins and Dr Bestor, with a somewhat romantic admiration of European academic traditions. Therefore, if he recommends greater differentiation and selectivity in the interests of justice and efficiency, and thinks this can and must be done without destroying the worth of the American school as a community, that is powerful testimony indeed.

Recognition that there need be no cleavage between quality and community in schools, even in comprehensive schools, has been growing in many parts of the world. The growth of comprehensive schools in an increasingly competitive world is an index. In Britain only 2 per cent. of the children were in comprehensive schools in 1956; in 1959 the figure was 5·5 per cent. It is expected that by 1967 the figure will be 11·3 per cent., simply through the maturing of schools or plans already in existence.[2] As we have already seen, the majority of English

---

[1] This question was increasingly asked during the closing stages of the Eisenhower administration. It was exemplified in the National Defense Education Act of 1959. The imaginative programme initiated by President Kennedy in February 1961 shows a lively concern for the encouragement of quality.

[2] For a more extended survey, see my articles on comprehensive schools in England in the *Comparative Education Review*, October 1959 and February 1960.

comprehensive schools are internally 'streamed' according to the proved attainment or supposed aptitude of the children. In addition to this 'streaming' there is a good deal of 'setting'. That is to say, children may be in particular groups (outside their general 'stream' perhaps) for special subjects. Theoretically a child might be in a top 'set' for mathematics, for example, but in an average 'set' for English, and a slower 'set' for a foreign language. Thus differentiation may help a child to find his own varied profile of abilities – and all without disgrace or glory.

One perhaps unexpected consequence of keeping children together longer in the same school, where their varied aptitudes and interests grow towards different futures by practically demonstrated endeavours rather than by tests, is the established fact that many more children stay on beyond the statutory school leaving age. Almost everywhere there is some tendency for this to happen, of course; but the trend is most marked in those schools where many abilities and interests are able to claim their appropriate tuition or pre-vocational engagement.

In Britain about 12 per cent. of the 16- to 18-year-olds were in fulltime education in 1960. Though this figure is the lowest in the English-speaking world, it is nevertheless a great improvement on the proportion staying on a few years ago. The Crowther Report of 1959 anticipated that by 1965 one child in two would be staying on voluntarily at school until the age of sixteen, and that therefore (as well as for other reasons of demography) 1965 would be a good year to institute compulsory attendance until the age of sixteen. The same Report, though in a number of ways it recommended the continuance of the English tradition of specialized courses, nevertheless echoed a general belief that the age of fourteen is still too early for final specialization. This belief should be assessed against the still prevalent practice of securing some forms of specialization by selecting children for different kinds of secondary school at about the age of eleven. This or a similar age of selection has, it is universally known, been the rule in most Western countries until very recently.

There are of course many obvious consequences of keeping young people longer in school; but as some of these are of a more social than strictly educational character, they will be considered more fully in Chapter 12. In the directly scholastic field we must now consider briefly the relation between longer schooling and the character of particular educational institutions. An example will help.

Before 1945, most children in Italy were lucky if they got a chance of schooling at all after the age of eleven or twelve. The majority were out of school after that age. If they did attend school after eleven or twelve, the choice lay between pre-university or pre-college courses for the few and directly vocational preparation for the overwhelming majority. That is to say, vocational futures were then decided unambiguously at the age of eleven or thereabouts, in three categories: (a) non-attendance at school, with work on the land or in other unskilled employment; (b) a vocational upper school until the age of fourteen; or (c) an academic upper school leading ultimately to public examinations. In post-war Italy (1961) as many as 50 per cent. may still leave school prematurely in the south, and perhaps 25 per cent. in the central districts not far from Rome. In cities enforcement of attendance is more satisfactory, and it has been made illegal to employ children of statutory school age – a provision often evaded, however. But the greater attendance of children at school has been accompanied by an alteration in the character of the schooling provided.

In the period since 1945, it is still true that Italian children are firmly on their way either to higher education or on their way to vocational training from the age of eleven upwards; but the emphasis should be placed on the phrase 'on their way'. There is less finality and restriction. For the majority (75 per cent.) of those still at school it is usual to attend a *scuola d'avviamento* (vestibule school) which combines a general education with thorough initiation into the practice of a particular occupation or group of occupations. Though purposeful indeed, this school is supposed to be less vocational than the strictly 'professional institute' beginning at fourteen for enterprising childen.

For the remaining 25 per cent. or so of pupils, the 11–14 school is a *scuola media* (middle school) of strictly general character, though of course much more academic than the *scuola d'avviamento*, which it parallels. At the end of the middle school, after gaining an all-important certificate, children can proceed to one of four alternatives. These are (1) the *ginnasio-liceo* or classical academic school; (2) the *liceo scientifico*, which despite the title is really a 'modern' academic school; (3) a training school for elementary school teachers; and (4) an *istituto professionale* or vocational institute, which also takes in a few bright children from the *scuola d'avviamento*, as we have seen.

From this example in a most conservative country we see a gradual broadening of the concept of 11–14 schooling, even where vocational preparation is included at that early age. For those whose vocational selection is now postponed until after the middle school, there is a common scholastic experience. The Italian 'Ten Year Plan' extensively discussed since 1959 seems likely, if implemented, to carry the broadening process further, and to impart to all children from eleven to fourteen a greater community of experience and orientation.[1] Some such intention was implied for the years 11–13 by the British Education Act of 1944, and by the French educational reforms from 1947 onwards; but it has never been possible in practice to achieve comparability of scholastic offering (let alone 'parity of esteem') while the existing, separate secondary schools survived in full force.

It is clear that any postponement of specialization must radically alter all schools' orientation and activities. Without running counter to what was said in the last chapter about vocational realism and developing a sense of purpose, we can see that much more schooling will become 'polyvalent' in terms of futures. That is to say, stratification and narrow specialization are tending to fade, making way for equivalent forms of realistic training which may be preparatory to several kinds of after-school enterprise. School careers can be realistic and in touch with life without acting as instruments of predestination. There is certainly no need to bring up all children on a vague educational diet simply because we are afraid that positive links with life will inevitably lead to particular careers or well-defined social positions. One of the most significant school changes in recent times has been the possibility of combining realism, and diversity of interest, with similarity of social opportunity.

Because we have so far been thinking primarily about children staying in schools, we might imagine that this has been an exclusively child-centred discussion overlooking the real need for child employment which still exists in many countries. At any rate, it might be supposed that we have forgotten the continuing public need for particular kinds of school-leavers. Not at all. When improvements take place in such things as soil fertility, agricultural methods, home conditions, or technical and industrial organization, there is a corresponding tendency to let children stay longer at school. Though ambitious parents emerging from poverty often think of schooling primarily in terms of the careers it offers, all the events just described tend to make children stay on in *less* vocationally directed courses.

[1] In 1960 a bill was introduced into the Italian parliament to establish a new 'unified lower secondary school' universally, in place of the existing *scuola media* and *scuola d'avviamento*. But once again it remains to be seen how far these proposals will be realized. Previous disregard of educational law in Italy is notorious.

The more complex industry becomes, and the wider the scatter of jobs available in it, the more likely does it become that prospective employers will prefer to have broadly educated children. Specific training in a narrow field is something they increasingly prefer to undertake themselves, for obvious reasons. Rapid changes in technique and marketing reinforce a natural preference for training in a firm's own methods. Therefore, for a combination of child care and industrial realism, educators and employers both tend to postpone vocational channelling – at any rate in an expanding range of school activities. Flexibility of futures is further safeguarded by the following influences: legislation forbidding the employment of young people before certain ages; generalizing or widening the scope of school-leaving examinations (see page 128); the development of further education on a part-time or full-time basis; and broadening the basis of recruitment for institutions of higher education such as technical colleges and universities. The universities, however, by insisting on highly specific attainments before admission to particular faculties (as in Italy and France) or to any faculties (as in Britain) present by far the most serious obstacle to the postponement of specialization in schools.

At the present point of our survey it is precisely this influence of the universities on secondary curricula that must be urgently considered – not only for its own sake but because so much of secondary school selection and early specialization for the *majority* of pupils is bound up with the possibility that a *small* proportion will go on to higher education. To see this influence more clearly, let us take two extreme examples – the English and the American. The English sixth form in grammar (i.e. academic, selective) schools exercises its boys and girls between the ages of about sixteen and eighteen in three or four main subjects which will be examined at the 'advanced level' of the General Certificate of Education. Supplementary courses are taken too, but tend in most schools to be eclipsed by the examination subjects. These latter are studied at a level comparable with that of much American 'senior' work in college, i.e. work taken about the age of twenty-one. They may even surpass that level in the case of candidates seeking admission to the universities, where competition usually demands a more than satisfactory mark. This is particularly true where scholarship papers are taken.

The English sixth form pupil has not only been selected initially for admission to the grammar school, and subsequently by having survived the drop-out of perhaps half the original enrolment before the sixth form; he is all too often already a narrow specialist. Not all head teachers take pains to correct this tendency, and many of those who do must admit defeat. Without some such specialization candidates would stand little chance of being admitted to English universities at all.[1] As far as subject-matter goes, the main part of their general education ended before they entered the sixth form. They are, however, much less widely schooled in varied, conventional subject-matter than most of their continental counterparts. They are also much less well primed with general non-academic 'know-how' than reasonably good American college 'juniors' or 'seniors'.

In strong contrast to the British example, American colleges themselves (covering the years from eighteen to twenty-two, as a rule) are traditionally expected to continue the process of general, liberal education rather than be specialist institutions for science, professions, or arduous academic disciplines. All such specializations are vigorously prepared for in American universities (sometimes more thoroughly than in British universities); but tradition demands postponement of narrowing down until the student reaches 'graduate school'. This is attended from the age of about twenty-two upwards, after the acquisition of a college degree. Thus American universities typically consist of a four-year general college, followed by specialist graduate institutions. The 'liberal arts' college adheres as strictly as it can to this tradition – a conservatism which is all the easier because nearly all the 700 or so liberal arts colleges are under private or religious control.[2] The huge growth in recent years of more obviously vocational schools and courses in American undergraduate colleges, particularly the state colleges, does not vitiate the general principles just outlined, for two reasons. Firstly, such vocationalism is considered by Americans to be a departure from the university ideal; and secondly, most such applied courses ought really to be compared not with university work in other countries but with non-university technical or commercial institutions.

[1] Furthermore, as is widely known, a powerful 'coaching' business has grown up to supplement the already rigorous curriculum of excellent grammar schools and Public Schools – chiefly to enhance the prospects of admission to the Universities of Oxford and Cambridge. In some cases (to quote 'the head of a famous crammer's, which expects to get 80 per cent. of its candidates through') '. . . the work the girls have to do for this entrance examination is harder than anything they will have to do if they get to the university' – i.e. in terms of slog, presumably, and not attainment ('Part-time Coaching': article in *The Times*, 1 May 1961).

[2] R. Freeman Butts, 'Basic features of American education', p. 9, in *Public Education in America*, edited by G. Z. F. Bereday and L. Volpicelli (Harper, New York), 1958.

Thus the contrast between the British example and the American ideal of general education – to be made available for as many people as possible at the college level as well as in school – is accentuated. As opposed to American practice, academic specialization is already markedly characteristic of the last two years in the *most favoured* of English schools (i.e. the Public Schools and the grammar schools), during which pupils are roughly 16–18 years of age. English universities are, generally speaking, specialist, professional places from first to last. (The post-war University College of North Staffordshire and the new University of Sussex are conspicuous exceptions.)

In the present chapter we are not considering universities and other forms of higher education as such. That will be the concern of the next chapter. Yet it is important to reflect on the influence universities exercise on the development of other phases or forms of education, either preceding them, or around them. If it is decided that universities should be fully autonomous as in the British tradition, then two conclusions may follow from the isolation which such self-sufficiency implies: (*a*) universities will be by-passed or supplemented if they fail to make provision for the full range of studies which need to be pursued *at that level*, and also for as many students as show they are entitled to receive higher education in terms of their own capabilities and their country's needs; (*b*) the universities have no licence to dictate to, or indeed to make weighty suggestions to, institutions which do not exist directly to serve them.

That is to say, universities may properly decide what kinds and levels of study are appropriate within themselves, thus behaving like learned societies; but in that event they cannot object to the development of alternative institutions at the public expense to do the necessary things they do not do. Though they may impose certain conditions of club membership and punctilio once university admission is granted, they are not entitled to say in advance what *secondary schools* should do to their pupils either in the best general interests of those pupils or in relation to the particular requirements of society at the time. Yet all these things have happened in many countries by implication, if not explicitly.

Furthermore, it is a matter of record that universities have all too often been tempted to pronounce (again in advance) that some kinds of study are not worth pursuing at an advanced level, or are incapable of contributing to the richness of civilization and the student's refinement. They thus weight the curriculum of many types of secondary school overwhelmingly in favour of particular subjects. Not only independent universities but even the state universities of some countries have sinned in this way. Thus, at different times, the following academic interests have been stigmatized as unworthy of the university: all the sciences except mathematics; modern languages; psychology; sociology; education; economics; business; and governmental administration.

The writer would resist any onslaught on the true independence of universities – subject to guarantees for the true and complementary autonomy of the rest of a country's educational system, without regard to the universities. Complete autonomy, however, could never happen unless neither the universities nor the rest of the educational system received a penny of public money, and unless the whole of education took place in some static pre-industrial society as a sort of rich man's dilettantism.

But formal education today is a business – part of the national economy and the social and political apparatus. In modern conditions, therefore, it is absolutely necessary to conclude that 'university independence' is far from being irresponsibility (quite apart from questions of finance). Though for reasons of intellectual integrity and to avoid manifest political dangers academic life must be independent in every possible circumstance, nevertheless the effective future of the *schools* (and of the universities themselves) depends on extremely rapid readjustment to actual educational needs today. This will necessitate a reversal of some tendencies, and an acceleration of some others. Preeminently it will demand of all university personnel an excruciating and continuous examination of conscience. Conscientiousness (and this is usually a mark of British universities) needs alertness and sympathy to be effective. It also moves more nimbly in response to public opinion and public financial prodding. The last instrument is the least worthy; but it is increasingly having to be used.

The unsatisfied demand for more university places, and the intolerable pressure on restricted facilities in universities, have made it seem necessary to look for applicants already well schooled in particular subjects. Yet these are not always relevant to the intended course of study. New entrants are required to be at an advanced level already – sometimes beyond the attainment expected in our fathers' time after a year or two spent at the university. Universities demand deeper and earlier specialization in Britain. Keener selectivity in nearly all other countries induces ambitious students to pre-select their field of most concentrated work even within an apparently wide range of pre-university subjects.

To return to our American-British contrast, both idioms have good and bad features. No evaluation should be indulged in which does not consider the whole background of social conditions and personal expectations in both countries.[1] The traditional European pattern or schooling as we see it on the continent is characterized like that of Britain by advanced work before the university level is reached; but on the continent it is a more usual practice for many subjects (e.g. eight or nine) to be taken to the immediately pre-university level, and for students to 'fan out' into their specialization only after one or more years in the universities. Thus there is a more extended exploratory phase; and early university level work is (outside Russia) seldom of the same intensely concentrated nature as in Britain.

Wherever the American style of leisurely, 'liberal' schooling is copied, complications often arise because of the inability of the adopting countries to incur American-size expense and wastage. There are other problems too. It is often felt that apart from any questions of economics the encouragement of genius presents special difficulty. Notoriously in mathematics and physics genius manifests itself most brilliantly from the latest 'teens through the early twenties. Similar precocity is also characteristic of excellence in the arts; and these remarks may also be applicable to some other subjects. Unwelcome though these early indications of genius are to sentimentalists and some social reformers, they clearly suggest that both for the sake of our abler children and to meet many nations' needs some kind of specialization may have to be combined somehow with egalitarian and 'liberalizing' influences. We are once again compelled to question the belief that equality and 'humaneness' are exactly synonymous with the postponement of specialization as such or with the early discouragement of brilliant differences. Those who wish to delay specialization wish to ensure, as a rule, that there shall be no evil social consequences of precocious exploitation or differentiation; but they may inadvertently recommend some educational evils.

Though, as we have said, purely social considerations arising out of such decisions are more appropriate to Chapter 12, it is relevant to remember here that serious malaise has arisen among students in Japan since the slower-paced American style of liberal college followed by graduate specialization was substituted for the pre-war pattern of

[1] See *Other Schools and Ours*, chapters 4 and 5.

specialized post-secondary higher schools followed by more specialized universities. To students in India, Turkey, and many developing countries, the prospect of an open but still uncertain future during their long un-vocational tutelage may cause anxieties grave enough to result in riots. Not only are these bad for morale; they can be a threat to international peace. The 'teen-age problem' can in different guises be a fearsome challenge to university assumptions and liberties.

Let us look at some Russian experiments which are relevant to these assessments, especially in relation to the question of vocational linkage. During the Stalin phase of Soviet development (i.e. until about 1953) there was a crescendo of endeavour to establish 'general education' secondary schools for everyone everywhere. These are often referred to as 'ten-year schools' because they took children to the age of seventeen, and compulsion began at seven. The 'ten-year' school was indeed a common school, comprising all children and offering them an identical curriculum (with insignificant differences between boys and girls, or to meet special language requirements). It was of the conventional, continental, academic type, with the important difference that everyone went to it. It was therefore non-specialist, though it is true that more directly vocational schools existed for the minority of villagers or backward children for whom a traditional, bookish schooling seemed too remote. The so-called 'labour reserve' schools associated with factories, farms, mines, or transport combined work with instruction for such children from the age of fourteen onwards. Again, there persisted a number of specialized institutions (including some of the *tekhnikumy*) which took off relatively able children (such as future elementary school teachers) from the age of fourteen. Yet on the whole the prestige-carrying 'ten-year school' not only was spread more widely under the Stalin dispensation until it took in almost all children in cities and towns and larger villages; it also became increasingly uniform in securing a straightforward academic schooling which was identical for all who attended it.

By the end of Stalin's life it was confidently expected that the 'ten-year school' of general, formal education would be the rule for everyone in the Soviet Union by the year 1960. Exacting and doubtlessly tedious though the curriculum often must have seemed, it was nevertheless keenly appreciated by nearly all parents, who saw what was formerly the rich man's schooling made available to their children. Not only parents but also many social planners and indeed educational theorists too relished the thought that Soviet brains would be developed, Soviet science built up, and Soviet plans for a supply of technologists achieved. (See *Other Schools and Ours*, chapter 6.)

It should however be emphasized that, apart from an all-pervading regimentation that was quite as much a legacy from pre-Soviet times as a Soviet phenomenon, modern Russian pedagogy is markedly humane in its consideration of children. Somewhat paradoxically in the circumstances it endeavours to make education a truly child-centred experience. (We shall consider these aspects again in Chapter 10.) Therefore, on logical grounds alone, and quite apart from doubts about deviation from the Marxist tradition of a work-centred education, it seemed obvious to many that uniformity of theoretical and 'general education' for ten years might be questionable. Hard-driven teachers knew the practical difficulties well. Only communists' great insistence on the 'collective', and Stalinist policies of planning scholastic productivity to suit the ever-expanding universities and institutes, caused the universal and identical 'ten-year' school to seem desirable on pedagogical grounds, though it was immensely popular on social grounds. For all that, it did succeed before Stalin's death in producing a far greater proportion of immediately pre-university quality candidates by European criteria than could be found in any other country in the world. So it was mechanically most successful.

In some ways it was too successful. It certainly produced an abundant potential of good scholars in the old-fashioned European sense, most of them ready with the long-approved pre-university scholastic apparatus of knowledge and study habits – and that although they had all spent all their juvenile years in completely undifferentiated common schools. The system produced many practical difficulties too, not least by creating a bottleneck. Despite the astonishing development of universities and institutes of advanced technological education (in all, more than 200, and many of them of great size) far more children left school with diplomas than the higher education institutes could possibly accommodate. The obvious device in such circumstances is to raise the entry qualification. This was done. First a silver medal diploma was demanded, then a gold medal. Even that is not enough now. Further indications of quality are demanded, especially at the more popularly sought after institutes. The professors seek to impose additional tests or inquiries, both before entry and afterwards. It is not surprising therefore that out of all those listed as students in higher education in the Soviet Union in 1960, about half were on a part-time (evening) or correspondence basis. All of them, we may be sure, possessed qualifications that a few years ago would have entitled them to go straight into universities.

Now that the Soviet school system can produce its university potential in such great masses and of more than satisfactory quality, the imperfections of conventional selection are made clear. There is no point in taking all those boys and girls to the threshold of the university and then rejecting half, particularly in a totally planned system where the numbers of various kinds of skilled worker are calculated ahead from the pre-school period. Old-fashioned European methods were all right as long as there was some doubt about getting the right categories and quantities, and the schools' output did not overtax the possibilities of higher institutions. Yet so much enthusiasm for scholastic prowess, combined with the traditional continental regard for academic professions, resulted in an over-intellectual bias that would be fatal in any progressive country and must have seemed like perfidy in the workers' state.

For some time the growing number of 'inadmissibles' to higher education was concealed by the growing practice of admitting them to evening departments or to correspondence courses, while they worked during the daytime in ordinary employment. A number of re-training devices were introduced, to divert seventeen- and eighteen-year-old would-be students to advanced work in industries and agriculture – with little success. 'General' pre-university education had done its job too well; yet the expanding supervisory and technician grades of employment were starved, despite the expansion of excellent *tekhnikumy* recruiting boys and girls of fourteen or seventeen at an attainment level below that appropriate for university or institute admissions.

It is in this context that we must assess the 1958–9 innovations often called the 'Khrushchev reforms'. In brief, these extend the first part of a Soviet school life from seven to eight years (until the age of fifteen), and then secure radical differentiation between the children. Since the new thesis was propounded first in October 1958, and made law in December of that year, many interpretations and practical modifications have been authorized. The scheme began to be put into practice in 1959–60; but it was then anticipated that from three to ten years would have to elapse before it could be fully implemented. However, certain of the initial forecasts and some of the subsequent modifications are important enough for separate consideration.

At first it was recommended that all children without exception should have some experience (perhaps up to two years full-time) in factories or agriculture, no matter whether they were going on to 'higher' or technical education or not. More recently, legislation and administrative interpretation make it clear that, although *all* children will have *some* work-associated 'polytechnical' re-orientation between the ages of about fifteen and eighteen, only about 50 per cent. will be diverted into actual full-scale working experience at that time. Even these will be strongly encouraged to improve their technical competence by in-service training and 'evening schools'. (In Russian, the word 'evening' includes the late afternoon.) This period of evening-school supplementation of a working life must last three years. It has been generally expected, by experienced educators no less than by the lay public, to result in cultural and practical attainments not lower than those of the old ten-year school. Evening schools give fifteen hours a week of instruction to the young workers.

Thus we must reckon the part-time three-year evening school (which in remote areas may be by correspondence, and elsewhere by a sort of part-time day-release) as the normal fulfilment of the eleven-year period of general and polytechnical education for the majority of children, or at least for about half of them. The directly vocational aspect of their working day will also be subject to training requirements. In all, up to eighteen hours a week of study of one sort or another was anticipated by Deputy Minister Markushevich of the Russian Federation, during conversation with the author in 1960. Time off work, on full or half pay, can be secured by these young workers for approved study and for the taking of examinations. Similar arrangements were observed in Czechoslovakia in 1961.

The selection of children in the category just described must never, it is emphasized, be based upon psychological or other tests as familiar in Western Europe and North America. It must depend upon a blend of three factors: (*a*) abilities and interests already shown in work and school; (*b*) the needs of local enterprises; and (*c*) personal choice after vocational guidance and interviews with the managers of industries or collective farms. In this connexion it is important to realize the value placed upon the pupil's record of work, with marks from one to five, throughout his school life. Those with an average of lower than three are in any case expected to repeat a year's work. Though Western observers will undoubtedly make up their minds about the selective principle at work here, it would be less than fair to overlook two relevant features of the Soviet system: (*a*) every possible attempt is made to encourage every possessor of any useful talent to develop it; (*b*) necessary differentiations are to a surprising degree robbed of their social or cultural stigmata by the very rich and welcoming provision of heavily subsidized 'culture' programmes. The pre-revolutionary sense of 'the people' has been intensified by two generations of insistence on 'the collective'.

For the other half of the children the choice at fifteen lies between two types of schools already existing but now modified. These are (*a*) the years nine, ten, eleven in a 'general education and polytechnical secondary school', leading to a school-leaving diploma offering the possibility of admission to higher education; and (*b*) *tekhnikumy* or other specialized secondary-technical establishments, mainly concentrating on the middle and upper range of non-university or non-institute technical occupations, but also allowing the possibility of recruitment to higher education for some candidates with uniformly excellent marks. Courses in a *tekhnikum* are of varying length, but normally consist of about 70 per cent. industrial training (with wages) and 30 per cent. theoretical instruction, while 'general' and social education takes place mainly through clubs and extra-curricular activities fostered by the school. In 1961 there were 3,684 of these institutions, training technicians or tradesmen in more than 800 occupations. Some of the programmes are of a short-term and elementary nature; but as the basic course begun at the age of 15 normally lasts for 4 years, it is obvious that a substantial level is reached in both general and technical education.

On the technical side, a further distinction is being emphasized. The old 'Labour Reserve Schools' were still vigorous enough in some cities during 1960 to have gold-medal exhibits at the Permanent Exhibition of Soviet Achievements in Moscow; but the more narrowly vocational trade or craft schools (*remeslennoye uchilishche*) for fifteen-year-olds are now clearly distinguished from 'technical schools' (*tekhnicheskoye uchilishche*) to which the more able and advanced children are admitted at the age of eighteen from the new eleven-year school. In addition to skilled craftsmen, the latter turn out specialists in technical control departments, designers, and the like. As from 1961 they are training specialists for work in increasingly automated factories and similar modern developments. Where this differentiation is made, the old generic term 'Labour Reserve' is abandoned, except as a survival in association with sports clubs. Perhaps the change suggests that all schools recruiting children under the age of eighteen are functionally part of the secondary school system. From this viewpoint, all teachers, administrators, and the like point out that the same 'core' of general knowledge, of subjects, and of 'culture' is made available to all children under the age of eighteen, no matter what their instruction.

Even the children in the 'general education and polytechnical secondary school' must devote the equivalent of two days weekly to working experience, giving twelve hours a week in all, while twenty-four are spent on general instruction illustrated more than previously with reference to real life work. Although practical demonstrations or experiments are almost unknown in classrooms (in keeping with the general continental tradition) there is some permeation of the material taught with the new 'labour' orientation. The effective work-linkage, however, is almost entirely confined to practical experience of labour outside. It is a cardinal principal that, even in the 'general education' pre-university school, children aged fifteen to eighteen should learn a trade too. Thus they have experience of earnest work under realistic conditions, and can obtain ordinary employment if they have to.

It is clear that this educational reform is a practical return to the true communist faith, as exemplified in Krupskaya. Although it is also useful in getting recruits for the middle ranks of the technical professions and aspirants for the lower rungs of industrial administration, it would be a grave mistake to evaluate it cynically – from outside and in alien terms. As a practical matter, it is clear from inside the Soviet Union that both work-experience before school-leaving and any extension of it afterwards can lead the enterprising boy or girl a long way ahead. It can result in further training at a high level, and lead to a distinguished position as a result of practical achievements. In any case it offers social and economic rewards which may be comparable with those in more esteemed professions in other countries. In the Soviet Union there are as glamorous careers in actual productivity as there are in the financing of it in some other parts of the world. But such observations are a digression from the 'polytechnic' principle, which is used as a new perspective and also as a sort of selecting device.

To assess the importance which Soviet educators attach to 'polytechnicization', we must not only take account of the last three (or more) work-linked years of the new eleven-year school period; we must also reckon in the two years of additional, full-time employment in *any* industry which school-leavers are now expected to have before they go on to any university or institute. By 1958, over 45 per cent. of all students in higher education had had this experience. The only real exceptions are future mathematicians, physicists, and some other 'theoretical' scientists, though about 20 per cent. of all university and institute places are reserved for specially promising children coming straight from school. Those with good work-experience, which does not need to be in a branch akin to the university specialization hoped for, receive preferential consideration for admission to higher education. So there can be no doubt about a genuine concern to give young Soviet citizens a taste of the farm and factory as part of their general education. Doubtless there is a hope too of stimulating an appetite for more.

Clearly, however, there is another aspect to this whole revival of the 'polytechnic' principle – and that is its possibilities for evocation and differentiation. Over and over again, teachers and administrators stress its value as an invitation to expanded interests, or as a real-life indication of children's inclinations and futures. This may not arouse much conviction in those of us who believe we have already secured such evocation in all kinds of activity within our own school organization; but we are then being insular, and forgetting the arid formalism of continental, verbal teaching found in Russia just as it is in Germany, Italy, Denmark, France, and elsewhere. Though some teachers trained in the academic tradition in the Soviet Union are no more enthusiastic about Khrushchev's innovations than we might have guessed on general grounds, many other teachers and more children are enthusiastic enough. Certainly it is a possible opening of horizons, and it can also present a more extended front of activities in which children can show their preferences, needs, and potentialities.

If we rashly conclude that school-time and after-school work is solely a device for selecting downwards the children of lower intellectual power, we are shown to be wrong by the very fact that all except future mathematicians and physicists are required to undertake it. Moreover, every possible encouragement is offered to 'employed' teenagers to get higher qualifications. What the Soviet system thinks it needs is more practical application to technology, as distinct from theoretical studies. It is part and parcel of the Marxist ideology that even the perception of 'truths' may be vitiated if not seen in a materialist and proletarian working context. Also, good communists should get to know each other as workers together. Yet these important factors in recent Soviet decisions should not blind us to the very thing we are looking for – the selective or differentiating principle. Undoubtedly, extra-curricular working experience and the more continuous periods of work from the age of fifteen onwards are highly prized as significant indices of children's varying needs and gifts; for the search for promising material goes on throughout.

We see this regard for ability most thoroughly borne out in another kind of extra-curricular activity – if that description can be properly applied to something that so thoroughly penetrates the whole of Soviet school life. The Party-operated youth organizations, from the young Octobrists to the Komsomol, are directly charged with two distinct but complementary responsibilities: (*a*) socializing everyone into the 'collective'; and (*b*) diagnosing and developing the special talents and particular abilities of individuals for the service of the community. In the first respect, they ensure that what we might call 'backward' children do not fall behind, but are helped in very many respects by their brethren and seniors. In the second, the hobbies or untapped energies and special interests of the enterprising are cultivated outside the formal, standardized curriculum. Pioneer circles, houses, and camps cater for children between the ages of about nine or ten to about fourteen or fifteen. At the latter age they can join the Komsomol (Young Communist League). Pioneer activities include not merely a Boy Scout style of corporate feeling and dedication, though they do manifest this in a peculiarly intense form: they also include all kinds of hobbies and studies, including foreign languages and a good deal of what in Britain would be called practical experimental work, though this is often very elaborate and extended into vacations.

Educators and Communist Party organizers make no bones about the fact that Pioneer activities (often in wonderful buildings with splendid equipment) pick out the talented and enterprising child – talented not just in social or hobby-like activities but in future genius of both practical and theoretical kinds. Moreover, the so-called 'Olympiads' [1] or nation-wide academic competitions are prepared for within the youth organizations. Thus distinction and diversity are selected, coached, and rewarded. Such special attention is worth coveting not only for its obvious, direct results in university admissions but also because to have been distinguished within the Pioneers or Komsomol is in itself an augury of future vocational success. Even office within the youth organizations depends considerably upon scholastic as well as personal distinction.

Increasing concern is expressed for the recruitment and fostering of really gifted students. My continued observation of what actually

[1] The term for athletic competitions is *Spartakiad* (from Spartacus, the leader of the slaves' revolt in ancient Rome).

happens reinforces the conviction of a strongly selective mechanism at work. For example, the first all-Union mathematics Olympiad reached their finals in Moscow in March 1961 (though there was a preparatory contest in 1960). Intellectual attainment contests of this type seem to be on the increase. At a Kremlin conference on higher education in July 1961, Mr Yelyutin, Minister of Higher and Specialist Education for the Soviet Union, urged more thorough scouting for talented students, and stronger encouragement of their university-level endeavours so as to develop creativity. (This clearly implies early selection.)

In this connexion, a note on the characteristics of examinations in the U.S.S.R. will not come amiss. To take the school-leaving examinations as an example, the topics are published long ahead and the actual themes of the questions are made known some weeks before the examination. Thus the test demands knowledge and insight, but in a straightforward way which enables pupils to make the most of (a) what they know, and (b) all resources for further knowledge. Such a test is clearly intended to make use of *all* types of person likely to succeed, because they are wanted; there is also a clear assumption that *all* pupils will easily obtain appropriate help.

By contrast, examinations in non-communist Europe might often be described as (a) eliminatory, depending on memory, cunning, and an eye for 'traps'; (b) dependent on a special type of presentation, especially in the past; and (c) a puzzle to the student, and a source of career anxiety to himself and his parents. Exemplifying this last characteristic is the French or Italian newspaper publication of solutions given by learned academicians to the examination questions. We should also note the alternative careers and later opportunities in Russia, which by-pass the 'needle's eye' of the end-of-school examination.

Thus, the differentiating principle is resolutely applied in what at first sight might seem an egalitarian and monolithic system. We should not convey our own background prejudices into this observation, however. For all its unfamiliarities, the Soviet school system evidently prizes and to some extent reconciles within the communist context two desiderata often at loggerheads elsewhere – differentiation, and parity of consideration.

The totalitarian nature of Soviet planning facilitates the transfer of a relatively old device to a radically different programme. Thus, the former 'ten-year' or 'general' secondary school is in full process of being transformed into a tripartite system of differentiation from the age of fifteen upwards. In this development, and in the years before selection markedly takes place, the para-curricular organizations are used in two overlapping but distinct ways. They encourage manifest ability from an early age, and allow children of all grades of talent to find conventional or practical activities to suit their aptitudes inside school or out; at the same time, because much differentiation is linked with work *outside* the classroom proper, the 'common school' ideal with its unusually uniform treatment is perpetuated until the rather late age of fifteen. The feeling of the 'collective' thus engendered is in turn reinforced by the markedly socializing opportunities of the youth organizations, not just in term-time but in the summer camps and other vacation activities in which almost all children actively participate. The new boarding school programme so rapidly developing also intensifies 'collective' suggestions.

In the new involvement of young people in productivity, the youth and Party organizations are conspicuous once more. They round up the dilatory and honour the enterprising. Invigilation and evaluation are continuous. In the Soviet system no part of the day, week, or year is really a Lockean 'private area'. Though qualities may be differentiated, deviationism from the Plan or the 'collective' is not permitted. Thus, though thousands of different careers are prepared for by the most far-sighted selection, the growth of 'élitism' and arrogance are guarded against. Though the ideological rigidities and formalism of the Soviet scene are indeed frightening to any liberal observer, there is something magnificently Aristotelian in the principle there exemplified: 'from each according to his abilities, to each according to his needs'. The actual embodiment of the principle at present in the Soviet Union is not such that many outsiders will wish to copy it. Nevertheless Soviet experiments[1] have shown that Aristotle's notions of distributive justice

---

[1] For up-to-date information the following are the best Soviet sources:

Novaya sistema narodnogo obrazovaniya v SSSR, (Moscow) Academy of Pedagogical Sciences, RSFSR, 1960.

Perspektivy razvitiya pedagogicheskoy nauki i koordinatsii raboty Akademii i kafedr pedagogiki pedagogicheskikh institutov (Moscow), 1959, by I. A. Kairov, President of the Academy of Pedagogical Sciences, RSFSR.

Kondakov, M. I.: *Education in the U.S.S.R.,* Moscow (Foreign Languages Publishing House), 1961.

The Humanities in Soviet Higher Education, edited by D. Grant, compiled in 1958 but published in book form in 1960 (University of Toronto).

The best commentaries in English, both rather critical, are:

The Changing Soviet School, edited by G. Z. F. Bereday, W. W. Brickman, and G. H. Read (Houghton Mifflin), Boston, 1960.

The Politics of Soviet Education, edited by G. Z. F. Bereday and J. Pennar (Praeger), New York, 1960.

can be applicable to an industrialized society. No doubt in a liberal context too the principle of functional selectivity can be reconciled with equality of consideration. What is decided about the selection in the scholastic arena of the liberal countries during the next few years may well determine whether the Soviet system or ours will seem preferable to the undecided majority of mankind.

BOOKS

See the general bibliography on Comparative Education, p. 369.
See also the *Year Book of Education* for 1958 and 1961, London (Evans Bros) and New York (World Book Company).

CHAPTER 8

Further and higher education

The words used as the title for this chapter are very often misunderstood. For that matter, so are the simple words 'education' and 'school'. 'Further education' brings in additional questions about what has happened before it. That manifestly differs from place to place. As we saw on page 153, what is a secondary school matter in one country may be something for a 'college' or university to tackle somewhere else; in yet a third place, apprenticeships or technical induction schemes give instruction that is the concern of schools or colleges elsewhere. Therefore any kind of statistics relating to 'further' education demand penetrating scrutiny. They can be understood only in relation to the one country or enterprise in which they were collected.

Primary schools may differ a good deal from country to country, and secondary schools more so; but 'further' and 'continuation' and 'higher' education must differ more, not only because their scope and character depend on the two highly idiomatic stages preceding them, but even more because of the remarkably different technological and social contexts which they have to serve. Yet the very complexity and unpredictability of further education are of great value to those who study the evolution of education in general, for it is in this highly fluid phase of it that existing preconceptions and institutions are least likely to prejudice people's conclusions. We see education in process of eager *adjustment*, and find experiments everywhere.

So a labyrinth of approaches and a Protean confusion of shapes need not daunt us. Among them we shall continually encounter familiar paths and recognizable features. Thus in some ways we shall be more at home in further education developments than when we are faced with other people's institutions of primary and secondary education, which may seem so monumentally alien as to affront us. The very resourcefulness of further education is part of a world-wide endeavour to come to terms with life in an industrialized society. The logic of industrialization is much the same throughout the world, though the discrepancies between it and previous social systems vary enormously, thus causing all those variations in further education. The growing resemblance of urban life in one place to urban life in another makes it all the more important that we should heed the lessons to be learned from others' experiments. Some indication of their importance may be drawn from the fact that governments throughout the world tend to watch, encourage, and sometimes control further education even when (as in Britain and the U.S.A.) they devolve the responsibility for primary and secondary education largely upon others.

As further education of any sort must be a fulfilment or correction of what has gone before, it gives us an indication of the natives' self-criticism or their unsatisfied ideals. Even if the study of further education did not have this usefulness it would still be necessary for any student of education to know something of the provision made for adolescents and adults. Otherwise he could never judge if the previous juvenile schooling was reasonably adequate for what was locally expected of it, or if it had any future in the years ahead.

Many a scholastic activity of our younger years has been of little more value to us in later life than hop-scotch or skill in other childish games, simply because it had no follow-up. Though such condemnation may seem irreverent to the conventional teacher, it is seriously intended. In many countries of the world juveniles and adults are made literate to no purpose. There is nothing for them to read later, or nothing suitable and profitable for them to read, so that they quickly relapse into illiteracy. They have wasted their time, and perhaps developed a distaste into the bargain. On these grounds alone, the prospect of some further education must be borne in mind when we evaluate whatever is done to children. We can see very readily that much contemporary schooling is basically a latter-day variant of centuries-old pre-university *vocational* preparation; but if the children are not now being called to church or university, does it really suit them? Futures must definitely be criteria for judging schooling in the present.

Two other general factors must be considered, one personal and the other social. Most of us fall in love, marry, have children, and are attended by all the problems of keeping a home and family in good order. But could we ever really learn about these things *in advance*? Obviously these and many kindred matters cannot be effectively considered (let alone understood) until we are actually involved in them. Therefore, the growing recognition that education is never a 'once-for-all' affair belonging to childhood, or a portmanteau packed for life during pre-adolescent years, makes it incumbent on modern societies to provide each man or woman with that personal guidance which comes from continuing educational opportunity. The diminishing influence of automatic caste punctilio, occupational stratification, village example – and indeed of family influence and religions – makes the provision and study of further education an infinitely more important matter than in any previous age. Liberty and mobility have given certain freedoms; but they have also removed certain supports. The mass media are probably not (without qualification) the best substitutes for these. Further education is clearly required in consequence of personal maturation.

The evolution of societies also introduces new and often pressing demands. Many of these have been touched on already; but they are worth a brief recapitulation here. The chief of them are: the develop-ment of quite unprecedented sciences and occupations, for which no previous preparation could be adequate; the rapid evolution of tech-niques and altered human relationships in the jobs that still persist in recognizable form; social mobility; political shifts of privilege and responsibility; and altered international relations. All these changes im-pinging on *adult* life make it imperative to transfer the emphasis in 'life preparation' from the juvenile phase of evocative or assimilative schooling to the later years of maturing comprehension and adaptation. A government which does not secure the fullest development of educational facilities for adults, as the British Education Act of 1944 demands, is bound to fail technologically. It will also become increas-ingly unstable politically and socially, for it is actually inviting all the 'hidden persuaders'[1] to take over the vital job that it has jettisoned. It will aggravate mental ill-health and crime too.

There can therefore be no doubt about the increasing importance of further education in the modern world. Before proceeding further, however, it will be convenient to set out in some sort of system the use of the various names applied to education made available for non-juveniles. 'Further' education seems to be the best generic term. It may be applied to any formal provision made by public or voluntary agencies (particularly in classes or discussions) for those who have terminated the normal complement of compulsory schooling. Thus, it does not strictly include such things as the elementary instruction of adult illiterates in a very backward country. For the same reason, we

[1] The reference is to the book of that title by Vance Packard (McKay), New York, 1957.

may exclude from it the extremely simple instruction in hygiene, home care, and social organization also frequently given in underdeveloped countries to the very poor who have never been to any school, though of course these same subjects (presumably at a more advanced level) might have to be taught also in a highly developed country to adults who have suffered an exclusively academic upbringing.

If by 'further' education we imply something added after the completion of the normal complement of compulsory schooling, we must therefore include in it the important subsection 'continuation education'. This term normally denotes something added to elementary or secondary schooling to make it more vocationally complete. Thus a short apprenticeship is a form of 'continuation education'. So in Britain until very recently secretarial courses and the like were mainly 'continuation' courses taken in evening institutes and other after-school centres, whereas in the United States and in the white schools of South Africa such courses have long been ordinary school activities.

As we saw in the last chapter too, much of the vocational instruction appropriate to a more extended apprenticeship in Britain may be part of the 'eleven-year school' programme in the U.S.S.R. It may also be found in vocational or technical high schools in some parts of the United States. In Germany, Austria, and Denmark the great majority of children leave school and go to work at fourteen; but all of them (if not in some full-time educational alternative) must attend one full day or two half-days a week at a vocational school until they are eighteen. Thus the German *Berufsschule*, the Austrian *Gewerbeschule*, and the Danish *Handværkerskole* are all clear examples of 'continuation' education. If ever the British county colleges, or the recommendations of the Crowther Report for part-time education to eighteen, are realized, they will be too. 'Further' education, of course, is an equally applicable but less specific term.

The description 'further' education comes into its own particularly with full-time vocational instruction given with the express purpose of attaining particular qualifications. These are sought by craftsmen or people at intermediate points in the business and administrative hierarchy. Technicians' training is a suitable example. Here again, however, international comparisons may cause confusion. Though the Russian *tekhnikum* exemplifies 'further' education very appropriately (and successfully), it also in its different forms trains teachers for the lower grades, journalists, dancers, and many kinds of manager. In Russian terminology and that of Europe generally, this kind of work is 'further' education of a vocational and less-than-university character; yet in the United States most of these occupations would be prepared for, though perhaps no better, in 'colleges' and universities.

There is generally a strong suggestion of bread and butter about the word 'further', and rather less of the odour of sanctity such as is implied in the term 'higher' education. From many points of view this status-seeking by terminology is very regrettable, especially when the liberalizing leaven that universities are supposed to impart is really absent from much of the *work* actually done there, being found rather in the circumstances of residence and human contacts, but not always even there. For example, the passionate pursuit of expertise in palaeography, a modern language, or statistics (or medicine or law for that matter) is *in itself* a technical and not a humane exercise. If it has humane influences, they are due to the infusion of perceptions and attitudes which might equally well leaven 'further' education.

As we have already noted, Comparative Education is not just a matter of laying two articles of the same name alongside each other and comparing this with that. We could not play this game even with two articles ostensibly performing the same function. To be real, and seen with real insight, such phenomena have to be seen in the totality of the living context – for the reasons given in Chapters 1 and 2.

The essential purpose of the comparative technique is to discover and use properly criteria which will diagnose for us the essence of a particular activity, or the force of a particular environment, or the crux of a particular problem. Each one of these must be diagnosed and studied in and through the living realities amidst which we find it. Comparisons will help us to get rid of any false idea either of uniqueness or of universality. That is to say, we avoid parochialism; but we also avoid the opposite error of believing we have isolated *the* causative factor or the universal panacea. When properly undertaken, comparisons can help us to avoid the entanglements of names and forms, so that we can make an examination of what really happens. Above all, we must determine never to compare incomparable things.

Pitfalls are nowhere more clearly seen than when we attempt to compare 'higher' education internationally. Risks are greatest when we consider the provision made in the United States. The astonishing range of occupations and interests ingeniously catered for by more than 1850 American colleges, mostly turning out graduates with bachelors' degrees or better, pays testimony to American specialization and admiration for the trained man or woman. But this is usually not 'higher' education as the rest of the world knows it, highly desirable though it may be. College-trained careers in the U.S.A. include teaching of all kinds, nursing, journalism, business and salesmanship, accountancy, and automobile engineering, not to mention the more bizarre examples.[1] These career studies are not usually pursued at the advanced level which might find a place in some of the world's universities or colleges of advanced technology, but at a standard considered by most non-Americans appropriate to the intermediate or preparatory *tekhnikumy*, *Berufsfachschulen*, *lycées techniques d'Etat*, technical colleges, or *istituti professionali*.

Reference is made to American institutions not to vilify them (for in their own right and in their remarkable suitability to the American context they are admirable), but to avoid absurd misunderstandings about the rest of the world's provision for higher education. Such misunderstandings seem all the more likely because recent publications of world statistics and several widely read education books fall into this very trap of measuring mankind's actualities in categories imposed by one nation's names. At home, no knowledgeable American is in any doubt about the kaleidoscopic range of interests and quality to be found in what is called 'higher' education in the United States. Hardly any harm is done domestically by the condescending extension of the term to almost any continuous instruction given after the age of eighteen. But irreparable harm could be done at home if Americans not merely claimed the right to go on and on until genuinely higher education is reached (an admirable and enviable possibility in the United States), but actually believed that all 'higher' education in their country was of equal standard and equal national importance. Tremendous harm can also be done abroad by this trade in misnomers. It is not merely that foreigners may be offended. A worse risk is that they may examine some of what passes for 'higher' education, and then consider the whole provision shoddy by contrast with what is available in other countries. In the delicate equilibrium between the communist world and the rest, such unmerited condemnation of American higher education as a whole is extremely dangerous. The best of American higher education is unsurpassed anywhere. It is therefore a pity that much mis-

---

[1] See Hofstadter and Hardy, *The Development and Scope of Higher Education in the U.S.A.*; J. L. Morrill, *The Ongoing State University* (Minnesota, 1960); and Gordon and Howell, *Higher Education for Business* (Columbia, 1959).

understanding is aggravated by ill-informed pseudo-comparisons originating in the United States.

From what has just been said it is obvious that 'higher' or university education in one country may do jobs that a less esteemed 'further' education provision may undertake elsewhere. Indeed the overlap may be considerable within one country – at least in function. Britain serves as a useful example. The British universities and university colleges of equal standing number no more than twenty-four.[1] Many or most of these are small by national as well as international standards. Yet the output of certificate holders from the schools continues to grow. It is obvious therefore that many school-leavers with good qualifications, which a few years ago would have enabled them confidently to apply for university admission, can no longer get in. They are thus headed off to alternative institutions where they can pursue the same or comparable objectives; but in Britain these are classified as 'further' and not 'higher' education, and they lack university status.

Such colleges include technical colleges, colleges of commerce, teachers' colleges ('training colleges'), and colleges of advanced technology. The last two will be considered later, and for the sake of convenience the colleges of commerce can here be reviewed with the technical colleges. There are in all over 340 technical colleges offering full-time study, and 220 more for part-time work. Though they do not have university status in any way, more than 175 of them give instruction in one or more technologies at the level of the Higher National Certificate. This does not count in British terminology as 'graduation'. Many colleges do however actually prepare students for the 'external degrees' of the University of London, making use of a device which

---

[1] The figure of 24 universities and university colleges relates to 1961; it includes the University of Sussex and the University of York. Additional universities have been designated at Norwich, Colchester, Coventry, Canterbury, and Lancaster.

University student numbers in Britain increased slowly from 40,000 in 1925 to 50,000 at the outbreak of war. Following the rapid post-war increase they reached 107,000 in 1960. Before 1970, it is anticipated, the number will be 175,000 or more. Sir James Duff has estimated that this 75 per cent. increase in a decade could be achieved without lowering standards ('University expansion in the United Kingdom' in *Progress*, March 1961). During the opening years of the 1960s, the number of pupils staying on in the last years of the grammar school – the 'sixth form' – has been increasing twice as fast as the university provision.

(It should perhaps be explained that in British usage the term 'university college' generally means a fledgeling (but regular) university under the tutelage of another, and maturing towards full independence. In the U.S.A. the same term regularly indicates a university-extension evening-course department of general education, mainly of a lower standard than on-campus courses.)

ensures a proper university graduation in a university-administered examination, though without giving students a university experience or such things as university library facilities. Formally, these graduates are exactly equivalent to 'internal' graduates of London University. Their examination is either the same as or equivalent to the ordinary examination for a degree.[1] Yet they have been in 'further' and not 'higher' education. Similarly, teachers' college students may prepare for external degrees, though without a proper university experience, and without university prestige.

The teachers' colleges themselves will be discussed in the next chapter, and the growing responsibilities and status of the colleges of advanced technology will be reviewed on page 180. But before going on to consider such easily recognizable institutions we ought to take note of the fact that in Britain many students in careers like architecture, engineering, and parts of the legal profession do not enter upon fulltime theoretical study in the way familiar in some other countries, but are 'articled' or 'apprenticed' at a high level of training and study without ever reaching university status or anything like it. In this instance we are not thinking merely of underlings or technicians, but of people who become really expert and who often claim with confidence that they are on the same level of understanding and professional skill as their colleagues who are college-trained.

It is quite clear that a profession such as the architectural and legal professions can very properly decide that a particular level of attainment is lower or higher than some other. No one can quarrel with that. Therefore there is basically no harm done when certain categories of legal men, architects, teachers, or cooks are stated to be less advanced in their professions than a few chosen colleagues. But in very many countries to this day, the sort of entry one makes into a profession may ultimately determine *for a lifetime* the amount of personal scope that will ever be granted, the opportunities for further learning in that field, and of course one's economic and social status. In the area of further education predestination of this kind is most marked. It is seldom possible to retrieve the situation fully by later study or professional enterprise. To return to the British examples just outlined, a university-trained architect or engineer or legal man still has a great pull over his colleagues trained in offices or firms, though he is frequently said to have less 'know how' in his profession. The distinction is breaking down somewhat in engineering, though even there it is alleged that an engineer

[1] For the newer Diploma in Technology, see page 180.

from a firm or a technical college knows *what* to do and when, whereas the university man does not know what to do in practice though he can give the reasons for the practice afterwards. Like all caricatures, this one has recognizable approximations to the truth.

The main point at issue here is not whether certain grades of person or of qualification are equivalent to others or not, but whether a progressive (not to say an equitable) further education system can afford to rubber-stamp people indelibly at the age of eighteen or sixteen, and then tell them they can never do better for themselves or their country's economy than cultivate the lowly allotment assigned to them at that stage. We have earlier seen that the 'eleven plus' diagnostic examination for secondary school selection has been under criticism in many parts of the world; yet nowadays the pressure on universities and on other forms of professional preparation has caused even more rigorous selection at 'eighteen plus', with less pretension to any supposedly scientific justification.

Stratification may result from mere historical accidents – as in the evolution of parallel forms of training, one or more of which has acquired special prestige. It may be the result of social as well as academic justification – as Oxford and Cambridge show in England, and the Harvard schools of Business and Law in the United States. It may depend upon parental incomes, or at least on the length of time parents can support a son or daughter without earnings. This is a world-wide matter of anxious concern. It may be caused by an unjustifiable lack of university places. In Britain, for example, the twenty-four universities could never accommodate those who leave school with qualifications that until very recently would have been far more than adequate. In France it has been necessary to add a very tough preparatory (and eliminatory) year to fend off about half of those who have passed the already difficult *baccalauréat* that gives them the legal right to enter universities. Shortage is often caused by financial shortage or mismanagement, as when the British government spends only £37 million in a year on universities, as against £47 million for egg subsidies, £52 million for cereal subsidies, and £85 million for fat-stock subsidies.[1]

Even with the best management in the world it seems unlikely that outside a totalitarian country all the needs of the modern Daedalus could be catered for by old-style universities. Though complex unpredictability does not excuse the plain stupidity just described, it does

[1] B. V. Bowden in *The Guardian*, 9 December 1959.

argue most strongly against the retention of unnecessary *social* dis-crimination between the various forms of further education into which the 'eighteen plus' steeplechase lands West European aspirants to the scientific or managerial professions. When all is said and done, the present universities and comparable institutions were not set up or perpetuated with present conditions and needs in view. New needs are being perceived every day on the job. New and complicated skills are developing on the job. New facets of knowledge or fundamental understanding are developing in everyday circumstances to supple-ment the traditional work of the formal, learned institutions. Many countries are already recognizing this, and to that extent breaking down some conventional barriers. Some set up separate technological uni-versities, or devise extra-university research activities. Good examples of adaptability are to be seen in the university-like work of the Depart-ment for Scientific and Industrial Research in Britain or comparable government departments, and in the willingness of the French govern-ment to grant official recognition to the diplomas awarded by non-governmental technical and technological schools – an astonishing con-cession in France.

For the purpose of appraising the coverage of further education, therefore, we should take account of various kinds of unofficial or 'off-beat' further education, and reckon in the quasi-official contribution of such bodies as the learned and professional associations (bankers, engineers, and various craft organizations in Britain) whose examina-tions or courses direct the studies of many thousands destined for high standing in their professions. Many of these would be university graduates or holders of important institutional diplomas if they had lived in other countries, without being any more widely educated or better trained. Thus we may also have to take account of correspond-ence and radio courses or similar supplements in a number of countries. These may be necessitated by the overcrowding of higher education institutes, by the need to work away from a university or similar centre (as in the Soviet Union), or because of geographical difficulties (as in Australia and Micronesia). Though such expedients do not result in students being added up in statistics for international boasting, they certainly extend the scope of further education in most effective ways, and they have the advantage of serving their countries' needs *ad hoc* and topically.

It is indeed one of the most striking features of all further education that it tends to serve specific needs directly and pertinently, without 'beating about the bush'. This is one reason for the universities' disdain, because what the sponsors of further education regard as topicality may seem mere narrowness to the universities. The trouble about this quarrel is the same as we often encounter – both sides are right, in part. In this respect as in so many others, their views and services are complementary. In the rather peculiar circumstances of today, therefore, with universities being asked to do the impossible in expansion and with extra-university institutions attracting more private and public support for utilitarian reasons, there does seem to be an overwhelming case for seeing where more fusion of overlapping functions and interests can take place. The more the universities and schools adapt themselves to today's personal and social aspirations, the less likely is the perpetuation of sectionalism and ignorance. The more likely are both sides to prosper, too.

Such co-operation is not merely a pious hope, or a prayer for peaceful understanding in a tangled and sectionalized country like the United Kingdom. It is manifestly demanded as common sense by a comparative analysis of educational evolution in many countries. Some misgivings about the universities' influence on schools were voiced on page 155. These should now be borne in mind once more when we think of universities' relationships with their own alternatives. Though it is true that not all universities or indeed all countries show the blemishes which are brought under criticism, there is enough of a universal tendency to justify generalities at this stage. Some university administrations have given the impression of trying to cut their universities off from evolution and trueness to context. They have all too often caused themselves to be superseded or by-passed in consequence. If, for example, future technologists are rejected either because there is no room for them or because they are not quite 'respectable', then alternative training opportunities are almost bound to spring up for them. In the United States, some of the institutes of technology have become internationally outstanding centres of higher learning, achieving a status which exceeds that of most American universities. These include the Massachusetts Institute of Technology, and its counterparts in California and elsewhere. Although, as we have seen, British technical colleges are not yet allowed to set themselves up on the university plane, nevertheless some trends are worth a closer look.

The seven 'national colleges' established in Britain for separate, specialized technologies each enjoy considerable independence under their own boards of management. In June 1961 the Minister of

Education gave similar autonomy to the nine Colleges of Advanced Technology (a tenth one has been designated), and made them independent of local education authority support by placing them on a 'direct grant' basis in relation to the Ministry of Education. These colleges are being developed for work exclusively at the university level, including postgraduate teaching and research. They already give a large amount of instruction at this level. So do the large regional technical colleges, already numbering more than 20 and likely to increase both in number and scope. According to a Ministry circular (13 March 1961), they will be fostered for the development of new advanced full-time and 'sandwich' courses in applied science and technology.

Students in all these colleges may actually graduate (p. 175); but many more now prefer to seek the Diploma in Technology (Dip. Tech.) established in 1955 and now the objective of thousands of students (3,800 in the C.A.T.s alone). The Diploma of Technology is awarded only after the conclusion of an advanced course in a technical college, and is declared to be the equivalent of a university honours degree. It should be borne in mind that two out of every three British engineers and about one in six scientists have obtained their professional qualifications in technical colleges for some years past. These new moves seem likely to confirm that tendency, despite the predominant output of scientists from the universities. The C.A.T.s and national colleges are not yet of university status; but they well may achieve this in the near future, especially as the Dip. Tech. is allowed like the existing B.Sc.Tech. to lead on to the Master's and higher degrees. Nearly 100 courses now lead to the Dip. Tech., in such subjects as mathematics, physics, chemistry, biology, and many applied studies. 'Membership of the College of Technologists' is a later, higher award.

The Colleges of Advanced Technology have more recently introduced a Diploma in Management Studies (established by the Minister of Education as a *postgraduate* award in 1960). This clearly means that they intend to continue their own preparatory studies to that level, and undoubtedly also suggests substantial recruitment of university graduates as candidates for it. As the aim of the new Diploma is stated to be the development of particular personal attitudes, and not just the acquisition of techniques, it puts a definitely university-like complexion on some of the colleges' ambitions. London University already has such courses; even Oxford and Cambridge have a 'fellowship in Management Studies' and a 'School in the principles of industrial management'. The provincial universities are naturally keen; but it seems possible that the para-university developments in the C.A.T.s and technical colleges may outstrip them in tax resources and industrial support. Some measure of the traffic to be anticipated in this field may be taken from the noteworthy proportion of American degrees taken in the field of business administration (50,000 per annum – 12 per cent. of all American degrees).

There is a constantly growing and highly specialized demand for work at a postgraduate level, in or after these colleges, by those who already hold degrees, diplomas, or Higher National Certificates. The nation needs full development of such work at this level, too. Under present arrangements it seems unlikely that universities could meet the demand, or that they would be willing to admit all those likely to apply for admission. Everything points to a build-up and upgrading of work in technical colleges. In the most advanced of them, very highly specialized courses already draw senior staff from industry both as students and as instructors. They work alongside regular university staff brought in for this very purpose. A Further Education Staff College was set up in 1961 to help the teachers and administrators of such high-level technical institutions to develop the highest and most experimental aspects of their work.

So much for the attainment of some technical colleges. How about their appeal? As technical college work at the top level is so manifestly vital to the future of a nation, it already attracts encouragement (in cash and otherwise) from industries and public funds – sometimes more readily than universities. This happens under governments of all political complexions. Firms also give scholarships and maintain students. Though working conditions in technical colleges and the like do not often compare fully with those in university departments, none the less there is a tendency for junior university teachers of considerable brilliance to be attracted to the salaries of technical colleges, which (age for age, and work for work) are often higher. Moreover, both with expansion and by reason of readier recognition, promotion prospects are often better. Further, the titles given to the teachers in technical colleges are the same as those teachers in universities (except, in Britain, the term 'professor'). As the financial claims of conventional university departments (which must be made in Britain at several removes through the University Grants Committee) are regrettably regarded by government exchequers and other financial supporters as somewhat donnish, they are neglected or postponed with depressing frequency. So the exodus of university researchers and teachers is a crescendo, especially when we take account of creaming-off by governmental and private research departments.

The example of Britain is not, however, the most striking one. Because some of the older and prestige-carrying universities in the United States would not or could not handle many of the newer demands for instruction, alternative colleges grew up to serve the people and interests turned away. Some of these became incorporated into colleges of useful arts, thriving on the land grants after the Civil War. Others became teachers' colleges and the like. In American conditions of expansionism the majority of them have passed through the stages (or titles) of being 'state colleges', 'state universities', and finally just universities. Many of them are able to attract excellent teachers, first-class students, munificent bequests, gifts of superb apparatus or whole departments, and indeed continuous tax support. Partly but not only because of affluence (also because of a go-ahead outlook) they have drawn into themselves many men and women of genius and integrity who a few decades ago might have disdained them. There is one other stage in this evolutionary process that must still be noted.

A time comes when undergraduates complete the early stages of their university education in the less honoured institutions (e.g. the state colleges in the United States) and then pass on to older, prestige institutions. Though this phenomenon looks at first sight like a dead loss to the former, that is not necessarily so. The connexion with a more venerable shrine of learning has its own publicity value, even if one is only a 'feeder' to it. It means, in turn, that young instructors of brilliance are more willing to serve an apprenticeship 'in the wilds'. This process grows like a snowball. It is obvious that by this time the older, once isolated, universities find themselves paralleled by academic institutions they once despised. They may actually have to include academic activities they once repudiated.

Far from being only a transatlantic phenomenon, this evolutionary process is in full swing, though in slower motion, in Britain too. Already the universities have been 'invaded', and with conspicuous success. The Manchester College of Technology has long been a greatly valued part of the University of Manchester. Between 1953 and 1960 alone its numbers grew from 645 to 1,863; they are still expanding very fast. Sheffield University has full professors of fuel technology, glass technology, and mining – not to speak of the more 'conventional' subjects in engineering. What is more, the whole university grew out of the amalgamation of a group of technical and 'applied' colleges. A similar tale could be told of Leeds, a fine university by any standard, but also boasting professors of textiles, leather technology, and colour chemistry. London University itself, in addition to the Imperial College of Science and Technology, has a college of agriculture, one of pharmacy, and a veterinary college. In addition to the less spectacular innovations now becoming familiar it has chairs in aeronautical engineering, aviation, and dietetics. It has not only conferred the coveted title of 'recognized teacher' (of the university) on particular members of the staff of colleges outside the university (as diverse as a college of estate management, colleges of music, teachers' colleges, and a Jews' college); it actually approves work done in an important technical college and some other centres as work done 'internally' in the University of London. Where does a university end and a college of advanced technology begin? In other words, where is that neat distinction between bread-and-butter 'further' education and liberally evocative 'higher' education?

This is not the chapter for discussing the training of teachers, which will come later. But as some parallels are pertinent, a brief mention may be made. In the United States the education and training of teachers were rejected by the universities at one time, as we have seen. The result has been that many institutions have mushroomed up from two-year 'normal schools', through all the stages just mentioned, to the full title of the university. Similarly, inside other universities the teacher-training departments have burgeoned out to mammoth size and complexity. At the worst, they dole out repetitious and protracted courses in the minutiae of school administration and teaching method; but some teachers' colleges are very good. As a rule, though, American professors who are not in 'Education' with a capital E despise the lot, often with good reason. For our present argument the main point is that these colleges do have professorial chairs, good facilities (if not always good 'faculties') and many students.

A happier *rapprochement* has been found in Britain's Institutes of Education. At the risk of over-simplifying we may say that these are devices by which teacher-training colleges are brought under the aegis of universities for the development of their courses, for examinations, and research. Though a compromise plan, this is clearly one way of breaking down some barriers. A closer historical research shows that the central college of the London University Institute of Education (now a 'central activity' of the University) was once a teachers' college, elevated to its present important position after being handed over to the University by the London County Council. A metamorphosis that could happen to one teachers' college could conceivably happen to others. Goldsmiths' College is already partly in the University as a school preparing for degrees and partly outside it as a teacher-training college. Moreover, other teachers' colleges make no secret of their university-level ambitions, and one of them has appointed a former university professor to be its principal. Evidently, the adjective 'Protean' can apply to universities no less than to other institutions in further education. All the auguries for the future suggest that some other distinctions (not all in Education colleges, but not excluding them) are destined to be impaired if the local education authorities in the United Kingdom have their way. The universities themselves, embarrassed by unmanageable responsibilities and a shortage of funds, are sitting tight on this question.

It would be idle to indulge in prophecy; but it does seem very likely that before the end of this century a large number of new universities will be founded in Britain and other Western countries. To tide over the intermediate phase in which they will be built up, it is probable that a number of 'half-way houses' will be recognized, doing work that is preparatory to, parallel to, or ancillary to the universities. Thus the universities themselves may become more like research centres, in a public relationship not unlike that of the Institutes of Education mentioned above.

In fact, the history of university development in the British Isles and the British Commonwealth is full of precedents which may be valuable for the expansion of universities anywhere, if only because of the exceeding caution with which very substantial development has been achieved. By contrast with the medieval Italian practice of establishing separate university centres in the capital cities of duchies and small principalities, which has left modern Italy with a rich heritage of ancient provincial universities, Britain's great stability under a London-based government left England with only two universities at the beginning of the nineteenth century. By that time the industrial revolution had been in full upsurge for more than fifty years, and the country was already an imperial power. Scotland had its old universities, of which St Andrews (1411) is among the most ancient in the world; but England itself was singularly lacking in facilities for higher education, not being helped particularly by the semi-torpor into which Oxford and Cambridge had fallen.

The first sign of regeneration was the founding of Durham University in 1823 – a rather late date when we consider that the United States had had nine universities established by Englishmen during the colonial period (see page 241). Americans had 'come of age' after the Revolution with the foundation of a number of additional universities and the upgrading of several preparatory colleges now cut off from the mother country. Of course, there had been centres of learning and research in England too, though they had not been brought to university status because of conservatism or indeed obscurantism in the academic hierarchy which had grown up in the older universities. For example, St Thomas's Hospital in London had been founded in the thirteenth century, St Bartholomew's in 1662, and Guy's Hospital in 1724. In the reign of Elizabeth I, the Gresham College in the City of London was established as a foundation (still active) to give public lectures but not courses, in much the same way as the University of Paris and the Collège Royal had initially done in France; yet it never became a University of London. Indeed, no such institution officially existed until 1836, and then only as a sort of corporation empowered to grant degrees to students of 'approved institutions' after examination. Until 1900, therefore, the work of the University of London was mainly confined to the examination of students. Where did they come from? They attended university-level colleges established in London almost willy-nilly, as the result of a clash of incompatible forces.

In 1826 a group of rationalists and other progressives sought to crack open the monopoly of Oxford and Cambridge by founding a 'University of London'. Jeremy Bentham was a prime mover. As a counterblast to that 'godless institution', King's College in London was founded by Royal Charter in 1829 for 'instruction in the various branches of Literature and Science and the doctrines and duties of Christianity'. In 1836 the two irreconcilable institutions claiming university status in London were administratively made capable of peaceful co-existence by saddling both ideologies with one examination system. Bentham's 'university' was re-styled 'University College'. Though not exactly team-mates, the two colleges appeared in double harness on graduation day. It was not until 1900 that the University of London was reconstituted so as actually to incorporate University College and King's College – and also, by that time, a number of other institutions which had grown up in or near London to do university-style work in preparation for the examinations of the University of London.

Some of the colleges thus incorporated with the cautiously granted

Royal Charter have then or subsequently included not merely the ancient and newer medical institutions of the capital but some women's colleges. London University was the first in Britain to grant degrees to women. There were also some remarkably varied newcomers. For example, Birkbeck College was once a Mechanics' Institute and working men's centre; but now it is fully part of the University, though it is still reserved for people fully employed during the day, except in their final year. Queen Mary College was originally founded in 1887 as the People's Palace Technical Schools in a somewhat depressed area of the city. The Royal College of Science was established separately in 1907 to give 'the highest specialized instruction' in 'various branches of Science, especially in its application to Industry'. It looked at one time like being a rival to the University of London; but it is now safely inside it under the title of Imperial College of Science and Technology.

Not to prolong the story, this pattern is somewhat matched by the development of the Victoria University in the North of England. Based upon Owens College, Manchester (1851), and at one time including University College, Liverpool, and Yorkshire College, Leeds, it has now resolved itself into the Universities of Manchester, Liverpool, and Leeds. In more recent years, the Universities of Exeter, Southampton, Nottingham, Hull, and Leicester have reached full dignity with the Royal Charter after having started as minor institutions preparing students for the 'external' degree examinations of London University. As long ago as 1904, Sidney Webb in his *London Education* (p. 67) looked forward to 'an indefinite multiplication of opportunities for undergraduate study' in the whole region near London, under the University of London superstructure. Subsidiary colleges and polytechnics, perhaps under local control, could doubtless act as 'feeders' for the University's higher courses and researches (though there might well be a problem of securing university atmosphere and evocation, as there is in technical colleges).

The same device has been particularly useful since 1945 in the scheme of 'special relationship' whereby overseas territories now maturing towards independence within (or outside) the Commonwealth have examination links with, and advice and assistance from, the University of London. In the course of time the staffing of African, Asian, and other universities with indigenous teachers transforms such colleges into truly national universities meriting international respect. Several African universities have thus become independent since 1960.

For want of space it is impossible to describe similar relationships established by the University of Durham, or to consider the interesting case of the University College of North Staffordshire. From its inception this college has granted its own degrees, under external guarantees. The University of Sussex (1960) is a similar example; but from the beginning it has enjoyed greater independence, and more flexibility has developed in consequence. The same seems true of the University of York (1961). All such experiments repay careful study by those wondering how to expand university systems without diluting the precious essence of scholarship and research. Parallel developments can be found in some North American cases, to suit the transatlantic scene. The University of the State of New York (1784) has been both a public education system and a nucleus of accretion for university-type institutions. There is excellent documentation on the trials and successes of such experiments.[1]

The examples given above once more show that the idea current in Europe that some institutions are universities and others just are not is false. It would be hard to imagine any grade of institution between the top university and the humblest aspirant to university status, and not find some actual example somewhere really evolving towards recognition or partnership. This does not mean that all would-be universities or advanced colleges should at once be promoted to full recognition. On the contrary, the 'free for all' scramble for the university title and university teachers in the United States should be a warning to all outsiders. A similar tendency may soon be a problem in India, as it already is in Japan. It should hearten us to think that kindly tutelage is often available from older universities to their younger sisters, even though it is a bit patronizing at times.

One last mention of a suitable expedient may be made. Without exactly entering into junior partnership, a rising institution can always invite some more established seat of learning to provide 'external' joint-examiners or assessors of the work in hand. This is now done in many parts of the world. The only sober alternatives to this 'guardianship' system (if we exclude the destructive scramble just referred to) are either state regulation of universities and technological colleges (as in modern France and the U.S.S.R.) or the very abolition of universities as such (as temporarily done by Napoleon and Stalin).

The growing governmental interest in higher and further education throughout the world makes it unlikely that public opinion will

[1] e.g. in *Government Policy and Higher Education*, by F. C. Abbott (Cornell University Press), 1958.

tolerate chaos in this sphere – even decorous chaos. One of the most insidious, but most effective, ways of bringing higher institutions under control without exactly seeming to do so is to give separate recognition and financial aid to the constituent faculties. That was, of course, the expedient adopted after the French Revolution and by Stalin for a period in the early 1930s. There are signs that many modern governments are already (by implication) moving in this direction. They include special grants made for specified researches, differential rates of pay or allocations made to particular faculties, and lavish expenditure on non-university further education.

Of course, not all governmental concern is suspect. Though some British university officials criticize the proposal to expand university places to 175,000 by the middle 1960s,[1] they are not supported by all their colleagues. It is certainly not proved that standards must be lowered. The result might simply be that excellent standards of intellect will be cultivated in somewhat different ways than formerly. We do not all, for example, try to prove excellence now by expertise in Latin or Greek verse. 'Standards' have previously been used to exclude the formerly 'banausic' subjects which now earn academic reverence and governmental cash – such as all the 'modern' and international studies and the sciences themselves. According to the ancient shibboleths many of our present academic titans would have been rejected for incompetence in the Classics.

Moreover, as Sir Geoffrey Crowther pointed out in 1960,[2] even the target figure quoted above meant that only about 4 per cent. (probably less) of the population would obtain a bachelor's degree. Commenting on technological and social needs of the coming century, he demanded: 'Can we conceive that it will be adequately run by a generation of whom only one in twenty-five will have reached even a first degree? Is this not, in fact, a formula for national decline?'

Room must be found for more people to prove their worth. It is manifest that much talent is wasted, and equally evident that once the frenzy of exclusion has seized those in privileged positions they invent more and more elaborate ways of showing why their preserves should not be disturbed. It is assumed all too frequently: that existing tests and subjects are everlasting indices of human worth; that sensibility in the ancient arts imparts unique sensitivity to the needs of mankind; that no new relationships between man and man, or between man and the

[1] University Grants Committee Report, 12 October 1960.
[2] On 9 December, in the 1960 Oration at the London School of Economics.

material world, need to be worked out for the future of civilization; that pragmatic or deductive minds are, humanistically speaking, too handicapped for proper university study; that the whole explosion of interest and endeavour implied by our accelerating industrial and social revolution can be coped with from stores of knowledge or aspects of perception that sufficed a generation or two ago. Looked at coldly, any one of the above assumptions must be declared false; yet they are often acted upon in the university circles of the Old World. (From the 'Old World' I exclude the U.S.S.R. and China.)

To be fair, much exclusiveness is forced on universities by reason of space and finance; but when rationing is forced on a country in wartime or famine no one thinks of making a harsh necessity sacred. Universities protest much more justifiably when they point out the perils which may arise when facilities for individual study, laboratory work, or basic inquiry are swamped by newcomers. Undoubtedly there is a grave risk here – but only if new populations and new needs are tackled by ancient methods. Adaptations that people forget about have already been made. In Britain, the U.S.A., and the U.S.S.R. (not to quote other examples) no one believes any longer that freshmen should be thrown into the ferment of university life without guidance or course requirements, as is the case on the continent under the sacred banner of *Lernfreiheit*. In Britain and the U.S.S.R. there is therefore far less student wastage, far less frustration, and far greater efficiency. If adjustments of this sort can be made once, cannot similar adaptations come now?

In 1961 the British University Grants Committee set up an inquiry into university teaching facilities and methods, which are widely stated to be unsatisfactory. Many university lecturers in many countries do not properly teach at all. Their talents could be far better used if they were trained to do so, and if the organization of universities throughout the world were modified to enable this necessary process to become more effective. The growth of knowledge, the world's sense of urgency and purpose, and the increase of competition make a mockery of the pretence of amateur pottering still widely indulged in. In fairness to the great conscientiousness of most university teachers in Britain it should be said that most of them realize this situation well enough; but they can do little about it and sometimes do not care to do so for career reasons. It is heartening that university administrations themselves are concerned to deal more realistically with the stern dilemma of the need to research and the need to teach. The harshness of this critical choice can be alleviated, however, by relatively simple innovations. Bibliographical and abstracting services can expedite inquiry, leading the researcher promptly to the point at which his scholarship comes fully into play. Instructional problems can similarly be coped with (i.e. mechanically, administratively, and by providing more helpful books or other material aids). All students crave for much more purposeful and much less absent-minded teaching. The last-named affliction all too often results from a grudging attempt to combine the lecturer's 'teaching load' with his 'real work' of research.

Amateurishness is proving as costly and incompetent in university life as *laisser-faire* was in economic life. Some necessary jobs are just not being done. The benefits are not being fairly distributed. Much effort is wasted, and much more still is unco-ordinated. Learning does not proceed fast enough or deeply enough in most of the several fields, and those fields are becoming territories foreign to each other. University teachers, devoted and grossly underpaid (except in the communist world), feel increasingly bogged down. Fortunately, this is one area of educational endeavour where much notice can be taken of internationally relevant examples. With more efficient and better aided teaching, the student load could be increased by some 50 to 100 per cent. By 'better aided' I refer not only to the administrative and mechanical aids of the last paragraph but to such intrinsically educative arrangements as the provision of assistantships, teaching fellowships, research fellowships and the like for senior students, on the American model. Teaching in a really good American university is a joy and a challenge unsavoured elsewhere, and mainly for these reasons; but a great part of the exhilaration derives from the double experience of having really adequate teaching at the lower levels combined with stimulating tutorial or seminar relationships at the higher levels.

Nearly all non-American universities assume that when a student graduates he is 'turned out' ready for the world and a career. Not only the increasing complexity of industry but also the development of research in universities themselves has shown this assumption to be outmoded. More than ever before there is a need for continued studies or at least re-interpretation. (This last is almost certainly better done if there is co-ordination or 'double harness' work with university researches.) In the United States, the rich development of graduate schools, where sound teaching is often undertaken as well as very diligent, systematic, and co-ordinated research, has made for conspicuous success at this level. Non-Americans sometimes wonder how it happens that, while an American bachelor's degree seems a modest attainment, the doctor's degree following it two or three years later has so often been based upon really excellent work – at any rate at the better universities. The reasons are simple enough. There is better oversight of M.A. and Ph.D. candidates, with substantial teaching for them (often too much, in fact); the teaching staff have better organized facilities for interviewing and graduate seminar work; and there are all the superb bibliographical, abstracting, and similar services referred to above. (The Russians also excel in these fields.) There are also abundant opportunities for the interchange of university personnel, or at any rate for meetings and conferences.

All these factors greatly affect the efficiency of university teaching; especially if university teachers are trained to teach. These aids manifestly enhance the value and profundity of scholarship too. There is no dichotomy. Indeed, one evident result is the sheer persistence in learning of an unexpectedly large percentage of the population. To use the American expression, they do not 'quit'. More people too would be involved in the total endeavour of universities if there were more opportunities for 'equivalence' to be recognized. That is to say, if there were fairer chances for people from technical colleges, teachers' colleges, and other para-university or peripheral institutions to approach the university-level studies of which they are capable. In the U.S.A. and Canada (which claims higher standards), such facilities exist. They are shown by the actual attainment of their beneficiaries to be abundantly justified. It is all a matter of determining what *is* equivalent; the rest depends upon the aspiring candidate. Success also turns on the attitude of the university teacher or admissions officer. Is he trying to exclude excessive numbers, or eager to develop *all* human potential capable of university pursuits?

It has been well worth spending all this time on universities and the higher reaches of further education, if only because of world-wide expansion and intensifying popular interest. To most students nowadays the notion of 'higher education' or 'the university' is immensely evocative – a symbol of the highest status. For underprivileged nations and classes it is also an 'Open Sesame' to technological prosperity. Those of us who live in ultra-conservative countries should realize that in other nations the university is not just a far-away privilege of a traditional ruling class or a latter-day haven for a small intelligentsia. It is a very real institution to which everyone leaving school at eighteen or nineteen with a certificate is entitled to claim admission. Of course, the *baccalauréat*, *Abitur*, *maturità*, and *Studentereksamen* are difficult; but so is the 'advanced level' of the English General Certificate of Education. Yet those continental examinations confer a legal right to enter the university. Furthermore, university tuition is now free (or available for a tiny, nominal fee) in several countries.

Unfortunately, this highly desirable provision of a free university education, combined with the existing overcrowding of narrowly conceived traditional universities, has caused many countries to limit admission in various ways. It has become so normal for certificate-holders to go to the university that pre-entry barriers have seemed out of the question. Therefore exclusive devices have been invented to take effect after the first year of university studies. These include the *année propédeutique* in France and the *philosophicum* in Denmark. In the Soviet Union there has been a toughening of university and institute admission standards and also a vastly increased turning away of less intellectual children towards industrial or other forms of training. Much attention is given to the provision of technological alternatives to the traditional university, but at the same level or higher. There are more than 200 such institutes in the U.S.S.R., and the number is growing. As we have already noted, the British Colleges of Advanced Technology are more and more tending to regard themselves not as weaker substitutes for the universities but as comparable alternatives.

The *grandes écoles* of France (technological institutes of university status or higher) have been an example ever since the *Ecole Polytechnique* was founded after the Revolution (1789). Holland has two technological universities, one over a century old. Two more are planned. Somewhat similarly, Germany has evolved the *Technische Hochschule* as a separate institution for the applied sciences, not following the Anglo-Saxon pattern of adding a new faculty to an existing university. The eight technological universities of the German Federal Republic have the same status and rights as the eighteen traditional universities. However, the problem of combining teaching with research, and the problem just referred to of ensuring a proper cultivation of talent in some more applied fashion (perhaps just below the traditional university level but not necessarily with loss of professional esteem and status), are among the urgent unsolved problems.

It will not be out of place to say a little about some differences in continental university systems which at once strike the observer from Britain or the United States. In the first place, continental students are very much on their own. There is little or no advisory service, and it is not uncommon for students to be 'lost' for as much as a year. It does not surprise us therefore that students may 'shop around' either in the same university or another before finally graduating. Even if a German follows the same group of interests throughout, he may attend several universities. This is characteristic of American students too.

German, Austrian, and many other students are not required to attend lectures; much less do they have 'tutorials' or written work. They just need to present themselves for examination when they are ready. They are required to complete at least eight semesters (four years) before graduating (e.g. by *Staatsexamen*, entitling them to begin teaching in secondary schools[1]). The whole experience will often take them five, six, or seven years – or longer – before they are ready. Tuition costs little; but the absence of support for residence makes it necessary for many of them to earn a living. Inevitably, this slows up progress. It also means that poorer students tend to go to university in industrial cities where jobs are easier to get, whereas small-town universities like Marburg are said to attract and retain an upper-class clientèle. This last observation does not apply in quite the same way to France, where Paris is the focus of all interests; but the other continental characteristics are found there. After the eliminatory *année propédeutique*, the student must obtain four certificates by examination before obtaining his *licence*, usually in two years.

In passing we may note that whereas the end-of-course degree in France is called a *licence*, in Germany it is either the eight-semester State examination referred to above, or the more exclusively university award of a doctorate in philosophy, Ph.D. Though this is theoretically obtainable after five years, in practice it nearly always takes much longer. In any case it is not awarded until after the printed publication of the thesis – a very expensive business unless some publisher thinks it commercially worthy of adoption. The names of university schools, activities, and awards vary immensely from country to country; so do the periods of time and the intensity of application needed to obtain the various degrees. One of the most deceiving of temptations is an understandable inclination to try to find international 'equivalents'. Before this can be done, a detailed and sympathetic study must be undertaken of one phenomenon in the whole of its own context.

In Denmark, Holland, and elsewhere, any person old enough may

---

[1] For fully qualified teacher status in a *Höhere Schule*, a probationary and supervised apprenticeship of two years (after the *Staatsexamen*) is followed by a second, confirmatory examination.

attend university lectures provided he is registered at the Rector's office; but he can sit for examinations only if he has a recognized school-leaving certificate. This 'open doors' feature brings the university closer into the life of the people. Similarly, when a candidate for a higher degree (e.g. doctorate) is defending his thesis, the townsfolk and relatives can attend. In Denmark, the public may also ask the candidate questions when the official interlocutors have finished.

Communal life is conspicuously lacking in the university systems of most countries. Most students live in lodgings. Occasionally, universities provide hostels or *foyers* ('dormitories' in American English); but these are not often popular on the continent. Furthermore in Holland, for example, the universities tend to have only one or two faculties, which restricts the educative value of students' social contacts with each other. There is a universal growth of official interest in the opportunities for residence and in the general welfare of students; though this growing concern is not often accompanied by suitable facilities. In the U.S.S.R., however, students often have superb accommodation, as at the new Moscow State University. As a rule, in most Soviet universities they pay 15 roubles a month (a little more than ten shillings or $1.50)[1] for their accommodation. In Moscow, the cost is double. Tuition is free. All who are in further or higher education can have cost-of-living scholarships too if they work hard. About 80 per cent. of them so qualify, on an average, though in the best institutes 90 per cent. get stipends. In 1960 the amount of these grants ranged from 300 to 500 roubles a month at the Polytechnic Institute in Leningrad named after Kalinin; but the students were expected to get about 150 roubles a month from home or from savings. For comparison, an unskilled or semi-skilled labourer earned on average 600–650 roubles a month.

Most students will have earned some money in their two years' working experience before entry; and those students who receive 'excellent' marks all round have their stipends increased by 25 per cent. These arrangements are general throughout the Soviet Union. It has already been pointed out that about half the students undertaking courses in higher education are at work in industries or other state enterprises, and have to study extra-murally or through correspondence. Hence, the full-time students are likely to be the best and to have

---

[1] Quotations in roubles and exchange equivalents (here and throughout the book) all relate to the end of 1960. The new rouble is officially worth 10 of the old; but international comparisons of purchasing power (to give the reader a fairer idea of what present changes mean) suggest 4 or 5 new roubles to £1, or 1·5 new roubles to $1.

enhanced stipends. It was officially stated in 1961 that a tendency was growing for the first two of the five university or institute years to be spent in part-time study. Indeed such students usually take six years overall, as their task is aggravated; however, many courses in higher education are directly related to work in the state enterprises, and much of the instruction relevant to the practical side is actually taken *to* the factory or farm for the benefit of extra-mural students. Moreover, promising students are picked out for transfer to full-time instruction; others are allowed to have time off for study with half- or full pay. In any case, all employees have had their working day reduced to six or seven hours, and a five-day week (it is said) will be universal by 1964–5, thus allowing more time for cultural pursuits.

Soviet students who have received stipends during their university life of five years are directed to a particular post for three years afterwards, according to the State Plan. After that they are free to take up any post. In France, students admitted to the coveted preserve of the *grandes écoles* are similarly treated. For example, a prospective teacher going to an *école normale supérieure* is not only taught free but receives payment as a probationary civil servant; part of this is subtracted for his living costs, but he receives a lump sum. In return, he must sign an *engagement décennal* to teach for ten years in France. Higher institutions of learning in France conclude their courses with competitive examinations, success in which binds the state to grant the applicant a position, which he in turn is bound to accept.

Until the end of the Second World War it was generally true that American university students were much worse placed with regard to scholarships than those in many other countries. More recently, an abundance of grants has been provided – so much so that in certain universities and faculties not enough students come forward with qualifications sufficient to claim the scholarships. Those requirements are usually slight, inasmuch as they often specify only being in the top quarter of a school-leaving class. Some state universities charge no fees to the children of their citizens. In other public colleges the fees are small by American standards, and many a student is able to earn enough during his summer vacation to tide him over his year's sojourn at an inexpensive college. Others earn their way by working while they study.

The hitherto exclusive and still expensive prestige universities like Harvard, Yale, and Princeton (where total costs average about $3,000 or £1,000 a year) now go out of their way to recruit able students from all kinds of backgrounds.[1] In many such instances they help students by giving them jobs on campus, as well as by aiding with grants and loans if outright scholarships are not available. It must be remembered, too, when comparing quantities, that the American high school is a non-selective school; that the overwhelming majority of American children complete it; and that almost one-third of all urban Americans go on to college, while about one-fifth finish it.

University numbers cannot really be considered except in relation to the school population and its distribution. In Britain the academic grammar school is highly selective, taking in 20 to 25 per cent. of the eleven-year-olds, and keeping rather more than half of them in school until they are about eighteen. Not all of the latter are university potential by British standards. Thus it was estimated that in the year 1958 the United Kingdom had some 75,000 children in school above the age of seventeen,[2] and of these the great majority were in the last pre-university year; yet in the same year the number of new university graduates was roughly 17,000. It is of interest to note that the United States, with $3\frac{1}{2}$ times the British population, had 1,700,000 pupils in the immediately pre-university year of school in that year. The Soviet Union, with four times the British population, had between 2 and 3 million schooled to the threshold of higher education. The 1958–9 Soviet reforms seem certain to lower that proportion.

On the other hand, questions of public finance directly restrict university expansion in Britain. British universities charge only about one-third of the cost price for tuition, or less, even to that small number of students who pay 'full' fees. Over 80 per cent. of all students get a grant as well. This at present (1961) varies according to parental income; but it seems certain that scholarship awards for middle-income groups will become more favourable than they now are. The grants already received not merely pay tuition fees, but in the majority of cases cover the full cost of residence. Similar arrangements are made for those following advanced courses in technical colleges and the like. The 1960 report already referred to anticipated that by the middle of the same decade there would be about 175,000 university students alone – a remarkable increase on the 1959 figure of 100,200. Yet no

[1] For an excellent all-round survey of expanding opportunities in the U.S.A., see *The Search for Talent*, New York (College Entrance Examination Board), 1960.

[2] The Crowther Report of 1959 ('15 to 18') indicates that 65,000 aged 17 and 18 were in school in England and Wales in that year (p. 6). A table in the *Times Educational Supplement* on 22 July 1960 shows 8·5 per cent. at school above the age of 17 in 1959; that would be 48,600 in England and Wales.

child in Britain is ever held back from education on financial grounds, though the academic hurdles and barriers are no laughing matter. Moreover, British university and college students, being subsidized, are discouraged from taking up paid employment during vacations (it would normally be quite impossible to work and study during term time anyway); though an increasing number do work in vacations. Thus, under these generous grant arrangements, university expansion is much more a public financial liability than it would be in the U.S.A., though of course less so than in the U.S.S.R.

This already unwieldy chapter has done no more than indicate the evolving shape of further and higher education in a variety of national idioms. The many experiments superficially sketched here will give an indication of some of the considerations that affect the after-school prospects of the world's youth. It has been impossible to piece together the last years of school and the first stages of higher or further education, for these must be studied in detail in each national context. Similarly, readers must be content to look back at previous chapters for accounts of the younger student's vocational education, even though it may be called 'further'. It has seemed more appropriate to exclude from this chapter the provision made for fifteen- to eighteen-year-olds, considering it as a culmination of the secondary phase, for that is what it often is in purpose or in the standards attained. In any case it overlaps work done in the secondary schools of other nations, e.g. the vocational high schools of the U.S.A. and those Soviet *tekhnikumy* which admit entrants at fifteen. Further and higher education as properly understood are not a second stage on the way towards an ordinary working maturity but a kind of tertiary education of an advanced, professional kind.

Many aspects of such advanced education (e.g. agricultural and commercial) have been omitted for reasons of space and in order to concentrate on a manageable field in which comparative analysis might have some play. For the same reasons, nothing has been said either here or in the subsequent chapter on teacher recruitment about the very important adjustments that have to be made in the presentation of instruction at this level, with all its special requirements of personal approach, different housing and equipment, and its use of the adult background of occupations, home, and leisure interests. At last many countries are coming to realize the very great need of special training for work with adults; but hardly anywhere is systematic preparation for this work studied and undertaken to anything like a satisfactory degree.

It has also been unfortunately necessary to leave out of this chapter that kind of mature education which is a particular interest of my own, and of mounting importance in an increasingly automated world, namely 'adult education'. This phrase is usually understood to indicate non-vocational instruction, or group study, or certain other kinds of systematically pursued cultural activities. Vocational interests may indeed be blended with an interest in the subject cultivated; but it is this interest in the subject-matter for its own sake or for its humanizing value that is emphasized when 'adult' is distinguished from 'further' education. This distinction may sometimes be spurious and unnecessary, and lead to other misunderstandings; but it is convenient enough administratively as long as we are not led to suppose that vocational interests should not or cannot be made liberalizing too. The adjective 'liberal' really refers to an attitude, and not to mere content.

Attendance at adult education opportunities is usually voluntary and non-professional. In its most highly developed instances, as we see them in the United Kingdom and Scandinavia, the U.S.A. and Canada, the Low Countries and Germany, adult education displays a multiplicity of adaptations. Its topicality and direct social purposiveness are specially marked. To that extent it is seldom completely 'general' or perennial, though some forms have persisted in full vigour for more than a century. Adult education usually springs from voluntary initiative; but many countries generously support it out of public funds. Sometimes particular bodies like the University Extension movement and the Workers' Educational Association receive specific recognition as providers, with much government financial support; but sponsoring organizations are exceedingly numerous and varied, both in intensity and status.

In Britain, the 1944 Act requires the local education authorities to ensure a complete coverage of all needs and interests in the field of adult education; but it expects them to support voluntary agencies which supplement the ever-growing work of the local authorities themselves in this field. In Scandinavia too the education authorities both centrally and locally co-operate generously and harmoniously with voluntary organizations. The folk high schools, religious and civic organizations, and the Workers' Educational Association work closely with public evening institutes to give a remarkable service to adults. In North America, cities and universities and in some matters the Federal government give tax-aided support to adult education. In the Soviet Union adult education is both very vigorous and greatly appreciated, in most encouraging circumstances. The concern of public authorities is not only humanitarian; it is connected with the growing 'problem of leisure' and the problems of rapid social change. Hence public interest is also utilitarian.

For want of space here, readers are referred for a fuller description and detailed analysis to *Adult Education – a comparative study* by R. Peers, London (Routledge & Kegan Paul), 1958.

BOOKS

See the general bibliography on Comparative Education, p. 369.
See also the *Year Book of Education* for 1959, London (Evans Bros) and New York (World Book Company).

CHAPTER 9

Teachers and their recruitment

What *is* a teacher?

Like most simple questions, this one has no simple answer. It is all the more difficult to answer because everyone knows what a teacher is, and everyone knows differently. What is more, everyone expects different things of 'the teacher' in differing contexts – from nursery school to university, from metropolis to missionary countries. The word 'teacher' is one of the most chameleon-like of words, changing not only its colour but its dimensions with every change of speaker or context.

We have already given thought to the demands made on teachers in needy communities (Chapter 4), and considered how these might change under the impact of social evolution. We asked ourselves about the fundamental problem of securing any teachers at all in such communities, and the secondary problem of making sure that they went where they were most needed. In this chapter let us forget such thoughts for the time being. So that we can think in more generally valid terms about teachers and their preparation, let us see if we can dream up a suitably composite figure first. Is that possible? How can we include in one amalgam the elfin American Miss straight out of teachers' college, our white-robed sister in Africa, and the tweedy type? What about the kindly mother-figure? And the real blue-stocking? As for men, we have all the masculine counterparts to the above, and a few extra characters. Can we include in our composite picture of men teachers the hearty games man, the perennial sixth-former, the dominie, the Perrins, the Traills, and Mr Chips? If we glance abroad, can we also envisage Signor Professore and Herr Doktor Oberstudienrat?

Our characterization is endless. We are thinking not of 'the teacher' but of mankind. Teachers are people, only more so. Their human qualities and quirks are high-lighted because they are, by profession, examples. They exemplify, and they are popularly exemplified. In the most crowded school, they are often isolated in their work. However, they are studied day in day out by generations of resilient children, of whom about one in thirty will one day be teachers too. Nearly all the children will become parents. They will pass on to their own children exaggerated anecdotes and some truths about teaching and teachers. For all these reasons 'the teacher' is both an example to his society and an artifact of it.

To the latter extent the teacher is typical; but in the sense that every teacher's work should be a personal response to other people's needs, that personal responsibility may accentuate distinctiveness and challenge. Distinctiveness is what other people (especially children) may call 'oddness'. If anyone is afraid of the stigma of eccentricity, he should never take up teaching.

On the other hand, if teachers are too peculiar the children (and their parents) will write them off as simply abnormal and irrelevant. Their message will misfire and their personalities will not communicate. The genius has no permanent place in the classroom, unless he is also a genius at public relations. (In that case, he may soon be out of it.) The teacher must be distinctive enough to be a challenge; big enough in personality and knowledge to command respect; and at the same time close enough to evoke partnership. Yet to be a complete success as a teacher he must not be too much of any one of these things, any more than he must be too little.

These truisms are important enough anyway; but for us now they are useful in cutting down our problem to manageable size. What sort of a teacher do we want? The potential teacher who is too much of any of the things described above may still have a vital contribution to make to education; but it will be outside the classroom in all probability. He may become an adviser to teachers, provided that he has enough experience of the actualities of the classroom to talk horse sense. He may work with adults, or as a stimulator of students mature and well-grounded enough to meet him on his own ground. Without that meeting of personalities and insights there is little effective teaching. 'Talking down' and talking over people's heads are equally examples of failure. There must be what Americans call 'immediacy' – the absence of any intervening vacuum or obstruction which might mar sympathy and acceptance.

Can we therefore talk about teachers and their recruitment in general? Obviously teaching varies with every person, both as teacher and as taught. It must equally vary with every group, every age, every level of instruction. Our own wish to study 'teaching', and perhaps our wish to establish a unified profession, may obscure these axioms; but they are still essential factors in the selection and preparation of future teachers. We must think of them all separately. We must also be prepared to see reason in other people's ideas about what a teacher should be.

With these rough and ready conclusions let us ask ourselves what else can be said about teachers and teaching in general. One of the most striking points of interest is the fact that in the later middle ages it was often supposed that no one would teach willingly. Pious people often took charge of a class or school with much the same self-sacrifice as others would take up a slum parish or run a lazaret. At any rate, that is the impression given by their writings. Nor was this charitable disdain felt only for contact with the underprivileged and malodorous poor, for these seldom had any formal schooling. Distaste was also expressed for teaching any young clerks. No doubt the ineffable tedium and recurring frustrations of the teacher's task in those harsher days made it a dreary substitute for contemplation in the monastery, scholarship in the library, or other priestly engagements. Indeed, references to this unwelcome purgatory with indifferent apprentices to learning survived the Renaissance, despite the occasional enthusiasms of educators such as that admirable clerk of whom Chaucer said: 'And gladly wolde he lern, and gladly teche'.

Why then did people teach – not just eager scholars and pious ecclesiastics, but people as unlikely as Rabelais and Madame de Maintenon? Both of these made a substantial and practical contribution to educational advance. They are only more extreme examples of paradox in the recruitment of good teachers. It could not have been for money that they taught. Teachers in all ages and everywhere have nearly always been underpaid. Nor could it have been for other prospects in this life, for similar reasons. Obviously there must have been some hidden ulterior motive or some concealed intrinsic satisfaction that induced teachers to go on doing what everyone (except the children, perhaps) wanted them to do, but which people would never reward them properly for doing.

The consumer demand for formal instruction has expanded since the middle ages from class to class until it has embraced whole populations. Now it is a world-wide phenomenon. Everyone wants teachers, and everyone expects more than ever from them. Yet the ordinary laws of economics seem to have gone quite astray, unless we are overlooking something. On the one hand we have this enormous demand; on the other we have a relatively small supply of well-trained people, many of whom express financial and social dissatisfaction – not to speak of downright boredom with teaching in some notorious instances. We should not credit all these grumbles too naïvely. The vocally reluctant teachers of Renaissance times might also have been chafing under monastic discipline. In more modern times we could hardly have expected teachers such as H. G. Wells, D. H. Lawrence, or some glamorous film stars to remain contented in the classroom.

Unless the generally accepted principles of economics are utterly without validity, we are driven to accept one or more of the following conclusions:

(a) many people are content to teach without prime regard to financial or similar rewards, mainly because they like it;

(b) there was and is no real shortage of people with at least minimum qualifications for school work;

(c) there are or were no competing occupations suitable for potential teachers, and likely to cream them off;

(d) most people engaged in teaching are just right for the job as they see it, and not for anything else;

(e) most of their contemporaries think they have found their proper social and economic level;

(f) most parents and politicians do not want a better or different schooling for most of the population than is at present available.

Unwelcome though all these conclusions may be, each of them has more than a shred of truth in it. Let us examine them one by one.

The teaching profession has throughout the ages been closely associated with religions. Teaching has often been undertaken as a near-religious mission. This very truth can all too frequently confuse our thinking about it. In the first place not all religions have been active in teaching – on the contrary. Some have kept their learning as secret as possible. Others, like Islam, have been characterized by high peaks of learning (of a highly specialized kind, as a rule) in a few places, while being marked elsewhere by an almost complete absence of concern either for education generally or even for the popularization of the special kind of learning most prized within that faith. Secondly, we need to look more discerningly at the kind of commitment to education which is exemplified in religious dedication to teaching. We can see this more clearly if we get away for a moment from the ordinary religious practitioners of education to observe the really great teachers.

Among the greatest teachers of all time we must undoubtedly reckon the Buddha, Socrates, and Christ. Obviously, ambition and money and other non-teaching alternatives meant nothing to them; but neither did education itself as the world now understands it. These were great teachers in the very special sense that they strove to communicate to people ready for them a distinctive world view and attitude. They spoke to adults, and their message came home only to those who were converted or ripe for conversion. These teachers were not at all concerned with knowledge in the ordinary sense of the word, much less with the processes of acquiring and imparting it. They did not directly relate their humane recommendations to any social policy, at any rate explicitly. They were even further from moulding a scholastic system to give shape to the implications of their message.

Constant references to knowledge and wisdom in the Scriptures should not blind us to the reiterated Christian requirement that all unregenerate knowledge should be emptied out, so that the soul may be flooded with 'the love of Christ, which passeth knowledge'. For St Paul it was the Greeks who sought after wisdom, and that vainly; for him, the ultimate truth was unapproachable in terms of men's words and human wisdom. An increase of knowledge or of intellectual dexterity might well be a snare. Though Christian and other saints throughout the ages have established seminaries and seats of learning, these have always been primarily places in which to prepare for the ultimate repudiation of vain earthly criteria.

No criticism of these great teachers is of course implied. The essential point is that their attention was concentrated *away from* the mechanics, the material, and even the wider content or context of education as we now think of it. They were teachers several removes away from any teacher we are likely to encounter. Therefore the example of these masters of mankind cannot strictly be related to questions of dedication in our classroom practitioner. An attempt to do so may lead to irrelevancies and harm. Let us see if the dedication we preach is really in keeping with the examples we quote.

A good example of the strictly dedicated approach to children's education is found in the practices of the Jesuit colleges. Their story may be most conveniently followed in the French context where we met them before. At the time of the Renaissance, French universities were decadent in many respects. They did not adequately serve ecclesiastical or secular needs. The Jesuit colleges developed rapidly throughout the seventeenth and eighteenth centuries, with such enterprise and excellence that they all but superseded the universities. Their example was matched by the growth of other academies, some of them Protestant; but Jesuit colleges were pre-eminently the training-ground for future priests and those educated Catholic laymen who would become knights of St Ignatius in the continuing counter-Reformation. Popularly speaking, they set out to recapture an increasingly indifferent or hostile world for Roman Catholicism by developing a 'fifth column' versed in all the enemy's techniques. It will repay us to see how this was done.

In Jesuit schools the 'new learning' was possessed – to defeat it. The young men were exercised in the languages and lore of the ancient world in such a way as to expose its ultimate fallacies, and to divert attention from its contemporary subversiveness. The thrust and parry of critical debate were pushed to the very edge of unbelief (like a skirmish in the dusk) – so that the bland peace of belief might be more gratefully welcomed. Thorough and technically excellent though Jesuit colleges have almost everywhere been, they have been specially marked by a peripheral hemming-in of inquiry, and by an ultimate repudiation of the last stage of the logic pursued – that is, the pursuit of inquiry beyond the safety of certainty as imposed by the Faith. If these bounds were set primordially, then all that 'education' was at best a pre-judged discipline for predetermined ends. At worst it was a perilous flirtation with the devil, the world, and the flesh – perhaps a necessary inoculation against the frailties of the human condition in a seductive, non-Catholic world.

Jesuit schools succeeded so well in France and other Latin countries not only because they were so vigorous, or because their standards were high (which was true), but because they cost so little. The universities already referred to were not only lackadaisical; they priced themselves out of reach. The Jesuits, vowed to poverty, offered all the prestige-giving and job-winning education the rising *bourgeoisie* wanted – on a sliding scale according to income, and always inexpensively. So city after city turned over its secondary and higher education to the Jesuits, or to similar religious orders with comparable aims and practices. The burgesses of those days, we may be sure, cared little more about the underlying educational aims than does the French middle class today. They wanted, and got, the particular kind of schooling they knew would advance their sons' careers. They seldom cared much about girls.

Now this story has been told not to belittle the Jesuits but to bring to a head some of the issues involved – particularly in relation to two important principles: (a) the matter of the dedicated teacher working for little money, and (b) the question of what kind of education will be demanded by any parent who does not belong to an authoritarian creed. These two principles directly affect our conception of the role and status of teachers. Jesuit aims and methods, paradoxical though they may seem to many, are logically defensible if you make the important supposition that nothing that really matters can be communicated to the pupils by the teacher *as a partner in self-discovery and self-expression.* ✗

not only Jesuits ✗

So teachers reflect, like a mirror, the unquestionable and intractable image of the God served. In this process the pupils' and the teachers' personalities should be passive. They are not engaged in anything more than complete self-effacement. The answers and the end are prepared in advance for the submission of the will. The exercises of the scholastic process are not of themselves important, except as leading to this climax. Nor are the personalities and perceptions of the pupils, except in accepting and reflecting the *externally* communicated verities of the Faith to the greater glory of God.

Worldly preparation, except in so far as it is intended to cater for the merely material needs of life, is essentially a preparation *against* the world; for by the criteria of eternity the world is one of 'the chief enemies of the soul', as the catechism says. It is obvious that we are here at a parting of the ways. No Protestant or agnostic educator can logically accept this view of the teacher's role or of the function of learning, though communists can. (We shall deal with the important question of 'ideology' in our next chapter.)

Protestants, agnostics, believers in non-Christian faiths, and most non-communist secularists will take the view that for human knowledge of things earthly and spiritual to grow it is necessary to cultivate to the full all aspects of the personality – including individual perceptions and judgement. To take one particular aspect, how can there be a Protestant ethic that is not based upon 'freedom of conscience'? And how can that arise except as a product of *inner* light (i.e. something implanted or immanent or at any rate uniquely personal)? How can this inner light shine aright if it is not fed with the fuel of useful information?

The characteristic Protestant answer to these questions has been to insist on literacy enough to enable the faithful to read the Scriptures in the vernacular, and also to cherish a firm regard for that 'useful knowledge' which would result in the living-out of Christian implications in a successful worldly expression. As a matter of political history it has also encouraged local community interpretations, either through the congregational 'communion of saints' or through democratic self-determination. In all these things the view is taken that each individual's world view (though not infallible) counts essentially towards the fullness of valid understanding. Each contributory item of knowledge and any exercise of personal 'understanding' must ultimately add up to a richer contemplation of God by the believer or of the human condition by those who are not so sure.

In other words, the educative process is an intrinsic part of any approach to goodness and wisdom. So is the encouragement of self-reliance. Far different demands are made upon the teacher for that kind of educational perspective. At this point of our survey we have reached a stage at which dedication and orthodoxy are not enough. Nor is knowledge or skill adequate if it strictly subserves a predetermined doctrine. Not only does it become imperative that every child shall have every faculty and viewpoint developed in terms of his worldly involvement; it is also necessary that the teacher as such shall achieve this through *personal* rather than sacramental or doctrinal support. Knowledge of the Creator and of virtues is communicated more through humane example and human expression.

A teacher of this sort must necessarily live in the very pulse of human affairs. He cannot be a withdrawn ascetic. Nor can he simply be 'an authority'. His knowledge and his dialectic must be adequate to communicate in the spirit of partnership, and also to withstand the exercise of criticism. There is thus a difference in pedagogical principle between the dedication of a teacher describable in these terms and the equal dedication of the Jesuits or any other religious order.

It is neither desirable nor possible that this new-style teacher should be markedly withdrawn from ordinary living. He cannot therefore devote his life to the austerities of scholarship in poverty – as many lay and clerical teachers formerly had to do. The dedication of early Christian teachers and the nearer example of the religious orders has long made the beneficiaries of education ask for sacrifices they were not entitled to, and could not logically have asked for in conjunction with the kind of instruction they wanted. Topical and progressive schooling cannot be expected on those terms.

We might as well note that in Roman Catholic countries not only teaching but much of the nursing is done by nuns. Indeed, in King's College Hospital in Protestant London the nursing was still in the hands of an Anglican sisterhood in Lister's time (in 1877) – very greatly to his inconvenience in developing antiseptic hospital techniques. Should we therefore now expect lay nurses and other hospital workers to work for next to nothing, or in terms of an other-worldly outlook more appropriate to days when the hospital was the very threshold of death for half the inmates? The modern hospital looks to life and positive health, with the co-operation of the patients in the context of their daily lives. The outlook of the nursing profession has changed its orientation, though not necessarily with any loss of devoted care.

These comments on the nursing profession apply even more emphatically to teaching, for teachers bear a greater and more direct personal responsibility in their world than nurses do in theirs. The basic question is whether we regard the teacher's task as one of helping to build a new world of goodness and meaning from within his pupils, with the help of material and perceptions drawn from others – or whether we think of him as a purveyor of external 'truths' which cannot be properly perceived (let alone decided) here below. In the former case we must certainly have good, independently judging, and well-informed teachers. Even in the latter case, unless we think of rational and personal processes as inherently misleading, we also need skilful and well-educated teachers to do the work of intellectual midwifery exemplified by Socrates in Plato's *Meno*. In that dialogue geometrical propositions are elicited from the unschooled slave by skilful questioning. Here is no rejection of earthly involvement, but the ostensible use of it for more abstract purposes. In seeking to secure the acceptance of revelation itself, wise teachers would use psychologically sound methods of co-operation. For all these reasons, though teachers are more than usually prepared to work for low pay and at a low valuation in other respects, it is one of the most foolish of false economies to allow them to do so.

It has been well worth while to anticipate at such disproportionate length some of the consideration of ideology which will be the work of the next chapter, for this is integral to any decision on the selection and training of teachers. But let us now look back to our second conclusion about the character and supply of potential teachers [(*b*) on p. 203]. Is there really no shortage of people with satisfactory qualifications for school work? Obviously, the more metaphysical our view of education, the less important it may be to look for good academic qualifications and strength of personality; for the external, inflowing perfections will come in well enough if only obstructions can be removed. This kind of attitude to schooling is not confined to religious people; it is found also in many pure rationalists, except that they are much more likely to insist upon two supposedly metaphysical qualifications. These are: 'mental discipline' achieved through intellectual exercises of any kind, but preferably in language and mathematics; and a thorough acquaintance with the fine, 'pure' abstractions of culture, preferably through literature and philosophy but also including 'non-decadent' art.

Now, it is a matter of historical record that the ancient grammar schools and universities of Christendom set out to give precisely or predominantly this kind of preparation for thinking and teaching. Therefore, presumably, anyone who had experienced a secondary or higher education was (as the French would say) *perfectionné*, or refined enough, to lead beginners at least part of the way along the same path. The canon of good learning was forever preserved in the corpus of approved literature; and the well-tried disciplines (being inseparable from equally abiding cultural values) were not likely to be improved upon. Therefore the best products of the best schools were all ready to hand as future teachers. They knew the unquestioned subjects as religious teachers knew the unquestionable items of their doctrine. Unquestionably, then, they could teach.

Though the verbs in these last few sentences have been written in the past tense, it is a contemporary fact that such outmoded logic is used to justify the employment of many secondary-school certificate holders as teachers in the minor private schools of England, and in the publicly provided elementary schools of France and other continental countries.[1] Indeed, on the continent the secondary schools turn out great numbers of certificate holders who are fit for little more than a regurgitation of the subjects they have so long been stuffed with. The market is so glutted that they are only too pleased to secure congenial repetition of their academic exercises in the schools – sometimes while pursuing their studies further at the universities.

After the university the problem is there again, perhaps in a more acute form. The university graduate is less likely than ever to turn his hand to unfamiliar enterprises in commerce or industry which openly or implicitly question the value of all that he has hitherto been good at. As we have already noticed, the overproduction of graduates unfit

---

[1] In 1961 it was still possible for the possessor of the *baccalauréat* to teach in a primary school or *cours complémentaire*, and to become qualified (*titularisé*) after five years' teaching experience, leavened with summer courses in 'pedagogy'. A somewhat similar arrangement prevails in some Canadian provinces.

for non-academic occupations is a real problem in many countries. Therefore, as the schools become increasingly competitive in the growing demand for university admission, they naturally seek the brilliant graduate – not *qua* teacher but *qua* pedant (for they do not see the distinction). Again, the graduate is glad to teach for a livelihood while pursuing some higher study at the university, or awaiting a university appointment. By these criteria there is no shortage of teaching potential.

In Britain too the 'better' schools (in the social sense) have predominantly disdained *trained* graduate teachers. No doubt because of the prevalence of this practice, it is possible under British law for an untrained university graduate to be recognized as a fully qualified teacher in the publicly provided schools. Ill-devised official salary scales and other financial disincentives induce many British graduates to go straight into teaching without further professional training. Although for some years the proportion of trained graduates grew, in some recent years more than half of all the new graduate teachers have lacked professional training. However, in 1961 the Minister of Education declared that all graduates teaching in all types of school must soon be professionally trained. No date was fixed, but it is anticipated that this requirement may be implemented between 1965 and 1968.

The situation is complicated by the vagaries of the market for academically qualified people [see (c) on p. 203]. The total of the graduates produced in Britain has increased by leaps and bounds since the war; but it is becoming increasingly difficult for academic secondary schools to get the good graduates they require – or, in some cases, any tolerable graduates in mathematics and science. The demands of industry, of scientific research programmes, of technical administration, and of the greatly expanded higher education provision all make inroads on the supply available to the schools.[1] Of course, all countries feel this shortage, though some do much more about remedying it.

It is not only scientists or those whose talents have been developed in an obviously applied form who are now drawn into non-academic occupations. For public employment and all kinds of business promising young graduates are recruited in very large numbers from the once neglected Arts field. At an earlier stage in a boy or girl's career, indeed,

[1] Some figures for Great Britain illustrate these trends. Of the total of 570,000 university graduates (or equivalent) in Britain, well over one-third are post-war graduates; only 7 per cent. are between the ages of 55 and 64. 17,000 new graduates are now produced yearly, and the number is increasing rapidly. By the end of the 1960s the 1960 total will have increased by more than 40 per cent. But so far from necessarily implying an increase

there is already some diversion from university courses in the Arts and traditional fields because of anticipated career requirements. All this means a diminution of the supply of suitable candidates for teaching, though the total number of graduates has greatly increased. Instead of thinking of teaching as a very desirable occupation, too, many new-comers now think of it as a second-best alternative or as a stop-gap. The supply of good graduates is still, however, fairly well maintained in those fields that are least saleable in non-teaching occupations.

Yet *any* good qualifications are now saleable. Thus we find, as we expect, that in highly technological countries such as Britain and the U.S.A. there is very little automatic drifting into teaching – except perhaps among young women who see teaching as a convenient career to combine with raising a family, or among the least ambitious or least qualified young men. Teaching is still often chosen deliberately; but people must now choose it with their eyes open. That is to say, people still take up the teacher's career (particularly in primary schools) because they think it worth doing or because they like it. Unfortun-ately in most countries the salary and promotion prospects are such that for the higher flights of teaching a positive deterrent is in opera-tion – the demand for personal self-dedication at the cost of a wife and family's living standards.

The more mobile society becomes, and the better the opportunities available to young children on their way up the scholastic ladder, the less likely is it that they will choose narrowly academic prospects or leave themselves 'trapped' with only teaching and like occupations as a future. So we have already noticed; but some recent and representa-tive figures are of interest. In the relatively prosperous districts of

of teaching potential, the great majority of these graduates are turning away from teaching towards industrial and commercial careers which are increasingly a graduate field.

The career choices of new graduates are listed below. It does not follow that they will all obtain their wishes; but the stated preferences are significant. They are as follows:

Business and administration	32%
Scientific research	15%
Engineering	10%
University teaching	8%
Secondary school teaching	8%
Medicine	7%
Law	6%
Church	4%
Other occupations	10%

(Figures quoted from a feature article by Dr Mark Abrams in *The Observer*, 4 September 1960.)

Surrey and Bournemouth only 25·4 per thousand and 20·1 per thousand of seventeen- to nineteen-year-olds enter training colleges (mainly for primary school work). From industrial Lancashire the proportion is 34·1 per thousand. From education-conscious rural Wales the proportion reaches 67 per thousand, the average for Wales as a whole being 47·1 per thousand.[1] At the higher level of graduate teaching, these trends are reinforced. The more socially and economically favourable the start given to children, therefore, the more likely it is that the people engaged in teaching will be those who are just right for the job as it now is, rather than for better-rewarded professions.

Of course, as teachers live long and are in any case working for about forty years, they usually find themselves before the end of their careers in an occupation that has been overtaken by rapid social and economic change to such an extent that it has depreciated like an unfashionable house. The older generation of teachers, which started out with brighter prospects, is often severely handicapped in its claims to recognition by the lower quality of many of the newest entrants. Here reference is made not so much to academic qualifications, though these are sometimes significantly lower, as to other personal qualities such as alertness, enterprise, and adaptability to any chosen career. Therefore, though conclusions (d) and (e) on page 203 are perhaps applied fairly to many young teachers, they are unnecessarily harsh judgements on many older ones.

In this lowering of esteem for the teaching profession as a whole we see some of the reason for the world's teacher shortage. But, quite apart from the known shortage of scientists and mathematicians, the problem of supply is never simple. As schools are now arranged, just any teacher will not often suffice as easily as in former times. The demand for specialized subject teaching over a very wide range of 'new' subjects accentuates the overall drop in the recruitment of good people. The increased provision of further education – not least in universities and teachers' colleges – is a further drain on school staffs. It is certain, other things being equal, that the best qualified teachers will be drawn away.

The clearest example of this is in the United States. There are now more than 1,850 colleges and universities for young people over eighteen, most of them with large enrolments. The teaching staffs of high schools, who are not well paid by American standards, have been creamed off into 'higher' education to such an extent that American

[1] *Times Educational Supplement,* 22 August 1960.

schools suffer perhaps the worst teacher shortage in the highly developed countries of the Western world. Moreover, especially in relation to the average level of American education (which is high), American schools have perhaps the lowest average quality of rank-and-file teachers among the more civilized nations – as far as learning goes. Britain has nothing like the same problem yet; but there is a crescendo of departure from the publicly maintained primary and secondary schools not only into further and higher education but also into the very important sector of the private schools. Among these, the most influential are the Public Schools. Migration is not always a matter of pay, either. Young teachers securing appointments in schools with prestige have a much better chance of promotion later in any type of school.

There can be no lasting solution to the growing shortage of teachers, especially of good ones, until there is a national policy for the recruitment, preparation, and engagement of teachers. (This does not mean they should all be civil servants.) The present embarrassment cannot be blamed on any one factor, like the creaming-off just mentioned, or the peculiarities of the English system whereby the non-denominational training colleges are usually the property of local education authorities which may not after all be lucky enough to secure the services of the trainees. World-wide trends in the distribution of occupations are as much to blame as anything else. No 'cure' will be real which does not take these trends fully into account. A wide range of commercial and public services now compete with teaching. The following figures show the gradual diminution of agricultural and manually employed categories in many countries, and the increasing proportion engaged in personal 'services' (including those in commerce, management, transport, and the professions). The figures are percentages of the working population, and relate to 1958.[1]

	Agriculture	Industry	'Services'
Italy	35	33	32
France	30	35	35
West Germany	22	43	35
Benelux countries	10	43	47
United Kingdom	5	50	45
United States	12	35	53

Within agriculture and industry also the number of jobs open to potential and actual teachers, and increasingly likely to attract them,

[1] *Progress*, Spring, 1958.

grows yearly. The whole position in teacher recruitment is hard to envisage 'at one go', because there is so much continuing change. This usually aggravates the demand. Children are staying at school longer; then they are more than ever trained (by teachers) in their first jobs; and residential and advisory services in education also call on teacher potential.

Yet the problems of urbanized countries are as nothing compared with territories like Algeria, where something like a quarter of the population is (by our standards) of school age, or Singapore, where there are 42 births per thousand per annum as against only 7 deaths. In India, nearly 40 per cent. are under fourteen years of age. In Mexico, half the population is under twenty. In such cases it is at least temporarily necessary to distribute the supply of the best teachers and other educational services in such a way that at least the rudiments are fairly spread. Provision may have to be made for supplementary opportunities as and when they can be made use of. This may also become necessary in a different way in some teacher-starved countries like the United States; but we shall return to the question of supplements and ancillaries on pages 216 and 217.

In the survey just made of occupational change in relation to teaching there is an implication that the teaching profession must look forward to decreasing popularity and a general worsening of quality in its new recruits. That seems bound to happen unless prospects and esteem are greatly enhanced. The sort of bright young man or woman who in France or Italy would have become a secondary school teacher now tends in Britain and the U.S.A. to dash off and join the managerial and scientific 'power élite'. It is undoubtedly true that many grammar school heads in Britain implicitly assess the teaching profession very low by channelling into it the duller boys and girls among the sixth-formers. Of course, they are here thinking of admission to the teacher-training colleges which do not rank with the universities. Some of the brighter pupils destined for the universities will also come back into teaching (about 8–10 per cent. of them). That is not enough, however, to maintain the supply needed. Moreover, if grammar school teachers and most university teachers are asked for frank advice, they are compelled in any objective appraisal to point out the snags and frustrations in their own profession, as well as its sometimes obscure rewards. Such advisers are seldom alarmed if their brightest pupils stay well away from teaching as a career. Instead, they shake their heads over a system which rates the public provision of education so low.

Hence Britain's teacher shortage is about 90,000[1] (1961 figure) if classes are to be reduced to a statutory size; and the wastage is about 2,000 a year. (The total school teaching strength is about 271,000 in England and Wales.) On the other hand, there are about 50,000 qualified women teachers who gave up their careers for family reasons and have not returned to the schools.

Thus we return to the last of the conclusions about the teaching profession listed on page 203 – that most parents and politicians do not *effectively* demand a better or different education for most of the population than it now receives. This is strange, for industrialists are convinced that before 1980 there must be a rapid shift towards a more highly skilled labour force; but the nation's leaders have not translated this conviction into terms of popular education. If they did, they would earnestly consider how things might be better organized in the teaching profession – not only in terms of money, but in the matter of securing the best possible disposition of the teaching talents that are available.

Though there is some progressive thinking and much muddle-headed humanitarianism, there is also astonishing blindness in high places to the actual inequities of the teacher supply system. In Britain in 1961 the majority of legislators (including 40 per cent. of the Labour M.P.s) and most senior civil servants and the like are university graduates; that also means that they were previously grammar school pupils, if not Public School pupils. The great majority of them take very good care to send their children to 'prestige and prospect' schools, most of them either outside or only partly associated with the public provision of education. It is still to these schools that promising teachers are drawn off, and from these schools that the future influences upon public opinion will come.

In the United States, though it still operates to a much smaller degree, a similar kind of trend is growing markedly among the intelligentsia and the well-to-do. There, well-tended pockets of 'public system' can also be appropriated by the upper crust because of the peculiarities of the district method of school control. Thus it becomes possible in both Britain and the United States to spare a crocodile tear for the shortcomings of the publicly provided school, while doing little more about it than agitating for tax relief for private school fees – which, of course, would be a direct hindrance.

[1] The National Union of Teachers estimated that, to reduce classes to a maximum of 30 children, 110,000 more teachers would be required by 1965.

It might be supposed that parents would be up in arms. That they are not is partly due to ignorance or lack of 'know-how'. They are also befogged by the very spread of educational opportunity. They see their children (if they belong to that lucky 20 per cent. or so) approaching the grammar schools and colleges to which they never had access themselves. In some other instances, they gladly settle for improved plans which spread secondary school opportunities in the less academic interests. But if present trends in all non-communist countries are followed during the next few decades, the future will belong to the graduates and those who compete successfully for formal qualifications of one sort or another. Freely moving teachers migrate to the schools most distinguished in this competition – if they have good qualifications to sell. As a matter of plain observation, they tend to avoid or even despise schools and subjects that stand low in popular esteem. This distaste seems to grow in proportion as some rather poorly endowed schools are boosted in advance of any real improvement in the equipment or – more important – in the personnel.

Though it is an unpopular thing to say so, the absence of worthwhile differentials in pay and prospects for well-educated and enterprising newcomers is one of the most serious causes of the downgrading of the whole teaching profession. It will be cumulative unless the publicly provided schools offer conditions and prospects comparable with those elsewhere. Of this there is world-wide evidence. In countries like Britain and the U.S.A. the parallel existence of prestige-giving and truly excellent private schools aggravates the whole situation. It is not the differentials which do harm, but differentials given for wrong reasons. We must consider our present neglect of them in the fullness of our context here, and with overseas comparisons. If we are not careful, we might ultimately find that future teachers would be predominantly drawn from the poorer human potential (as in the U.S.A.), from poorer categories of school (as in the French *cours complémentaires*, and the Dutch *Hogere Burgerschool*), or the depressed classes of society (as in the case of most elementary teachers in Britain before 1939). We should certainly find that the teacher's function would be belittled, with increasing reliance placed upon pre-digested pabulum in the shape of 'outlines', recommended syllabuses and methods, all kinds of audio-visual aids, and special lessons by experts given with the expectation of a humbler follow-up by mere ordinary teachers. For much routine work, indeed, ancillary 'teachers' helpers' may be used. All these things are already with us, not to speak of 'teaching machines'.[1]

Let us now return to what was said on page 201, that teaching must be varied to suit every group. According to the purely academic view of the teacher's function, criticized in this chapter, this has traditionally meant that teachers with the highest formal qualifications of a university type have been recruited for the oldest and brightest children, while less well schooled or pedestrian people have been thought good enough teachers for the youngest or dullest children. Therefore, this latter category of teachers have been recruited from such categories as the oldest of the children in the elementary school without further apprenticeship, as in India now; from among the pleasanter matrons whose family-rearing practice has made them good child-minders; from clerks and craftsmen and others with vocational skills usable in school;[2] and (in more recent years in some countries) from those who have had at least some sort of post-primary education followed by a short course of general and professional education.

It is only in a very few countries, chiefly Britain and the United States, that graduates of real universities have taken up teaching in the primary or non-academic post-primary schools. Even in the United States and Canada, the apparent usualness of this practice is quite misleading, because by international standards most of the American graduates engaged in teaching in such schools would not be counted as real university graduates, but rather as comparable with the teacher's certificate holders soon to be considered. In those very countries too it is usual to insist on degrees above the basic teaching qualification (if possible) for recognition as a genuine post-primary teacher. Unfortunately many such study extensions concern classroom routine and mere method; but they are additional studies after all. So it may be said to be a world-wide rule that, until very recently, at any rate, the

---

[1] Teaching machines operated on Pavlovian principles by reinforcing the 'conditioned reflex' have been a special study of Dr B. F. Skinner, professor of psychology at Harvard University. They apparently induce no particular feeling of discomfort in the 'patient'. Items can be learned with half the effort and in half the time taken by direct oral instruction or by the private use of texts. Mechanical teaching (or self-instruction and self-correction) devices are used in a number of universities and in the U.S. Army, e.g. in learning foreign languages.

[2] No despite is implied for such people, provided they are properly oriented and trained for their new responsibilities as teachers, as has happened with great success in many countries in post-war schemes of emergency training. Criticism is confined to the assumption that elementary literacy or vocational competence will suffice for primary school teaching.

younger or less successful children have been worst served in terms of teacher preparation.

Before pursuing this matter further, we should try to disperse some emotions with a cold douche of realism. Both in individuals and in communities it is important not to squander resources and activity but to direct them where they are most potently applied. Though it is no doubt desirable to have a potential brain surgeon or violin virtuoso playing bricks with nursery school children, they would not only be wasting their talents but probably not doing as well there as other people who could relieve them for work ultimately of greater value to all concerned. Most grumbling about infants and geniuses not playing together in Arcady is not really about that, but a concealed complaint about two other things: the failure to provide underprivileged children with people properly trained to serve their needs; and an outmoded identification of the *amount of subject-matter taught* with the amount due to the teacher in salary.

By one criterion (e.g. that of the school psychologist or the paediatrician) the care of infants and backward children is as demanding a study as the care of adolescents or seniles, and should be as well recompensed. But in making this comment we are comparing paediatricians with their specialist colleagues – and not children's needs with adult needs. We should therefore compare teachers with teachers (or with competing occupations where their professional skills might be used), rather than the mere age or competence of the children involved.

Now, it is a matter of common sense that some teachers are more skilled, more learned, more expensively and extensively trained than others, and very much scarcer than others too. Though it is true that mere amounts of subject-matter are not of themselves a guarantee of demands made upon teachers, nevertheless it is obvious that some teachers' tasks could never be done by most other teachers. Such teachers cannot be substituted for, and they are not expendable without peril to the whole educational system. They must therefore be retained at any necessary cost, deployed to the point where they are of most advantage, and loyally supported at appropriate levels by less well requited colleagues. That is the whole point of differential recruitment for universities, special schools (e.g. for the deaf), and for such posts as those of principal and supervisor. If it is true that many passed-over teachers could do those jobs just as well (and it seldom is true), then their protest is against the system used in selection and against the imperfect use of resources, not against the point of principle.

More grumbling is caused about the differentiation of teachers because of ignorance of what actually goes on in the grumblers' own countries and abroad than by any other factor. For example, North Americans often point with pride to the fact that they have a graduate teaching profession – which is in the main literally true in terms of what North American graduation means. But very considerable grading goes on within that profession. The rates of pay and vistas of opportunity vary tremendously from district to district, in complete contrast to familiar patterns in Europe, where standardized rates of pay according to status and responsibility are commonly established throughout a country. So no one can pretend that there is any homogeneity in the North American teaching profession for that reason alone. Furthermore, teachers' graduation or state recognition again varies greatly in the degree of scholarship and competence which it implies. Canadians and Americans know this; others do not.

Outsiders may also be ignorant of the usual North American requirement that high school teachers must have qualifications above those considered satisfactory for elementary school teaching, for example a Master's degree. What is this but the same distinction between primary school teachers and secondary school teachers that has now been abandoned in Britain? As if that were not enough differentiation, we should also note the prevailing custom in many countries (including the United States) of recognizing teachers only for particular grades or classes, or for particular subjects. They are well and truly categorized. To be given a higher class or an additional subject may count as a promotion, and may bring higher pay too. Europeans are often astonished to find how minutely a North American graduate profession can grade itself. There is no solidarity whatever in consequence of graduate status as such. An even more striking grading is found in France. Inspectors on a periodic visit to a school are required to award a performance mark to teachers, after hearing lessons. This mark can have an immediate effect on salaries for better or worse. A similar arrangement has been tried in some Australian states, and still persists in a modified form both there and in New Zealand.

So it may be childish and unrealistic to object to differentiation in principle, and in advance of detailed information. It is usually more appropriate to stigmatize the reasons given for the grading, or the social and economic system which brings about grading without good reason, or malpractices within the grading system, than the principle of giving differential rewards for difficult jobs or scarce skills. Now it is a matter of history that most countries have doled out elementary education 'on the cheap' for generations. It is also true that securing education and training as a prospective teacher has been in many countries for many years about the only easy way of scrambling out of humble status. Though this is no longer true of such countries as Britain and France, the objectionable memory of it survives to affect judgement now. But judgements in the field of teacher recruitment are critical for the successful establishment of a teaching profession with real status and competence in the future. If we do not secure this, with a full variety of all the teachers required in the publicly provided schools, we may have allowed our shudders at the past to give private schools all the prestige and prospects for generations to come. It is not suggested that pay and prospects alone will secure a good and diversified teaching profession; but these may help considerably, and we must weigh them.

Just as in hospitals there is a functional hierarchy of skills and status from orderlies and nurses upwards, so most countries grade their teachers and teacher training. Both the principles invoked and the practices followed are sometimes good, sometimes bad. More often than not (as we saw above) they have not yet disengaged themselves from mainly historical entanglements. The typical continental method of securing primary school teachers has been to take bright pupils from a senior elementary or intermediate school (e.g. *Hauptschule* in Austria, *Mittelschule* in Germany, *cours complémentaire* in France) and give a further course of instruction for periods of two to five years until the age of about nineteen or twenty. In many continental countries this used to be in an institution running roughly parallel to the prestige-giving academic secondary school; but it hardly ever reached the same level of attainment, and certainly never the same social status. This is still true in Italy, for example; and the practice survives in many African and some Asian countries.

A trend in many countries in recent years has up-graded these teachers' institutions by raising their certificates in relation to university admission. In France it has become the practice to take the *baccalauréat* as an integral part of the *école normale*'s programme, before going on to strictly professional studies.[1] In Austria and Italy a certain amount of admissibility to universities has been conferred on those who leave the pedagogical institutes with a teacher's professional qualification. In

[1] See, however, the footnote on p. 209.

practice so far this does not seem to help the young teacher much, and the French pattern has more to recommend it.

Prospective teachers in such continental training institutions are almost invariably addressed, referred to, and treated as children. They are normally called 'pupils', and not 'students'. They are often addressed in the singular, familiar forms of speech (e.g. 'tu' or 'Du', instead of 'vous' or 'Sie'), in marked contrast to university students. A change will doubtless come when, as increasingly happens, countries admit candidates to teachers' colleges only after completion of the full secondary school course. This is now true in Germany of the *Pädago-gische Akademie*, and in Britain of the training colleges. If we take the United Kingdom as an example, such colleges include a double purpose in their curriculum: the extension of the student's general education, with advanced work in one or more fields; and studies in the theory and practice of education. British teachers' colleges now have a three-year course – the same length as that in a university. Students can sometimes extend the college course by one year and prepare for a university degree. Though these colleges are not part of universities, they are associated with them for advice and examining and other purposes through the Institutes of Education. This is a kind of mentor-ship system whereby a regional association of colleges, largely auto-nomous, has the guarantee of a university for its standards and cer-tificates, under a central Director who has professorial status in the university. The lecturers in the constituent colleges serve on important committees and boards of studies in the university, and a close two-way traffic is maintained in other ways. The British Institutes of Educa-tion well repay study for possible adaptation to the evolving needs of other countries.

By contrast with these long-standing arrangements for primary and middle school teachers, few countries have done much until recently about the training of university graduates for the teaching profession. The practice is growing, however. It is now well organized in France and the U.S.S.R., though in different ways; a number of other countries are following suit with one-year schemes; but for the training of university graduates for secondary school teaching the United Kingdom, the Commonwealth countries, and the United States remain the most obvious examples. In England the usual pat-tern is to have one year of professional instruction and training in a university department of Education after graduation in an Arts or Science subject. The professional qualification is called either a 'post-

graduate certificate in Education' or a teacher's diploma. In Scotland
the procedure is similar, except that the professional course is given
in a teachers' college outside the university proper, and may result in
the award of a second degree (B.Ed.). In Wales, Education may be
included (even as a major subject) as part of the first degree programme;
but students must obviously also reach a substantial standard in one or
more 'straight' academic subjects. Alternatively, the professional course
may follow the first degree in Wales too.

The American pattern is, very roughly, similar to the Welsh
wherever it takes place within a real university department or college
of full standing; but in all fairness we must note that most American
colleges of Education are not considered by American scholars generally to enjoy that standing. At Harvard and Yale and one or two
other very distinguished universities the English fashion of a postgraduate professional year is the rule. In that case, however, the
Master's degree is awarded on conclusion of the one-year course,
whereas in British universities a Master's degree (in Education as in
other fields) takes longer, and follows more advanced work. Some
American universities have also conducted noteworthy experiments
in the training of lecturers for universities. Several have admirable departments which train instructors for adult and further
education.

There is no space here to indicate the detail of teacher training patterns in various countries. It seems more important to content ourselves with seeing the main trends outlined. Yet, because evolution in
the Soviet Union is in full swing, and that is an educationally radical
and egalitarian country, there are interesting features to note in the
system of teacher preparation. Here we see the oldest of the Old World
turning rapidly into the newest of the new. Before 1954, teachers
for the primary grades in rural schools were usually given a four-
year preparation in a pedagogical school (or pedagogical *tekhnikum*)
beginning at the age of fourteen, after the completion of the ordinary
seven-year school. (This arrangement is similar to that once common
in the rest of Europe.) A number of these were still in use in 1960,
though Ministry officials were apologetic about them. Also, some such
teachers were trained in a two-year course, but after the completion of
the full ten-year (now eleven-year) school and obtaining a good diploma there. In 1959 there were still 150 of these two-year institutions
in the Russian federation (R.S.F.S.R.). This pattern resembles the
French admission of those with the *baccalauréat* to the *école normale* for

a shorter, two-year course, or the British admission to a two-year training college before courses were extended to three years in 1960.

A noteworthy move towards the provision of a genuinely higher education for all types of teacher in the U.S.S.R. was made in 1958. Since that year, thirteen of the pedagogical institutes (hitherto only for secondary school teachers in training) have kept more than 1,000 places for future primary teachers. In 1959 this number was augmented. A number of such places are also reserved for those responsible for vocational or 'polytechnical' subjects in the upper end of the eight-year school and later. It is anticipated too that some promising kindergarten teachers will be allowed to pursue their special study at the institute level. This is said to be the goal for all future teacher-training.

The pedagogical institutes just referred to are part of the provision for higher education, and run exactly parallel to the ordinary university faculties. University officials, indeed, are at pains to point out that there is little or no distinction between universities and institutes in point of attainment, but only in emphasis. Pedagogical institutes have typically recruited first-class students at the age of eighteen (now often twenty because of the two-year work period[1]), for a full-time course of four years or a part-time or correspondence course of five years. A 1958 announcement anticipated that all full-time courses in pedagogical institutes would be extended to five years too, to bring them into line with the five-year courses of other kinds of institute and of the university. The instruction formerly offered by correspondence to teachers in remote areas, with periodic residential visits to an institute for one or two months at a time, is now being brought slowly to a close; but there is still a heavy volume of part-time attendance. For example, the State Pedagogical Institute for Foreign Languages[2] in Moscow has 2,000 full-time day students, and another 3,000 evening and correspondence students. The teaching staff ('chairs') state how many students they think they can cope with; but the government often exceeds this quota.

[1] Some still come straight in from the eleven-year school at eighteen; they are said to be 'the most brilliant' in languages, science, or some other subject.

[2] This is a very highly esteemed institution with a strongly competitive entry (see below), of which the professors are understandably proud. Similarly, the 'Kalinin' Polytechnic in Leningrad and some other institutes impose their own selective process on top of the minimum published requirements of the state. In any case, the whole question of selectivity at this level must be considered in relation to the 20 per cent. admission of brilliant pupils straight from school, and the less obvious but equally selective influence of success in certain schools or courses.

Students specialize in accordance with abilities they have already demonstrated, and also to fit the requirements of the State Plan. Like all others in higher education, they have compulsory instruction in dialectical and historical materialism. Specialization can be in subjects, or particular skills, or types of children. Since 1958 there has been much more emphasis on practical work. This begins in the third year, as a rule; but experience in camps, &c., may precede it. Careful studies are now made by the Academy of Pedagogical Sciences and other bodies of the example of the most successful teachers. Students are allowed a certain amount of latitude in their choice of specialization; but as they have been preceded by reports from their previous schools and have also been submitted to exhaustive pre-entry examinations and interviews, prospects seem fairly cut and dried. It is said that there are between three and five applicants for every place (fifteen for each place in some departments), so the selectors can be strict.

The impending extension to a five-year curriculum had not completely taken place during the 1960-1 academic session, at any rate at the Foreign Languages Pedagogical Institute referred to above. Half of the time is spent on linguistic and literary study of a broad but intensive kind; and another one and a half to two years are spent in specialized study of a more senior kind in preparation for the presentation of a thesis on a topic to be approved by the whole faculty. A huge list is distributed of books which must be thoroughly studied. Seminars, discussions, and work assignments of various kinds, make the student's life more than full. There are four formal examinations on the way.

The uniformity of treatment in class that is characteristic of Soviet schools is also found in the institutes. Students receive marks for their work on the familiar one-to-five scale; but all progress together towards the final diploma. There is a pass list; but it is not officially graded. However, in the allocation of jobs there is no doubt attention is paid to known excellences or the opposite. To a foreign visitor, even in ordinary class routine, it seems obvious that the instructor asks the bright students the hardest questions, and vice-versa. Still, every attempt is made to shepherd them all along together, and differentiation is often combined with some equality.[1]

Exceptionally able students – a handful – may stay on for a further three years in the pedagogical institute or elsewhere to prepare the dissertation on which is based a claim for recognition as *Kandidat Nauk*

---

[1] See my article 'Differentiation and equality in Soviet schools', in the *Anglo-Soviet Journal*, Autumn, 1960.

('Candidate in Science', roughly equivalent to a Ph.D. in Britain or the U.S.A., but probably not always as high an attainment as the former). In the preparation for this ordeal there is close co-operation with the staff of the institute. Some of the instructors themselves may also be preparing theses, though mature teachers of excellent quality. Before defending the dissertation, examinees must have published three learned articles in substantial periodicals. The research may be academic, or methodological, or be concerned with instruction in such circumstances as industrial training. For candidates with such an external purview there may be leave of absence or scientific exchanges for as much as a month at a time.

Some idea of the standing of the instructors in the pedagogical institutes is obtainable from salary comparisons within the U.S.S.R. Senior engineers were paid 1,800 roubles a month in 1960, or 3,300 roubles if graduated as *Kandidat Nauk*. Senior institute teachers received 2,000 roubles a month, or more than 3,000 roubles if *Kandidaty Nauk*. To avoid any possible misunderstanding, it should be pointed out that the lower figure is the normal one. There is no question of the degree of *Kandidat* being a simple journeyman's ticket. It is rightly regarded as an exceptional attainment.

All university students and students in non-pedagogical institutes must now include some 'pedagogy' in their undergraduate studies, with the exception of particularly promising mathematicians and physicists. These are destined for advanced researches. There is no shortage of good, sound mathematicians and scientists for the schools, particularly now that some courses in what we would call 'Education' are imposed on all. In any case, under the Soviet dispensation any civil servant (and they are all that) can be called on to serve anywhere, at least for a period of three years. So the schools are not likely to be short of good graduate teachers.

Universities understandably pay less attention to educational theory and practice than the institutes, though they do include both for future teachers. In the institutes some 20 per cent. of the time is now practical. They cultivate subjects less deeply than universities. But otherwise there is said to be no difference between students or institutions in status, rights, pay, or ultimate prospects. Institute students, like others, are strongly encouraged to add to their qualifications later. They can also move to non-teaching jobs in due course.

In addition to the long-standing Soviet practice of teachers' conferences, there are now in-service seminars and 'refresher courses' conducted by specially successful teachers. Thus improved methods are encouraged. Teachers are also encouraged to write textbooks, and can make a lot of money doing so; but there is a risk in this because of possible re-interpretations of what is orthodox. However, much lively examination of current trends goes on, not only in schools but in Pioneer work and other forms of instruction. All teachers are highly paid and esteemed; but there is an ascending order of prestige in the terms: *master* (technical instructor), *uchitel'* (teacher), and *professor* (advanced specialist in a subject).

In all the countries we have examined, and in many others for which unfortunately there is no space here, bridges of various sorts are being built between the previously segregated preserves of the teaching profession. In some countries, perhaps least in Britain of all those examined here, bridges are also being built between the various forms of education available to teachers as a whole and the prestige-giving studies of the universities proper. It is right that this should be so (provided that genuine equivalence of attainment or aptitude can be shown), for two reasons. No matter what start is made by a prospective teacher or any other learner, it is manifestly to the advantage of all that he should continue to the fullest development of his capabilities, and not be held down by time-honoured protocol. Not only is that restriction a personal injustice; it dates from a time when the teacher's task was narrowly conceived as a restrictive one – an elimination of distraction from the pure, approved ration of enlightenment to be ingested by purified and captive children in their predetermined stations.

But school is not an isolation hospital for clinical inoculation. Any reasonably up-to-date view of the teacher shows him engaging children's existing interests and helping them to evolve. This aim is incapable of fulfilment unless the teacher himself is also engaged in expanding his own interests – evolving himself as he helps civilization to evolve. Therefore the teacher's task itself should be seen as a continuous personal education.[1] That does not mean continuous instruction; but it does call for encouragement in every possibility of development. In all countries greater flexibility is needed in the recognition of 'equivalence' (i.e. an entitlement to further study from the point of readiness already reached, without undue attention to outmoded requirements). This is particularly necessary in the case of teachers. If study and formal professional review are not exactly called for, there must nevertheless

---

[1] Many states in the U.S.A. insist that teachers take some additional in-service training or other courses at periodic intervals. A similar requirement is emphasized in the U.S.S.R.

be a real feeling of continuing personal adventure. That is exactly what present hierarchies and awards seem designed to kill.

A second good reason for eliminating arbitrary dooms imposed on teachers is the growing fusion between types of school – or at any rate the fading of that traditional segregation between interests and levels once identified exclusively with particular types of establishment or child. The best educational practice no longer thinks it good that children should be isolated in restricted pockets of perception; their ambitions should be as wide as society, and their horizon as distant as the world's ultimate prospects. That goes for teachers too. It will be ultimately to the advantage of all teaching even if this eventually leads to a more mobile teaching force. As a corollary to this view, there seems to be little sense any longer in segregating future teachers from other students, or from the actualities of mature living conditions.

Thus education will be severely braked if it is not seen as a partnership (of all concerned, and not just teacher and child) in the continuous exploration and rebuilding of the human phenomenon. We hand on tradition, as we cannot help bequeathing the countryside – a rich legacy of man's cultivation with a promise of richer harvests to come. Man is an *unfinished* artifact of his past, of spiritual traditions, and of his present endeavours. Platonist, Christian, Marxist, and social biologist all agree that man must complete himself. The teacher's job in this evolutionary process is impossible unless he himself is the very exemplification of life's ferment and all its eagerness. The teacher's role is greater if he does not claim to exercise the whole or the major responsibility in education. For the child, education should be a venture into a wonderland where his share is real and significant, even if it is not El Dorado. For the teacher it must also be a personal and social unfolding. All teacher recruitment, training, and engagement must be undertaken in this spirit.

BOOKS

See the general bibliography on Comparative Education, p. 369.

See also the *Year Book of Education* for 1953, London (Evans Bros) and New York (World Book Company).

The *Year Book of Education* for 1963 will also be on the teaching profession in a changing world.

The Study of Education
as a Personal and Social Leaven

CHAPTER 10

Ideologies and systems of control

'I just don't see it!' How many times have we used this formula of dis-agreement? It turns up every day in school. It is the crux of many tragedies. It is the pivot of politics.

'Eyes have they, and see not' complains the psalmist. Both he and the evangelists make constant reference to 'the hardness of men's hearts' (i.e. in modern parlance, 'minds' [1]) or to the deafness which prevents them from hearing the words of truth. Bacon in his turn says:

> The 'idols' and false notions which have already preoccupied the human understanding and are deeply rooted in it, not only so beset men's minds that they become difficult of access but, even when access is obtained, will again meet and trouble us in the instauration of the sciences, unless mankind when forewarned guard themselves with all possible care against them. [2]

In all these cases one contestant believes he is propounding *the* truth about a matter, while the resister seems to be already possessed by the spirit of error. Karl Mannheim calls this kind of involvement 'particular ideology'. [3] He says: 'We are sceptical of the ideas and representations advanced by our opponent. They are regarded as more or less conscious disguises of the real nature of a situation, the true recognition of which would not be in accord with his interests.' Mannheim then proceeds to give examples of 'total ideology', whereby a whole web of related and persistent ideas or obsessions are believed to be characteristic of a par-ticular class or period. Beliefs and philosophies are not to be taken at their face value but are to be understood in relation to the background of the speaker. In evaluating a total ideology we critically analyse not only the content of what the speaker says but the whole personal, social,

---

[1] In the ancient world, the heart was the seat of the intelligence; the emotions were centred in the bowels.

[2] Bacon, *Novum Organum*, section 38.

[3] Mannheim, K., *Ideology and Utopia* (Routledge & Kegan Paul), 1936, p. 62, and the whole of chapter 2. (My page reference is to the Harvest Books edition.)

and conceptual context in which he seems to be enmeshed. We are not really thinking of errors in his reasoning, or peculiarities of his psychology. We see him not as obtuse or as an ignoramus, not as a liar or as 'resisting the known truth', but as penetrated by a tangle of false understanding which victimizes him.

We arrive at this level when we no longer make individuals personally responsible for the deceptions which we detect in their utterances.... We more or less consciously seek to discover the source of their untruthfulness in a social factor.... We sense in his total behaviour an unreliability which we regard as a function of the total situation in which he finds himself.[1]

It is some illustration of this point when we mitigate blame or diminish responsibility on the ground of class views, 'vested interests', womanly weakness, or national characteristics. We may oppose the error, and even hate it to the extent of persecuting it; but our onslaught is directed against *it* as a social phenomenon, rather than against the erring person as a person. Some of us feel more like praying for him, or liquidating him, than tackling him directly with supposedly objective reasoning; for we all feel our opponent to be possessed by a totally false outlook warping everything he sees. He cannot see 'the facts' of the case. As education by its very nature includes a lot of persuasion, and turns significantly on what we believe to be facts, the notion of ideology demands detailed consideration.

Marx has given us our most thoroughgoing examination of the concept of ideology, and (with Freud in a somewhat different way) has very profoundly shaken all subsequent thought about 'absolutes' and 'pure reason'. Those who believe in these things are now dubious about our access to them. Marx attributed not merely the content and the order of our thinking but also its whole conceptual activity to the functioning of our social (i.e. economic) roles. Merely personal or family history, such as Freud stressed, could for him have no real consequence. Such an isolation of social element (e.g. a person, a couple, or a family) would have seemed to Marx a fallacious selection of one product of the whole economic process. It seemed necessary for him to envisage that whole process in long-term historical perspective – and in accordance with that distinctive ideology (or interpretation and way of life) which we have since come to recognize as Marxist. No one needs to have any sympathy for Marxism as a political faith to see well

[1] Mannheim, K., op. cit., p. 63.

enough what an important influence Marx's method of diagnosis has had on our interpretation of 'understanding' and 'world views'.

All sincere and earnest persons seek 'objective truth' and 'reality'. It is possible that they may find it. But as we look around we often suspect that our neighbours, individually or together, 'live in a different world' from our own. As we approach wisdom, we may eventually recognize that all the apparently conflicting ways of thought and evaluation *may* be reducible to different ways of expressing our variously conditioned experience of the same things we observe. In other words we, instead of being absolutely or certainly right, may only be expressing a partial truth that at best is complementary to other points of view (or 'ideologies').

So far in this chapter we have been considering the influence of ideologies in somewhat negative terms – as hindrances to supposedly pure understanding. Yet ideologies must also be seen from a positive point of view. They can, so to speak, be the master interpretation or 'vision of the whole' that enables the entire jigsaw puzzle to fall into unexpected order. The little boy working on a difficult passage of translation grumbles that 'it doesn't make sense'. He really means that *he* does not make sense of it until the critical clue is given; thereafter the passage begins to 'make sense' with dawning clarity until even the most puzzling parts can at least have their meaning surmised. So it is with all learning, of course. The *Gestalt* or overall concept of relationships appears to be essential to orderly and speedy learning.

So far, at this elementary level, we have not reached the full realization of what a total ideology means to those who cherish it. It is the master interpretation of the whole medley of human existence, most clearly exemplified in the great religions. It comes to life in behaviour and institutions. In order to establish the New Jerusalem (or its equivalent in other faiths) men have not only argued and preached; they have also set up societies and systems in which they (perhaps all people) could rehearse, extend and intensify their 'understanding' and their acceptance of the gospel.

Such institutions include, of course, churches and meetings, special ceremonies and music and forms of address, special language, special uniforms or clothes, special pictures (or the equally special absence of them), special food, special careers, and ultimately special instruction or initiation in special places. In the final triumph of a faith, all these things seem no longer special but the only true way of doing things. They may even be 'natural'. So great is the force of habituation, and so great the human craving for a well-ordered routine – including methods of perception and analysis.

Compulsive and satisfying though the suggestions of a religious faith may be, particularly if it 'makes sense' of morals and emotions and the social order in which it is enshrined, it is still not quite an ideology in the full latter-day sense of that word. For it is obvious that in the final analysis the 'world view' of faiths is an 'other-world view', in so far as the 'certainty' of which they are the inheritors is achieved only on the supernatural plane. The earthly application of those principles may be fallacious because of the intractability, temptation-value, or downright wickedness of things on earth. Thus such a near-ideology as a faith maintains itself in pristine purity by various devices of exclusion and repudiation.

The true believer can therefore say (as I have heard them very politely say): 'We know that . . .', while saying of others that: 'They believe that . . .' Believers are, by their own logic, entitled to surround themselves and their young charges with protective devices such as special schools for special instruction, enriched with all kinds of special symbols and indeed with reminders in all kinds of studies (particularly history or any subject remotely connected with cosmogony, such as biology). Moreover, some risks and contacts will be particularly avoided. An emotional welcome or distaste for particular words is cultivated. Such diagnostic words include 'holy', 'faith', 'charity', 'science', 'reform', and 'progress', because reactions to these tend to distinguish whole profiles of attitudes from contrary attitudes.

Eventually, if the implications of a way of life become explicit in the institutions through which it has worked its logic out, then the whole governmental, economic, social, philosophical, and artistic self-expression of such a way of life becomes closely integrated as a culture. If it is vigorous enough, it may stand for centuries as an abiding civilization. Then, instead of being simply explicit, the whole value and perception system becomes so implicit that it seems natural. In Chapter 3 we noted that a culture is a well-established and institutionalized way of life, supported by a characteristic technology or social order. Powerfully formative though such cultures are, they have usually been localized rather than world developments, especially in pre-industrial times. Much more pervasive value-systems or civilizations are exemplified by pre-Reformation Christendom (in its many different forms) and Hinduism.

In considering these instances we come much closer to full appreciation of what the word 'ideology' really implies; but there is more to an ideology than we have so far expressed. Anyone using the word 'ideology' to full effect implies not so much that a sectarian view – even of the chosen elect – looks *outward* upon some unenlightened external mass, but that all the phenomena and activity 'outside' the faith should really be imagined as internally penetrating and indeed constructing that faith with *their* own system. It is not a case of God-given light shining outwards. The suggestion is that theologies, values, and the like are all constructed by environmental forces or by the reactions of human beings to such external realities. Thus, according to the concept of 'ideology', religions themselves (like fashions in art or etiquette) are by-products of a bigger pattern of perception and reaction which is more comprehensive than they are. Hence a thoroughgoing ideology would hold that the web of its 'total understanding' literally *gives* meaning to all the activities going on within its purview.

The ideologies of Hegel and Marx are particularly deterministic. They suggest that human systems are externally made by outside forces which, as it were, possess them. Only one interpretation is possible. The one answer, the one force, is the one truth. It must reach out and ramify until every detail of every activity and every study is permeated by it. Elements which resist it are said to be effete and purposeless. There is no room for alternatives or unpredictable reactions – if only the logic of the ideology has been thoroughly worked out. Thus every shred of life must be scrutinized and purified; and if it cannot be satisfactorily contained within the ideology it must be repudiated.

It does not necessarily follow that every ideology must be deterministic and intolerant. Determinism implies that there is really no freedom anywhere; every event is directly caused, and particular results must inevitably follow particular causes. Because of the obvious consequences of such a view, Professor Karl Popper has bitterly attacked ideological systems and has also tended to deny causation in history.[1] Yet, as I hope to show shortly, one can be a democrat and have an ideology. Indeed, it seems necessary. Moreover, the fault of the systems attacked by Professor Popper is that they are deterministic in suggesting inevitability. Human affairs are undoubtedly caused; but they have multiple causation. It is the multiple reaction of human beings that introduces uncertainty, and therefore makes choice or varied consequences possible. But choice and will can neither develop nor be strengthened if they are *not* engaged in a system which helps

[1] Popper, K., *The Open Society and its Enemies*, London (Allen & Unwin), 1957.

to make them sensible and gives them the prospect of future consequences.

So allergic are the adherents of deterministic ideologies (and of some faiths) to the supposed threats of alien systems that they become embattled against them as soon as they reach a position of strength. Since the Reformation this reaction has led to the Thirty Years' War in Germany, one of the most disastrous and unfortunate recorded, and all the more lamentable because fought on the grounds of religion. It has also led to the rise of Mussolini and Hitler on one side and to communist revolutions and purges on the other.

Fortunately, liberal countries have eventually come to see that conversion by the sword or by expurgation is not the most desirable form of securing the code they cherish; yet that mellowing is itself due to the rather special ideology they have developed – one based upon tolerance and living empiricism rather than on the preaching of any form of 'dead certainty'. It is an ideology none the less.[1]

The social and governmental customs of the English-speaking world are indeed teaching instruments for this 'Third Way' ideology. Thus it may be difficult (for example) for Britons or Americans to understand how intimately and disturbingly felt are arguments in France, Belgium, and Italy about the control of school systems. The protagonists there are not arguing about religion in the sense that English speakers usually understand it; they are goaded into implacable hostility because of perverted and nonsensical attacks (as they see the situation) upon all their most fundamental values and their most cherished ways of doing things in all departments of this life (and the next, perhaps). It is a very concrete, personal, and un-academic matter. The slightest slip may by implication make the enemy's victory surer. English words like 'compromise' and 'working agreement' seem stupid milk-and-water affairs when you are deciding between unimaginable heavenly bliss on one hand and diabolical possession on the other.

In these circumstances there can therefore be no real compromise, because there can be no compromise with falsehood and perdition. What may be necessary, however, is an armistice – a cold war instead of a hot one; but the battle is still on behind the scenes. It may take another form; but its objectives are ultimately the same. Thus what we delude ourselves into thinking of as our Anglo-Saxon habit of 'compromise' is really no such thing. It really has become a third ideology, logically

[1] It is exemplified in K. Mannheim's *Freedom, Power and Democratic Planning* (London, 1951), under the name of the 'Third Way'.

opposed to the other two contesting interpretations, even if we tell ourselves we are only willing to live and let live. In fact, we are relying on our own ideological interpretation of how knowledge and education grow. We prize tolerance, because we implicitly say that understanding is evolved empirically by the day-to-day co-ordination of increasingly valid approximations to truth. In time, we think, understanding will shape itself.

To safeguard this peaceful process we think it sufficient to point out objective error about matters of simple fact, to invite complementary co-operation, and to rob the 'hidden persuaders' of some of their disruptive powers by exposing them for what they are. Yet it is highly likely that we thus ignore some basic human needs in our negative programme, namely the need for securing 'understanding by stages' and for built-in reminders of our system of values (Chapter 6.) Tolerance and reminders are not enough, either; we must evoke as positive a commitment to our way of building up the human future as other ideologies evoke within their own bounds. In keeping with our own ideology, however, we shall avoid excessive exclusiveness and 'holier-than-thou' smugness; for, according to our logic, any self-assured orthodoxy is inherently suspect in the long run of human affairs.

It is by taking the long view that we can often see a proposal in perspective, harmless enough though it may seem at first. For it is not always the essence or logic of an idea that is perilous, so much as its practice when it becomes institutionalized. These trite observations have special validity in relation to schools and other educational mechanisms. Let us therefore see where exceeding protectiveness can lead us. We have already had some indications in the last chapter (p. 205), when we considered the Jesuit colleges of France and their skilful enlistment of post-Renaissance learning in the paradoxical service of a pre-Renaissance way of life. The Jesuits, of course, are not alone in this; they are instanced only because of their great and systematized skill in doing so. The somewhat comparable practice of bowdlerizing Shakespeare and the classical poets for school textbooks seems well enough; but have we always done well when we close young minds not simply to bawdiness but to a balanced view of human emotions and prospects as they are? To go one stage further – are we to agree with Plato that Homer and other masterpieces shall be banished from our schools because of the unseemly behaviour of the gods as there described? Or that certain kinds of music and poetry shall be banned because they are not austere enough? And will our censorship stop there?

Historical evidence suggests otherwise. In Roman Catholic schools any book that has a direct bearing on matters of faith or morals contains (if it is approved) a printed notice in Latin to the effect that 'Nothing stands in the way', and a further injunction that it may be printed. We cannot grumble at that. After all a church is entitled to indicate what is or is not contrary to its teachings: and those who take note of this indication are its own flock. To carry the process one stage further, an *Index* of books and other publications is drawn up in Rome by the Holy Office (or Inquisition) to show which reading matter is forbidden to the faithful without sinful risk of their souls' well-being. This *Index* proscribes not only salacious writing, inaccurate representations, and the like; it also includes the entire production of certain authors whose works reflect a hostile ideology. Obviously, certain scientific and philosophical theories are banned too. In addition to these general embargoes, the clergy are also often submitted to particular restrictions by their superiors in different countries (like being forbidden to attend any theatres), so that they may not taint their parishioners.

A study of the *Index* can be astonishing, both in its inclusions and in its omissions. Its existence cannot logically be complained about, if we believe in educating for orthodoxy; but we can wonder at the administration of the censorship in practice. Outsiders may also perhaps be forgiven for questioning how far this supernatural ideology can tally on earth with tolerance, or effective co-operation with other people in possibly non-approved programmes of reform. It is after all somewhat disconcerting for others to be by implication suspect as part of 'the world' – an 'enemy of the soul'.

Partly for these ideological reasons and partly also because of more practical or administrative fears about the standards and control of schools, the governments of many countries are unwilling to co-operate financially or in other ways with the establishment of church-associated schools. But as there are other factors involved, we shall postpone our examination of this particular problem for a while.

It is not only churches, of course, which try to impose a censorship in the interests of orthodoxy. Governments do it too, though with the exception of the communist countries they seldom venture to do so unless there is solid church support behind them. To take but one instance, the state of Tennessee in 1914 demanded that no teacher should take drugs, drink, or smoke. More recently in the Scropes case it decided that to teach the Darwinian theory of evolution in any aspect was contrary to Christian orthodoxy and must therefore be illegal. The state of Mississippi in 1956 required all its teachers to submit a list of all the periodicals they read, for fear they should be tainted by anti-segregation literature. In the Deep South it is axiomatic for many people that such subversive literature is a betrayal of Christian purity and a sober social order. In the Union of South Africa there is a closely similar feeling. There the God-given mission of the white man in the Dutch Reformed Churches must be rigorously maintained against the creeping corruptions of all forms of darkness – new-fangled and emancipated relationships for girls, non-patriarchal orientation or urbanized ambitions, and the pigmentation of the majority of the population. Television too is forbidden (1961), though it exists over the border in Rhodesia, and could be received from there. When the hordes of Midian encircle, such governments try to legislate the 'threat' out of existence.

The supreme example of government and planning in accordance with an ideology is, of course, the Soviet Union. There communism is not just the label of a party; it is a whole way of life, a philosophical world view, and an educational principle. Scientific studies, economic activity, politics, and education are different aspects of the same thing, we are told. Therefore not only is every item of instruction (every definition in every book) under the strictest scrutiny; every alien intrusion of non-communist interpretation is also carefully guarded against. If any such intrusion takes place, it is 'contained' and corrected. This ideological safeguarding is far from being merely negative. It acts as an internal leaven or stiffening throughout all subjects and extra-curricular activity. The 'spirit of communism' enthuses and vivifies Soviet schools (particularly the boarding schools) in exactly the same way as a 'good Catholic atmosphere' is characteristic of most convents and Catholic colleges in the Western world. The children have the same serene, unquestioning look and the same full commitment. In every room (in every book for that matter, and as far as possible in every exercise or problem) are the reminders of the faith. Here is the child Lenin at three years of age. There are the great episodes of his life, his missionary activity. Those are the notable texts. Here is his statue or picture welcoming the children; and there are the records of the dedicated children and adults who have triumphed in his cause. 'Study as Lenin studied' begins the lesson in arithmetic (or English, or geography). 'Children, live and work and think and speak like communists!' say the banners.

This, to an astonishing degree, is what the children do; and they seem remarkably content and successful in the process. Of course, the immense material achievements and social amelioration that have followed 'the Great October Socialist Revolution' (as it is almost invariably called) carry the real inner conviction of their own success story; and the invitation to an expanding personal and public future is certainly inspiring to the children. Moreover, the parents of most of the children now in school are themselves the beneficiaries of post-revolutionary reforms, either scholastic or economic. Those parents have in the overwhelming majority plenty of reminders that their lot is better than that of previous generations, no matter what it seems like to us. They are mostly anxious to avoid prejudicing socialist progress. They are assured by every word they read, and by every word they hear from official sources, that to impair communism in any detail is to put the brakes on that progress. Their own memory of encirclement and intervention makes them ready to believe the constant story of a hostile and perverted non-communist world outside.

Many potential liberals and critics in the Soviet Union are therefore more afraid of the destructiveness of non-communism (as they see it) than of the oppressiveness of their own régime, which is in any case not more oppressive than that which preceded it. In so far as they know they are under constant, censoring supervision, most of them would justify it as a sort of purposeful paternalism. It certainly is a close surveillance. Not only is there an external, ideological *cordon sanitaire*; there is also (for example) space on everyone's library ticket to show the last fifty books he read. There must be no accidents inside, either!

Shocking though the writer and his readers may find such invigilation, that is not the point. Contained in the concept of education for any orthodoxy are the germs of such control. The essence is the same, though the methods and degree of efficiency may differ. There is only one big difference in principle: that most pre-communist orthodoxies did admit the possibility of 'private areas' or irrelevant oases where 'self' could be unquestioned. Yet in practice even these have often been suspect, particularly in the realms of philosophical speculation and political or scientific inquiry. The greatest difference between a modern political ideology and other 'orthodox' ideologies is one of degree, and of field of interest. The others have not been so thoroughgoing in institutionalized control, preferring the subtle controls of conscience; and they did not concern themselves like communism with the technological field which gives such superb opportunities for control.

And officially they left material enterprises alone. Within the more limited realm of their competence, however, some previous ideology-conscious communities have similarly exercised all the control they could.

As we have already seen, the development of public education systems in the post-Reformation period has been intimately bound up with attempts to shake free from the ideological completeness of the Roman Catholic interpretation and from the contemporary patterns of centralized, hierarchical forms of government. Hence Knox's schools for every Scottish parish, recommended as early as 1560 and actually established in 1691.[1] When radical Protestants emigrated to the New World they were equally quick to set up schools and colleges. The latter include the following: Harvard (1635), William and Mary (1692), and Yale (1701). Nine colleges (now great universities) were so founded during the colonial period alone, in contrast to the existing two in England. Similarly, when Scots settled in Otago in New Zealand in 1848, they promptly decided to open public schools for everyone. However, the teachers were required to have a minister's certificate of Presbyterian orthodoxy. On the continent of Europe too the deliberate propagation of Protestant faiths was attended by the establishment of parish or town schools for this and related purposes. In Lutheran countries the control of both ancient schools and the more recently established public tax-supported schools stayed in the hands of ecclesiastics for a very long time. Even now the Ministry responsible is often called 'Church and Education'.

Particularly where a Presbyterian or congregational type of church administration has been dominant, the local and self-determining type of school control has been characteristic, if only because of suspicion of the king's ecclesiastical connexions (as in the Church of England or its counterparts elsewhere). In England itself, the Anglican neglect of popular education and the burgesses' reliance on private or semi-private education prevented the evolution of any effective public control of schools as they developed; hence scholastic enterprise and supervision stayed a parish matter. The decentralized pattern of control in the U.S.A. and the United Kingdom is a consequence of these events. In England it is especially marked in the present internal autonomy of each school, whether that school is independent or maintained out of taxes.

[1] See N. Hans: *Comparative Education*, London (Routledge & Kegan Paul), 1947, chapter 8.

W.P.E.—Q

However, the increasing complexity of the demand for popular education, and the impossibility of providing it adequately in the rapidly developing urban industrialization of the nineteenth century, showed up the inadequacy of existing resources. Valiant efforts were made in many places to spread popular education on a basis of local self-sufficiency (as they still are throughout the less urbanized parts of the United States); but the whole momentum of technological development and social demand really makes nonsense of such a pre-industrial concept. It becomes a matter of simple arithmetic that local taxes cannot alone supply equal opportunities for all, now or ever.[1] Both the consumers of schooling and the political and industrial planners are now determined that fuller opportunities shall be provided. Education is now a national priority in most countries. This means co-ordination and concentration. If we take the example of one rural state in the U.S.A., New Hampshire, we find that in 1923 there were 800 one-room schools; in 1959 there were 16 of them, and these quickly to disappear. The United States affords the outstanding example of de-centralized educational responsibility; yet we find Federal encouragement, prodding, and support of scholastic improvement from the North-West Ordinance of 1787 and the Land Grants of 1862 and 1890 to the National Defence Education Act of 1958. 'National Defence' is right. A concerted drive for continuing national self-development must be based on a strong national system of schooling.

That is indeed the way that governments in Europe have long seen it. Modern France is the product of Napoleon's scholastic code, itself based upon the revolutionaries' adaptation of the Jesuit and similar colleges. Modern Germany has been made by educational expansion from the first quarter of the nineteenth century onwards. Soviet growth is of course inseparable from its school system. In the Far East Japan leapt forward even faster than the former Russian Empire after 1868, through the use it made of its schools. There is no need to multiply examples. It is already clear that nation after nation has been impatient of unaccelerated evolution and voluntaryism, taking over or superseding existing scholastic provision with a well co-ordinated system of its own. Where the existing provision has been retained, it has usually been aided to such a degree that the former 'owners' of the

---

[1] The classic instance of this is New Zealand. Despite obvious reluctance to abandon provincial control (1852–7), or the authority of District Education Boards at a later date, financial embarrassment gradually caused the transfer of powers and responsibility to the national Department of Education. Australian states had a similar experience.

schools are really little more than government agents in the greater part of their activity.

At this point a grave difficulty can enter in. If the outlook of the general population is entirely in keeping with the ideology of the previous administrators of schools (as it was in the Lutheran Scandinavian countries at that time or Catholic Eire now), there need be no conflict at all. The public school will perpetuate the ethos (and perhaps even teach the doctrines) of the Church. Officials can teach or supervise the secular and vocational content of schooling without doing violence to anyone's susceptibilities. Satisfactory standards are maintained; equitable distribution of opportunities can be secured; and there is no sectarian discord. If there are dissenters on religious matters, but they are still few enough not to matter much, they may well be provided with tax-supported schools of their own, as happens in Denmark and Eire. But for this to happen, there must either be an absence of previous ideological discord (rather a rare state of affairs), or else an unusual sense of being an international example.

Some countries whose population has traditionally insisted on a religious backbone to any public instruction have solved the problem of sectarian jealousy by equally supporting two blocks of denominationally oriented schools. Examples are to be seen in Scotland, the Netherlands, and parts of Germany. In Scotland the bulk of the population in the south and east is Presbyterian (or of very similar persuasion); in parts of the west and also in cities with an immigrant Irish population, many are Roman Catholics. When the parish-controlled schools were transferred in 1918 to the control of education authorities, an agreement was reached whereby officials would be satisfied on educational standards and ecclesiastics would satisfy themselves of religious orthodoxy. As long as the population continues to maintain roughly the same proportions and the same degree of influence in government, and as long as it is still convinced of the need for a doctrinal basis for schooling, harmony can be maintained.

This desirable state lasted a long time in Holland, partly because the Calvinist and Catholic populations tended to live in distinct areas. But with the development of urban growth and the exploitation of the new lands reclaimed in the polders, areas of mixed population have become increasingly conscious of sectarian rivalry. The position has been further complicated by two other factors: the proportional predominance of the Catholic birth-rate and the growth of a secular-minded body of townspeople. Thus, while the ideological affiliation could initially have been given as approximately 60 per cent. Calvinist and 40 per cent. Catholic, ideological defection and demographic change now give us approximately 40 per cent. Calvinist, 40 per cent. Catholic, and 20 per cent. neutral or secularist. The secularists are entitled to set up tax-supported schools.

A consequence of these divisions is that there are Calvinist boy scouts, Catholic boy scouts, and a secular equivalent; Calvinist parties, a Catholic party, and a secular party line; Protestant trade unions, Catholic trade unions, and left-wing secular trade unions. Children tend to find their playmates and school companions not in accordance with the class or local distinctions of other countries but by ideological criteria. Dutch officials of undoubted religious sympathies are often deeply disturbed by the growth of these divisive forces, and still more by the uncertainties of the future. Many openly express regret that unintentionally disruptive influences were ever given not merely recognition but also financial support. In the long run, many believe, true religion is not served thereby.

For similar reasons the deeply religious colonists in North America soon decided that, although religion must be in their view the paramount influence in life, it must be a home-based influence and something to be kept out of a public school system. Therefore the tradition of the public school in the United States has been a secular one – a remarkable development, but not altogether surprising in the light of the settlers' early sectarian rivalries and their very strong sense of having often suffered from persecution themselves. In a not dissimilar evolution, the public system of education in Australia and New Zealand has departed from the English tradition of religious schooling and its own early beginnings, to become entirely secular. Church-associated schools exist, particularly for Roman Catholics; but they are not tax-supported.[1] In Canada, too, though the provinces first settled had Church-associated schools (so much so that in Newfoundland there are five separate systems), the more recently developed provinces to the westward show decreasing patience with sectarian instruction, until in British Columbia the public system of education is secular.

In Britain too, though a 'dual system' exists, the Free Churches (i.e. Protestants not belonging to the established Church of England) surrendered their denominational schools from 1870 onwards. They not only believed that all publicly financed instruction should be neutral in

---

[1] At the time of writing a vigorous campaign, mainly by Catholics, may possibly result in a modification of this statement in parts of Australia.

religious matters, but also thought that religious teaching should be a parental responsibility. In fact, however, the retention by Anglicans of many schools founded as 'local schools' in the nineteenth century, and also the unwavering independence of Roman Catholics, resulted in the present compromise. Now there are non-sectarian 'maintained schools' both built and currently financed out of public taxation. There are also many tax-supported 'voluntary' schools, of which the most important category is that of 'aided schools'. These are schools established and repaired out of private or denominational funds, but having all their actual teaching costs (except for religious instruction) met out of public taxation, so that about 90 per cent. or more of their recurring expenses are a local government responsibility even if the school is entirely staffed by priests, brothers, or nuns. About one-third of all tax-supported schools in England and Wales are 'aided' schools. There are also other schools in varying degrees of independence and/or religious affiliation, with financial support in proportion.[1]

The Churches and other non-official but aided bodies run teachers' training colleges in addition to schools in Britain; but they do not have their own universities, trade unions, or radio stations (as is the practice in Holland and elsewhere). Nor, as a rule, do they play any part in technical education. All schools in England and Wales must by law impart some religious instruction (non-denominational in all the 'maintained' schools) and have a daily religious act of worship; yet the majority of the British population are extremely hazy in their religious connexion, if not indifferent altogether. The gradualist and evolutionary approach characteristic of British social development generally is responsible for the comparatively peaceful development and uneventful persistence of the dual system there, as contrasted with the turn of events in the British Commonwealth and the United States. Though church membership and attendance are much more widespread in the United States than in Britain, all public schools there are entirely secular; and church schools get no public support.

The 'separation of Church and State', however, has never been such a fanatically held doctrine as by anti-clericals in the nominally Catholic countries of Europe and South America, especially France, Belgium, and Italy. In each of these countries, successive changes in government have profoundly affected the question of the schools' status in relation to the Church. In Belgium in particular there has been continuous oscillation between favouring secular schools and supporting Catholic

[1] For details, see *Other Schools and Ours*, p. 81.

schools. The see-saw has been complicated by the loose identification of Catholicism with the Flemish-speaking northern population (more agricultural and maritime), and of secular partisanship with the French-speaking Walloons of the south, where most of the mines and manu-facturing towns are. Bitterness is often intense, and the by-play of the schools problem is constantly felt throughout the whole of political and social life.

In France, the history of the post-revolutionary period has been similarly chequered, though if anything the rivalry is deeper and more widespread. It draws into itself considerations of politics, occupation, place of residence, and the like. *La question scolaire* more than any other single issue in France is diagnostic in determining ideology in the widest sense – and the 'schools question' means nothing more or less than whether Catholic schools shall receive financial support or not. For generations, republican governments have refused it; but since about 1954 a small amount of aid has been given directly or indirectly, chiefly the latter. It never amounted to more than 10 per cent. of the costs before 1960.[1] The immediate self-alignment of French Catholics with a whole set of purely French partisan attitudes (almost as though these were part of the very essence of being Catholic) shows once again how thoroughly French Catholics, like French rationalists, are part of the culture in which they live – to such an extent that their reactions and priorities may seem utterly alien to their co-religionists in, say, Britain or the United States. Once more we are reminded that an inter-national phenomenon like a world faith (or even a more extensive world view like an ideology itself) defies proper consideration unless it is seen in the significance of the context in which it is being studied. French Catholic reactions are part of the history and institutions of France.

From the scholar's point of view no less than from that of the sectary, therefore, the identification of familiar names and apparently familiar events in other countries with what seem to be their counterparts at home may be most misleading. Such identification would be risky in

---

[1] According to the as yet unimplemented bill of 31 December 1959 (the outcome of the Lapie Commission), three new relationships between private (Church) schools and the French state are envisaged for the future:

    (*a*) the integration into the state system of private establishments which wish for it;

    (*b*) a contract of association giving full or partial financial support for such classes or courses as conform to the rules laid down for public education, with similar possi-bilities for the teachers;

    (*c*) more flexible arrangements for partial co-operation with the state, and smaller amounts of aid in proportion.

any case; but with the rapid social and ideological changes of recent years the risks are greater still. It has frequently happened, for example, that temporary exiles returning to their homeland after an absence of perhaps ten years during the post-war period have been astounded by changes in the climate of opinion in the land of their birth – and that often without any overt re-shuffling of interests and politics. Italy in the 1950s is a case in point. Such change is sometimes attributable to an alienation of sympathy for the elders on the part of young post-war adults or adolescents; sometimes it is due to increased purchasing power and more inviting prospects; sometimes there has been profound political change; more often the alteration cannot easily be ascribed to any one cause or cluster of causes. But the ideology has clearly shifted, and with it the whole educational emphasis. Thus we see that comparisons along a time-scale can be just as important as those made internationally.

One expedient for cutting the Gordian knot of ideological and sectarian wrangling is for governments to preserve a neutral status in relation to it. At least, 'neutral' is what the status is called by its advocates; yet we have seen that such a stand is a positive rather than a strictly neutral one – positive, in the sense of negating the claims of some others. That is one reason why in France and Belgium and parts of Australia the 'secularists' who want impartial public schools are so strongly attacked by Roman Catholics. The French revolutionary slogan 'Education is a function of the state' is bound to be objectionable to a church which feels conscious of a mission to teach all nations. None the less, government after government coming to responsibility for setting up public school systems has adopted an inter-sectarian and inter-partisan position – not strictly negating any point of view, but not supporting any. To uphold this position it is not necessary to claim a teaching function for the state as such. The obvious example of this is India. The Indians are a very religious nation; their whole way of life rather than their faith or observance can be described as Hinduism, which is the allegiance of some 85 per cent. of their population. Some 10 per cent. are Muslims, and the rest belong to minority faiths. Yet it has been decided that all public schools and all functions of the government shall be secular. Religious schools are not forbidden, however. Some attendant complications were reviewed on page 112.

In the Soviet Union and nearly all communist countries, religious schools of all complexions are strictly forbidden.[1] Also forbidden are

---

[1] In Czechoslovakia and Poland, at the time of writing, religious instruction may be given by priests (who are paid) to children attending the otherwise secular schools, but

other kinds of private school, with the limited exception that in certain cases seminaries for adults are permitted to prepare candidates for the priesthood. This embargo clearly has an ideological basis. In some other countries restrictions or an embargo are sometimes placed on religious schools, not exclusively for the obvious reason but because these must usually charge fees to maintain themselves. This financial difference may mean that such schools will then attract the children of the well-to-do to a privileged future which correspondingly shackles other children. Alternatively, it may mean that shortage of funds and other embarrassments may make the religious schools very much worse in quality than their publicly supported counterparts. (Both extremes are true in different places.) A secular, neutral solution commends itself to many fair-minded people in these circumstances; but we should not be so naïve as to suppose that that is all there is to it. Sometimes a 'government take-over' is a thinly disguised sectarian or partisan take-over, as may well be the case in Ceylon in the present phase of identifying Buddhism with Ceylon nationalism. To tell religious schools that they can still be independent if they do not charge fees may be egalitarian, and may be a desirable manœuvre on other grounds; but no one can pretend that it is not tantamount to an embargo on them.

How do state intervention and control come to be welcomed? People with plenty to eat feel a peculiar horror at the idea of rationing. People with too little to eat will welcome rationing if they think a more equitable distribution will result, as usually happens if the rationing is both realistic and efficient and there is enough of the basic commodities to go round. In times of real emergency the ensurement of this basic supply may have to be undertaken by government agencies or some other centralized board; mere chance and speculation are inadequate. All these considerations have a special relevance to education in the modern world. Nations are nearly all convinced of the need for public education in much the same way as all are convinced of the need for public health and a prosperous economy. They cannot afford not to have it; yet they are unable to ensure it on a purely localized basis. By its very essence, it has to be everywhere to be effective anywhere. Therefore in varying degrees nations secure the basic supply of education by regulating it. Just as governments pass pure food laws, securing

only if parents expressly ask for it. All kinds of difficulties and discouragements may be put in the way, however; and even in these traditionally Catholic countries the number of clergy available is now too small for widespread instruction of this kind. Facilities for Sunday schools and the like continue to exist in the countries named – outside the official school provision. In other communist countries they may be forbidden altogether.

certain basic minima without actually telling people what pure food to eat, so many of them reserve the right to inspect all schools, whether private or not. In Britain this right was confirmed by legislation in 1944, but was not exercised until after 1957. Even in the absence of such inspection, independent schools may be required to register themselves with the education authorities (as in Britain).

The next stage comes when all teachers too (like all medical practitioners, midwives, and pharmacists) are required in the public interest to be registered. In certain cases, specified minima of training and skill may be demanded – at least for service in the publicly provided schools, though educational and professional standards are not always scrutinized for employment in private schools. In nearly all states of the United States, in France, and many other countries, unqualified persons are not allowed to teach in the publicly provided schools, though a blind eye is turned towards the private sector. In Britain there are a few unqualified teachers in the publicly maintained schools also, and many university graduates lacking the formal training as teachers which is a prerequisite for recognition in some parts of the world.[1]

Naturally, such control over the standards and efficiency of teachers is more easily exercised where there is some or complete financial support for the schools. That is not, however, the only mechanism for ensuring compliance. In France, for example, though there is no scrutiny (except on moral grounds, &c.) of teachers in unaided schools, the state has a monopoly of important public examinations. To approach any career in public employment, which covers a large field in France, the possession of a recognizable qualification is imperative; the higher one climbs, the more important this becomes. Thus the Catholic schools, for a long time unaided, have nevertheless closely approximated to the state schools in curriculum and orientation, so that comparable standards could be achieved by the somewhat smaller proportion of their pupils entering for the state competitive examinations. Moreover, the social *cachet* conferred by these examinations is considerable. The state's supervisory influence thus extends informally beyond the boundaries of its own preserve.

It is well known that the French administrative pattern in education and other state matters is pre-eminently the example of government-based centralized control. The Minister of Education will usually be changed with every succeeding government; but his permanent officials maintain a steadfast direction of the rationale, content, and practice of

[1] See p. 210 and footnote on p. 226.

French schooling from the pre-primary phase to the postgraduate field. Its efficiency, within its terms of reference, is a world-wide example, though a good deal of inflexibility or unadaptability has been criticized in recent years.

However, this fault may be attributable to an underlying and characteristically French philosophy, which suggests that true 'culture' must be always and everywhere the same. Thus deviation from the norm or from traditions may be regarded pedagogically with much the same revulsion as the faithful feel against heresy. Despite the diehards, some very significant stirrings of change in orientation and application have been noticeable in the post-war years; but a much greater sense of danger is felt in all experimentation if this implicitly commits the whole apparatus of the public system. Radical self-justification may therefore be demanded of such experiments before they are approved, instead of the interim workability which would satisfy less rigidly organized countries. It would not be so bad if the state system regarded itself merely as a basic purveyor under a scheme of rationing – a device for guaranteeing minimum standards and efficiency everywhere. But the French labour under the incubus of having a secular 'teaching state' always on guard against being untrue to itself or assailed by the armoury of the teaching Church outside.

All teachers and administrators in the French system of public education are civil servants. As public employees they can be sent where they are needed, though primary school teachers are recruited and engaged on the local basis of the *département* (more or less equivalent to a county). In consequence, the standards throughout France and the French Community are uniform wherever possible, though there is undoubtedly a gravitation of the best towards the centre. For centuries the attraction of Paris as a lodestone has been a feature of French life. Inversely, this phenomenon tempts all administrators to measure provincial needs and the needs of the ignoramus by the criteria of that aristocracy of the intellect now deemed to be truest to the spirit of France. In the long run, as we have seen, to give everyone the same treatment is not the same thing as giving them fair and equal treatment.

Geographical and similar difficulties in ensuring a fair supply of education have however caused many countries to admire the centralized efficiency of the French dispensation. Perhaps the most telling testimony comes from Australia and parts of Canada, where it might have been expected that the decentralized traditions of government brought from the home country would have been accentuated by the centrifugal emotions of emigrants. This certainly happened in the United States, for example, and thus might have been looked for in Canada. Instead, the difficulty of ensuring equal opportunity and standards has caused reliance to be placed on centralized direction within each autonomous province. In Canada (for example, in British Columbia) particular items of knowledge are expected to be covered in particular 'grades'. Pupils are not supposed to pass upwards from one grade to another until the requirements have been fulfilled. (Such conditional promotion has, of course, been characteristic of many European countries. It persists in Holland and the Soviet Union now, for example; and it is really implied in the now less familiar term 'standard', used as synonymous with 'class' or 'form'.) Recommended approaches to the various items of the curriculum are also a feature of such centralized systems. Sometimes the 'advice' given to teachers is felt to be mandatory, in so far as inspectors look for its fulfilment.

In Canadian provinces a certain amount of centralized recruitment of teachers is undertaken, particularly when immigrant teachers are sought in Britain. The various courses and approved grades of teachers are normally decided in each provincial capital, as are the prerequisite courses of study leading to such recognition. But as a rule the different school districts or cities within a province undertake their own teacher-hunting campaigns, vying with each other (if necessary) in offering higher salaries or 'teacherages', as school houses are unfortunately named. This competition sometimes nullifies the intention behind the centralized provincial administration of the curriculum.

Probably to avoid difficulties of this sort, the usual practice in Australia is to recruit teachers as civil servants of the particular state in which they work; to require them (wherever possible or necessary) to work in less favoured districts as part of their professional experience; and to plan promotions in such a way that, for example, a first principalship may be offered in the 'outback'. The acceptance of a less popular assignment may be a condition of ever receiving any urban or metropolitan offer in future. The difficulty of providing teachers or indeed more spasmodic instruction for children in the remoter areas makes it more necessary than ever to keep a close eye on the progress of education; for the supplement offered in correspondence courses and broadcast lessons depends for its effectiveness on comparability of standard in different places at one and the same time.

Other considerations too influence administrators towards centralization. The unequal financial resources of different districts and indeed the locally varied fertility of parents in relation to resources both make some sort of levelling-up necessary. This did not take place in Britain until 1948, and educational expenditure is still uneven in many respects. States in the U.S.A. have attempted some equalization within themselves, not always successfully; but equalization as between the states is so far non-existent, despite increasingly generous Federal aid for the stimulation of bright children and unpopular but nationally important subjects like mathematics and physics.[1] Yet another factor in countries with a large immigrant population is the need to assimilate new citizens, who would certainly be deprived of first-class opportunities if their approach to the schools were commensurate only with their parents' resources or their understanding of what educational opportunity in their adopted country meant. The comparative ineffectiveness of home demand or of local stimuli makes school boards more keenly concerned to keep standards up – which all makes for centralization.

We have already had occasion to remark that an ostensibly decentralized system like that in the United States may, within each decentralized unit, exercise a very tightly co-ordinated control over the appointment of its teachers, their work, and the schooling available to the children. Some of these units within the United States are more populous than European countries which Americans sometimes criticize for centralization. Yet this may be less coercive than what the Americans can see operating in a number of their own cities. Likewise, the governmental responsibilities of the London County Council are on the domestic side greater than those of some whole countries. Its problems in the engagement of teachers are therefore comparable; but in accordance with the English tradition there is no direction of studies, and the head teachers of schools exercise an autonomy which is not matched in the publicly maintained schools anywhere outside Britain.

Another aspect of the devolution of responsibility not often touched on in this connexion is the varying degree of parental choice. Parents in the United States have a great say in the running of their public schools, both through the elected school boards and by representations to the teachers themselves. Most American teachers from time to time feel parental intrusions to be a headache, if not misguided interference; but the 'grass roots' tradition is so strong that political liberty seems to be assailed when educators ask to be allowed to carry on their own business. In Britain, county councils and education committees are power-

---

[1] President Kennedy's 1961 programme, and President Eisenhower's National Defence Education Act, are examples of this aid.

ful democratic instruments sometimes reacting sensitively to electoral pressure. Parent–teacher associations on the American model are not always found in Britain, and seldom display the same exuberant sense of being a group in control; but at one remove an important localized influence may be felt in Britain in the activities of schools' boards of governors, which are usually made up of nominated representatives of various elected or locally rooted official bodies. Few other countries outside Scandinavia have proceeded so far with 'watchdog' committees connected with schools. Many of those introduced in other countries during the post-war period have little more than potential influence.[1]

It will be seen that all the examples of state intervention and centralization considered towards the end of this chapter have arisen not strictly because of ideological reasons at all but because of administrative necessity in the interests of efficiency and fairness. These basic necessities of a civilized way of life must obviously come into conflict here and there with the time-honoured and sometimes very honourable institutions bequeathed to modern times. More often than not such clashes are caused by differences of idiom or clientèle rather than by onslaughts on the central ideology of the older system.

Friction can arise, however, between apparently homogeneous ideologies. For example, the very Christian Commonwealth of Pennsylvania annually finds itself in conflict with some of its most conspicuously Christian citizens, namely the Amish sect. This denomination, fundamentalist in Scriptural interpretation, considers that compulsory school attendance until the age of sixteen violates parental choice and does harm to the Amish way of life, which is describable as a preindustrial one. Particularly sensitive to parental and sectarian representations though American officials usually are, they nevertheless in this and comparable cases feel justified in deciding that the children's ultimate interest and their own proper interest in public education entitle them to impose compulsion. To a greater or lesser degree problems of this sort recur wherever public instruction is offered. The solutions imposed or agreed upon mark the steady evolution of a newer ideology, taking account not only of traditional faith and mores but of the integral adaptation of these to the reality of modern circumstances.

[1] It is worth placing on record that teachers in centralized systems sometimes declare that there are compensations for the formal officiousness of control from above. They list the following 'freedoms':
  (a) from the shortcomings of autonomous principals;
  (b) from the dictation of local superintendents eager to be noticed;
  (c) from the interference of local pressure groups.

We return a little closer to the ideological field when we see how expanding concepts of education (for example, insistence on a proper follow-up in vocational guidance or some kinds of youth work) may extend beyond the view of education hitherto familiar to Churches, private schools, or other voluntary organizations. It may be necessary in such cases for the public education authorities to give direction, or to bring about liaison with employers, non-scholastic enterprises, and the like. Similarly, new concepts and opportunities in the care of neglected or handicapped children may make demands beyond the resources or awareness of hitherto exemplary charitable organizations. All kinds of unexpected supplement may be called for by industrial and social developments. In all such instances it would be unfair to stigmatize what has happened as 'state interference'. It would be fairer to say that an almost autonomous growth of the concept of education in relation to expanding opportunities demands a better deal for children than that which had been tolerated under the older ideology.

In long-established societies reacting peacefully to change or challenge, such differences of pace and interest are peripheral rather than of the essence of the matter – unless, as in France, a whole concatenation of entanglements is involved as soon as any reform is suggested. But in societies which have lagged behind the progress of the West (not necessarily through any fault of their own) impatience or destitution makes it seem inevitable that total planning shall be effected. Then at once the basic questions about education and its function in society are urgently asked. They cannot be asked as in a philosophical discussion, either. They are inseparable from economic development, political education, and so forth. This is clearly the situation in most African states. In the absence of alternative educative institutions powerful or discerning enough to help at the pace required, the state must understandably take the lead. Thus in some countries (like Iraq) we find a 'Ministry of Guidance'. Ill-omened though such names sound to us, they are only to be expected in the state of their countries' development. 'Guided democracy' too may be better than no democracy at all, and at any rate better than the chaos which makes totalitarianism more patently a possibility than ever.

In any case, all industrial and commercial organizations in every country have undergone a very rapid process of centralization and rationalization from about 1875 onwards. The number of individually run shops, factories, and the like diminishes yearly; similarly the number of separate labour organizations dwindles as they are absorbed into larger amalgamations. Most of the apparently independent enterprises are so closely associated in interest if not in direction that one may properly speak of them as closely co-ordinated. Not only does this change in itself cause administrative thought to be more consistently centralized; it also reinforces the trend towards centralization because of two changes in the career prospects of our leading men and women. These tend to be 'managers' rather than owners or otherwise endowed with a private interest; secondly, they tend to see their careers in national if not international terms. Thus people who a few generations ago might have been expected to be powerful local worthies with deep roots somewhere now move around more during their careers. They cannot so readily be expected to exercise local and parochial control over public concerns like education. Even if they are localized, they are probably distracted by membership of many other committees already. Many of them are 'commuters', living in a dormitory suburb, shopping in other places, doing their business and finding many of their amusements in still other centres. Their children more often go away to nationally recruited institutions like prestige schools, colleges, and universities. More rather than less centralization of thought, planning, and control therefore seems inevitable.

The risks and promises inherent in any educational activity demand unquestionably that teachers should see their daily work as taking place within the framework of an ideology, whether they are conscious participants in it or pawns. If they allow themselves to drift, doing faithfully what other people before them or now have suggested, they simply reinforce an ideology without questioning it. That ideology may have been a great civilizing influence. It may be one now; but on the other hand it may simply be a sort of automatism arising out of the convenience of particular methods of administration, or of supplying particular kinds of textbooks, or of communicating through some mass agency. The slightest sense of responsibility in their vocation should make all teachers the opposite of docile. They must at all costs avoid automatism, either personal or public.

In this chapter we have reviewed very superficially two great ideological systems and sketched in a third possibility. The two major ideologies are those of unquestioning religious orthodoxy and of equally devoted submission to the totalitarian controls which are simultaneously more powerful and easier to slip into. The suppositions which people in Western democracies take for granted have had a very short life in human thinking, and are still undergoing imperfect experimentation.

If they are worth safeguarding, and if we think they can contribute significantly to life in old and newly developed countries, then we must work with the same positive commitment to them that other teachers show in other ideological systems. For we represent not a dilettantism or dallying with both; we stand for a 'third way' because of the simple fact that we question the total veracity of the other two ideologists. We try to make understanding grow by encouraging multiple, diverse, and responsible contributions to it. We consider a harmony of personal responsibility and social evolution to be the creative principle in all human development. It is the key to understanding.

Not only for this reason, but also in the hope of achieving objectivity in ourselves and fuller scope for our children, we must not merely note that 'ideology' exists as a force in *all* thinking; we must constantly try to disentangle the constituent parts of our own. Then we can choose and help to shape futures. We shall be not only better educators, but better educated too.

BOOKS

See the general bibliography on Comparative Education, p. 369.
See also the *Year Book of Education* for 1957, London (Evans Bros) and New York (World Book Company).
Mannheim, K., *Ideology and Utopia* (London and New York), 1936.
Mannheim, K., *Freedom, Power, and Democratic Planning* (London), 1951.
Stark, W., *The Sociology of Knowledge* (London), 1958.

Philosophy, psychology, and programmes

On Marx's tomb in a London cemetery are carved his words: 'Philosophers have only interpreted the world in various ways; but the real task is to alter it.'[1] He succeeded more than he realized.

So much stress has been placed in this book on environmentally influenced perception that philosophy as such has not so far been fairly dealt with; nor has psychology in its conventional textbook guise as a study of individual mental activity. Indeed, the word 'psychology' has hardly been used – not because it is a naughty word itself but because it is so often naughtily used to mislead its users and hearers. In fact, a great deal of attention has been given already to social psychology, though not under that name. Likewise, the familiar concerns of social philosophy have been reviewed almost *ad nauseam*, if not under textbook headings. The excuse for this omission must be that academic people all too often practise their exercises as though they had sprung to their present position like Athene from the mind of Zeus – unengendered by this world, uninvolved in it now, and not earthbound in their future. Such lack of realism is always dangerous, and particularly in connexion with education – a specially potent instrument for altering the world.

Reinforcement of what has already been said about ideas and involvement on pages 231 and 233 may be found in a quotation from Bertrand Russell:

Subjectively, every philosopher appears to himself to be engaged in the pursuit of something which may be called 'truth'. Philosophers may differ as to the definition of 'truth', but at any rate it is something objective, something which, in some sense, everybody ought to accept. No man would engage in the pursuit of philosophy if he thought that *all* philosophy is *merely* an expression of irrational bias. But every philosopher will agree that many other philosophers have

---

[1] Marx, K., *Eleven Theses on Feuerbach*, 1845.

been actuated by bias, and have had extra-rational reasons, of which they were usually unconscious, for many of their opinions.

He goes on to say, speaking of Marx's notions of economically-determined ideology: 'Marx, like the rest, believes in the truth of his own doctrines; he does not regard them as nothing but an expression of the feelings natural to a rebellious middle-class German Jew in the middle of the nineteenth century.' [1]

One of the harshest disagreements between communist Russia and communist China turns on this very point. The Chinese insist on regarding the Marxist-Leninist scriptures as gospel, now and forever. The Russians know only too well that Marx and Lenin themselves saw with the eyes of their times; they preached in the idiom of their times. Their very words and programmes have since helped to change the world out of recognition. When they spoke about propaganda, coercion, and war they did not speak in terms of modern methods of communication, control, or destruction. So both their subjective entanglement and the objective change of events have flawed the supposedly universal applicability of their philosophies. If it comes to that, Marx and his contemporaries could hardly have envisaged their manifestoes in terms of applying them to the Tsarist Empire itself, which seemed too unready and underdeveloped. They thought of Britain and Germany as ripe for communism. Still less could they have foreseen the emergence of underdeveloped and often ex-colonial sovereign nations in Asia, Africa, and the Americas - even though they dreamed of the final vindication of communism in ostensibly global terms.

That is why it is so important not merely to give the fullest consideration to the worldly entanglements of an ideology, but also to use what I have called a 'three-tier analysis' on all philosophical arguments (p. 48). Even when soaring in the philosopher's heaven we should see that a philosophy must be examined (*a*) as a principle, (*b*) as a set of corollaries or deductions, (*c*) as a working guide for practical programmes in one or more particular contexts. There is no wish in this chapter to suggest that absurd conclusions are bound to be revealed by using applicability as a touchstone for most theories; but if absurdity is made manifest, it is well out of the way. If, however, the metaphysical philosopher's stone turns base matter to living gold, so much the better. The first hunch or central principle of a philosophy then obviously has a promising future. What educators must look for is a philosophy with

---

[1] Russell, B., *History of Western Philosophy*, London (Allen & Unwin), 1946, p. 813.

a future, a philosophy that comes down to earth. All philosophers should think of their words in terms of programmes.

This is, of course, what all teachers and students demand of Education lecturers – and what they do not always get. Undoubtedly those who prepare and counsel teachers should be down-to-earth in terms of good experience and homely communication; but that is not the same as asking for everything to be spelt out in simple rules-of-thumb. The whole point of the three-tier analysis recommended above is that the working examination of philosophies must be done empirically by the practising teacher no less than by supposed philosophers – and that not only in the classroom but in the self-unfolding of the teacher referred to earlier (pp. 226–7).

Such a day-to-day examination of conscience or study of perspective is impossible unless the teacher himself has had professional education – and not just training. One of the most astonishing illustrations that this does not always happen was given by the supposedly successful principal of a large American high school attending one of the author's courses at a distinguished American university. She defended the teachers' college which she had attended more than thirty years before by saying that in all her teaching and administrative experience she had never encountered a situation for which she had not had a practical preparation in college! 'Teacher education' in her case had not added up to much more than circus training for a static world of nearly identical people, such as existed only in her unaroused imagination.

Naturally, the young teacher or student wants a working guide at first. There is no harm in that, any more than in the very proper longing of a learner-driver for the time when driving 'comes naturally'. Then a routine of ordinary control has become so well established that it seems almost effortless. So it is with all activity skills. Much initiation of this kind can be given to the beginner by experienced teachers, whose daily practice keeps them more in touch with 'the tricks of the trade' than university and college lecturers can be. A certain amount of this kind of apprenticeship is good for young teachers until they develop sufficient skill and competence to express their own personalities and that creative distinctiveness referred to earlier. At this point they depart from 'tricks of the trade' far enough to wonder if the tricks are worth doing after all, or whether the trade envisaged by the old hands is quite appropriate either to the young people or to the world they are in. Teaching is not an expertise, when all is said and done, though expertise of course enters into it. It is a personally exacting profession. It may also be the embodiment of a philosophy-in-action such as Marx looked for – one that will help the world to change for the better.

Obviously, such an educative development in the teacher himself does not happen easily or quickly in the best of circumstances. Circumstances are far from being always at their best, especially where school systems are being rapidly built up, or before they are developed to full stature. In the latter case, the teacher is still often under someone else's thumb.[1] In the former, quick results are demanded with maximum economy; therefore detailed instructions and curricula are mass-produced, from which teachers depart at their peril. Some of these are farcical and degrading. Fortunately, most school systems are well above this level, though not all are. On the other hand, many subjects or items of behaviour all too quickly become canonical, and thus beyond question. Some of these have survived within living memory in our own countries: copper-plate handwriting; spelling perfectly rather than writing creatively (teachers knew how to spell, but not how to create!); sitting with hands folded or clasped (as in many countries now); learning all the rivers and ports by heart, in order. To abandon each one of these things meant lowering the flag; but why not? A braver flag was ready. Yet the decision to change allegiance was a difficult one for many people, because it entailed that most difficult of exercises – standing back and seeing oneself in context.

This solitary exercise is pre-eminently a crisis where the philosopher can be of help. His work is one of analysis and evaluation. The various ingredients in a situation are distinguished so that the principles can be seen. The claims and counterclaims can be disentangled; the priorities are set in some sort of generally agreed order; and the judgments of leading thinkers on general principles are compared. But the final judgement and application must be personal. By abstracting the essence of a problem from its particulars, philosophy can help those facing a problem to see that they are not alone in their dilemma, but may be helped by the experiments and perspectives of others who have had similar difficulties elsewhere. Thus it is a sort of shorthand or symbolism; but by that very token it cannot be a practical do-it-yourself kit with full instructions, any more than an algebraic or physical formula is so many apples and pears. The translation of theory into programmes, and of programmes into practical achievements, must always be an intimate adjustment. Like other intimacies, it is a two-way experience.

[1] See Tropp, A., *The School Teachers* (Heinemann, London), 1957, especially chapters 1–3.

Unfortunately, 'principles of education' (or the equivalent under different names) are sometimes in some teachers' colleges ostensibly brought to their classroom application in a way that reduces the lecturer and the trainees to the circus level. 'General principles of classroom administration'; 'principles of teaching English' (or some other subject); 'principles of parent-teacher relationship' – all these courses and hundreds like them are the main fare in the worse kind of American teachers' college. To be sure, the better kind of college eliminates this sort of hack-work or reduces it to a minimum; but such a decision is not easy when so much weight is attached to the principle of student choice or to courses made to suit the quality of students actually enrolled. Any teachers' college worth its salt offsets its 'how to do it' courses with others which might be categorized as 'why?' courses, or 'to whom?' or even 'why bother?'

However, young teachers and students often find it easier to lap things up than to think about themselves and their surroundings critically. They are thus equivalent to the worshippers of copper-plate handwriting brought up to date. Fortunately, teacher training colleges in Britain and the more estimable in the United States acknowledge that any interpretation of 'principles' as 'rules of thumb' must be discarded. They recognize in their curricula that the illustration of 'principles behind the practice' is really an attempt to examine personal and social fundamentals. There is no real dichotomy between being 'good at teaching' and being 'a good educator'; the aspects are complementary.

So the principles must always be sought behind the practice. In recent years some excellent work has been done in showing the profile of philosophical implications behind some ordinary classroom routine or teaching activity. It is inappropriate to re-cover that ground here. Readers are referred instead to R. L. Brackenbury's amusing and perceptive *Getting Down to Cases*, New York (Putnam), 1959. But it is worth our while to reflect in passing that in the long run whatever we do as teachers or parents or ordinary people probably fits in with a whole set of personal attitudes and perspectives, if we are mentally and morally sound. (Otherwise, instead of possessing a reasonably harmonious 'self' we are tricked out in second-hand attitudes that do not match each other, and may make us a playground for conflicting ideologies.) Unconsidered words and preferences will always 'touch off', even if they do not overtly reveal, our psychological and philosophical patterns of association.

In these circumstances the only real way in which we can hope to remain free and responsible agents instead of mere indices of social causation is to try to detach ourselves reflectively. We can return to the words of Lord Russell quoted at the beginning of this chapter: 'No man would engage in the pursuit of philosophy if he thought that *all* philosophy is *merely* an expression of irrational bias.' Our lives, thoughts, and values are not *all* so much social causation; neither are they self-evident. But we do need to check on our philosophical involvement so that our 'free conscience' and consciousness of 'self' can be at least nearly free, and so that our children can continue to grow.

A first step in the examination of philosophical implications for education should be to understand something of the main schools of thought whose deliberations or manifestoes have had direct application to school organization and practice. We should compare them for their direct influence, and also look for indirect implications. For a quick and reliable summary it would be hard to beat *Education and the Philosophic Mind*, edited by A. V. Judges, London (Harrap), 1957. The essays in that book were contributed by scholars not only expert in the various philosophical and psychological fields surveyed but able to illustrate them sympathetically.[1]

In the portrayal of a philosophical or psychological system it is of prime importance to communicate at least some of the emotional complex surrounding it. Without doing so, we cannot see the logical outcome or at any rate the empirical outcome of it. Let us take a very simple example. If we reflect on the Aristotelian basis for social philosophy 'Equal treatment in equal circumstances' and its corollary 'Special consideration in special circumstances', we can hardly be said to appreciate what is involved unless we also think not only of *institutions* but of *emotions* too. Such institutions include the jury system and ration books, which embody the first principle; an appropriate emotion for the second is the shock we feel if children or old ladies are made to struggle for places in a bus queue, being refused the generosity to which their weaker state is believed to entitle them. To a much greater degree the faithful adherent of a supernatural ideology feels shock and sickness at sin or apostasy. Thus institutions and emotions are alike teaching instruments for our philosophy, as well as the results of it. Of course, we must 'bring philosophy down to earth' not only in such homely and familiar examples but (if possible) in universal per-

[1] The *Year Book of Education* for 1957, London (Evans Bros), surveys Philosophy and Education internationally.

spective. After all, one essential feature of social justice is that judgements must be universally applicable to similar circumstances. How does our philosophy affect mankind?

It will be advisable to ask ourselves what impact the main schools of philosophy have made on those thinking about schools. There will be no attempt here to summarize *Education and the Philosophic Mind*; but for the sake of fuller comprehension the systems of thought described there, and several others, will be set out briefly in their family relationships. This lining-up for comparison makes it easier to see what sort of travelling companions we find ourselves with in our various philosophical pilgrimages. We must suspect them. Some paragons of logic ask us to 'clear our minds' (whatever that means!). Others put a great deal of stress on such abstractions as 'conceptual thinking'. But unless 'conceptual thinking' and the like are primarily thought of as 'short-cut' devices like mathematical symbols, we run the risk of trapping ourselves in our own inventions. As Professor M. V. C. Jeffreys has said: 'Some kinds of truth have to be *lived into* and not only *thought into*.'[1] One might go further and say that some theoretical notions are not perceived in their fullness until we try to bring them to fruition in experiments, institutions, and emotions. Whether 'truth' and 'absolutes' exist or not, it is certain that our approach to them is that of very earthly human beings. It is equally true that any mistakes we make will be revealed by their unwelcome impact on other human beings.

For our convenience in this book the main philosophies affecting educational attitudes may be grouped under four headings:

(*a*) revelation and 'supernatural' philosophy, which may however be reinforced by natural inquiry;

(*b*) rationalism, or access to perfection by the use of the mind;

(*c*) philosophies of experience; and

(*d*) philosophies based upon scientific or historical 'laws'.

We should note at the outset that there may be considerable overlap between these categories, because some philosophies appear to owe allegiance to more than one. We should also note that most of the philosophical systems have been evolved with adult men and women in mind. We must therefore ask ourselves throughout if any special modification or examination is demanded because we are considering them with reference to young children and their futures.

The force of conclusions drawn from *revelation* can be seen most

[1] *Education and the Philosophic Mind*, ed. A. V. Judges, London (Harrap), 1957, p. 70.

familiarly in Christian theology. God is all perfection, infinite, ever-lasting, everywhere; God is the first cause, and the end. Man (since Adam) is a flawed reflection of his Creator, whom he can never know properly in this life; he is the bearer of immortal possibilities through the unfortunate entanglements of the world and of his own being; he can attain the blessed vision of God only by curbing himself at least to some degree, so that his final redemption depends on the submergence of his will and reason for the acceptance of the external, eternal light. Each human being, despite profound and perhaps ineradicable in-equalities, has access to God's light, love, and mercy. In some churches these are felt to come direct; in others they are considered to depend mainly (or ultimately) upon the mediation of the Church itself through particular observances or beliefs. In some churches, again, a refusal to comply with the latter is as final a barrier to the divine embrace as are infractions of the ten commandments. Subject to these variations, the Faith (a revealing word!) is of universal validity. Its fulfilment in the Kingdom of God can never be achieved in this imperfect world, but only after death. This summary, I believe, is a fair representation of Christian principles as they relate to human access to truth and per-fection. Though churches manifestly differ greatly in the amount of emphasis they place on evil and on the implicit condemnation of the human status contained in the very word 'redemption', their differ-ences over the points summarized above are mainly a matter of degree.

The spokesmen of the Christian churches have from time to time been in disagreement about how far all men (in Adam) have fallen from grace and divine wisdom. But since the thirteenth century it has never been widely felt that faith and reason must always be irreconcil-able. St Thomas Aquinas (1225–74) thought that the 'natural law' discernible by human reason alone was in its most perfect state a lower manifestation of the divine law taught by the Catholic Church. There-fore, there need be no conflict between them. Since his time much attention has been paid by churchmen to the task of reasoning out the faith, so as to convince the believer more fully and to win over the un-believer. At some stage, of course, 'the gift of faith' must be divinely bestowed; but the acknowledgement that the human mind (as distinct from the will) can be educated in its own 'natural' terms towards God is of profound significance.

These educational possibilities of the human reason were often con-sidered to need restriction to the already well initiated, or to future leaders of the 'Church militant', like those we encountered in the pre-revolutionary French colleges. For most ordinary people faith, trust, and good works sanctified by the ministrations of the Church would be sufficient. This latter approach is education by habituation – a potent force in many Roman Catholic, Islamic, and Buddhist countries, and surviving in some vigour in the religious aspect of British 'character training'.

We shall later return to some of the consequences of combining such a 'world view' with that of Plato; but for convenience we can temporarily omit this consideration in favour of another important aspect, namely that of *renunciation*. If much emphasis is placed on the fallen state of mankind (or in other faiths on our entanglement with material concerns), then it follows that education in spirituality depends upon catharsis, or the rejection of some of our human endowment. 'The devil, the world, and the flesh' are then enemies of the soul.

Consequently whatever is being educated is really part of the soul; and in so far as anything else is being schooled, it is being weaned from its 'natural inclinations'. There will probably need to be coercion of some sort – perhaps external (such as the threat of excommunication from the Church, or punishment, or 'authority'). Alternatively, coercion may be internalized (in the form of asceticism, dedication to duty, and the like). The expression 'self-denial' should be carefully pondered over. The sense of an ever-present risk to salvation often haunts those who cherish such attitudes. To avoid this risk, the Amish in North America and many members of the Dutch Reformed Church in South Africa shun industrialization or its consequences, finding the true embodiment of their faith in a pre-industrial, agrarian life. These are only extreme examples of a widespread and often unsuspected tendency. The virtues most prized according to this view are connected with self-effacement, like 'resignation', 'modesty', 'trust', and passive contemplativeness rather than pushful activity.

Such views are far from being confined to Christianity, much less to any one aspect of it. They are characteristic of many Eastern religions – not only of Buddhism and Islam already mentioned but of Confucianism and its derivatives. They are associated with 'mystery' religions like Orphism and Mithraism, and with some philosophies like Stoicism and certain aspects of Epicureanism. Job too said: 'The Lord hath given, the Lord hath taken away; blessed be the name of the Lord.' 'The body is a tomb (*sōma sēma*)' said one school of Greek poets. In times of particular crisis or upheaval, the sense of benightedness is strong. 'Hell is ever filling with these very souls' ran a once popular hymn. John

Wesley, in founding Kingswood School (which now excels at games), forbade the pupils any physical sports for fear they might idle or play the Devil's game. The Puritan ethos (or its equivalent in other religions) has usually been a stern, 'stiff upper lip' affair. If it has not been afraid to exercise the conscience freely, Puritanism has certainly suspected all things carnal.

In one way or another in different climes a 'renouncing' pattern of religious or near-religious thinking has limited educational interest in self-expression, ambition, and competitiveness. Christian Puritanism, for reasons soon to be given, was an exception in this last respect – at any rate in the sects which prospered through industrialization. An almost Carthusian self-enclosure is very often found, also reinforced by strict community rules. Such faiths and ways of life have tended to neglect or think little of material and social improvements, though this latter kind of neglect was often tempered by the virtue of 'mercy' – a more familiar notion than earthly justice. Authorities have included mystics or those learned in 'the Law', rather than those given to systematic inquiries about justice and humaneness. Moreover, in many Eastern countries today the familiar assumptions made in Northern Europe and the U.S.A. about the claims of personality and learning are considered to be quite strange, not only because of a different order of values but also because of different ideas about 'personality'. My 'self' may be seen as part of a 'world soul', or part of an eternally reincarnated procession of souls, or simply as a status related to membership of a family. Thus our Western assumptions about unique personal responsibility, unique personal claims, ambitions, and self-fulfilment seem so much selfishness or misconception.

The implications for education of philosophies of *rationalism* (or access to perfection by the use of the mind) are more obvious and penetrating. Plato is usually considered to be the prime example. Probably more has been written about him or in consequence of him than about any other writer. That is one good reason for saying little about him here. As readable and efficient a summary of Plato's influence on education as could be required is Sir Charles Morris's essay in *Education and the Philosophic Mind*. There is, however, another reason for not attempting to survey Plato 'in one go' within the space available here: it is so hard to distinguish Plato the rationalist from Plato the aristocratic mystic. Much of the time, Plato writes as though knowledge were wisdom, and wisdom were virtue; but for much of the time too he appears to overlook reason in favour of education by habituation and character-forming discipline, or of educating the emotions. He also speaks of allegorical and myth-like communication between those who really perceive the truth and the purblind people below. Thus for our purposes it is more convenient here to by-pass the study of Plato proper, and to pay some attention instead to the different ways in which his implications have been worked out (a) in rationalism, and (b) in paternalism.

The clearest consequences of rationalism are seen in the manifestoes of the American and French revolutionaries. It is seldom recognized just how much the American declarations owed to the 'universalization' of British political principles in the secret salons of the French intelligentsia. Those gentlemanly plotters on the continent, unable to secure any foothold in France for British political practices or institutions, worked them over theoretically and generalized their applicability in world-wide terms. Though it is interesting to trace the lineage of some of those revolutionary ideas back to 'supernaturalist' sources, no divorce could be greater than that between the supernaturalist's 'Lord, I believe; help my unbelief' and the mentality of those rationalists who could say: 'We hold these truths to be self-evident'.[1] For St Thomas Aquinas 'It is clear that Natural Law is nothing else but the participation of the Eternal Law in rational creatures';[2] but many of the revolutionaries on both sides of the Atlantic were much more sure about the power of reason than about God's participation. The stress for them was placed on the limitless perfectibility of man through the mind. The perennial truths, the everlasting absolutes, the universally valid and inalienable rights were perceptible to everyone if his mind had been trained aright – no matter what his background or condition.

This view, that truth and intellectual certainty could be available at least to any well-trained person, was not a sudden or new idea, though it was striking in many of its conclusions. For example, as we have seen earlier, Socrates in Plato's dialogue *Meno* could draw geometrical truths out of the unlettered slave. St Thomas Aquinas himself said that 'even if we were to grant that God did not exist' the Natural Law (i.e. principles of justice discerned by reason alone) would retain its validity. What was revolutionary in the claims of the French *philosophes* was

[1] The American Declaration of 1776 and the French of 1789 are so close in conception and terminology that many phrases and ideas are interchangeable. Both also bear a remarkable likeness to Thomas Paine's *The Rights of Man*, published in 1791 but well known in essence before that date because of its author's political activity and pamphleteering.

[2] Aquinas, St Thomas: *Summa theologica*, 1a, 2ae; quae. 91, art. 2.

that 'the natural, inalienable and sacred Rights of Man' and all proper claims or complaints were 'based upon simple and indisputable principles'. 'Simple' said the Frenchmen; 'self-evident' said the Americans. That is to say, the ordinary citizen could see them.

Obviously, from Descartes (1595–1650) onwards the paramountcy of pure reason alone had been proclaimed; but for Descartes himself the base, animal side of human activity had seemed a drag on man's higher self. Plato some two thousand years before had been utterly convinced of the power of reason to see and interpret the essence of the good life; but such access to perfect understanding through knowledge and training depended on ascetic preparation. It was certainly not given to the despised commonalty. Even the future guardians of the commonwealth needed an arduous education, followed by a kind of spiritual retreat. After all that, they saw only as if seeing shadows. To guard against ultimate error, we are told at the end of the *Laws*, a nocturnal council must exercise a kind of censorship. This is privileged access to truth indeed.

That is why the French revolutionary declarations, though in some ways their educational conclusions owe much to Descartes and Plato, must be seen as opposed to Plato in some of their implications. At least the germ of perfect rationality is supposed to be found in every man. The French word 'perfectionner' is far more optimistic than the English word 'train', with its suggestion of limited skill imparted from without by a trainer. An exuberant optimism with regard to human perfectibility by the use of reason and education was widely shared in revolutionary France and America. Of course, many (like Thomas Jefferson) had doubts about how far this process could extend; but few doubted that it could be extended far beyond what had previously been thought possible. Many were prepared to believe that in this respect as in others 'all men are created equal'.

In understandable reaction against the excessive bookishness of the pre-revolutionary curriculum, the French *encyclopédistes* wanted to install an all-round learning which would include much useful science. Thus one of the most promising innovations of the revolutionary period in France was the establishment of the Central Schools. Unfortunately, these lasted only six years. The sort of science and applied learning looked forward to by Diderot and Condorcet soon faded out of the secondary schools, though they survived gloriously in French higher education. The reversion in the secondary schools was no doubt due in part to that 'absent-mindedness' of all institutions already discussed in earlier chapters; but it must also be attributed to the existing prestige traditions and to the absence of people able and willing to teach the new subjects. Napoleon's dispensation too in 1808 reinforced conservative influences in the matter of curriculum orientation, even though it broadened the basis of recruitment socially. Every boy's marshal's baton had to be won by dint of the time-honoured exercises in the classroom – the well-proved exercises in the great books, to sharpen the mind for mastery of those universal certainties which must always be the same.

Though it is obvious that Napoleon's centralized and almost military monopoly owed something to his personality, a great deal of centralization had already developed under Louis XIV, Louis XVI, and Cardinals Richelieu and Mazarin. But it was specially implied too in the ideological antecedents of contemporary educational philosophy. Neither the French revolutionaries nor Napoleon himself could be described as good Catholics; but for all that they were, so to speak, part of the Catholic 'stream of consciousness' in France. The Church claimed universality and infallibility of doctrine, with privileged access to truth intellectually, sacramentally, and morally. The system of values accepted by the Church was seen as a perennial if not static one. The supreme good was the highest spirituality. It is not altogether accidental that the good secular French for 'mind' is the same as the word for 'spirit'. It is as though the old ascetic disciplines for the soul have been appropriated to the 'perfecting' of the Republican mind. 'We are priests of the mind', says the secular teachers' spokesman.

In French circumstances it was easy to adopt or adapt approximately the same philosophical outlook either for schooling the mind or for saving the soul. It is all there either way: catholicity, infallibility, a hierarchical approach to true knowledge, the neglect if not the repudiation of the body and worldly sympathies, and the fierce struggle for salvation. Though at first Napoleon's system was not popularly dispensed to recruit the young of all classes, at least in his emotions and by implication the future *corps d'élite* might be recruited from the populace, in much the same way as cardinals could be recruited from behind the shop counter. Modern French education ostensibly offers equal opportunity to all classes in society, and all types of background (black or white or brown).

Unfortunately, as we have seen, an identical scholastic offering is certainly not an equal offering, if taken by itself. When the peasant and the African have to compete on identical terms with the child of the metropolis, there is no equality at all. Nor is there much possibility of evolution when all, peasant or African, in the eighteenth century or the twentieth, have their schooling devised in terms of an unchanging heritage of civilization – as though the outside world (outside the ivory towers, that is) were as uncontributory to humane understanding as Plato's 'money-grubbing mob' and Descartes' 'automata'.

The French curriculum looks very much like the 'humanistic' curriculum everywhere else in Latin countries. It also closely resembles that traditional in Germany and other continental countries. There is the same reliance on theory and 'pure' knowledge. The distinctive French ingredient is both philosophical and administrative at the same time. The French, at least in principle, acknowledge that all men and women in differing degrees can make their way to 'culture' by the same paths. They must therefore have the chance opened up to them. In keeping with this philosophical attitude, the French have devised a bureaucratically controlled competitive mechanism that on paper works perfectly and economically. It therefore commends itself to many impatient or rapidly emerging countries, as we have seen.

In all such organization, the most esteemed teachers are remote, Olympian exponents, having little or nothing to do with 'school life' as we understand the term, for that is practically non-existent. Order is usually kept by inferior assistants, who may also do the teacher's marking for him. The most successful teacher is the one most likely to leave his school and take up a university appointment. That is a common way of recruiting university teachers. Before actually securing a full-time university post, many a French *professeur agrégé* will find himself giving a part-time series in a university or in some teachers' training course. In France, Italy, and many Latin countries substantial additions can also be made to incomes by coaching assignments. In so far as these principles (if not the practice) are modified in the French system of education, that reform is being achieved at the cost of repudiating a revered intellectual tradition in favour of other considerations. In other words, the rationalist approach to education is being to that extent abandoned.

Belonging to the same general philosophical family, though looking different at first sight, are the *paternalistic* outlook of Thomas Jefferson during and after the American War of Independence, the British tradition of the Public School, and British imperial rule.[1] These too owe

[1] For a general review of British attitudes see R. Ulich, *The Education of Nations* (Harvard University Press), 1961, chapter 5, especially pp. 97 ff. See also *Other Schools*

much to Plato, with their ingredients of 'superior' classes, 'governing', and a generally condescending approach to the foibles if not the 'lack of breeding' shown by others. Once again we see that apparently chance words may be profoundly significant. 'Breeding' is ambiguous, as used in England, referring simultaneously to the activities of the stud and to those of the Public School – not the same thing at all. What may be called a Pindaric view of excellence, as something inherited and peculiar to the 'best' families, forms an inexplicable amalgam with the supposition that excellence is induced by participation in the best institutions (Public Schools, the older universities, and the right clubs or regiments).

Although until recently little regard was felt in Britain for intellectual eminence alone (indeed to be a 'swot' like a Frenchman, German, or scholarship boy was 'bad form'), nevertheless if intellectual eminence could somehow 'happen' to a pupil in combination with excellence on the playing field, it was rather a good thing in its way. (The past tense is used now, because the ever-increasing competition from grammar schools and technical colleges has caused all Public Schools to raise their sights academically.) According to the older view, academic excellence could be just one acceptable aspect of excellence of character. *That* is the main thing. Until the later 1920s and the early 1930s a surprising proportion of Public School boys did not go on to universities. They had no need for that to secure a good future. Therefore they did not feel outclassed by those who did carve out university careers.

Though such a lordly attitude does not look at all like intellectualism, in a way it is associated with it; for the patrician 'knows what's what'. He has had a 'liberal education' even if not through cerebration. He has grasped the great principles of the Classical tradition. He is aesthetically sensitive, appreciating Homer and Horace as well as the metric psalms and the Authorized Version of the New Testament. He is often distinguished by a sense of obligation, both towards the perennial, universal excellences and towards his fellow man, no matter how lowly. Though much frightful exploitation of underlings has gone on in British history, it has not strictly been attributable to the paternalistic ethos perpetuated in the Public Schools but rather to the surrounding social and economic structure. Within the schools' own purposes, philanthropy and patient condescension have been dominant – provided

and Ours, chapter 4, and my essay 'The gentleman: the evolution of an ideal' bound as an appendix in the present volume.

they were allowed to dominate, and not be subverted by malcontents who did not know their place.

This last proviso has always been the snag with any tradition of privileged access. It has been tacitly assumed that true refinement was the birthright of children born in the right families; yet, almost in contradiction of this view, the class system which allowed mercantile success to ennoble British entrepreneurs also allowed their sons to be made gentlemen by getting the right schooling. As we have dealt with this phenomenon at length before, reference is made here only to put it in philosophical context. By exposure to refinements (rather than by a life-and-death struggle in intellectual crises), generation after generation of raw young boys (and later girls) have been processed into gentility. Ethically, Christianity was the leaven of this life. Philosophically and aesthetically, the Classical world and Platonism were and are its distinguishing marks. In recent years a good deal of modernization of instruction has gone on, without always affecting the social outlook.

A first departure from true Platonism was found when we encountered the Public Schools' power of assimilation of newcomers from below. Though Plato's *Republic* did notionally make place for 'golden' children who might be discovered in the lower classes, much more is said there about demotion than elevation. A second departure from Platonism is a consequence of this first defection. Whoever can 'make the grade' can be adjudged worthy of some place in the hierarchy, not by identical intellectual criteria as in France but by serving a sort of lowly or marginal apprenticeship under patronage until the neophyte has proved himself. Still, the fags belong to the school, and the N.C.O.s belong to the regiment. This time we are not talking only of schooling or rational processes that will actually *identify*. We are considering also that ripple-effect of 'good breeding' which reveals itself in good manners and 'good form' generally. Thus a servant can be a 'gentleman's gentleman', having profited by an initiation in the right circles, though he is still considered to be an inferior who must know his place.

At this stage we have brushed against another philosophical school – empiricism, or the school of experience. We shall postpone our review of it for a moment to round off what can be said in this brief space about paternalism. The idea that underlings, the lower classes, subject races, coloured people, and all those not born in the right place can share in the universal values of 'civilization' is Platonic and Christian in the sense of supposing that the qualities admired are universally admirable and unquestioned. It is Platonic too in supposing that not all people are equally ready to perceive these abstract perfections; but it parts from much of Plato and from Aristotle's views on servility in acknowledging that, in time perhaps, all men are capable of being uplifted by education. That education, however, is thought of in conventionally British terms; it is seen as character-habituation and practical initiation rather than as the assimilation of *culture* in the French fashion.

In terms of school and any other aspect of improvement, therefore, the British paternalistic tradition of education (though almost incredibly cautious and smug) does by implication admit the possibility of being adapted to a different clientèle and a different idiom. That is no doubt one reason why British imperial administration has been one which sent out 'gentlemen' all over the world, distinguished by firm loyalty to the standards of their class and school, equally distinguished by a regard for 'universals' such as justice and integrity, but humanized (even if made exasperating) by their paternalism. They have been almost unforgivably slow to give the white or coloured 'lower' classes the chance to show what they were capable of; but, so far from supposing them to be for ever unregenerate, they have gradually initiated them into at least the minor orders of their hierarchy, and have admitted them freely to their schools and universities on these terms. Thus, what has happened in the Southern states of the U.S.A. and in South Africa is distinctly at variance with the example shown in West Africa, India, and South-East Asia. A long apprenticeship is always irksome, especially in politics; but 1960 showed that hasty emancipation (as in the Congo) is not always preferable to a slower paternalism such as Ghana and Nigeria had experienced; for the latter is an apprenticeship with prospects, rather than a futureless manumission.

In so far as paternalism in education has earned a meed of praise here, it is only by way of compensation for the general neglect it has encountered. There is no intention at all of praising the kind of static paternalism shown in philanthropy (often with good results); that patronage has all too often suggested to the 'lower orders' that their 'betters' permanently 'knew what was good for them'. A lasting wrong is often done when anyone sets himself up as a sort of perennial Father Abraham, with patriarchal sway over bond and free, life and limb. We are concerned with short-term paternalism in relation to education – in itself a forward-looking thing. Therefore it follows that we must by implication condemn any overlordship that makes the ruler a grandee, no matter how kindly. Still less can we tolerate the sort of exploitation which has often accompanied the best of philanthropic intentions. We are simply trying to give a fair due to that paternalistic attitude which can perhaps be described as a 'nursing' approach.

When Nigeria became independent on 1 October 1960, her new prime minister went out of his way to praise the apprenticeship through which his country had achieved not only its maturity but its readiness to take on world-wide responsibilities. We should not overlook the endeavours of both the Soviet Union and the United States to foster similar paternalistic relationships with the underdeveloped countries lying within their reach, for quite different purposes and with markedly different results.

Some educational consequences of paternalistic benevolence, both good and questionable, have already been touched on. They will therefore be no more than mentioned here. In Britain they include: access by scholarships to Public Schools – but to a limited number of candidates who can prove themselves; scholarships to universities – but to a number of universities inadequate to serve any large-scale influx; the system of school prefects; the 'house' system; the tutorial system; the scheme of 'special relationship', whereby colleges at home and abroad are groomed for independent respectability under some unquestionable, traditional aegis; the almost universal copying of at least some Public School norms by the publicly maintained grammar schools; the conservative respect for the trappings of the 'gentleman', even to the extent of insisting on Latin for scientists at the ancient universities in the middle of the twentieth century; the general neglect of the sciences and 'useful subjects' until relatively late; and, of course, the traditional British emphasis on standards – of character, of performance, and (more recently) of intelligence.

Although we have already encountered *empiricism* (i.e. emphasis on the value of experience in philosophy), that phenomenon has appeared in our survey of paternalism almost like a recurring but regrettable contamination from below – as though some workman kept walking through the club. In fact, however, from William of Ockham (or Occam) onwards, empiricism has been the most persistent feature of British political and scientific thought. The aristocratic Platonism which the world thinks characteristically British seems by contrast to be almost a sort of self-conscious Sunday behaviour put on by boys who know they are being observed. That character-training compulsiveness so distinctively British has induced the educated classes 'to put on the new man' (as St Paul says) almost artificially or out of character. (Hence the American expression: 'a stuffed shirt'.) The ruling classes have, traditionally, identified themselves with the armoury of attitudes they have put on (including values, conventions, and such trivialities as speech), to such an extent that they have slipped back into plebeian pragmatism and empiricism only with reluctance or forgetfully. One might therefore try to clarify the relationship between the opposing philosophical attitudes (not altogether accurately) by drawing a distinction between the upper-class and Latin-French affectation of paternalistic humanism, and the lower-class or Germanic tradition of down-to-earth empiricism. Though not an exact portrayal, this cartoon bears a recognizable likeness to the truth.

Why call it a Germanic tradition, when German academic philosophy itself is exceedingly abstract? The reason is that the old governmental institutions that developed in the British Isles during a long period of Norse and Germanic invasions were characteristically local and self-determining meetings. They could hardly be called democratic; for only the elders appear to have had much say. That is not quite the point, however. In course of time, adjustment to the local conditions of life and farming in quite varied districts of Britain (often with marked variations within a small compass) made British institutions very much a parish-pump and rule-of-thumb affair in the majority of cases. Not even the developing influence of London during the Wars of the Roses and the great period of mercantilism was able to combat altogether this centrifugal tendency. Therefore, when the time came, British Protestantism was characteristically nonconformist and congregational in type whenever the weakness of the centrally established Church permitted, or whenever emigrants escaped the royal reach in other lands. I have had something to say about these features of British (and later American) life elsewhere; so there is no point in repetition here. But we should note that a whole way of life grew up that was pragmatic enough to find sufficient justification for conduct in satisfactory results, and empiricist enough in philosophy to mistrust theories not demonstrably validated by experience or experiment. It comes as a surprise to an English speaker to learn that in many other languages not only are the words for 'knowledge' and 'science' identical but the word for 'scientific' may carry the same implication of abstraction as our word 'academic'. To the Anglo-Saxon science and theorizing are inseparable from experimental testing and 'know-how'.

Yet we all know that this last feature is more marked in American life than British. *Pragmatism* elevated to the level of a philosophy may be said to have been engendered by the American frontier out of British empiricism. 'What works is right' is an acceptable conclusion in frontier circumstances; but to claim that 'there is no truth, only truths', as Dewey did, looks like a bit of transatlantic revolutionary talk. It is not, however. Quite apart from the ancestral traditions of the home country, some more recent antecedents of Dewey are discernible in the very vigorous contribution of utilitarians such as Jeremy Bentham, James Mill, and John Stuart Mill. Like Dewey, these men dispensed with theory, as so many 'fictions'. 'Actions are right in proportion as they tend to promote happiness, wrong as they tend to promote the reverse of happiness.' That is plain enough; though we might overlook the preoccupation with *actions* in our familiarity with the quotation. So is the principle of 'the greatest happiness of the greatest number' a pragmatic rule. The principle of utility is obviously the antecedent of Dewey's insistence on 'signposts' in philosophical inquiry, and his evaluation of it in terms of its instrumental possibilities. To say so much is not to quarrel with Dewey, but to laud him for being the faithful European he was. What was distinctively American about him was that he speedily exploited his thought in a practical conclusion. He also incorporated in his democratically organized activity schools the utilitarian principle: 'Everyone to count for one, and nobody more than one'. Yet he was paternalistic enough too in his practice to recognize that the teacher must, so to speak, pull the strings behind the activity and 'spontaneous' interest.

Clearly, an important outcome of pragmatism and empiricism is a recognition that each person's perception may be valid as a contribution to a generally true understanding – at least to a local and topical extent. ('No truth; only truths.') Thus any effective democratic system (not just an occasional free vote) will gather up a constant flow of suggestions and views from below upwards; it will also maintain a flow of understanding downwards. That is true in politics; it is also true in schools, in universities, in research enterprises, and even (where possible) in factories and armies. No one needs to embrace empiricism as a philosophy to see that in practice any ideal 'goes over' better with that sort of concerted co-operation. When dealing with adults we see that the development of personal and social responsibility is best ensured by simply allowing people to be responsible – effectively and constructively responsible in enterprises they understand, and under guidance or with assistance if necessary. Their views are not so much wantonness; they are part of the building of civilization. They are not automatically acceptable, of course; they need piecing together with the knowledge and understanding of others, let alone factual support. Seen in this light, effective democracy is an experience that both demands and ensures further education.

These empiricist conclusions are directly applicable to schooling. So-called 'group dynamics' means nothing but chaos if it is a case of the ill-informed arguing with their peers. But where it is well conducted, as in a university seminar or a systematic adult education class, it is invaluable – not just in eliciting facts or comment (important though that is), but in civilizing the participants. They come to recognize the complementary constructiveness of well-considered views. What is true of adults is also true of younger people, within the limits of their perception.

Therefore far less reliance is placed than formerly on formal exposition ('chalk and talk'). More use is made of discovery ('heuristic methods'), partnership ('group activity'), and of the body (audio-visual aids, manipulation, dramatization, visits, and activity methods generally). All forms of co-operation, from American-style 'student government' to joint consultation in industry, embody this philosophical attitude. The true empiricist maintains that all these activities and aspects of participation are an integral part of getting at the truth; but many who disagree on that point will willingly admit that such operations are psychologically useful in getting the truth over. Thus we see that a programme may be acceptable in practice, even though there may be profound disagreement on the principles invoked to justify the procedure. For these reasons many politicians and philosophers use man and human activities as a practical, if not the only, criterion for evaluating ideas.

At this point it is worth while to pause for a moment to consider an often overlooked distinction between British-style empiricism and American-style pragmatism. Pragmatism as the moving principle in American schools has certainly encouraged Protean adaptability and a confident outlook. There is no doubt that most of the world's schoolchildren would be better for more of this. The averagely successful product of the system looks like a true citizen of the world. Unfortunately, it may only be the world as mirrored in the opportunities and problem-situations of the United States. Wherever industrialization and urbanization repeat outside the United States situations which look familiar, Americans react responsively and successfully. This response is not automatism – not quite; but there is a tendency to recognize superficial stimuli as 'the total situation' in accordance with which a response is called for. Of course, it is not. 'Familiar' situations seen in Tokyo or Wiesbaden are not familiar at all. Therefore the specifically conditioned responses somehow seem wrong. Inner uncertainty may therefore plague the confident cosmopolitan. Hence the perpetual 'need to be loved' that is the American's special cross. Pragmatism's constant preoccupation with specifics and manœuvrability may neglect the need for some permanent standpoint or consistently pursued objective. Men need more than pointers and experience; they need a permanent *system*. The bitter self-reproach of so many Americans in failure is like the panic of men on a foundering raft, or of mariners whose compass has gone wrong

Empiricism, by contrast, is less adaptable than thoroughgoing pragmatism. By definition the well-tried thing may seem admirable. Hume's philosophy looks radical in parts; but in other parts it looks as conservative as Burke's. Therefore the reaction of the empirical Briton when he fails is often either to pretend that he has not done so, or to go back to the well-tried routine for some slight modification. The associated vice is 'humbug' (a British word); the corresponding virtue is indomitable (if sluggish) resourcefulness.

Now we must pass on to *humanism* proper. The true humanist says 'Man is the measure of all things'. This view is compatible with a belief in a perpetually valid Natural Law, at any rate in a fairly static pre-industrial society in which 'the rules' can be imagined as perceptible to man, and as permanently applicable to all human problems. It is compatible with utilitarianism (which forms part of it), though in utilitarianism it is distinguished by requiring social and political evaluation, e.g. greater happiness, better laws. In scientific humanism a further ingredient is found: the contention that man is not just detached and looking at life as though enjoying a painting; he is considered to be incapable of understanding data or himself without both scientific training and a fair appreciation of some scientific facts. Scientific humanists will therefore insist on at least the elements of physical and biological science in the curriculum. They will demand that habits of observation, recording, and critically testing be built up. They usually suggest that although knowledge must be used for progress and happiness, no such evaluation may rely only on subjectively 'human' judgement but should be determined wherever possible by the objective study of needs and behaviour. Thus the study of man has moved from introspection and metaphysics to include at least some psychological content and some social science.

Many persons of profoundly religious conviction share the caution of the secular humanists just mentioned, in requiring empirical testing of conclusions on the basis of known facts. Though they believe that the ultimate truths and perfections are of divine origin, nevertheless they recognize that throughout history many astonishingly different views have been put forward as 'revelation'. Either because of humility, therefore, or because they acknowledge the need of a programme based on psychology and practical politics, they may share many of the scientific humanists' views on school and social organization without wavering in their allegiance to religion. They are thus called 'religious humanists'.

It is impossible to consider all the 'isms' in relation to education; but before passing on to the fourth and last category listed on page 263 we might note in passing *logical positivism* and existentialism. The first of these suggests that moral judgement and the like are really statements of emotion-linked approval or disapproval; that judgements can be clarified by acknowledging the social causation of these emotions; and that many issues can be divested of obscurity or reaction first by carefully analysing the terms used, and then by testing the conclusions. This sounds very radical; but most logical positivists and verbal analysts actually behave in a most conscientious way, as though they were conventional humanists. Their programmes therefore resemble those of the scientific humanists in insisting on the training of the young to discover facts, think clearly about them, and 'debunk' questionable traditions of judgement and practice.

Existentialists, almost on the contrary, feel that most philosophy has been over-intellectualized; not enough of the stress and strain of living experience and emotion has been incorporated into men's systems of value. They therefore emphasize the constructive importance for human understanding of 'living out' each occasion in which we may find ourselves. I matter; what I am doing matters; my whole feeling and commitment matter. Therefore existentialism suggests the importance of cultivating at least three things: sensitivity and emotion; a sense of personal integrity and commitment; an awareness of social responsibility and partnership. It will be seen at once that these aims do not depend exclusively upon existentialist views, but are compatible with other philosophies. There may simply be a 'hunch' that they contribute to good teaching practice.

In fact, much good teaching method is a very eclectic agglomeration of what has actually been found to work with young people. Good teachers and organizers are those who make the best possible use of whatever opportunity offers. Yet they do not rely only on expediency. Expediency might on occasion seem to justify a nice, easy lie or at any rate a myth or other deception. It might (according to unrelieved utilitarianism) seem to justify 'making an example' of someone even by punishing unjustly; yet no conscientious person would ever do it, on principle.

On what principle? Though not pretending to any philosophical foundation, such a refusal is eminently a philosophical one because the teacher implies that instead of expediency he must rely on some essence of justice. Some universally applicable principle is felt to be at stake, even if the principle itself can only be fumbled for. Similarly, in exercising 'authority', whence does the teacher's authority arise? Because he is older? Or stronger? Or has been to the university? Or because he speaks 'authoritatively'? Or can quote statistics? Or because there is something recognizable in the essence of the situation that calls for the pupil's acceptance of the rule? It is at least good teaching method to ensure that the pupil understands the main principles involved, with their claims and counterclaims. He should know what light can be thrown upon a problem by the great thinkers. Thus, not only will sound judgement be more likely on the spot; it will have a future in sound judgements later.

The last main category of philosophy will be dealt with very briefly here, though it has been of incalculable practical importance in many parts of the world. That is the group of *philosophies based on supposed scientific or historical laws*. Though scientific humanism might seem at first sight to fall into this class, it does not for the simple reason that it insists on trial and error rather than on the vindication of 'laws' which, by the nature of things, could never be proved or disproved until the end of human existence. Such 'laws' are therefore not laws as science understands them; they are the basic hypotheses of a doctrinaire ideology.

The 'laws' which most obviously fall under this condemnation are those advanced when theorizing about the supposedly economic nature of all human activity (as Ricardo and Marx did), or about the dependence of human nature and judgement upon man's sharing in the 'real' soul of the state (like Plato, Hegel, Mussolini,[1] and Hitler). All

[1] 'The Fascist State', said Mussolini, 'is the soul of the soul.'

of these and their earlier variants have by implication been considered in my reviews of totalitarian ideologies already. No more need be added here except the obvious corollary that according to such ideologies the individual, the occasion, the 'principles' and the purpose must all be judged by the ultimate end envisaged by the 'law'. Of this the governor is custodian. For all practical purposes, therefore, the fulfilment of the 'law' is the achievement of the state's programme, whether this be some economic millennium, or world power, or 'perfect political wisdom'. History too must be seen and rewritten in these terms. Marxists not surprisingly teach that 'what is before us is for us'. Education in these circumstances is not what is elsewhere understood by the term, even though it may be most efficient instruction and perhaps humane in many practical respects. It is dictation and dogmatism. The Kremlin's (or Peking's) indignant repudiation of 'revisionism' and 'deviationism' should remind us just where we are – on the plane of an orthodoxy which proscribes heresy as a blasphemy against revealed truth.

In these circumstances no real philosophic discussion is possible. One might just as well try to argue away a deeply held religious faith. But to recognize this impasse is not to say that we have then finished our appraisal of the ideology. A faith may be basically erroneous or heretical in minor ways, and still help people to be good and charitable. For these and similar reasons most believers would prefer to encounter some opposing religious doctrine than no belief at all, not to speak of indifference or atheism.

Likewise, neglect and ignorance are usually worse enemies of mankind than the positive effort that has gone into social and educational improvements on unacceptable ideological grounds. Even an ideologically biased instruction with good practical results *may* in the long run be more charitable, and indeed more humanizing by our own standards, than the frequent alternative – total neglect. Once more we come back to our earlier point about programmes. People will often do many excellent things for unacceptable reasons. We are then delighted with the good deed to such an extent that we not only tolerate it but welcome the chance of any participation that does not altogether compromise us. If we are quite honest in our observations, we see many things done in the Soviet Union (for example) which are clearly the result of excellent planning, technical expertise, and a genuine concern for people. In other words, a good *programme* is carried out. Communists explain their actions exclusively in terms of their own *ideology*. We should not let them get away with that, any more than we accept the claim of other religions to have specially created or fostered the virtues we regard as shared by our own way of life.

We have already noted that utilitarianism pure and simple is not a finally acceptable answer for any moral decision (p. 280). In other words, as a philosophy it will not hold water. But that does not stop its being welcome to us as a short-term criterion with which to judge our policies. We welcome its utility in programme-making, without accepting its ultimate logic. To return to our example of the Soviet Union – there is no suggestion here that we should accept communism (an administrative device) or Marxist theory (an ideology); but if other people find these developments impel them to serve a large part of mankind better, then we may have to welcome what is good in their programmes and repudiate what is wrong in their policy-making, just as we did in partly accepting and partly rejecting utilitarianism. Such a distinction is easier if we remember our three-tier analysis: we reject the basic principles; we question or reject many of the systematic deductions, though not all of them (e.g. social, educational, and economic complementariness); and we may be able to welcome a considerable part of what is done in practice.

We must always remember too that one and the same theory may not work to the same effect in different contexts. It is hardly necessary to recall that the revolutionary manifestoes of the eighteenth century worked out differently in the U.S.A. and in France, or that (despite identity of the faith and the moral code) North American Catholics and Central American Catholics are no more the same than are Italians and Irishmen. What really makes the difference is the embodiment. Here we may approve; there we may disapprove. But we must never accept naïvely the claim that what we encounter has the straightforward cause the speaker imagines.

To bring this chapter to a close we may reflect once more that only some sort of philosophical evaluation can rescue us from mere routine and precedent, from purposeless dilettantism, from totalitarian subservience, or from self-contradiction. Philosophies endeavour to make us stand back and see what we are involved in – not just in terms of here and now but by more universally acceptable criteria. Many schools of philosophy have claimed perennial or indeed universal validity; but such changes as the advent of industrialization, the emancipation of depressed people, and the opening up of a new world of knowledge have all made much philosophical 'certainty' seem an ephemeral idiom.

Yet at least there have been helpful approximations to the truth. Indeed, some patent fictions like Natural Law have contributed immeasurably to the better ordering of human affairs. It is unquestionably good that we should be required to justify our conduct not just in parochial and familiar terms but with as transcendent a perspective as possible.

The gradual building up of psychology into something like a science has shown us that the study of 'mind', 'reason', and the like need far more than introspection. The more recent study of social science has reinforced this evidence. There is no such thing as pure, disinterested thought; there may be no 'self-evident' truths. Yet when we have said the last available word about involvement, motivation, and so forth we have still not really accounted for the human craving for 'the good life'. Philosophy can throw some light on that, at least by illustration. We thus assemble our criteria for comparative analysis, and we evaluate what *is* comparable.

We must not fall into the error of supposing that psychology is necessarily more detached than philosophy, either. It is no accident that measurement of individual 'intelligence' began in Paris; that Freud's work began in Vienna and later found its home in Paris; that Pavlov's work on environmental conditioning was done in Russia; and that social psychology, industrial psychology, and the like have come to us from the United States. Psychologists (and their inquiries) are just as involved in the social nexus as other observers of human affairs.

But when we acknowledge involvement, we have not said or implied that inquiries are like a circular perambulation in the desert, leading nowhere. One thing is certain – that effective progress depends upon *programmes* realistically adjusted to local and topical needs. People will agree on programmes when they will fight battles over principles. Policy gradually shapes itself as satisfactory achievements are reached. It is then that provisional working principles can be formulated, compared, and analysed. It is here that philosophy is vindicated as a criterion of comparison. Religions disagree and ideologies disagree in the last justification. Philosophy at least approaches a universally acceptable language for man's evaluation and improvement of himself.

BOOKS

See the general bibliography on Comparative Education, p. 369.

See also the *Year Book of Education* for 1957, London (Evans Bros) and New York (World Book Company), and the books recommended for Chapter 10.

See also Russell, B., *A History of Western Philosophy*, London, 1946, and Whitehead, A. N., *Adventures of Ideas*, Cambridge, Mass., 1933.

SECTION V

Teachers in a World of Change

CHAPTER 12

Social and family change

Is school a limited-liability enterprise? Can we put up the shutters and sit behind the shop? Clearly not, as we have seen. We now recognize very well that our responsibilities are by implication unlimited. But do we stop often enough to examine dynamically the interaction of scholastic and social change through which our 'ripple effect' is expanding? We may remember how wide our commitment is; but do we remember how long it lasts? Do we let the actualities of growing up reveal inadequacies in our preparation for it?

It is true that in Chapter 6 we thought about the changing responses to technological need, and thus considered the future of children in relation to an expanded horizon of careers. We have also given thought to altered relationships with parents and teachers, and we have noted the public disquiet that may arise from culture conflict or simply from the fact of surviving into a different world from that which became familiar during infancy. But we have not so far given due consideration to the more strictly personal and intimate consequences of extended or more elaborate schooling. That will be the work of the present chapter. We shall also take careful account of the altered prospects of women and girls, and heed the implications of marital change. We shall observe these phenomena not simply as large-scale events, but mainly as personal influences.

The length of children's schooling (identified all too often with education) is usually taken as an index of civilization in a nation, and of prosperity in a family. It therefore has symbolic status. Sometimes the symbolism is about as useful as a repulsively fancy ornament. Sometimes it has the same virtues as an absurd hat – valued not for its protective qualities but because something happens subjectively in the woman who wears it. If the consumers and displayers of educational concoctions feel different because of them, then these are phenomena of real functional value, no matter how questionable they may be intrinsically. Thus we have to consider education too, not as though we were totting up accounts but in terms of what it does internally to people. What, then, have we started?

'A college education for your children' is a slogan that daily sells insurances, mortgages, and loans over the American radio. A college education to the age of twenty or twenty-two is a 'must' for all middle-class Americans, and all Americans are notionally middle-class. (Ask them.) Are they athirst for learning? Certainly not many of them. Is it purely a case of so much 'school' adding up to so many more chances in the employment lottery? We are closer to the answer here, though we have not reached it yet. All kinds of career are open to the really enterprising climber in the United States, no matter where he came from and whether he has had a college education or not. Of course, it is easier to climb from some positions than from others, and a college education certainly counts.[1] But the real point is surely the feeling of assurance that comes from consciousness of having made an adequate start – one that is like a send-off with a pat on the back, and may be as intoxicating as an unexpected invitation to meet the great and powerful on their own ground.

Jonesmanship finds different idioms from country to country and from Jones to Jones. It is a universal phenomenon extending downwards at least to the fishes, and probably beyond. The notable thing in the human species during recent years is that no prestige criterion has been more publicly vaunted than education. The extent of this boasting is seldom realized in countries like the United Kingdom, where it is still not fashionable to flaunt education except that received at the more expensive private schools and the two oldest English universities. It is no idle boasting of merely ego-inflating significance, either. Throughout the world schooling is prized not so much as the basis of being civilized or refined, as for being the highly utilitarian key to technological success and abundance. A second value attributed to it by nearly all successful countries is that of perpetuating the essential virtues of each country: the American way of life, the communist faith and morals, the spirit and intellect of France, and so forth. A third value is added by the underprivileged, who make up the majority of mankind;

[1] According to the calculations of Professor Schultz of the University of Chicago, a college education is worth $100,000 in a lifetime to its possessor; but as Mr John Vaizey and others have pointed out, such financial profits can hardly be attributed to the college education as such. Recognition and recompense of all kinds depend heavily on the social connexions of the recipient, and on the social and economic complex into which he ventures forth. Alleged cash values of education cannot therefore be calculated in terms of a family or personal investment for private profit.

they think of it as a proof that, although underdeveloped, they are not 'backward'. They are not left out of the characteristic human endeavour. No form of appreciation is more passionate than this. In formerly subject countries it combines the gnawings of hunger with the relish of equal acceptability. In still depressed social classes elsewhere, any schooling has the value of an 'Open Sesame' – meaningless rigmarole, perhaps, but giving access to treasure.

But what of all those people who are the recent beneficiaries of educational largesse in the more highly developed countries? In earlier chapters we saw that the length of publicly provided schooling is an international status symbol. Hence all those statistics in UNESCO reports. Since about 1957 merely quantitative comparisons have lost favour, however. More attention has been given to the vindication of quality. Much money has been spent in the United States, for example, to demonstrate (if possible) that the American recipe is as good as any continental prescription. But in noting all this concern for more and better schooling we have hardly encountered so far the children to whom officious elders dole it out.

More and more pupils stay longer and longer under instruction. (Until the Soviet reforms of 1958 we might have said 'at school'; but it now seems possible that many countries may diversify the last few years of the compulsory period of formal education, combining with it some apprenticeship to work or some constructive experience in life. The Danes are an example of a nation's long-standing preference for this link.) Already in Chapter 6 we noted the malaise which afflicts the pupils and students of many countries when tedious and apparently purposeless schooling regiments youthful energies and curbs youthful ardours. In Chapter 7 we considered some forms of life-linkage and diversification designed to relieve frustration and turn youthful exuberance to good effect. But all educators must realize that we are only just beginning to size up this problem in terms of its personal implications for effective schooling, let alone provide answers. We must pay more attention to long schooling as a personal *problem*, as well as an advantage.

Under the influence of supernatural teachings and paternalistic philosophy, three ways of coping with 'wantonness' or waywardness have been devised for use in those social classes where the formalities demanded a long immaturity for young scholars. They may perhaps be described as constraint, supervision, and 'the blind eye'. As people nearly always think of sexual behaviour when anything like wantonness is mentioned, we may as well deal with that first. We see constraint both in the extremely widespread practice of keeping girls amazingly ignorant of sexual matters (not omitting England's 'better' boarding schools until fairly recently), and also in such things as maintaining a Spartan régime with a sparse diet, hard exercise, cold baths, and the like. More excessive but not unknown constraints include beatings or expulsion as a punishment for offences, and the use of saltpetre in the diet to depress youthful sexual appetite. In time, of course, the advocates of stern constraint have always supposed that 'discipline' would internalize itself and become habitual. Sometimes it did, to good effect; sometimes it did, with lasting ill effects; and sometimes it has been notoriously temporary.

Supervision has of course always been continuous wherever constraint has been used; but it has also been practised very thoroughly on its own. At no time were boys in many boarding schools ever allowed to be really alone, or to go about in pairs. They must always be three or more together, preferably under the eye of a senior boy or a master. The organization of the 'companionship' system in the Society of Jesus was designed to provide assistance to each member in all kinds of spiritual or physical need; but it lent itself very well in practice to close supervision of the kind just mentioned. In other circumstances, chaperonage of young women served the same ends. It also quietly titillated lasciviousness, as can be seen from the fact that if a couple were left together for a few minutes unchaperoned the girl might be considered 'compromised'. Though the past tense is used, in many countries these observations are true of the present.[1]

It is often noticed that when over-protected young people have their first experience of mixed company at the university or 'in society' their reactions are disconcerting. They cannot therefore be said to have been educated; but that hardly matters if they scarcely ever escape from invigilation throughout life within their own social entourage. Often, of course, chaperonage is very ineffective. Some chaperons are complaisant, like Juliet's nurse; others are eagle-eyed in the ballroom but cannot see outside. This last failure seems particularly evident at some campus balls in the United States, though in many colleges chaperons are carefully recruited from the 'faculty'. Educationally speaking, chaperonage is mainly negative.

What I have termed 'the blind eye' is the technique of taking no

[1] See, for example, Levi, C., *Christ stopped at Eboli*, London (Guild Books), 1953, p. 73.

official notice of what is suspected of happening. Properly brought up young people in cool northern climes can hardly realize how inevitable it seems in more southerly regions that adolescent boys will have sexual experience, even boys of good family and from virtuous homes. Of course, some cynical fathers frankly tolerate these events, if they do not actually aid and abet. Good girls are kept carefully cooped up; but there are others, either in licensed houses or in domestic service or otherwise accessible. So matter-of-fact are these unproclaimed norms that if a girl walks anywhere alone, or with her head uncovered, or if she looks up at a man, she may well be considered abandoned. That is why English and American girl visitors to southern France, Italy, and Spain are sometimes misunderstood. They certainly perplex the inhabitants. Though loose behaviour is not recommended here, it must nevertheless be observed as a device commonly used for dealing with some of the problems of adolescence. It must indeed be examined a little more closely in some of its implications.

One implication is, as we have already observed, that girls can be kept under constraint but that boys cannot – at any rate, not so easily. Another is that boys undergoing protracted education in a college or university will have, so to speak, privileged access to some young women who do not belong to the same social category and 'do not really matter'. Sometimes these are organized prostitutes, and sometimes camp-followers. They have for centuries been a feature of university cities in Europe, so much so that within living memory visiting foreigners expressed astonishment at the relative absence of such hangers-on from British university cities. Humanitarians generally, and religious people too, object to prostitution or its equivalent on both moral and humane grounds. Socialists and communists in particular campaign against it as a sign of social and economic exploitation. The gradual emancipation of women and the improved social and educational opportunities for the less privileged have certainly made prostitution seem much less inevitable for many young women; and destitution as a contributory cause has practically disappeared from North European countries. But this highly desirable change has been fraught with consequences for education in many countries of the world, not excepting the cooler Northern lands.

Instead of thinking of 'the lower classes' mainly as being available to serve in various capacities, those who receive an extended or intensified education must now think of them as at least similar to themselves – perhaps identical with them. They cannot, therefore, get rid of their troubles and then forget about them as previous generations did. Furthermore, instead of thinking of 'the lower classes' as 'lower' in moral fibre and sensibility, the young men of privilege have recognized at last that what their elders encountered on their prowls was perhaps ordinary, but uninhibited, womanly behaviour. There is much literary evidence from the period between about 1910 and 1935 of the surprise felt when it was realized that good women were after all exactly complementary to men socially and emotionally as well as biologically.

Fortunately, north-western European countries and the United States developed educational opportunity for girls almost quickly enough – quickly enough, at any rate, to let boys get to know girls as responsible and real people and not just as female fantasies. Crazy though co-education was originally felt to be by the upper classes (elementary schools for the poor have usually been co-educational for reasons of thrift), it has certainly put a stop to the 'blind eye' technique in its crudest form. A much more relaxed social atmosphere for teenage boys and girls has also contributed to a quite different understanding of how the sexes grow up. But it has in some ways intensified problems by forcing adolescent society to work out its answers to unprecedented questions within a social system that includes everyone and does not leave unfortunate recipients of 'wild oats' outside, or otherwise suppose that adolescents' problems are best dealt with by ignoring them.

It would be foolish to pretend that everything is happy now that girls may be judged by what were formerly boys' standards, or that proximity and naturalness have quietened all rash romance in favour of epicene quiet familiarity. But it does seem true that much head-shaking and lamenting over decadence arises simply from the ignorance of some older people about what probably used to be normal for men in their own circle, or certainly used to happen among their poorer and less sophisticated contemporaries.[1] Moreover, juvenile love interests now get greater publicity. A much better informed attitude now forbids us to try and cure 'calf-love' by bread-and-water methods or other threats. We know how serious and how intense it is. We also recognize the great need for love and understanding and above all patience that every adolescent experiences. We therefore make more of teenage teething-troubles – psychological and social, as well as sexual. In fact, every parent of teenagers must often feel he or

[1] Hoggart, R., *The Uses of Literacy*, London (Chatto & Windus), 1957, p. 76.

she suffers greater pangs than they; and it is as well that we do. Consider the alternatives.

Youngsters have to work out a colossal readjustment to life, in terms of new despairs and delights, new powers and responsibilities. If we their elders do not understand them, or do not seem to, they will write us off as 'not mattering'. From time to time in every family, no doubt, some tempest arises in which this happens temporarily; but the real risk comes when the severance of sympathy is chronic or permanent. All over the world this is happening on a gigantic scale. Sometimes the contributory factors are confined to temporary cultural and emotional conflicts of the 'crabbed age and youth' variety. But sometimes the kicking-over of parental traces is complete and lasting.

Students everywhere are notoriously radical (though they seldom are so now in the United States and the Soviet Union). Therefore it is easy for observers to ascribe any revolutionary change to the short-lived hotheadedness of youth. However, when university students defy rigid ancestral tradition to the extent of breaking loose from home ties and setting up house with some young woman student (with marriage or not), the personal results of the liaison are likely to be permanent for both partners, whether or not pregnancy results. In Hong Kong, for example, free-and-easy disregard for all the old people's precepts and values is common among the students. In Japan, young boys and girls go off in large numbers to live under canvas in youth camps. The results are similar. Altogether apart from the direct impact they may have on the traditional family economy and authority system, such changes less directly teach girls to claim partnership with men, to go sailing and dancing and mountain climbing with them, and before long to demand marital and parliamentary equality. It would be absurd to assume from the two examples given that they are unique. In fact, they are matched (though less surprisingly) in many European and American countries. China and Japan are mentioned only because the revolution is so marked.

In considering such behaviour, there is the greatest danger that we who are not Chinese or Japanese may miss the major significance of what has been described. The strict sexual code of the official Christian tradition makes Westerners concentrate their emotion of shock on the lasciviousness of young people; but for many Eastern people such waywardness is little more than a by-product of a much greater wrong (if indeed pre-marital relationships are worried about at all in the case of boys). The real wrong as seen locally is the attack on the source of all authority in the father; the second great wrong conse-quential on this is the attack on the family system, in refusing to con-sider the advice (or perhaps orders) of the family elders on careers, place of residence, choice of wife, and the like. Promiscuity and un-welcome pregnancy are hardly more than symptoms of a more gen-eralized wickedness. To understand what we see, we must appreciate where the indigenous people find the crux of the delinquency com-plained about.

We must omit consideration of delinquency as such; but to drive home the point just made, reference to a film about delinquency will be relevant. *Tokyo Twilight* is ostensibly on this problem. When it was shown at an international seminar to a specialized audience considering documentary films on social problems, some of the Americans present asked where the delinquency was. The story had described the rake's progress of a Japanese girl student of upper middle-class emancipated family background, who fell into free-and-easy ways in the teenage coffee-bar society of post-war Tokyo, became pregnant, procured an abortion (quite legally, but without the knowledge of her family because she was so ashamed), and was jilted. Her married sister, also emancipated, had become estranged from her husband. The father, preoccupied with business, was rather neglectful of his paternal duties of guidance and care. The whole film is a tragedy of family break-up and the frittering away of respect for authority – a great wrong. 'But where is the delinquency?' repeated the Americans. They were looking for guns, gangs, drugs, robbery, rape, and killing. The idiom of delinquency varies. One delinquent may be a criminal, or unhinged; widespread delinquency is a *social* symptom. We abhor the crimes, of course; but the essence of the teenage rebellion is in estrangement and repudiation. That is the focus of our concern. Disrespect for parents and elders shown throughout the film described must have been a crescendo of shame for Japanese viewers; most foreigners did not notice that at all.

Thus rock-and-roll and all that goes with it may be little more than a noisy nuisance in a country like our own; but it takes on a totally altered symbolic significance if the mere presence of girls of good family background is in itself boldness and immodesty. It may be also a casting off of ancient associations, like the discarding of a kimono for slacks and a Palm Beach shirt. Out go all the ancient decorum and the religious tradition of inner quiet exemplified by over a thousand years of Zen Buddhism. In putting on the contemporary teenage uniform, the young Japanese are assuming a way of life in which they know the older people cannot share – and they are glad about it. This loss of cultural sympathy is markedly accentuated in Japan by the students' adoption of a quite different way of talking – not just in slang or in the topics talked about, but by deliberately abandoning traditional circumlocutions, polite forms of address, and 'educated' style. Schools do not teach rock-and-roll and all the rest; but they are certainly instrumental in preparing a state of disaffection for which rock-and-roll may be locally emblematic.

I have of course no intention of passing judgement on rock-and-roll as such, though it is interesting to read what anthropologists and such psychologists as Sargant have to say about 'abreaction' [1] brought about by dancing. Nor is there the slightest implication here that the young are necessarily more 'decadent' than their parents or ancestors. They may be, or may not be; that depends upon the evidence and the circumstances and the state of intention in which these activities are undertaken. What our examination must fasten on to is something deeper than the prevalent mannerisms of youth. It is something different from the perennial and proper 'teenage rebellion' through which all young people learn that they too can 'act grown up'. It is more than the everwidening 'gap between the generations' aggravated by the speed and scale of technological change. We must fasten on to what the symptoms reveal – failure of the educational provision which our society makes for youth.

We are really faced with the symptoms of a need. What sort of induction into maturity do we give our sons and daughters? Our 'teenage rebellion' and the more spectacular signs of culture conflict manifested overseas become much more significant if we stop thinking of them in purely physiological or psychological terms and see 'the youth problem' mainly as a sociological one. That is the field in which we can cope with it practically. What is wrong with our social arrangements? Are our schools unsuitable? Is our 'link with life' a fraudulent fantasy? Are we actually provoking conflict by blowing now hot now cold on our young people's craving to be significant adults?

This last characteristic of all parents, no matter how well intentioned, is a collective as well as a parental failing in our world. Let us gather up in one place some of the points made earlier, and add a few of special significance here. Our children, in staying longer at school, or in serving long apprenticeships, and certainly in waiting to be married,

[1] Sargant, W., *Battle for the Mind*, London (Heinemann), 1957, p. 62.

are kept 'marking time' longer than young adults have traditionally been throughout human history. To take but one example, the age of marriage in many countries follows close upon puberty. To take another, the early stages of industrialization usually absorbed workers during adolescence and very soon let them reach the maximum work and wage they would ever achieve during their lives.[1] In other societies, elaborate religious, social, and sometimes physical ceremonials mark very clearly the transition from childhood to manhood or womanhood. Once in the adult fold, there is no going back. By contrast, our young people not merely have to wait longer; they have very many different and conflicting levels of initiation into maturity, and no initiation carries certainty.

The onset of puberty in well-fed Western countries is earlier in succeeding generations. That is a plain enough manifestation about which there can be no doubt. Consciousness of maturity is not only an internal, personal matter; it is externally played upon by advertisements for clothes, amusements, and all kinds of activities. Girls particularly become anxious if they are slow to mature. Yet we have no Samoan permissiveness towards adolescent sexuality, and nothing comparable to the 'bachelor's house' of the Trobrianders.[2] We let our advertisers or our children's peers remind them constantly of their physical interests – more vividly than ever because of our great interest in 'romance', which is markedly absent from most human communities. Yet the most we permit our teenagers (if we can manage it) is a remotely supervised flirtation, or dancing, or occasional parties. These devices are helpful at times, at times inflammatory. In the United States, 'dating' is an elaborately socialized instrument of personal and community initiation;[3] but in recent years it has tended to give place to a more permanent 'going steady' which, of course, brings new frustrations to teenage lovers. 'Too young' is the theme of many plaintive songs; but that is not what the advertisers say. Films, books, entertainments, and public example develop a higher expectation all round – personal, social, and sensory – together with a more impatient demand to 'have it now, and pay later'.

In our increasingly custodial schooling, and in our demand for ever-longer training which postpones the attainment of a really adult job until the mid-twenties, we inevitably accentuate the natural anxiety

[1] See Hoggart, R., *The Uses of Literacy*, London (Chatto & Windus), 1958, pp. 41, 62.
[2] See Seward, G. H., *Sex and the Social Order* (Pelican edition), London, 1954, p. 85.
[3] See my *Other Schools and Ours*, p. 183.

of young people for their present and future status in all kinds of relationships. How can we therefore expect them (unless we provide and cultivate an opportunity) to be firmly 'committed' and responsible? In days of greater social injustice, adolescents were passionately political. (Think also of Cyprus, the Arab countries, and China in more recent times.) Nowadays, in the social democracies especially, we often hear that they 'could not care less'. It is a strange thing too to note that our own idiom of youthful disturbance is not always particularly characteristic of the poorest and least educated sections, but often of the better-placed children in ambitious or comfortable homes. Yet it cannot be said that our children really lack interests: boys often have great technical knowledge and resourcefulness, and most girls take a keen interest in making a successful career out of marriage. Furthermore, evidence suggests that teenagers in vocational training are less likely to give trouble than others. These considerations make us look back to the vocational linkage in teenage instruction about which something has been said already; but it is probably not the practical ingredient itself which counts, so much as the more obvious purpose ahead and the sense of commitment.

Young people continuing under instruction find themselves at quite different points of the social 'pecking order' in the various aspects of their life. In the academic hierarchy of a selective school system they may be persons of consequence, or alternatively 'duffers';[1] but in organized extra-curricular activities those roles may be reversed. In a society which prizes competitiveness rather than complementariness, friction may be set up here. The teenager's world of the week-end and holiday brings about a still further readjustment. Most of all, the disparity existing between those who stay on in highly esteemed forms of instruction and their contemporaries who have already started working and earning like adults can establish a profound sense of cleavage, not only as between people but also in one and the same person. In the park or the pub he seems a man; on Monday he may return to pettiness.

Let us look at this more fully. Every advertiser knows the enormous profits to be made from appealing to the teenager, who, without family responsibilities, is likely to spend proportionately far more on 'having a good time'. The very same things that adults want, these employed youngsters can often have in greater abundance. Despite themselves, good boy and girl students cannot fail to be impressed by such

---

[1] Nearly all languages have a word for this, e.g. 'passengers'. The Russians say 'sitters'.

conspicuous consumption, with its socializing possibilities. The same sort of problem which faced underpaid and drably clothed British or French soldiers during the war, as contrasted with their transatlantic allies, faces many teenagers today. They are at a disadvantage not only in the obvious matter of buying presents or paying for dances, but also in belonging to sports clubs or having cars or even in more obviously educative experiences such as going abroad.

Working teenagers themselves can often afford these things; their families are even more likely to have them. By contrast, those teenagers still in full-time study are hard-up themselves, and likely to find that their families for various reasons must live much more thriftily than less education-conscious neighbours. Incidentally, the 'sliding scale' assessment of university scholarship awards still persisting in Britain often means that the middle-class scholarship holder is markedly worse off during his student days than his colleague from a poorer home, with unfortunate effects on his participation in student activities. He is also more sensitive about such things as the need to get a vacation job.

In saying so much we have not told the whole tale. Increasingly ostentatious self-vindication is natural in the working teenage group, partly because they feel in some way blackballed from the exclusive circle of the pre-professional student. Certainly that is true in some Western European countries, including Britain. Resentment is, of course, seldom admitted; but it shows itself in the ridicule which is in some places heaped upon such targets as school caps and uniforms. Without any crude and obvious hostility of this sort, indeed, the natural distaste which maturing girls feel for school clothing and discipline (an impatience often shared by boys) is aggravated by the natural comparisons to be made with the clothing and mannerisms of employed contemporaries. The latter, in fact, often make capital out of such comparisons. Their sneers may sometimes be justified; they may indeed be more wide-awake to 'the proper study of mankind' than those remaining at school.

In countries where a paternalistic tradition imposes unusually juvenile clothing and deportment upon the pupils of prestige-carrying schools, these trends are accentuated. They can, of course, be fairly easily mitigated – either by improving the current regulations about clothing and submissiveness, or (perhaps better) by altering the school administrative system so as to provide a clear break of some sort at about the age of fourteen or sixteen for admission to a comprehensive further education college, which will permit all kinds of adolescents to face young adulthood in mutual acquaintance and fuller self-appreciation. It is unrealistic too to overlook the adult background to our teenagers' sensitivity. Growing protest against all kinds of Olympian condescension is implicit in the organizations of pensioners, hospital patients and consumers generally.

In school circumstances proper, anything that will remove the imputation of juvenility or inferiority from all or any section of the adolescent group is to be welcomed. The sense of being privileged can certainly exercise a marked effect on a small group whose futures seem marked out for them; but the corresponding effect on other people is often one of frustration. Indeed, it might be suggested that any sense of educational and vocational predestination in any part of the social spectrum has a deadening effect overall. There is much to be said for uncertainty enough to encourage enterprise and adaptability. That means adequate promise, and a demand for effort all round.

The characteristic smugness of the British, for example (especially when it is assessed in conjunction with excessive conservatism on 'both sides' of industry, or dilatoriness in the application of the country's own researches[1]), may doubtless be attributed in large measure to that atmosphere of being 'foredoomed' which so markedly distinguishes England from the supple evocativeness of the United States and of great dominions in the British Commonwealth. Fatalism of any sort is demoralizing; but it is worse when it is almost accidentally developed fatalism. Many British categories are little more than by-products of school types that developed piecemeal. At least in older dispensations a whole ideology and social system accompanied the stratification or

---

[1] Criticized directly or by implication in the recommendations of several immediately post-war commissions on training for management or training within industry; and criticized more directly in the *Times* supplement on the use of computers in industry, 4 October 1960. Also the subject of a front-page paragraph in the *Times Educational Supplement* on 7 October 1960. These strictures were even more vigorously and directly applied to the important and characteristically British craft of shipbuilding by a report of the Department of Scientific and Industrial Research published in the same month. This condemned on a wide scale (*a*) technical backwardness, (*b*) 'demarcation problems' (i.e. disputes between employees about who does what job), and (*c*) antiquated personnel methods. During the latter part of 1960 several public reports in Britain made similar criticisms of parts of the national economy; but no one seems to have recognized industrial shortcomings as *social* symptoms which must be linked with educational inadequacies, until Sir David Eccles (the Minister of Education) publicly said so much in February 1961 (*The Times*, 14 February 1961). Separately and together, these failures are the results of the educational and social attitudes of non-incorporation and unimaginativeness criticized here.

categorization enforced, with an appropriate welcome and future in each category. Now in Britain there is very widespread willy-nilly drifting, except for the privileged and hard-working minority whose ambitions keep them at their studies. (Even these do not work as hard as most of their counterparts overseas.) But how to incorporate the *majority* into a nation's shared efforts – politically, economically, or socially – that is a serious problem linked with the general lack of educational evocation. How to develop imaginativeness and zest is really the same problem.

Incentives can no doubt be provided, sometimes meretriciously, by such devices as the institution of some examination or other for every type of school. It is noteworthy that in 1960 the national secondary schools examination council recommended the British Minister of Education to set up such a pattern in the less academic and non-professional schools, recognizing in effect the widespread practice of taking both academic and practical examinations in very many such schools already. Certificate-hunting is almost a national pastime in countries as diverse as France, Holland, and Denmark, and for a multiplicity of objectives.

Useful though these inducements can be, are they the whole solution? Certainly not. Boys and girls during their teens may often be idle; but they are also capable of intensive work entirely outside the purview of examinations. If a sense of adventure natural to those years can be developed through any expansion of horizons, that may be more lastingly effective than trophy-hunting. After all, some of the most coveted trophies, such as a good marriage, are imperfectly prepared for in school, if at all. Moreover, the traditional concentration on examinations can be harmful or deadening, even in such natural territory as the English sixth form or the French *classes préparatoires*. In the desire for a university award (or for becoming a prefect or head of the school for that matter) many a pupil stays an extra year when he would probably be better in the outside world.

There is of course no reason why the education of youth should be thought of primarily in terms of school, particularly in those countries where formal schooling finishes early. Indeed, as we have seen in Russia, Germany, Holland, and Denmark, much of the systematic continuation of education beyond the age of about fourteen is already undertaken in factory or farm, in apprenticeships, or in some indirectly scholastic venue. A slow increase of residential and/or club-like provision is also noticeable in many countries, very often with the support or encouragement of official bodies. Long- or short-term boarding facilities are increasingly common features of all school systems. Churches and party organizations too seize the opportunities afforded them by the sense of 'conversion' or 'the need to belong' which is so usual at this age. An official youth service is maintained by governments of all complexions, either to provide youth leaders and 'animators' for voluntary organizations or indeed to educate the young people directly. In the latter category the Pioneers and Young Communist League (Komsomol) of the Soviet Union and the Yugoslav People's Youth may be mentioned. These are an official, integral part of those countries' educational systems, and have already been described as such.

Yet in varying degree nearly all the organizations mentioned in the preceding paragraph are organized by officers outside the ranks of young people themselves. Obviously, it is one thing to provide facilities, and to give help or advice or instruction where these are asked for; but it is another matter to undertake control of youth to the extent of guiding its development – as we see it in the operations of totalitarian parties or the proselytizing zeal of most Churches. It is quite clear, on the basis of world-wide evidence, that young people want to be able and need to be able to organize their own pursuits to the limits of feasibility. Any firm or obvious tie-up tends to be resented. That is why in such countries as the United Kingdom and the United States as much initiative as possible is left to voluntary organizations, which do however receive blessings and a little financial help from central government sources.

Unfortunately, voluntaryism generally produces patchiness. The strata or areas which most need help very often get least. Moreover, it is easy for officials to make the mistake of looking around and counting up organizations, many of which do truly distinguished work. What of those sectors of youth or of youth interests which are not covered by them? In a country like England, where so few people are regular churchgoers, it is no uncommon thing for youth clubs to be church-sponsored. Nowadays, not much propaganda work is directly undertaken; but the association with an unwelcome ideology is often enough to deter recruits. It must also be admitted that, despite the excellence and rightness of many youth clubs, the self-conscious virtue or brotherliness of others militates against their real success.

Very few towns or other educational districts have anything like a good non-sectarian youth provision in any part of the world; and in some places where this does exist it is primarily concerned with reclamation. Delinquency control is admirable and may be necessary; but no club member likes to think of himself as merely being saved. In fact, most teenagers loathe the connotations of the word 'youth'. In order to make the carry-over from school childhood to free adulthood effective and happy, a totally new and nation-wide appraisal of self-administered and self-directed education (formal and informal) is essential. It is spontaneous self-education we want to integrate with the formal system, rather than 'youth work' as such.

So far, no democratic country approaches this objective really closely, despite such surveys as the British Albemarle Report of 1960. It is true that standing conferences of voluntary youth organizations exist in many countries and also internationally. But the great majority of their constituents are frankly what they are called, i.e. youth organizations, in the conventionally accepted sense of those words. The intra- and extra-curricular activities of schools, colleges, factories, and the like are all tangential to the official youth programmes of non-totalitarian countries, if they touch them at all. What is indispensable for success is that 'youth work' of any sort should be seen not separately but as a maturing self-fulfilment outside school of all the life potentialities that first began to display themselves in school.[1] To this extent the Pioneers and Komsomol of communist countries, though they are not autonomous and evolutionary youth organizations of the type desired here, have very much to teach us in their personal, social, academic, and generally cultural constructiveness. The Party controls all 'truths' and objectives, of course, like the Church in some other countries; but within this powerful limitation there is very much self-determination of interests and expression, resulting in a strong sense of appropriateness and purpose.

Though the numbers of those taking part in our Western youth organizations are impressive, they might mislead us because of the temporary nature of much membership and also because of the general flimsiness of the connexion. Furthermore, there is a steady overall decline in numbers. Figures for the mid-1950s were given in the

---

[1] In Britain, a National College for the Training of Youth Leaders was set up at Leicester in 1961, roughly on the lines of a short-term teachers' training college. Much more to the point, perhaps, is a current proposal to combine the training of teachers and youth leaders in a single institution in London. This harks back to some of the original recommendations of the McNair Report (1946), and takes account of the 1959 Crowther Report's emphasis on a more 'club-like' atmosphere for teen-age pupils everywhere.

UNESCO study (number 35) *New Trends in Youth Organizations* (1960). The percentage of young people taking part in some organized youth movement at some time was as follows:

United Kingdom	54%
W. Germany	30%
Netherlands	18% (but 24% in sports organizations)
United States	5%

It is clear that these figures say nothing whatever about the degree of socialization of youth undertaken in the various countries. Obviously, the American high school and college discharge the very functions of welcoming and initiating that the youth organizations of Europe are intended to do, and they also prepare the youth of the country for careers and universities. Though giving well-deserved credit to this feature of American life, and though taking account of the extensive counselling system which operates in all schools and colleges of the United States, I still cannot feel that here we have a universally acceptable blueprint.

In the first place, 'school' in the United States (the term includes everything, to the university level) is acknowledged by many Americans themselves to be custodial and too juvenile in character. It is felt by students to be a long corridor of waiting, passing through life but cushioning out its sounds of anxiety and competition. No other nation can afford such protracted guardianship, even if it wanted it. In any case, what we are looking for is not a continuance of the *pupil's* status, but a phase-by-phase awakening into adulthood, with gradual appreciation of *all* the concerns of life in proportion as these are experienced and organized by the young adults themselves.

We must ensure that work and obligations are appreciated, as well as opportunities. Our general prescription includes at one end the bright future genius following his academic or technological apprenticeship; but it extends at the other to the young woman knitting a pair of tiny socks. Neither today's college nor the youth movement as normally understood is a medium comprehensive or elastic enough to include both kinds of interest. Something is left out of our concept and provision, even when the future genius and the young knitter are one and the same person. Both intellectual and emotional experiences are of the profoundest educational value to young adults; they should both be comprised in the vision of life ahead. How many educational organizers have seen the possibilities and duties of extended education in those terms?

Without going over what has been said earlier, we may remind ourselves that job-getting, job-changing, courtship, marriage, home-making, and parenthood are each new awakenings. Each new plane of experience gives a new educative opportunity, both in the narrow and in the wider sense of 'education'. For some less academically interested or less technologically competent learners, those experiences may be almost the only incentives and the main 'Open Sesame'. Most of us share them, whether we are academic or not. Therefore, any educational provision which fails to take account of them, and to co-ordinate them with the rest of our formative experiences, is merely disjointed. In failing to help us construct it is in fact destructive, because it tells us that highly significant parts of our lives are meaningless, one to another. This is educational hysteria.

More than for centuries, we are all coming to realize the inseparable bond between the various aspects of our lives. We have a better understanding than our ancestors' entirely supernatural ideology permitted them to have, because our appreciation is empirically supported by scientific and social observation. As well as the expert, the man in the street sees social and personal changes that must obviously have tremendous educational impact, demanding a radical reappraisal of the content and purpose of education. The most obvious factor is that we are now compelled to educate everyone by formal means and for lengthy periods, allowing far less to 'happen naturally'.

As half our population is female, and as most of them will not only marry but make marriage and maternity a responsible and enjoyable career, it follows that any system of schooling that leaves this fact out of account is a misfit. Not only children will suffer, but husbands too; for marriage as a career and consciously appreciated way of life is now a masculine as well as a feminine concern. If ever it was 'a thing apart' for men, as the saying goes, it is not so now in these days of conjugal partnership and psychological need. I am not asking only for preparation for the married state in the sense of 'home economics', any more than I should be satisfied with elementary arithmetic as a preparation for a business career. What is called for is an effective appreciation that the married career gives an important *perspective* on the whole of life. In these times of extended and enriched education we should be educated and oriented in respect of it, not just trained or informed.

Linked with these obvious generalizations is the important and special new fact that young people expect to marry much earlier than had recently been the rule. In every recent decade, the age of marrying has crept forward a little. In the United States, says Peter Drucker, women are marrying at an earlier age than they have for 200 years. He has also pointed out that it is the relatively underprivileged girl in the factory who marries late; whereas the more highly educated marry early, start having children first, and have larger families. In Britain, the average age of marriage is younger by far than it was before the war, especially for girls,[1] most of whom are married at or soon after the age of twenty.

In contrast to the American pattern, British university and technical college students marry later than their less academic contemporaries for economic reasons; but they are still marrying earlier than they did, and married students are not the almost unknown thing in universities that they were within living memory. In some continental countries a fair amount of pre-marital cohabitation of students is tolerated, even in student hostels; and careful surveys also indicate that older ideas on sexual abstinence are jettisoned elsewhere much more often than marriage (or 'common-law marriage') statistics would suggest. Yet the marriage figures themselves also generally show a more marked lowering of the age of marriage among students and professionals than among other young people in nearly all countries.[2] Thus marriage is for these couples very much part of preparation for a career and of the career itself. If professional and life preparation is to be *educative* (as distinct from arid training), how important it is to take note of these marital actualities in devising study courses or orientation for the students themselves!

It is even more important that teachers and others responsible for the education of non-students should take account of the huge significance of the marriage ambitions and problems of their young charges, especially the girls. The widespread precociousness of adolescents in sexual matters accentuates the absurdity of anything like a spinsterish approach to them. So many of the conventional ingredients in the curriculum offered to adolescents a generation or two ago now seem a pathetic and namby-pamby insult to a girl who, rightly or wrongly, is more experienced sexually than her teachers. Bridling against what

---

[1] The Crowther Report 'Fifteen to Eighteen' (Her Majesty's Stationery Office, 1959) said that 4 per cent. of the girls concerned in the report were already married women (p. 29).

[2] UNESCO study number 35, *New Trends in Youth Organizations*, 1960, p. 10.

she considers baby-talk may make her less inclined than ever to retain sympathy enough with her elders to consider or take counsel from them. That, at least, should always be possible. The quickest way to make 'lost girls' is to lose them. Though these remarks apply to boys too, the inevitable interest a boy must take in bread-and-butter learning[1] does give another point of contact with him some time. Girls of this age, particularly if not successful in traditional academic subjects, quickly become out of sorts with school and with refining influences generally – except for the generally helpful influence of the better women's magazines. An estranged girl may soon mean a difficult home; and it is a pity if scholastic inadaptability contributes to this decay.

The changes described above have several further consequences. Well-schooled girls not only become intelligent and socially responsible mothers; they also increasingly add to the family income, either to raise the living standard (perhaps in terms of a car or domestic appliance), or to secure some less material boon such as a more expensive education for the children. A great many mothers who have had a good education resume their careers (particularly as secretaries or teachers) when their children are old enough to be at school. So their previous vocational training has not been wasted. It may in fact be enriched by their maternal experience. This last point is one of special significance for the teaching profession.

In underdeveloped countries or other places like Switzerland where women do not have identical political and economic rights with men, it is understandable that they should vindicate their claims to equality by pursuing studies and careers hitherto dominated by men. Sometimes this has incongruous results, especially when we contrast the home-conscious U.S.A. (where even men students often take courses to help them be better husbands and fathers) with countries like India, where the smoky hearth and baby-filled kitchen are so dreaded by many emancipated women that they avidly lap up all the scholastic aridities which other school systems are trying to jettison even in the case of boys.

Any educational welcome, any sort of educative realism, that can give young people roots and significance must be specially welcomed in the great changes of today. Delinquency has many causes, and is too

---

[1] Yet we must not assume because of our own social background that girls must be oriented only towards domesticity. In the U.S.S.R. the majority of doctors are women; so are one-third of the engineers .More than one-third of the physics students at Moscow University in 1961 were women too.

complex and thorny a problem to tackle here; but one aspect of it – that inexplicable and apparently despairing delinquency of the well-cared-for child in a progressive country – must fill us with misgiving. It seems as though over-protectiveness (or is it better described as enforced juvenility?) can cause outbursts of youthful iconoclasm just as destructive as the resentment of former generations against injustice. Instead of the bacchanalian 'letting off steam' which was characteristic of student 'rag days' in Britain, and the wild but good-natured post-graduation carnivals of some continental countries, we now often hear of an apparently compulsive and hysterical destructiveness – sometimes solitary, sometimes *en masse*. It occurs widely in Britain, Germany, Japan, the United States, and Sweden, for example. The keynote seems to be not the old braggadocio and exhibitionism, but an uncontrolled and unhappy repudiation of immaturity and insignificance.

If this is a true diagnosis, as is credibly suggested, then rock-and-roll and dream-world fantasies can be useful cathartics – though of obviously temporary therapeutic value. The long-term cure for all forms of wantonness however is clearly to tap and use the energy, by letting it be purposeful in a double way: in terms of genuine acceptability in the adult world, and in terms of constructive significance to the world the young people will soon be responsible for as adults. Countries like India and China, with disproportionately high numbers of very young people, often afford striking examples of youthful enterprise and co-operation. China is sometimes described as 'a country of the young', not only demographically but because the young are making it. In several parts of the world, about half the population are under twenty-five. Our North European and North American countries by contrast are ageing countries, with an embarrassing proportion of pensioners. A good many middle-aged people too, such as parents and teachers, are often felt by young people to be in need of immediate superannuation. All such countries have a growing 'youth problem'. It therefore seems likely that not only our attitude but the grudging and significance-lacking opportunities we afford the young are in urgent need of radical transformation.

Our complicated technological society demands long and tedious apprenticeship in one form or another of study or initiation. But as it has not proved beyond our powers in a modern democracy to give equal consideration and opportunity to citizens who are functionally and educationally unequal, why should it prove impossible to recognize maturity and readiness wherever they can be found among young people, while continuing our necessary guardianship and instruction of them in other spheres? The problems raised by universally extended schooling have clearly not been faced, as long as we go on thinking of education according to a prescription which may once have suited the unrepresentative élite of a pre-industrial oligarchy. In any case, in those days it was not school which really gave the education, but society. In these times, however, society is so complex, and modern enterprise so scattered, that scholastic and professional training must incorporate consciously what centuries once organized empirically.

The obvious conclusion is that, as adolescents explore their way towards status, mature expectations, and the realization of their interests as men and women, so our school system or its successors must forever try to initiate them significantly into the society which will soon be theirs, not ours. This must be tolerantly done in terms of their needs, not of our perquisites. No longer can we plan an 'approved course' of so many years or so many activities. That may be all very well for younger children; but the teenagers we are concerned with are older than Juliet and as old as Alexander the Great. They are nearly as old as Mozart, Newton, and Einstein at the moment of their genius. Has our paternalism helped or hindered their attaining such stature? Without risks on our part, their adventuring into life will be stillborn.

Or will it? Not in every case, we may be sure. The world-wide 'youth problem' tells us that. In those idioms of youth we complain of, a new instrument of exclusion is being devised. We are being excluded, not they. Two reactions on our part are possible: we can claim the infallibility of totalitarian ideologies, and canalize the energies and zeal of adolescence into the construction of a predetermined society, statically conceived; or we can work the other way round, by sharing with our young people in the continuous and expanding *adventure* of their growing up. It is not of course suggested that their norms will be right (at any rate in any perennial sense); but as educators we are concerned with communication, sympathy, and co-operation. Any alienation or deadening of youth instigates the repudiation of all we stand for. Crusades and commitment will then be truly 'old stuff'.

In such circumstances, as history has repeatedly shown, totalitarian dedication may ultimately seem preferable to chaos. Yet our young people's directionless wandering may have been unintentionally caused by barriers to understanding and co-operation which we ourselves have set up. As parents, teachers, and organizers of education we must earnestly consider how different a thing extended and widespread schooling is from what would have sufficed in the much tinier scholastic enterprise of pre-industrial times. Above all we must acknowledge that the prescription on which we were brought up must already seem parochial in a world of incalculably wider horizons.

BOOKS

No books are specially suggested for this chapter and the others in this section, for two reasons. Firstly, the author is not aware of any that he cares to recommend without qualification. Secondly, it seems more important that readers should formulate their own resolutions for the future, rather than read about someone else's.

CHAPTER 13

Barriers in education

A great deal of attention has already been given in this book to problems caused by barriers in education. For the sake of convenience, these may be listed here, so that reference can be made back to previous chapters, while more acute problems or new manifestations of educational isolation will be dealt with in the present chapter.

We first considered what may be called geographical or regional remoteness from educational opportunity. Account was also taken of the near-fatalism which makes some people 'not even think of' school opportunities for their children or themselves. Linked with this is the indifference which for one reason or another is often felt when opportunity is made known. This indifference is often the result of a lifetime's conditioning or a long tradition. In its extreme form it can amount to outright alienation, as when *solidarité ouvrière* makes left-wing partisans repudiate what seems like a schooling dedicated to *bourgeois* decadence, or when extremely religious traditionalists shun the 'materialism' of unwelcome instruction. Fortunately, such barriers are being crumbled away gradually; but they are still important in many places.

On a much larger scale we considered the influence of ideology and religion, not so much in imposing handicaps on their adherents (though in some cases this is an important consequence) as in separating the adherents of one 'world view' from others, both in school and outside. It is one thing to form a kind of earthly sanctuary for the safeguarding of a faith's purity; but it is quite another matter to keep outsiders vividly aware through such esoteric manifestations as special clothing, hair, language and the rest that they are a huge 'out-group' whose taint must be avoided. Outsiders like 'holier than thou' attitudes even less. Many of us live in fairly tolerant countries, where Jew rubs shoulders with Gentile, Catholic with Protestant, believer with unbeliever in an atmosphere of unostentatious co-operation for the achievement of certain agreed objectives. We hardly realize to what extent and with what fanaticism and persistence group is made hostile to group elsewhere. Sectarianism is easily tolerated; but sectionalism and downright non-co-operation in the building of civilized understanding are in the truest sense inhuman. All world views are necessary for the full study of the human phenomenon. To say so much is far from indifferentism. Communication is surely necessary for any one aspect of education or civilization to be sober and well informed. In a world of diminishing distances parochialism may still befog the realization of our common humanity.

The most spectacular forms of isolation associated with ideology and religion are those which derive from totalitarian forms of government. Nearly as dangerous are those which preach theories of racial superiority, or impose a stratified caste system on the social order. All have been briefly reviewed. In a less spectacular form the same general attitude is revealed in theories of privileged access to 'truth' on the part of particular classes, or of particularly 'intelligent' persons (to the effective exclusion of others), or indeed in stratified or over-departmentalized school administration. Some methods of selecting children can almost mechanically achieve the same isolating effect that others would propose on theoretical grounds. Paternalistic management and finance of industries, which have had a long run and are still vigorous in many parts of the world, have had the same depressing educational effect, which in time is recoiling on the industries themselves. Another isolating influence can be detected in the supposition that some forms of knowledge are of axiomatically refining value, or that some kinds of activity (variously named, for example, as memorizing or scientific observation or sport or artistic dexterity) are so special for 'humanity' that persons lacking them must be of less account. In our own day of well-publicized and centrally co-ordinated enterprises (whether socialist or capitalist makes no difference), a pathetic trust in a hierarchy of 'experts' also has a deadeningly isolating effect.

All too many headmasters, inspectors, and professors in a pyramidal system become unwitting enemies of progress because of inertia, dread of 'irregularity', or their own pathetic vanity. Personal inadequacy of this type can occur anywhere, of course; but disservices done in the context of education become generally perilous. If we are to avoid senility in our civilization, there must be regeneration. It is therefore incumbent on all in positions of authority to go out of their way to encourage growing-points and creativity. Particularly in our industrialized world, some counteraction to mechanical 'processing' and 'leaving it to the big wheel' is absolutely necessary – not to speak of the risk that the 'big wheel' is out of gear.

That this is no mere pious talk is proved by the concern shown in one international conference after another – at Harvard, in Moscow, and at Oxford – for promoting conditions favourable to 'creativity in science' or equivalent 'continuous creation' in the arts. The growing emphasis on research by teamwork is another pointer in the same direction. Even where teamwork is not formally organized, it is obvious that what is often called 'cross-pollination' is more essential than ever for the discoveries of today and tomorrow. Encouragement for imagination and enterprise is sadly lacking, however, in many industries and universities. These remarks, of course, are far less applicable to the U.S.A. and Canada than to European countries, among which Britain is an arch-offender. The mere removal of outmoded hindrances – long overdue – will not be enough; constant vigilance must be exercised to secure the positive *promotion* of conditions favourable to imagination, discovery, effort, and the flow of ideas. At a time when communist youth and the newly emancipated nations seem seized with a new dynamic, it is particularly important to free our own progress from the impedimenta of ancient protocol, and from erroneous suppositions about how civilization is advanced. The great re-births in the history of culture (like the post-medieval Renaissance) have been characterized by a multiplicity of growing-points. By contrast with our present reliance on one capital city, one acknowledged group of scientific or artistic leaders, Renaissance Italy alone reaped a harvest of beauty and genius from proliferating creativity in many small towns.

Concerned as he is with communication and evocation, the educator must be perpetually on guard against all such handicaps or barriers. The hidden hindrances to mutual understanding and appreciation are in some instances more potent than the obvious barriers, simply because they are unnoticed; they seem 'natural'. Behind them, people fence themselves in with the idea that they alone are 'true' to human ideals, while all others are benighted or mistaken. If this self-adulation stopped there it would be merely a disagreeable nuisance. But in addition it has obvious international dangers; it all too often issues forth to the world as some universalized theory of supposedly perpetual value.

Much more easily recognized are the barriers of *language*, which are critical in many countries. It is obvious that many a state includes more than one nation in its boundaries. Sometimes, indeed, what was once one nation may in the course of time have learned to speak two or more languages. Difficult though this division is from the point of view of national unity, it is all the more intractable if one of the languages is associated with political or economic dominance. This often happens because of invasion or cultural penetration. An example is seen in Ireland, where English in the course of time almost entirely superseded Gaelic, which was however consciously revived for nationalistic reasons.

Scotland and Wales provide similar instances, except that in the islands and highlands of Scotland Gaelic has persisted with greater vigour, while in Wales the native language not merely held its own in many less accessible places but has actually flowed back into former areas of English exclusiveness. In each of these cases we are reminded that the language itself, important though its strength and emotional evocativeness are, can hardly ever be considered alone. Almost always there are additional complications of religion, or culture, or technology and trade, as well as the more familiar association with claims to home rule and the like. In fact, these cultural connexions and the languages themselves are often prized as a political banner or defence against external control, being revived or refurbished to that end. So fiercely cherished may the language and rituals of the forefathers be that after generations of living in a distant land the descendants of the original emigrants may make more fuss of these tokens than their kinsfolk left behind. In Nova Scotia and other parts of Canada the Scottish connexion is more assiduously vaunted than in many places at home. In Pennsylvania there are still small Welsh-speaking circles keeping up their integrity against Americanization.

It is more understandable that the ancestral language should be considered sacred if it is the medium of traditional worship, as Welsh is for many. Thus Lutheran parishes in the mid-western states of America may cling to German, Norwegian, or Danish. But it very often happens that the ecclesiastical language is not the current language of the ethnic group. Thus classical, religious Hebrew is not the modern, revived Hebrew so often learned; more strangely still, the Yiddish widely spoken in the world's cities is not a Hebrew or Jewish language at all, but a dialect of German hammered into international suitability in the ghettoes, and written in Hebrew characters. Similarly, the Greek of the Orthodox liturgy is not the language of the ancient Greeks, nor the language of any part of the mainland or the islands; but it is of course surrounded with emotional associations and linked with the New Testament. It will thus be clung to even after expatriate worshippers hardly know what the words mean. Somewhat similarly, Indian Muslims often retain the use of Urdu rather than another modern language in the home and for some observances, even though their cultural connexions are Persian and their religious links with Arabic, and though they live in non-Urdu-speaking areas. That is because Urdu was predominant in the Muslim parts of what until 1947 was the Indian Empire.

So far from being isolated or untypical examples, the foregoing serve to introduce us to the world-wide phenomenon of multilingualism (i.e. the speaking of several languages by one person or community). Before seeing what scholastic morasses this may lead us into, it will be profitable to consider a few examples. Let us take the difficult problems of a child growing up in Bombay. Three distinct languages are currently spoken by the major groups in the city; but let us suppose that the child's mother tongue is Gujerati. For obvious reasons of trade and daily contact he may also learn Marathi. For national reasons he will almost certainly learn Hindi or Urdu (probably the latter if his family are Muslims). There is perhaps a further language for public worship, e.g. Arabic, or Persian, or Sanskrit, or Latin, depending on his religious affiliation. He will almost certainly learn English if he goes to a secondary school, and he certainly will if he wants to go to the university, enter public life, or engage in international trade. If we add up our score, we see that our child will learn five languages, perhaps six or seven to some degree.

This is not only an arithmetical problem in terms of parcelling out the curriculum and energies. It is a personal one in terms of the emotions, and a social and political one in terms of one's aspirations. For example, speaking Urdu rather than Hindi may simply indicate family origin, in showing what part of Northern India they came from. Careful speakers of either language can soon understand each other, for there is considerable overlap – so much so that both the British administrators of the former Indian Empire and such nationalist patriots as Mahatma Gandhi advocated the use of Hindustani as a *lingua franca* eliminating the more Persianized ingredients of Urdu and the more Sanskritized elements of Hindi. But sectionalism is such that for religious or regional reasons many speakers shift the character of the language they use towards or from the Persian or the Sanskrit pole. Others do not realize how partisan in one direction their own speech is; for example, Mr Nehru himself (a northerner) has been heard to complain that he cannot always understand the generalized Hindi of

All-India Radio. If such unintentional partisanship is carried to excess, it can easily cause a generally understood language to become separate sub-languages which in time will be mutually unintelligible or at any rate mutually unacceptable. Chinese is a conspicuous instance. Very shortly we shall return to consider the illustration Norway too affords of this very development; but just now we must go on to think more about language problems in India.

Great though these problems are, they could (in the eyes of an out-side observer) either become quickly much smaller or quickly much bigger. For example, Hindi and Urdu are closely akin to each other, but are written in very dissimilar scripts; the former uses the Devanagari script hallowed by the Sanskrit scriptures, and the latter uses Arabic characters reading from right to left. For expressing the sounds of Indian languages the Devanagari script has much to recommend it; but to adopt it universally would mean rejecting not only the Urdu script but those of other equally Indian languages, particularly in the south. These are sometimes declared by their speakers to be no less remote from the northern languages than the English tongue is. Bengali too, though not very dissimilar, has a different script hallowed by a very rich and ancient literature. Thus, we have not only a problem of what the national Indian language shall be out of the fourteen major languages and approximately 200 minor variants; we have also the question of scripts.

Scripts may be loved not only for religious associations but also because of their long-standing use in ancient and beautiful literatures, or indeed in other forms of visual art, as is the case with the now abandoned Turkish script and the internationally used Chinese characters. Sacred buildings and textiles, for example, would promptly seem vested in a foreign garb, if a radical changeover of writing were affected. However, what script to use is a special problem on its own, which will be postponed for fuller consideration. Just now we must note that the notionally distinct problems introduced by the existence of different scripts are emotionally entangled with considerations of language choice.

If we come back to our Indian child who has to learn five or more languages, we can see that the burden placed upon his schooling is almost intolerable. Memory work on an unprecedented scale is called for; and this in turn affects the complexion of the whole field of learning. Other subjects are administratively crowded out of the curriculum; and linguistic competence rather than any other sort is at a premium.

Moreover, all learning tends to look 'foreign' to children not born into well-schooled social groups, not only because of the incubus of foreign languages but also because the whole perspective of ambition is away from the vernacular concerns of field or hearth, and out into the alien territory of other places and communities. A resulting ambivalence of affections is one reason why Indians can be at one and the same time both internationally tolerant and domestically parochial in support of the community to which they belong.

In immediate relation to schools, this complicated state of affairs all too often means that education is inevitably bookish (quite apart from the prevalence of other factors). It looks unrealistic in terms of daily events and developing future needs, and is emotionally beyond the horizon of villagers or poor townsfolk. Of course, very many poor parents are ambitious for their children; but even if they can afford the loss of income or the positive expenditure which may be necessary, they still have to envisage their children's being schooled away from them in alien speech and mannerisms. Indeed, that is what they imply in having them schooled. That is one reason why the very sensible proposals of Mahatma Gandhi, Sir John Sargent, and others for 'basic' and home-based education were pooh-poohed by many rich and poor alike. They did not want their children to stay attached to farm and village concerns.

Problems of language and curriculum are very far from being solved in India. However, some guiding principles are now established. As far as possible, state boundaries are re-drawn along linguistic lines. Borderlines of any sort are notoriously hard to draw; in this case geographical tidiness is impossible, because of linguistic enclaves and other cultural factors. The number of states has notably increased for this reason since independence, and campaigns are afoot to add to their total. Within this general framework, however, the principle now adopted is the sensible and humane one that primary instruction shall be given in the mother tongue wherever possible. However, for those numerous groups whose home language is not the regional or state language, it will be necessary even at this stage to make sure of elementary proficiency in it as a foreign language.

In the secondary schools, to which at the time of writing only a fair-sized proportion of the children go, Hindi is taught in at least a simplified form, for this is the national language adopted. Unfortunately, the populous and important states of the south contain numerous ardent campaigners for English rather than Hindi as the official language of government and inter-state higher education. Foreign though it is, English is at least known by about 1 per cent. of the population (the most highly educated group); and it has international utility outside the Indian subcontinent as well as inside. Thus, without attempting to forecast the outcome of this debate, it is clear that the English language too will have to be widely learned for many years to come.

It is natural and proper to look for some universally acceptable national language. On general grounds it would seem regrettable to choose a completely non-Indian language for this purpose, though English is undoubtedly important. More than 60 per cent. of the Indians are already able to speak or understand Hindi or Urdu; a considerable number of others speak languages with such affinity or so much borrowing that it would not be too difficult to make the necessary move linguistically, except in the south. We still have problems of religion and of literatures. Thus children of all grades of achievement and from all kinds of background are faced with problems both pedagogical and emotional whether they are 'in' on a language or not. We should certainly not make light of such anxieties.

As we have already noted, the position is complicated by the privileged position of canonical religious languages like Sanskrit, Persian, Arabic, and Pali, and the 'classical' curricula associated with them. Not to make too much of the more obvious complications thus introduced, we must note simply that the choice of particular texts, or the sayings of particular prophets and sages, are bound to attach particular value to certain kinds of educational aim, and by implication to detract from others. The great compensating advantage that Indians have for the resolving of their problems is that for centuries if not millennia the Hindu way of life has been one of cultural synthesis. Some further *modus vivendi* may therefore be evolved.

Though India is the classic case of linguistic problems, it is far from being the only country so involved. Independent Nigeria, to take but one example, has three major languages and perhaps more marked regional differences of culture and religion. Within each major linguistic group there are dialects and variant ways of life. The making of a nation depends on the adoption of certain things in common, even at the cost of suppressing deeply cherished traditions (including language) at the national level. Since the introduction of European influence it has been no uncommon thing for immigrant missionaries, traders, and administrators to use their own languages as a *lingua franca* amidst this babel, to such an extent that for generations much primary schooling has been offered not in the vernacular languages but in English, for example. (This also happened in missionary schools in India during the experience of many people still only in middle age.) Though it is now considered good practice to use the language of the home for primary instruction, the inter-community use of English has taken such a hold that it is now the official language of the country, as it also is for Ghana. After the first two school years, instruction is gradually given through English, so as to unify the country. Independence is indeed bravely achieved if such difficult decisions, in view of the recent past, can be so resolutely taken. Independent Malaya rightly encourages the learning and use of the Malay language by her polyglot and racially mixed population; but English is still the language of law and commerce, and still prevails in education.

Though, of course, Sweden has never been dependent in this way, the purposes of international understanding (and utility) are served by the requirement that all Swedish children shall learn English. No such rule applies in Denmark and Holland, but the number of children who learn it is surprisingly high. Of course, these are small nations; but they are proudly independent and fully conscious of a glorious history. They are homogeneous in race; yet their geographical and mercantile position has made them adept at language learning, to a degree that might put others to shame. In such cases, however, there is no culture conflict, because the mother tongue is fervently admired and cultivated, while foreign languages remain foreign no matter how friendly international relations may be.

Deep cultural cleavages may occur within one and the same homogeneous racial stock, even with the use of what is basically one and the same indigenous language. To appreciate the extent to which fragmentation has gone on in Scandinavia, we should look back a little. Despite the extreme geographical and economic isolation of many parts of the Scandinavian countries, and the development of dialects in association with isolated groups, a generalized literary and ecclesiastical 'Scandinavian' could probably have been acceptable in most parts of those northern countries, if it had not been for local 'crystallization' in the sixteenth century. To this day, Swedish, Norwegian, and Danish are mutually intelligible to those who have had a little practice, even though they have been separated by literary and administrative forms to become distinct languages. (For example, Swedish is formally taught in Danish schools; and there are Danish–Swedish dictionaries.)

Norway, which was subject to Danish rule until 1814 and was thereafter united with Sweden until 1905, not only has a linguistic inheritance from old Norse but has acquired cultural additions from both political connexions. In recent years these have been something of an embarrassment. Under Danish rule the royal government of Norway, its courts of law, the Church, and the school used Danish for four centuries. For utilitarian and prestige reasons this 'royal speech' or *riksmaal* spread throughout the towns and business circles. But in the country the farmers and fisherfolk continued to use the 'country speech' or *landsmaal*, which is closer to old Norse or modern Icelandic. Since 1814, literary nationalism has produced the Norwegian equivalent of Robert Burns's rural protest in Scotland; it has formalized in popular literature a distinctly non-Danish Norwegian. War-time tensions and antagonisms accentuated people's affectation of one language form rather than another; but in post-war years a strong attempt is being made to establish common forms and common sympathies in *Nynorsk*, or 'modern Norwegian'. Of course, the widespread use of broadcasting and peripatetic agencies for adult education is bound ultimately to bring into closer linguistic proximity the scattered three and three-quarter million Norwegians of this extremely long and mountainous country.

If such acerbities can be raised between what are really formalized variations of dialect in Norway, where people share the same religion and socio-economic outlook, it is not surprising that distinctly foreign languages in one and the same country can cause deeper cleavages, particularly if there is little religious sympathy and if each language tends to be associated with a distinctive way of life. This is conspicuously the case in Belgium. This small country, the most densely populated in Europe, came belatedly into being in 1830 after being attached to Holland after the Napoleonic wars. Its sudden achievement of independence from the Netherlands was partly instigated by two demands: the Dutch government's double insistence that the Flemish language be used in all schools, and that all schools should be secular. Thus French-speaking Liberals and French-speaking mining or industrial communities in the less fertile regions of the Ardennes tableland (with a predominantly secular outlook) were united uneasily with Flemish-speaking farmers and seafarers of the north (who are passionately Catholic in outlook).

Though Belgium has had international guarantees of inviolability since 1839, she has never had peace within. The east–west line near

Brussels divides not merely linguistic groups but ideological partisans, especially in relation to the question of secular or religiously controlled schools with tax support. At times neutralism nominally prevails (as now, with opportunities for Catholic, Protestant, or Jewish instruction – or none – in the schools); but there has been constant chopping and changing. Each encroachment of any sort is suspect. French-speaking Belgians usually want Church and state to be utterly distinct; culturally they look to Paris. They can hardly be induced to learn Flemish. The Flemings now call their language 'Dutch' (*Nederlands*), and tend to look northwards and east – a tendency exploited by the German occupying forces during the last war. They are bound to learn French, not only because of official bilingualism but for international utility. The soreness of Belgians on the linguistic score is shown by such things as the regrouping of regiments on linguistic lines, the quarrel about which suburbs of Brussels the ever-expanding Flemish population may live in, rivalry for control of the bilingual civil service, and so forth. The bitter quarrels over the royal family, over taxes, and over withdrawal from the Congo in 1960 drew much of their rancour from these underlying cultural cleavages.

The French-speaking Walloons know they are as right as the French are. The Flemish-speaking Catholics have infallibility on their side; and if the secularists succeed in establishing non-denominational 'lay' schools they will boycott them in favour of their own under ecclesiastical control. This is exactly what we find in France. Such troubles are often endemic in Catholic countries. In these circumstances a 'third force' usually creeps in – that of atheistic Marxism, which gains ground in battles between conservative Church and liberal state. Belgium's language problems, though important enough in themselves, assume much greater dimensions because of their intricate connexion with ideological conflicts.

Switzerland has a different story to tell. This very small country of under 5 million people is a confederation of distinct ethnic and language and religious groups, originally banded together for self-protection in a mountain fastness. There are twenty-two cantons. Dialects of German are spoken by a majority in sixteen of these; French is dominant in five; and Italian in one. Linguistic frontiers are far from being neat, however; and in addition to the three main languages a fourth (Romansch) is found in some mountain areas. The three main languages are all official, are all used for parliamentary debates, broadcasting, and the press. They are not written in the usual spoken form, however, but in good French, high German, and so on. An exception to this rule has recently arisen, to help small children with their first stages in reading. Books are now available in Swiss-German; but a transition is soon made to German proper. Thus, except for some small and isolated Romansch communities (who must use German or Italian in school), it is possible for a child to be educated in his vernacular or a close approximation to it.

Primary education has been free and compulsory in Switzerland since 1874. The decentralized pattern of educational administration makes cantons responsible for their own primary education, entirely so; consequently no primary school may be biased towards a particular faith. Catholic cantons so keenly resisted this arrangement in 1874 that federal intervention was necessary; but after much bickering peace now obtains. About 58 per cent. are Protestants, and the rest nearly all Catholics. Complete freedom of worship prevails. Secondary and higher institutions may have religious associations. There are seven universities, one of them Catholic (Fribourg). As between the languages, amity is characteristic. French enjoys prestige far beyond its native speakers; the German-speaking 75 per cent. are quite eager to learn French or Italian. In post-war years many Italians from south of the Alps have entered the country to work in textile mills, adding indirectly to the significance of the native Italian-Swiss of the Ticino canton. Despite the many vicissitudes of history and religious strife, the long-standing inter-communal peacefulness of the Swiss in their multilingual confederation is an example to all. Liberal social welfare arrangements and other encouragements, especially for the development of technical resourcefulness, help to break down any other barriers that might arise socially or economically.

More like the situation in India is the linguistic complex of the U.S.S.R. There are 15 Union Republics,[1] of which the Russian republic proper (or R.S.F.S.R.) is by far the largest, with 74 per cent. of the national territory and over 110 million inhabitants, including 58.4 per cent. of the total Soviet population. The other 14 Union Republics are (under centralized communist party control) nominally sovereign in many important cultural matters, particularly in such concerns as general education and anything affecting language or indigenous cultures. Within or adjacent to some of these Union

---

[1] These are: R.S.F.S.R., Ukraine, Byelorussia (White Russia), and the Uzbek, Kazakh, Georgian, Azerbaijan, Lithuanian, Moldavian, Latvian, Kirghiz, Tadzhik, Armenian, Turkmen, and Estonian republics.

Republics there are administrative and cultural enclaves. These include **17** Autonomous Soviet Socialist Republics, and 9 autonomous regions. Within the Russian republic proper (the R.S.F.S.R.) there are also 10 National districts.

Though this looks at first sight like a highly complicated and decentralized *administrative* machine, it is not really any such thing; it is simply an index of the cultural and linguistic sub-units of the Soviet state. The economy and politics of all these divisions are under the tightest control of the Party and the Federal State Plan. However, their cultural and linguistic self-expression are fostered within that framework. In fact, the Soviet state comprises some 177 different minority groups, speaking more than 125 languages, sub-languages, or dialects, and traditionally attached to some 40 different religions.[1]

In each of the 15 Union Republics the national language (e.g. Ukrainian or Uzbeki) is used as the medium of instruction at all stages, including the university; but the Russian language, as the federal medium, is obligatory as a school subject throughout the Soviet Union. It is also the medium of command in the Army; and it is essential for anyone wishing to go far in the party or in public life. Tremendous pride in the participation of the different nationalities in the Soviet Union is fostered, however, by such things as the Permanent Exhibition of Soviet Achievements in Moscow, where each republic has its sumptuous pavilion, and in many other ways down to the printing of major languages on the federal paper currency.

Each Union Republic had its own Ministry of Education and its own university as a kind of repository of national culture, as well as for other academic purposes. Obviously, though, higher technological and professional education must rely very heavily on federal opportunities and textbooks, which are in Russian. The Moscow Ministries of Higher Education and of Culture have all-Union responsibilities, though they have subsidiary ministries in each of the Union Republics. It is noteworthy too that, in addition to the formal institutions of government, such important organizations as the Academy of Sciences of the U.S.S.R. have to use Russian. Indeed, the Academy of Pedagogical Sciences of the R.S.F.S.R. and various other organizations of the Russian republic proper now serve (through the medium of the Russian language or in translation) as all-Union (i.e. federal) services.

In varying degree, according to their importance, the minor Auto-

---

[1] *Education in the U.S.S.R.*, Bulletin No. 14, U.S. Department of Health, Education, and Welfare (1957), Washington, D.C., p. 7.

nomous Republics have been encouraged to develop teaching and research in and through the indigenous languages. At first their higher and vocational education (and indeed even secondary education in the less well developed territories) had to be in Russian, because there were no teachers and books suitable for vernacular teaching. In recent years progressive attempts have been made to foster the development of Ministries and comparable organs at the level of the Union Republics, Autonomous Republics, national districts, and the like; but such linguistic and cultural diversity is strictly co-ordinated towards federal harmony either by the all-Union organizations already referred to or by joint Federal-Republic instruments. (In Russian these are called 'union-republic' ministries, &c.; but the term is avoided here to remove any possible ambiguity.)

Complaints are sometimes heard from two contradictory viewpoints. It is sometimes said that indigenous cultures have been 'steamrollered' and Russified; on the other hand visitors sometimes complain that children in Tashkent, for example, do not speak good Russian.[1] Both comments may be justified, to the extent that foreign languages are not easily taught to all the children of any country; and it is undoubtedly true that such indigenous but opposing cultural manifestations as prayers in the vernacular have been discouraged if not altogether forbidden. No doubt those whose native language and culture are not Russian are at some disadvantage, as is shown by the fact that certain school programmes have to take a year longer where linguistic difficulties are felt; but Soviet policy is more humane in this matter than its imperial predecessor.

China's case is most unusual, in that it shows a common *written* language used both in China and outside it (e.g. in Japan) to express ideas rather than sounds. It is thus usable for quite different languages. That is indeed what happens in China itself; for there are at least three major kinds of Chinese which are mutually unintelligible, not to speak of many dialects. Singapore alone boasts three or four different dialects of Chinese. To understand the usefulness of the ideographic system of writing, we should think of arithmetical numbers. The symbol '5' is variously recognized as *cinq, five,* and *pyat'* by speakers of European languages; but though they cannot understand each other's speech or written *languages,* they can all understand the symbol. To communicate in this way, however, a phenomenal number of symbols

[1] *The Changing Soviet School,* edd. Bereday, Brickman and Read, Boston (Houghton, Mifflin Co.), 1960, p. 230.

must be mastered. There are about 23,000 Chinese characters. They are aesthetically prized; but several thousands are necessary for reading a simple newspaper or book. Students are in worse case. Chinese and Japanese students can often be seen memorizing characters. Obviously, the general use of a *spelling* script (or even a syllabic 'half-way house' such as *Kana*, or the *Kanamajiri* used in modern Japan for newspapers) would save the Japanese very much time and effort. But in China it would mean that national unity of communication would be broken down, and that the classics would be unintelligible.

To make the best of things, the present government in Peking has used its influence to induce the Chinese to learn the Northern dialect of the capital (formerly called 'mandarin') in a simplified form. In Singapore too the Chinese schools teach this common dialect, which is however unfamiliar to the majority of Chinese homes there. This revives the proposal of James Yen in the 1920s, but carries it further. Yen suggested that a select list of 1,000 characters would be used for a 'basic Chinese' (*Pai hua*); but this number is both too large for many illiterates and too small for wide utility. It is not altogether surprising that in the past decade proposals for the use of a modified Latin script should have come to the fore again. Grave difficulties are found here too, because a single sound with different intonations carries widely different meanings in the monosyllabic Chinese tongue. On the other hand, the extremely rapid industrialization and modernization of China cannot brook the encumbrances caused by the traditional script; and the increasing familiarity of Chinese with Russian and Western sources of scientific information is acquainting larger numbers every year with the more expeditious alphabets of our countries, imperfect though they are. No one can say what will happen; but the most recent information indicates a determination to Latinize writing as soon as the Peking dialect (*Kwo Yü*) is a basic national language.

Though so much has been said here about languages as barriers to understanding or social and educational mobility, we should not think of such handicaps as far-off, exotic things. They are close at hand. Apart from such manœuvres as the widespread exclusion from schools and universities of people knowing no Latin or French, we should also think of exclusion on the grounds of dialect or accent. In Germany a provincial accent is little or no handicap; in Britain it can be very serious indeed, especially at the all-important competitive interview.[1]

Thus we see that though in some countries the relation of language to

[1] *Other Schools and Ours*, p. 87.

problems of communication and of establishing school programmes is immediate and obvious, we must be on our guard against supposing that that is either the major difficulty or the only one. The essential problem for the educator (in the widest sense) is the breakdown of communication between persons and groups. This can happen where there is basically very little language problem, or where the barrier to communication is one of class sympathy and personal smugness, as in Britain. Differences of idiom and accent are used, in Britain especially but not exclusively, just like clothes and examinations elsewhere – to indicate whether people have been assimilated (or are assimilable) into the prestige group or not. In Japan, in addition to questions of accent, we must also consider the elaborate forms of address and 'educated style' whose presence or absence marks off the Japanese into social grades and political parties. In Italy, some northern industrial areas and many country districts regularly use the familiar form *tu* for 'you' (instead of *Lei*); but the general use of it in Florence or Rome would make the speaker suspect as a communist. The manner of exclusion can make an interesting and worth-while study; but the essence of our concern is the *fact* of exclusion. To a greater or less degree nearly all human communities share this failing, usually to protect the selfish interest and self-esteem either of the whole community or of those who make privileged use of the advantages of the community. To fence in their privilege, they accentuate natural or cultural dissimilarities.

At this point, before going on to discuss other barriers, we should pause for a minute to clear up possible misconceptions about such things as 'nationhood'. Any anthropologist or political scientist knows that *nations* are culturally consistent or administratively manageable groups of people. They may or may not be 'races'; usually, they are not. Homogeneous 'races' are a great rarity on the earth, when we consider the very mongrelly make-up of the approximately 3,000,000,000 members of mankind. Such ostensibly 'pure' races as inhabit parts of Sweden or various mountain strongholds or islands have probably become 'pure' only by the inbreeding of a few clans during the past few millennia. A genetic examination shows much previous inter-mixing, and mankind has never been very pure or eugenic in its choice of mates. Countries like Britain, Germany, and France (not to speak of obvious immigration territories like the United States recently and the lands of the U.S.S.R. until the end of the middle ages) are just about as mixed as can be. If 'race' simply means long-settled popula-tion, we can accept the term; but that is the only way. Biologically pure races are so remote a possibility that we can exclude them from our reckoning.

Clearly, though, there are nations. What are these? We have just defined them, and we might add to that definition the criterion that nations both recognize themselves as nations and are so recognized by others. 'Just like a Frenchman' or 'just like an American' is as recognizable a description as 'just like Tom'. Being Tom is partly a genetic thing, of course, in that Tom may have red hair or may be prematurely bald; but in saying 'just like Tom' in terms of *character* we are not paying attention to these things. We are referring instead to that 'self' which Tom and his teachers, parents, and environment have made. This is partly an unconscious artifact; but the more important part of it is a conscious *ego* or *superego*, used by Tom himself as the measure of his own perfection. In human affairs myths can be important motives, with nations just as they are with Tom.

National character is one of the most important of these myths-become-facts. We have already noted that national characteristics are culturally changed; they can therefore have no predominantly genetic or climatic determination. Yet there is no doubt that, while not taking too literally such clichés as 'the Frenchman's clear mind', we must pay proper attention to the norm-making system which causes national character to be recognizable, and thus act as a sort of signpost to others. Personal character is subject to very strong environmental and historical influences; but even more, because it acts so markedly on people of many personal types, national character can be described as:

(*a*) the concerted rehearsal-effect of familiar institutions and practices; and

(*b*) conscious or unwitting self-identification with widely publicized norms and ideals.[1]

So it is that nations have an idealized image of themselves. In this idealized image they often see the whole ideal of man. Thus they combine what others might call an *eidolon* or fanciful image with what Bacon meant when he spoke of 'idols' in the quotation used at the beginning of Chapter 10, i.e. almost in the sense of 'ideology'. Therefore it is not surprising that differences from a national norm are supposed to be tokens of inferiority. Those tokens may be idioms of

---

[1] These ideals, though extremely influential and persistent, can change imperceptibly – both in their content and their application. See the Appendix, p. 360, for 'The gentleman: the evolution of an ideal'.

manner or diet or religion, or they may be physical characteristics such as the hairiness and long noses of white men, the flatter faces of Eastern people, or the dark skins of Africans. A primitive but natural enough distaste for the unfamiliar (not as a rule shared by young children) is exaggerated when culture conflicts arise (e.g. through war or religious intransigence), or when one group seeks to take advantage of another economically. At such times, all that men consider to be brutal or excessive is promptly recognized in the 'out-group'. Thus Englishmen look round and find 'Dutch courage' and 'French leave' are typical of their near neighbours; while others further afield are notorious for stilettos or idleness. Equally, continental neighbours find Britons hypocritical, cold, and a nation of shopkeepers.

Though these stereotypes are very important in putting up barriers to communication and sympathy, or in keeping nations uncritical of their own shortcomings, they are as nothing compared with the terrible consequences of racial or colour discrimination. Nazi theorists found the Jews hereditarily decadent and untrustworthy; they found non-Germans were servile to a greater or less degree; and coloured peoples they thought of as only marginally human. We are easily horrified when we remember the dreadful results of these theories; but we forget that we too cherish in our midst a good many prejudices which are the germ of Nazi practices. There is no need to go back a century or so to scan old comments in *The Times* and *Morning Post*, which reveal the Englishman's almost farcical jingoism. People still talk about things being 'in the blood' or part of 'the national character' in terms which suggest that a nation is a *person*, and a person indeed whose whole essence and future were determined at conception. Aristocrats and aristocratic nations, according to this prescription, come into being like pedigree albino Angora rabbits. The genius of a man and of a nation are, it is claimed, hereditary.

Now it is common knowledge that eugenics are not the guiding principle in love-making. Even if they were, we cannot produce 'genius' as easily as a pink-eyed rabbit; for many more factors than one are involved. Supposing genius to be linked with intellect, it is still not to be identified with gentlemanliness, or sympathy, or aesthetic potentiality, or perseverence and hard work, or business initiative and orderly behaviour – or any other of the many things necessary to a viable civilization. Even if it were, indeed, our aristocrats are not a homogeneous bloodstock, like Arabian horses or polled Jersey cattle. Their very names tell you so. No 'aristocracy' in any human community can seriously lay claim to genetic superiority. Indeed, it would be highly questionable whether any single family could show much if any genetic advantage, despite all the often-quoted examples of mathematical and musical families. Where do genes preponderate, and where does stimulating environment?

We have examined some of these matters superficially in Chapter 7. For fuller treatment, if required, the nearest simple book on elementary psychology will suffice. But though it is easy to refute ideas of genetic predestination for greatness or servility, it is very difficult to rid ourselves and our neighbours of the implications of these ideas in practice, at any rate when we are thinking in terms of other nations and colours. Patriotic pride in national achievements and virtues may possibly be justified; but the person nourishing that pride may have contributed nothing to it himself. Therefore he ought to feel small, instead of puffed up. Observation of racial discrimination suggests that it is these self-inflated puny men who are most arrogant. In any case, why make the elementary mistake of identifying nation with 'race'? In praising a nation, we are praising its culture. That is to say, we are praising acts (which can be praised anywhere, anyhow); or else we are praising its educational system. If the latter, we must surely believe that spreading the self-same educational opportunity to others may civilize those others. That is what the French do, though we may not agree with their rationale and methods. There is no sense in withholding educational opportunity, or evocative opportunities of other kinds.

The reason usually given for withholding opportunity from other *colours* (or types) of people is that they are wholly or partly ineducable. The chance to show whether they are or not has usually not been conceded to them in any effective way that would link a genuine opportunity with the problems and promises of their starting-point (which is what all children need). Therefore theories are produced in advance to show why they are unsuited to education. Not one such theory stands up to systematic logic or practical experiment.

It is doubtful if more than an extremely minute proportion even of mental defectives in any community can be described as 'ineducable'. Imbeciles are educable; and many patients in mental hospitals who were formerly thought ineducable in any effective way have had their performance on 'intelligence quotient' tests raised twenty to thirty points by a little suitable help. So much for ineducability; but large blocks of humanity are not backward hospital inmates. In any nation or ethnic group we find the same scatter of intellectual potentiality. You cannot say anything at all about a 'race' or community as a whole, in terms of what they are or might be in respect of educational potentiality – except to say that they are all equally educable, given the same or equivalent suitable chances.[1]

Not all European nations have a bad record of discrimination against coloured people. The French may be intellectually and culturally arrogant; but they are not so on grounds of pigmentation. Other nations, like the Danes, so seldom see dark skins that they may go out of their way to look at a coloured man or woman. This they do with curiosity, of course, but with respect and friendship. Of the Russians the same might be said (since the Revolution) as about the French, except that in their case self-admiration is on ideological and technological grounds; yet before the Revolution the Russian government had a bad imperial record in Asia.

In southern Europe, the Portuguese and Spaniards feared the Moors, and hated them on religious grounds; but they were bound to admire their military prowess, their fine buildings, and their science. Therefore they have not usually felt more objection to North Africans than they had for any other enemies, especially heretics or infidels. Miscegenation as such has never seemed abhorrent to them. This fact has affected the colonial practices of both countries. Spaniards in the Americas freely interbred with the indigenous peoples and their slaves; and in Brazil every conceivable kind of mixing takes place, except perhaps economic. The colour bar, as understood in some other places, does not operate. Hispanization in the former Spanish colonies was ruthless; but though this was often cruel the fact that it took place proves that no serious bar of colour or race existed as such.

Complications have undoubtedly been introduced into the relations between peoples of different colours by the harsh fact of slavery. But to get this factor in its right proportion we must remember that white people kept other white people as slaves in Greece and Rome; slavery is taken for granted in the Old Testament and the Koran; people were

---

[1] See Bibby, C., *Race, Prejudice and Education*, London (Heinemann), 1959.

For studies of the psychology of discriminators and those discriminated against, the following are recommended: Richmond, A. H., *The Colour Problem*, London (Pelican Books), 1955; Dollard, J., *Caste and Class in a Southern Town*, New York (Harper and Bros), 1937; Cash, W. J., *The Mind of the South*, New York (A. Knopf), 1941.

For studies of particular areas see the following: Little, K. L., *Negroes in Britain*, London (Kegan Paul), 1948; Glass, R., *The Newcomers*, London (Allen & Unwin), 1960; Robb, J. H., *Antisemitism in a Working Class Area*, London (Tavistock), 1956; Myrdal, G., *An American Dilemma*, New York (Harper), 1944; Ashmore, H. S., *The Negro and the Schools* (University of N. Carolina Press), 1954.

bought and sold by the Chinese until recently; and the Africans themselves not only kept other Africans as slaves, but made a fat living out of selling captives to anyone who would buy them. This went on certainly until the abolition of slavery by Brazil in 1888, and is suspected of continuing now.

Excuses that white Christians could advance for dealing in slaves included the following: the supposed natural servility of some races; the rather hypocritical belief that slavery or serfdom as an institution was so widespread that its practitioners were doing nothing extraordinary; the belief that in the natural state the enslaved populations were either so harshly treated or such superstitious pagans that paternalistic bondage would be preferable. But why go on and on? Men will always find excuses for what they want to do; and better excuses are needed for doing a wrong thing. The main point is that this combination of excuses made out that black people especially were only on the fringe of the human condition, unable to claim the respect that humanity demanded, and in any case extremely backward. Slavery moreover (irrespective of the brutality of slave masters and dealers) broke up marriage as understood in Africa and Europe, encouraged lechery between slaves and between master and slave, and reduced the morality of the slave compound to that of the barnyard not only in sexual matters but in such things as fighting, stealing, and the rest. This was an imposed 'morality'; but it was comforting for white ladies and some sanctimonious people to pretend that it was natural to coloured slaves.

After emancipation or urbanized demoralization as we see them in the Southern United States and the Union of South Africa, the man of colour tends to be used exclusively as a hireling. That is his status; he must be kept to it. Otherwise he becomes an economic competitor. Thus reasons must be found not only for keeping him down, but also for showing him to be inferior. Ingenuity does not fail. The guilt complex of the masters, and all kinds of sexual legend, are used to impose segregation. Dirt, drunkenness, and disease fester in *any* segregated slum. These phenomena are all capitalized by segregation's exploiters or defenders. They are described and discussed in the books referred to. We must look at some of their scholastic consequences.

If it were true, as it seldom is, that formally equal schooling were provided for segregated populations, the judgement of the United States Supreme Court in 1954 must still be heeded: that segregation of any sort is by itself a denial of equal opportunities. All the evidence gathered by observation in many parts of the world shows this to be true. In any case, ostensibly equal treatment and facilities are usually the result of a belated attempt to make up for all-too-obvious existing inadequacies. This is certainly the case in Louisiana, Alabama, and Georgia, where some remarkably fine schools have been built for Negro children in recent years. People see buildings more readily than they take account of the internal scholastic opportunities, the supply of teachers, career prospects, and the whole matrix of home and society in which unequally treated children and parents have to live out their lives.

Colour prejudice is a complex telling much more about the segregator than about the segregated. It can be studied as a phenomenon in itself; but the *practice* of having schoolchildren segregated either by law (still an important factor in the South) or for other and more accidental reasons (in the North of the United States) is inseparable from other considerations which have essentially nothing to do with colour, because they are social and economic.

In considering the Negro segregated by other things than law (which is his position in some Northern cities) we are dealing with factors which in other situations equally affect Italian, Mexican, or other poor immigrants, but which are more intractable in the case of the Negro because of his ineradicable colour and all the backlog of legends used to justify slavery and other forms of exploitation. The resentment of the coloured man against such calumnies can be relieved only by an acknowledgement that similar calumnies were used, for example, in Britain against the white slum dwellers in English cities until the end of the nineteenth century (and sometimes later). In the Southern United States, resentment surviving from the Civil War is still an important factor impairing the prospects of racial equality and national co-operation.

The existence in the Americas especially of so many people of African (and sometimes of Indian) origin is due to the development of cotton and sugar growing or to the use of cheap labour for use in near-tropical or tropical conditions. But we must note that these same crops were first cultivated in many areas by white men. In the Southern states only a very small proportion ever owned slaves; yet the majority of rural people grew cotton, tobacco, and other cheap-labour crops. 'Poor white' cheap labour is still one of the Negro's worst foes. In Australia, sugar is a crop using exclusively white labour. In South Africa, the role of the Bantu in mines and farming is one which is played by machines in Canada, or was divided between Mexicans, Poles, Germans, and other immigrants in the United States. Machines and labour legislation can give them full status. There is no doubt that with greater mechanization and modernization of outlook most of the reasons for the present maintenance of segregation in any country could quickly disappear. Thus educational advance, in the technological as in the humane sphere, can greatly alter the prospect for segregation. It is noteworthy that most segregating areas of the world are markedly conservative if not backward (like Mississippi) in the development of educational opportunity for their white as well as for their coloured populations.

We should briefly set out some of the world facts about segregation, and its disappearance. In the Union of South Africa, where *apartheid* is segregation in its most radical form, neither the white people nor the Bantu are indigenous. The early natives (bushmen and Hottentots) were reduced or driven out by the immigrant Bantu from the north, who arrived about the same time as Dutch settlers, during the seventeenth and eighteenth centuries. Now there are about $6\frac{1}{2}$ million Bantu in rural areas, of whom 3 million live in tribal reserves. An additional 2 million Bantu, approximately, live in towns and cities, where they are not allowed to own land. Africans are 68·8 per cent. of the population, occupying 13 per cent. of the land. In 1951 the white population was 2,643,000; of these, only 670,000 are rural dwellers. In addition, there is a large 'coloured' population consisting of about 1 million descendants of mixed marriages or liaisons between white people and others. There are also 300,000 Indians, mostly in Natal, who are the descendants of indentured or contracted labourers. A majority of the white population (60 per cent.) are of Dutch descent; their mother tongue is a simplified but now vigorous form of Dutch, called Afrikaans. Their church is one or other variant of the Dutch Reformed Church, fundamentalist and conservative. A very large minority of the white people, however, are of British descent or are immigrants who speak English. Afrikaans and English are both official languages. The indigenous languages are not. The 13 Bantu languages had originally no alphabet until European scholars provided them; but now their literature is growing.

The principle prevails that primary education 'is free to all'. It is compulsory for white children from seven years of age to fifteen. The medium of instruction is the mother tongue (for white children) though this is sometimes very officiously decided against children's and parents' wishes. White children are supposed to know both English and Afrikaans; English-speaking children are seldom bilingual however. Schooling is also nominally compulsory for coloured children and Indians (but not for Africans). Only about two-thirds of the coloured and Indian children effectively attend school, and about a quarter of the Africans. They obviously have language problems where instruction is given in European languages. Even this small proportion of the Africans attend only for two or three years as a rule, and that only in the extremely basic 'sub-standards' where the barest elements of literacy and number are taught. The prospects for Indians and coloured children are a little better. The whole outlook for non-whites has however been made bleaker by tighter control of the missionary schools, which are now brought under government regulation. Previously they were more tolerant and generous than the official schools, particularly in the matter of *apartheid*.

At the secondary school level the opportunities for the different sections of the population are even more unequal. At the universities and technical institutions a strong resistance to increasing segregation was maintained; but now the 'open' or integrated universities are forbidden to non-whites. Higher education for Africans is now limited to facilities at Fort Hare and other segregated colleges, which even with the greatest of determination can hardly hope to compare in their unfortunate isolation with the standards and facilities of the nine white universities. These acts are justified by many South Africans not usually in terms of undoubted self-interest but in terms of a crusade for a 'white civilization', preached in the Afrikaans churches in Abraham-like terms. In the highly mobile and enthusiastic Africa of today, the Union of South Africa voted in 1960 for a republican constitution to safeguard the privilege of the eighteenth century and the ethics of the Old Testament. In 1961, the Union left the British Commonwealth.

The situation in the United States, though unsatisfactory, is much better than that in South Africa. It also shows a vast improvement upon what was usual in the United States a generation ago. Of about 180 millions (1960 census), some 12 per cent. are coloured. In the U.S.A., as distinct from South Africa, this term indicates all recognizably non-white persons. The great majority of these are descendants of imported slaves; but a very high proportion of them have some or much white ancestry. Of the fifty states, seventeen in the South have persisted in maintaining formal and legal segregation of Negroes and whites, despite the Supreme Court ruling. Some difficulties should be noted. Some segregating states declare people with a minute proportion of coloured ancestry to be Negroes (e.g. one thirty-second, or one six-teenth); others are less doctrinaire. Many Negroes look very light, or white; and not all have African features. Other administrative difficul-ties should be mentioned. Many of the so-called 'border' states (i.e. in the Civil War) and some Southern states like Texas have unsegregated districts. Arkansas, so much in the news, had some desegregated col-leges, clubs, and schools before the 1958–9 trouble at Little Rock. Each year since 1954 has shown much swinging over to integrated schooling in many districts – Southern, border, and Northern.

Most Northern states have no official segregation at all; but in the poor areas of large towns and cities (New York, Chicago, Detroit, Cincinatti, for example) segregation is effected by residence. Federally aided housing estates do not have segregation, any more than the armed forces or the Federal administration of the United States. Socially a great deal of discrimination is shown in housing, club membership, the professions, and business generally; but to be fair we must note that a remarkable change has taken place since the beginning of the War. This has been not merely in recognition of the educational and social advance of many previously backward slum dwellers, but also in recognition of the justice of their claims. Integrated war-time military service helped a great deal.

The activities of the National Association for the Advancement of Colored People (N.A.A.C.P.), the evidence of a world-wide scandal, and the fear of Russian competition in non-white countries have all contributed; but two other considerations must also be weighed in. Mechanization and industrialization have given Negroes such a high purchasing capacity that, though lower than the white American average, their average standard of living is higher than that of nearly all white nations elsewhere. The coloured trade unionist counts for a lot. The coloured purchaser and (in all but the Deep South) the col-oured voter exercise direct influence. The example of some of the finest independent schools and universities in admitting all able students equally has recently been very influential. Polls now show that the overwhelming majority of Americans feel that all segregation is evil and must be ended, as the Supreme Court said, 'with all deliberate speed'. The only snag is that ambitious or snobbish parents want desegregation to start somewhere else – not next door or in Junior's school.

So much has already been written on this problem that in the limited space available no more can be said here. The difficulty of ensuring the actual change-over that now seems ultimately inevitable is discussed fully in Ashmore's *The Negro and the Schools*, and in an article of my own.[1] Problems of removing barriers caused by less organized and unofficial discrimination must however be seen in a wider world context of unfair treatment. Mrs Glass's survey[2] shows racial prejudice as it appears in England. We must never forget too that discrimination on the ground of colour exists markedly among coloured people themselves.[3] It is found not only in the United States and other parts of America but also in India, where newspaper advertisements for desirable marriages leave no doubt at all about colour prejudice. This was manifest long before Europeans came upon the scene. To say so much does not excuse discrimination in any way. It simply testifies to the universal use of any locally available excuse for social, economic, or educational stratification. Schools and public example are the best means of combating prejudice intellectually and emotionally. Through career opportunities and the institutions with which they are linked they can also quickly transform the prospects of segregated populations. There is no overlooking the international impact of Soviet example and propaganda, either.

In addition to the relatively prejudice-free examples of France, Brazil, and the Soviet Union, we should also give credit to the white New Zealanders for an enlightened and amiable relationship with the Maoris. After misunderstandings, warfare, and injustice the Maoris are fully New Zealanders in educational, occupational, social, and political rights. At first an attempt was made to integrate them to the white man's ways – an acculturation they can still freely have if they wish; but now it is recognized that Maori schools with Maori instruction in Maori ways are equally their right if they wish. Maori schools can be and are attended by *pakeha* (white) children. Maoris not only have M.P.s but have provided an acting prime minister. The Maori population declined for decades, but has risen again to about 127,000 out of a total of about $2\frac{1}{4}$ million.

We can find a clue to the solving of many racial and social problems in a very familiar phenomenon. In previous chapters reference was made to the unfair treatment of women in many parts of the world.

[1] 'Segregation and American society', *British Journal of Educational Studies*, November 1956.

[2] Glass, R., *The Newcomers*, London (Allen & Unwin), 1960.

[3] This can readily be seen in the advertisements and 'socialite' gossip of the American Negro journals *Jet* and *Ebony*. It is a growing factor in the West Indies, perhaps more so with the departure of white domination.

This has been the consequence not only of their biological links with domesticity but because their menfolk regarded them as 'special' rather than as equivalent human beings, even after outright bullying and ownership had ceased. Women are different, but equal, and men need their difference. Surely this gives us a clue to our future treatment of formerly owned and bullied populations with a different colour or culture. The shocks and prejudices which we all share to some degree when we encounter the unfamiliar, especially if an outsider seems a rival to us, are caused not so much by the unsatisfactoriness of others as by the canonization of our own way of life to a point at which it seems unquestionably the only way. That kind of ritual-making and formalization is found in children. It is also a symptom of pre-senile decline, in societies as well as people. Which diagnosis suits our own undue rigidity?

Shall we open ourselves up to a more adult realization of Terence's old saying: 'I am a human being; therefore I think that nothing of human kind is alien to me'? Or are we to go the way of the unadaptable empires of the past? We seek technical improvements in living and schooling. We open up opportunity to quite a surprising degree. But is that enough? Might we be only broadening the social basis of the old sterility, as some over-intellectual school systems have seemed to do? Change means what it says; it is not enough to add more people to the unadaptable hierarchy of an *ancien régime* or to build up a new 'meritocracy'. Change implies total flexibility, though it does not imply flux. Flux comes when we are so rigid that others flow around us, leaving our standards behind yet being uncertain of new ones.

To suggest as radical and continuous a breaking down of barriers as possible is not to abandon the past. Indeed, the more conservative we are in wishing to conserve the best of the past, the more must we try to find ways of sharing it with others. The traditions we value are great because they have lived and grown. They have arisen out of living solutions to human problems in such a way as to find perennial but fresh re-expression in succeeding ages. We must carry on that continuity in time; spatially we must also be eager to spread the sharing of values that industrialization, science, and communication have now made accessible to all mankind.

CHAPTER 14

Understanding our world

Public education on a mass scale is a relatively new invention, at any rate in the sense of something formally provided by public bodies in and outside school to influence the intellectual and cultural development of the people. This invention is as yet only at the beginning of its career. From securing simple literacy and technological preparedness, public education has progressed through the encouragement of orderliness and health towards conscious preparation for world understanding.

The use of this term must not be misunderstood in our present context. Hardly any nation consciously sets out on a deliberate programme of developing 'world-mindedness' as such in the schools, though statesmen everywhere talk a lot about it and though educational advisers sincerely advocate the extension of children's horizons. It is this last, semi-conscious endeavour on the part of individuals and groups which has prepared the way for the formal campaign that some crusaders for international understanding would like to see carried on. Campaigns for international understanding are seldom given really effective support; yet in one sense much progress has been made. Internationally important events have greatly widened everyone's horizon. Let us think about this less overt preparation of young people for civilization in world terms, so that we can see where we stand.

Some countries, especially the U.S.A. and the United Kingdom, have huge international commitments and anxieties – not to speak of trading interests. Yet the popular awareness of the world in these countries is still so limited that it would be laughable, if it were not so tragic for the whole of mankind. In the case of the United States this widespread ignorance is peculiarly regrettable, because of the admirable rise of an immigrant population to international prestige and power through the use of new techniques that could equally advance the rest of the world. The venerable values of Western civilization are sincerely revered in the American way of life. More than that, they have caused the advantages of freedom, education, and prosperity to be more widely diffused through the population than has proved possible in those older countries whose technology still moves in low gear, often because of the braking effect of long outmoded social assumptions. The example of the United States is one of the major constituents in any thinking about the future of civilization anywhere.

On top of the example of American social experiments at home, we must add the influence of the United States' international example. The Federal government has been generous to other countries on an unprecedented scale. Much of this aid has been undertaken for humanitarian reasons; yet statesmen are not blind to the fact that enlightened self-interest would often prompt similar moves. In these circumstances, when the eyes of half the world are upon the American scene, it is paradoxical that district or state influences on school systems sometimes cause children to be well primed on local history and institutions, informed of constitutional rights and such matters, but only half aware of what life adds up to even in other regions of the United States. Texas is an outstanding but not isolated case. It is the more ridiculous because Texas is a rich state whose prosperity depends on exporting oil, beef, and fruit – the very stuff of other people's lives. Many parochially brought up children consider that life in the rest of the Americas is an un-American rivalry. Europe, Asia, and Africa are either effete places, or liabilities to the American taxpayer. These fanciful world pictures, so dangerous in the present international situation, are conjured up by the official or semi-official weighting of the school curriculum in favour of local interests; but they are sometimes made much worse by the cultivation of what passes for 'social studies' in place of old-fashioned geography or new-style 'study of mankind'.

However, schools can work only in the social context woven about them by adults. Parochialism of the kind described above is only to be expected where newspapers devote more than half their space to local news or scandal-mongering, with only about a quarter allotted to genuine national news, and even less for matters of international importance. That is characteristically the case with most American newspapers, for these are preponderantly provincial because of the geographical nature of the country and the 'grass roots' tradition. British newspapers are not so localized; but some of them are as sensation-ridden as the worst anywhere, and a number of them are conspicuously parochial in another sense. It is all too often assumed that only one way of life, one expression of human interests, is the 'right and proper' interpretation of the great drama of mankind. It would be bad enough if that were a generally British way of life. Unfortunately it is but a one-sided evaluation of that in most of the large-circulation periodicals. True, some British newspapers and periodicals take their international and humane responsibilities very seriously; but those most conspicuous in these matters are plagued with anxieties about circulation. If it were not for the extremely disturbing nature of recent international events, bringing threats to peace and disturbances to trade (which make good copy), it is doubtful whether the popular press would open many windows on the world.

Television has been very important in Britain in breaking down many barriers. The sobriety and responsibility of both B.B.C. and independent programmes deserve high praise. Cumulatively this awareness adds up in children's minds. It is extended in school, both in formal lessons and in educational broadcasts and films. Yet slow progress seems inevitable unless there is a conscious and concerted drive to remind all children constantly, everywhere, of their interdependence. This can be done in many countries of the world in association with nearly every bite eaten, every item of clothing or other article used. In time, we hope, the major media of popular information may respond to such a deliberately induced awareness. It is undoubtedly preferable to encourage it through the interchanges of peace than through the threat of war. In any case, the only defence against war is to prevent it from breaking out; and the way to ensure that is to build up an all-pervading sense of our complementariness to each other at all points.

Western parochialism does not stop the eyes of the world from turning constantly towards the American example. In the circumstances of today a very obvious polarity has developed, as between the U.S.A. and the U.S.S.R. The countries of Europe are still important not only for what they have been but for what they can still offer in the future. But several of them have a lot to live down, and most of them suffer to some degree from marked international purblindness. This blinkered state does not altogether shut out the rest of the world, as a rule; it is as though some emotional block prevented a straight view of it in terms of common humanity and mutuality. The rapidly emerging countries in the rest of the world are profoundly suspicious of European manœuvres for the future. Not all their awareness of indebtedness for governmental forms, for democratic ideals and the rest, can allay fears of future selfishness. For these reasons we must come back again to the destiny of the United States, especially as affected by internal parochialism.

The great American exceptions to the parochial tradition in journalism, like the *New York Times* and some of the big regional papers with a wide influence, show up the inadequacies of the typical publication. If this *national* unawareness can be so marked in a highly mobile nation of travellers, it is hardly surprising that international interest (and still more, insight) is so poorly developed. No nation has more generously tried to help the rest of mankind in the post-war period than the United States, as a governmental corporate body; but for many Americans as persons it is still true to say that all this humanitarianism seems little more than an unprofitable drain on the exchequer. In other words, official humanitarianism is not yet personally humanizing for the average American. This is all the more regrettable because the non-communist world looks to the United States for an example, not least because a great power and a new civilization have been built on an amalgam of many nationalities.

The exigencies of nation-building, the period of isolationism, and the almost complete economic self-sufficiency of the United States have all contributed to this intellectual parochialism. Not even the fantastic tourist activity of the post-war years has done much to break it down. Americans are often astonishingly well 'adjusted' to their own system and mores; yet they often break down or fail to make contact as soon as they leave the system. It is to be hoped that such purblindness will be as temporary an affliction as some others of which Americans (to their great credit) have rid themselves. When all is said and done, the foreigner visiting the United States is extremely well looked after by official or voluntary agencies of international co-operation, whose enterprise and multiplicity cannot fail to impress him. There is nearly always a wonderful unofficial welcome too. But how little aware some homespun Americans can be of their compatriots' international activities can only be ascertained by inquiring in schools and homes. An extreme case I once encountered was in an admittedly rather dull but nevertheless graduate class in a Southern university, where only two students had ever heard of UNESCO, in 1956. Fortunately, change is on the way; but it still has a very long way to go before Americans as a whole are as internationally conscious as most Europeans. That is not always saying much.

In the Soviet Union at a first encounter we seem to find internationalism on a grand scale. There we see the 'international' league of this and the 'world-wide' campaign for that. However, the severe limitations on this world perspective promptly spring to the eye. Co-operation and friendship are often expressed and (I honestly believe) felt by the people themselves; but contacts and perceptions are effectively circumscribed not only by ideological differences (which may, after all, be a two-way barrier) but by the unilateral embargo placed by the authorities on 'corrupting' contacts with the non-communist world. There are signs that, if given their way, some elements in the Kremlin government might be prepared to take risks now that they feel so sure of the ultimate triumph of the communist system throughout the world. Scholars and researchers, as well as well-groomed delegations, are now finding their way abroad or welcoming foreign contacts; but the 'world-mindedness' of more junior citizens is carefully screened. Correspondence about sputniks, for example, said to be 'world-wide' was really all with 'socialist' countries or 'socialist' circles outside – and by 'socialist' the communists do not mean at all what you or I mean. The selection of foreign-language books and newspapers is extremely biased. Only communist or unfavourable portrayal of non-communist countries is allowed in literature or history, as a rule; and seemingly neutral books or papers in the English language seen in a Moscow Palace of Pioneers in 1960 had been published in such places as Bucarest. (The Rumanians use the same alphabet!)

We do not help either communists or ourselves to understand our world position if we smoothly accept or glibly use such terms as 'the free world' in contradistinction to 'captive nations' and the rest. Now it is true that our political organizations are free in the sense that we spontaneously organize ourselves in the most wayward fashion – a circumstance which I feel is necessary on epistemological no less than political grounds. To that extent we are free. We are also not forbidden to make contacts with people in other nations or other ideological systems, either in writing or personally. These are very important freedoms. But we often lack some other liberating opportunity that the Soviet citizen may possess in abundance; in our different countries these may be economic, social, medical, or educational. We are not always *free to* do all we are capable of in our own or others' interest; and we are certainly not always as *free from* certain severe handicaps as Soviet citizens generally are. We of course think our freedoms are of a higher priority in human affairs than theirs; but they do not always agree with us, and if they tacitly cherish our evaluation they may feel that our political freedom is as hamstrung by economic or social interference as theirs is by government controls. They may indeed believe that their embarrassments will evaporate more speedily than our own. This view challenges consideration in the West; and it is infinitely more impressive when seen from the viewpoint of the underdeveloped or otherwise handicapped populations of the world.

Thus, instead of feeling absolutely sure that our political self-congratulation is self-evidently justified, we should try to see our own world position as others see it. Otherwise we can never influence them. Our almost axiomatic acceptance of 'the only possible' viewpoint referred to at the beginning of the first chapter is no longer inevitable abroad. It may even be difficult for others. Our astonishment that others can think otherwise can only contribute to the decline of our international prestige and influence. Others can see our ideological shackles much more clearly than we can.

Why cannot we learn to see the limitations on our understanding – for our own selfish purposes, and quite apart from any effect we may hope to produce in the international field? To try to see just where we stand may feel like a sort of nakedness, or even vulnerability; but there is no reason why it should be in any way a self-destruction. In psychoanalysis or any other therapeutic confession, self-recognition is the beginning of a new personal growth. This may require some self-criticism. It must certainly be freed from self-deception.

In Britain, self-deception is practised on a colossal scale. We have the evidence of those distinctively British words 'smug' and 'humbug'. As has been said before, British newspapers include some of the best journalism in the world, and some of the very worst. Britain's cultural pattern is such that the great majority are still more attuned to the latter than to the former. The emphases of amusements and advertising seem determined to accentuate this polarization. Despite extended educational opportunities (which after all are on a scale that would have seemed like a pipe-dream in the 1930s), and despite hopeful evidence of a new basic recrudescence of cultural development, the majority of people do not seem to feel they are *partners* in any of it. At best they usually wear it like surburban gentility. Even their champions are worried by an apparent lack of enterprise or response on the part of those they are trying to advance. The protests of the 'Angry Young Men' tend to be patronized like some fashionable eccentricity.

The well-to-do and traditionally educated in the United Kingdom often openly express resentment against the popular aspirations and culture of the day. Their attitude to the majority, who leave school early, can sometimes only be compared with the resentful arrogance of those who show colour prejudice – as though the newcomers from the lower orders were alien undesirables poaching on private property. This is clearly shown by all the silly talk about 'making them pay' for necessary education. Another person's poor education is my peril. To restrict public education is as benighted a policy as attempts to restrict the public health provision a century ago. Cholera and typhoid were not class-conscious then; nor are disaffection, irresponsibility, and non-co-operation now. A little ignorance, or a little feeling of 'otherness', grows as quickly as a little disease. If any section of society attempts to live off others' endeavours, or to ride on others' backs, or even just to 'get their own back', that is a disease of the whole society.

That it is a very widespread disease is shown by the immediate recognition and acceptance of such expressions as 'I'm all right, Jack' (or coarser equivalents). It reveals itself too in the restrictive practices and outmoded 'sitting tight' of both producers and employees. It is noticeable in growing incivility, and in increasing untidiness and dirt in public places. (These once unfamiliar accusations are now beginning to be a by-word abroad. Comparisons are made not only with the amazingly public-spirited tidiness of Russia but with improvements made in Austria, Italy, and perhaps less expected places.) The British post-war revival has been much slower than that of other European countries worse hit than Britain was. There has been a great and sudden increase in delinquency, and an even greater one in general shiftlessness. In many ways positive wrongdoing seems more acceptable than amoral shirking. It is not such clear evidence of *general* cultural disintegration.

This demoralization, already considered as a phenomenon of youth, is also an adult breakdown found in all classes. It is indeed not confined to Britain. 'I couldn't care less' was a transatlantic import, popular though it became in Europe. In Germany the cry was *Ohne mich* ('Leave me out'). In France cynical *je-m'en-foutisme* expresses the same repudiation of social responsibility. The Danes too are greatly worried by indifference; so are the Swedes, and the Dutch. The Americans have their beatnik problem (as well as severe delinquency); and the Russians are worried (though less) by 'non-positive' attitudes and 'even religion'. A two-headed bugbear is seen in each of these examples – withdrawal from responsibility towards society as a whole, and retirement into a separate order of things that lends greater significance or meaning to one's routine of life than the approved norms of the community.

These are all symptoms we have discussed before. What we have to consider now is how far our scholastic assumptions and arrangements may contribute to them. In other words, we must see how far the 'first round' of public education on a mass scale has failed, and what must be done to make it a success in future. It is very difficult to secure a sudden turn-about of elaborate administrative arrangements, or to divert expensive plant to unfamiliar and untried purposes; but in the preparation of the future teachers themselves it is at least possible to secure a quite different interpretation of the function of teaching.

The teacher's attitude can never be one of acceptance, or of handing-on, no matter how traditionalist our views – because of the very simple truth that educators must hand on the past *to another public in another context*. To get others to accept it (if that is the right thing) we must not only speak their language but also enable them to claim all that the past can offer as their very own, or – if they wish – to modify it to suit their purposes. Only thus do we recognize the dignity and relevance of all human beings. That is the basic condition of being truly civic or religious, or both. Therefore, if we exclude any section of society from the opportunity to learn and develop, we are undermining the past as well as the future.

How can we do that? How can ignorance *grow*, as was stated a page or two ago? The answer to both these questions is substantially the same: if relevant information or interpretation is shut off from any group in society, we promptly repudiate the very essence of all civilization and religion – that we should be recognized as relevant to each other, or members of one another. Ignorance or indifference festering in a corner of society causes mortification of that area just as certain as the atrophy or necrosis of a member cut off from the circulation of the blood. To say this is in no way to preach the 'organic' theory of the state. It is simply to recognize a quite different truth: that communication and sympathy must be continuous and fluid throughout society for *any* of it to be real. If we cut off other people, we cut off ourselves.

Therefore a class-structured or otherwise sectionalized educational system is perilous. It is not essentially perilous for that reason alone, because some long-standing class systems associated with well-ordered cosmogonies have still communicated to succeeding generations an acceptable 'world view'. But then that 'world view' has been shared by all persons and classes within the culture. In our multiple society, adhering to no one religious, political, or other organization of experience, all constituent 'world views' are essential to the whole awareness of our culture. Yet they can never be anything other than so much discord and contradiction, unless we positively secure the communication of many kinds of 'awareness' and sympathy. We must provide opportunity for self-formation and self-expression. We must also make it clear how each idiom is relevant to the whole, to be shared and judged by the whole, even though it may not be accepted.

Thus, if it does prove necessary for any scholastic or social system to establish competition or a hierarchy of any sort, it should nevertheless be an open competition. Any functional differentiation must remain *complementary* to the functions and needs of everyone else. There need not therefore be a 'mass culture' in the literal or monolithic sense; but any viable civilization must be popular in the sense of including all the people in its opportunities, purview, and aspirations.

Now a system like the present British pattern of education does not satisfy these requirements. There are privileged schools which, though scholastically excellent in most traditional ways, are largely cut off from real experience of others and are out of the reach of others. (I say nothing about unequal access to jobs here, concentrating here on the matter of awareness and 'membership'.) There are other schools, like the grammar schools, which do an excellent job in imparting knowledge and other forms of personal training; but despite continuous evolution their sensitivity and adaptability to modern needs have been handicapped by the isolation of the 3 per cent.[1] above and the 75 per cent. below. (For that is the way nearly every Briton sees the position.) It is not only a matter of 'above' or 'below'. The question of *types* of interest and approach to the problems of living is highly relevant to the establishment of a modern British culture – attuned to all actualities and ready for world-wide significance.

Nearly everyone training teachers for work in the different kinds of school, or discussing school work with experienced teachers in any one of them, will have noticed many times that their comments on such things as 'the child', 'the school', 'the community', or 'the working world' reveal different worlds of awareness – or, in another word, isolationism. It is assumed that only the speaker's world is real. Anything else is of less significance, even if it is not altogether ignored. Others are, so to speak, foreigners. Such isolationists forget that we are *all* foreigners.

People who speak or think in this way are very ready to condemn any supposed 'lowering of standards' or 'abandoning of principles' or

---

[1] 3 per cent. is the figure usually given for the proportion of schoolchildren attending Public Schools; but that entails stretching the latter category to its utter limits. In 1961 the Headmaster of Eton calculated the proportion in Public Schools as not more than 2 per cent. Professor H. C. Dent put it at substantially less than 2 per cent. in the years preceding 1944.

'treason towards culture' (it depends which country you are in). They forget that the supposed maintenance of particular standards and so on in one quarter may actually be accompanied by a widespread crumbling of general standards or other disintegration elsewhere in the body politic. There is no logical reason why it should happen, of course; but it is a painful fact that isolation or rejection usually does have this effect. Moreover, the almost mechanical judging of 'standards' (i.e. quality) by the mere *amount* of *the same stuff* that happens to be present in the different kinds of school programme is arrogance as illogical as if we were to persist in judging gentlemanly quality by the amount of lace or wig displayed.

We can have creditable 'standards' expressed in many different ways. Though a certain amount of knowledge or skill is absolutely necessary, of course, for some highly indispensable occupations, so that we can properly insist on standards *in that respect*, we are not then concerned with 'standards' in any absolute sense. Yet that is usually implied. To know what 'standards' are in any general or valid sense, we must gather up information about all the *different kinds* of standards that may be actually required in all parts of our corporate activity, and take steps to see that they are all secured. Otherwise it is we who are neglecting standards. We are also making the attainment of our own cultural objectives impossible; for we are destroying the social matrix in which they have to be achieved.

The gathering up of all relevant viewpoints is not automatically achieved, of course, even by the most alert minds. It needs to be prepared for not only by careful study but by constant vigilance too. No local experiment such as our own entire public provision of education during the past lifetime can tell us very much about educational desiderata in general. No one national system can tell us much about itself, unless we are at pains to recognize our experiment as the local and short-lived affair it is. We must look around carefully at others' example. Thus we may see what we have done wrong. One of the hardest things for us to do, however, is to see our own omissions. What have we left out that other people take care of? What can we discover that is better done by other people?

It was questions like this which, in the early days of public education in Europe, prompted administrators and supervisors (but hardly ever the poor teachers themselves) to go abroad and spy on neighbours. Disconcerting reports were often brought home of how much better the neighbours managed, especially in terms of the technological education so vital to the development of enterprises in the nineteenth century. Some books call this activity 'Comparative Education'. It is not that, of course, but the study of foreign educational systems (in German, *Auslandspädagogik*). Such a study can be of immediate practical utility in special cases; but it is much more fundamentally important to teachers or other students of mankind to learn what makes other cultural systems tick, or what interferes with their working.

One of the factors in personal and social development is the school system, of course; but this in turn takes its significance, aims, and effectiveness from the whole social matrix in which it is found. It is that that imparts the cultural dynamic and resources which make schools successful or failures. Therefore the study of foreign educational systems and practice is meaningless or misleading unless we prepare ourselves for it by a more humane background study of the nation or people concerned. Such a survey is part of the study of mankind – and of ourselves. It will never be effective unless (for the time being) we make ourselves as neutral as possible. That is to say, we do not look at *foreign* educational systems, and we do not even look at foreigners. We look at one local and topical experiment in the whole kaleidoscope of human experimentation, a full view of which is essential to our self-understanding – supposing that can ever be fully achieved. The answers so far evolved by the whole of our national system are as partial and incomplete by total human standards as the several parts of our own system are in relation to its entirety. We should therefore try to see ourselves too as remotely as possible. One of the best ways of doing this is to fasten our attention on to two very far-away cultural systems, which every inhabitant there took as much for granted as we do ours.

Little more than a hundred years ago the sole mediator between man and heaven, namely the Emperor of China, was forced at British gun-point to accept the presence of representatives of European governments at the imperial court (1860). This was just one more example of barbarian aggression, for how could the personal embodiment of the world's finest civilization really believe that the foreign devils were able or entitled to hold equal discourse with him or his servants? China had known the right way for some 2,500 years. Previous concessions to barbarians had merely been a sort of staving-off or bribery; there was no question of reciprocity. Therefore it was not for many years more that Chinese ambassadors were sent abroad with any effective powers; and the presence of foreigners in China was regarded as little better than a temporary expedient, if not a disease. We should note that

Chinese distaste for the foreigner was not just a matter of race or descent, but was strongly influenced by considerations of merit; for the imperial administrators had for many centuries been recruited by merit as displayed in competitive examinations. The barbarians were irrelevant and undeserving.

At about the same time (1853 and 1854) the Americans forced another infallible mediator between man and heaven to open up his country to trade and other contacts. This was the Japanese Emperor, the descendant of heaven. As a matter of fact, it was the impact of occidental influences which finally brought about the overthrow of the shogunate (a clique of military regents) and the restoration of the Emperor to full powers. In 1868 the Meiji restoration ('Meiji' means 'order of enlightenment') introduced the period of large-scale copying of Western skills and activities already described in Chapter 5; but the point to notice here is that despite all this remarkable re-education the Emperor remained divine and infallible. This can be seen from the Imperial Rescript on education of 1890, twenty-two years later. The Rescript starts with the words: 'Our Imperial ancestors established Our Empire on broad and eternal foundations and implanted . . . that virtue whose beauty has been demonstrated from generation to generation by Our subjects ever united in loyalty and filial piety.' It then commands obedience and self-sacrifice so as to 'safeguard and maintain the prosperity of Our Imperial Throne, co-eternal with heaven and earth'. The proclamation continues: 'The Way here mapped out is in truth the teaching handed down by Our Imperial ancestors to be observed alike by their Descendants and by their Descendants' subjects, infallible throughout the ages, true in all places.' [1] Infallible and certain though the Japanese value-system was, and dedicated to unchanging standards, neither the Japanese administrators nor the Japanese people have been afraid to admit that other countries were ahead of them in technical or other detail. By large-scale copying and domestic reorganization they have brought their country out of the middle ages to modern world-power status in a lifetime.

If infallible 'ways of life' can bring themselves in the very short space of a century (for what is that in a recorded history of millennia?) to re-assess their social and educational tradition in the most radical way, why should it be difficult for us or anyone else to measure our present assumptions and practices by world criteria? After all, we pride our-

[1] See Stoetzel, J., *Without the Chrysanthemum and the Sword*, London (Heinemann/UNESCO), 1955, p. 102.

selves on empiricism, evolutionary progress, and multiple growth. With every handicap of infallibility both the Japanese and the Chinese have learned from those whom they formerly despised. We do not claim infallibility, and we pretend not to despise each other. We have good examples before us if we want to set out to copy this or that item of other people's school systems. Marc-Antoine Jullien, Matthew Arnold, and Michael Sadler spring to the mind.

What is recommended here is not the slavish copying of any item, much less the whole system. On the contrary. Every living school system, and every re-appraisal of that system, must be an evolutionary process within the context in which it finds itself. Some items may doubtless be adopted, but only by being adapted. The crucial part of our study is the resolution to determine *our* present position by comparative examination, to re-appraise *our* present orientation by similar criteria, and to start out again in a more appropriate direction.

So much for the modification of school systems. Even if we do not structurally modify our system, we must still remember what has been said here about atrophying our growth by cutting ourselves off from the sources of information and understanding available to us abroad. 'The school', 'the child', 'the teacher', 'the home', 'the curriculum', and even 'the essentials of education' are understandable only in terms of mankind. Therefore, as part of their professional preparation all teachers must have some genuine acquaintance with people and schools in other countries than their own.

This is not always possible at first hand, though that is becoming increasingly easy. Teachers must therefore undertake study and sympathetic examination of other school systems – organization, aims, and difficulties. Otherwise they remain unacquainted with activities which may demonstrate the falsity of what they do, or may corroborate their preference in some moment of uncertainty, or may show that an additional viewpoint is necessary for the full complement of understanding. Only in this way can teachers understand their jobs, deal intelligently with their responsibilities, and go on educating themselves through their work.

Quite apart from any slavish adherence to mechanical routine, (which kills children's alertness), and quite apart from some unfortunate insistence on the wrong subjects for the wrong reasons, much school work is vitiated by the blinkered state of people's knowledge. Educators are not exempt from this failing. Many geography and history textbooks are notoriously partial. This we readily see when we examine the material used in Soviet and East European schools. But we can see it equally well when reading different accounts of the American Revolution (or the War of Independence, if you prefer) on opposite sides of the Atlantic. Many previous differences of presentation are being smoothed out; but numerous obstacles remain in different countries.[1] For accuracy no less than for the sake of international understanding, they must be attended to. In this matter as in most others, what may be mistrusted by some as 'international understanding' is really only self-understanding in truer terms.[2]

In the field of self-recognition through international contacts, all kinds of school visit or exchange of personnel *may* be fruitful. On the other hand they may not. It all depends on the degree of preparedness of the students, teachers, or other people involved. Mere tourism and gaping at 'foreigners' are often harmful. The foreigners we should gape at are ourselves. Given some self-awareness we may benefit very greatly by purposeful travel or by taking part in some world-conscious organization. In many countries a wide range of activities cater for all kinds of internationally humane interest. Because there is no space here, and because this chapter must deal with other aspects of developing world awareness, reference is merely made to two excellent sources of information about these activities: *Education for International Understanding*, London (Parliamentary Group for World Government); and the American publications of the International Information Administration, the International Educational Exchange Program, and the U.S. Office of Education in the Department of Health, Education, and Welfare.

One of the most remarkable developments of the post-war period has been the supply of technical assistance and the lending of experts, primarily but not exclusively to hitherto underdeveloped countries. The effect has been obvious in actual fact; it is also noteworthy that most such territories now prefer to call themselves 'developing countries'. In other words, uplift has been social and psychological as well as technical and economic. It is thus indirectly educative, and it provides the material basis for much formal education too. UNESCO, the Food and Agriculture Organization of the United Nations, and many assisted

---

[1] See *History Textbooks and International Understanding*, J. A. Lauwerys (UNESCO), 1953. See also Dance, E. H., *History the Betrayer* (Hutchinson), 1960.

[2] See also *A Handbook of Suggestions on the Teaching of Geography*, N. V. Scarfe (UNESCO), 1953; and *Suggestions on the Teaching of History*, C. P. Hill (UNESCO), 1953. Other advice is contained in *Teaching for International Understanding*, C. F. Strong (H.M.S.O.), London, 1952.

self-help schemes like the Colombo Plan are cases in point. In addition, such countries as the United Kingdom, the United States, and the Soviet Union have made direct subventions in many ways.

The British scheme of 'special relationship' with overseas universities has already been mentioned; but it is only one of many such devices for letting educators at home and abroad work in 'double harness' until new countries can stand on their own. For example, at the end of 1960, despite a home shortage of teachers, the British government set up a National Council for the Supply of Teachers Overseas. This supervises the organized expatriation of valuable personnel, and also brings overseas students to training colleges in Britain.

In the United States, the Foreign Operations Administration undertook much assistance of this kind very soon after the war, and the precedent established has since been continued on a most generous scale by public and private agencies. The Fulbright scheme, so well known, is only one of numerous instruments developed for this purpose. Private foundations and public and private universities maintain a constant interflow of academic personnel. They welcome academic visitors from all parts of the world with great hospitality. Conferences and seminars are also conducted for journalists, politicians, and others likely to influence public opinion. The smaller American colleges, as well as the most famous, contribute richly to the vital interchange of goodwill.

Though such services are undoubtedly of first-class importance in the development of international understanding, they are indeed delicately balanced services. It is not unknown for students to return home with a bitter taste in their mouths after training in the United States or Britain, not because their hosts have done anything wrong but because some of their hosts' compatriots were so unsympathetic, if not hostile. Colour prejudice may sometimes be influential here; but it is far from being only a matter of colour. Sometimes the blame may be attributed to poor orientation of the visitors; sometimes the fault is the other way round. Patronage is so often offensive, no matter how well meant. There must always be reciprocity in any successful human relationship Therefore we see once again that partial education is never enough. International understanding may be pioneered among the intelligentsia; but to be effective it must extend throughout the whole of a country's school system.

On 1 October 1960 the Soviet Union opened a brand-new 'University of Friendship' in Moscow. There were over 35,000 applications for the 500 vacancies to be filled from Latin America, South-East Asia, and

Africa and the Middle East. Another 150 from all parts of the world will arrive every year henceforward. Sixty Soviet students were admitted to keep them company and communicate the essence of the Soviet way of life. This was only the culmination of a long programme of admissions to Soviet institutions. In the new university, in addition to general and preparatory courses, 80 per cent. of the students are offered training in the faculties of engineering, agriculture, and medicine. It is clear what an appeal these facilities will inevitably have throughout the world. In the course of learning the Russian language during the preparatory year, and subsequently, much will inevitably be communicated about the communist way of life and its international plans; but there is no direct insistence on Marxism-Leninism or on atheism, for example. There is no doubt that these visitors will find the Russian peoples friendly, and wholly committed to international friendship – within their own frame of reference. Their 'world view' includes the concept of 'service to humanity' – again within the terms of their faith. Soviet expatriate technicians and advisers in other lands are doubtless carefully groomed also to show the same attitudes. In the face of this contradiction of the Western pattern of political and social assumptions, it is clear that anything we can do to develop a greater international amity may be a safeguard for our own civilization.

Without any doubt, the development of the European Common Market and other economic and political associations will of themselves contribute powerfully to international awareness and sympathies. The Organization for European Co-operation (O.E.E.C.) already undertakes directly educative work, and has a fine series of publications to its credit. Several proposals to establish an international university have culminated in the designation of a site and constitution for one in Florence by the European Parliamentary Assembly in 1961.

Not only great nations are thus involved, perhaps for semi-strategic reasons. In Luxembourg an international school with internationally valid leaving certificates has been established since 1954.[1] Israel has an Afro-Asian Institute for Labour Studies and Co-operation, to train future trade union leaders from abroad. It is clear that in such cases honest and mutual appreciation must be more potent than an entirely one-way propaganda intention. This is the way it should always be with all teachers.

[1] See McKinnon, R., *Progress*, 1960, p. 296. Though this school has strong functional justification in serving the children of employees of the European Coal and Steel Community, it is capable of a much wider adaptation to suit similar circumstances elsewhere.

If teachers and administrators want to avoid being tradition-bound mandarins in the service of the unquestionable Way (like the Chinese of 1860), they must be positively restless in their search for a fairer view of issues in education – the very field in which we most actively shape humanity. Yet busy teachers have many disadvantages in this further-ance of global understanding. Though they are usually intelligent, sincere, and well behaved, they do not normally enjoy great prestige or power. Therefore they cannot shout a new gospel from the housetops, or sell it with their personalities from the television screen. Many teachers too (especially women) are over-conscious of others' authority, and fight shy of being victimized. They hesitate to prejudice their promotion prospects (rather small, as a rule). They often work hard to earn extra money in evening classes or other ways. They all too often clutter themselves up with marking. Though they are in a learned pro-fession they do not always read very much or very widely. They do not get much chance to see what other teachers do, though involved with them every day. In proportion as they are undogmatic (and therefore good teachers), they tend to have a larger than average share of the prevailing state of moral and social uncertainty. In teaching and in preparing for examinations, they must usually rely on textbooks de-vised by others, though they may not care for them. (This is true where they have an entirely free choice of books – and that does not happen in all countries.) For all these reasons the majority slip imperceptibly into routine or diffidence, and do not 'stir things up'.

All this is lamentable on any account, and most of all because teachers as a whole are dedicated to the development of humanity in every sense of that word. It would not be enough for them to sink themselves into even the best organized school system; for some of the most competently organized school systems manifestly show poor understanding of their own countries' needs, let alone the needs of man-kind. Therefore any teacher worth his salt must reach out beyond the system; he must fulfil himself by communicating his own sense of par-ticipating responsibility. There is no need whatever for him to repudi-ate his present context, his school as it is, or his personal patriotism; but it is imperative that he construes these as constituent parts of a wider commitment.[1] Thus, even without preaching or campaigning, the leaven of his humanity will be passed on to his young charges. The widespread lack of responsibility, about which there is so much

[1] Teachers can find some encouragement, and some clarification of the issues involved, in Peters, R. S., *Authority, Responsibility and Education* (Allen & Unwin), 1959.

W.P.E.—Z

complaint, may thus be dispersed. But no teacher can impart this sense of partnership and complementariness if he does not feel it. It is in early training that a new view must be cultivated. Hardly any teacher-training programmes in the world do much to foster this commitment in any global sense, partly because the majority of them have been devised to produce a lot of teachers (within a limited specification) quickly and cheaply.

Now that more time is being allowed for teacher training in many countries, and with a general attempt to up-grade the personal education of teachers, there is at last a real chance that teachers' preparation may be itself a humane study, objectively and subjectively. That is to say, teachers in training may have a chance to know the world in terms of 'the concept of mankind' (as Professor Robert Ulich puts it); and they may also realize themselves more fully in relation to their job. In this last connexion every teacher can recognize his commitment not as something petty and local (i.e. only in terms of teaching this subject to these children for specified purposes) but as a transcendent dedication. That is already mirrored in the selfless self-expression of a great musician, the self-submergence of the keen researcher, and the ambivalent love which parents feel for their children. Very many teachers feel this already. So far from being pious fantasy, this kind of commitment is the only way to satisfaction. It is one of the few things that will prevent the teacher from becoming hidebound.

A sense of vocation is something personal, and part of the character; but it can certainly be induced by college methods of acquainting the future teacher with his profession. In any case it needs reinforcement, and must be made richer by genuine insights. The mere study of foreign educational systems will do little; but an effective analysis of the type properly known as Comparative Education will do much. Even where that is not possible, at least the attempt should be made to present all problems affecting the teacher in a world perspective.

Comparative Education studies are not always as successful as they might be, because instructors overlook the fact that the students' requirements are not exactly the same as those of the comparative sociologist, professor, or other research worker.[1] As in all teaching, it is important here to communicate with the student in terms of (a) his own readiness, and (b) his prospects. Therefore the kind of book or presentation that is suitable for him is seldom the same as what will

---

[1] I have previously developed this theme in a somewhat different way in the *Comparative Education Review* (New York), June 1959.

satisfy the advanced researcher. Unfortunately, many Comparative Education textbooks are found almost unreadable by students for this reason. Furthermore, we have to take note of the fact that students in Education usually come from very many different backgrounds, and in different states of readiness. Yet their very lack of homogeneity can be a great gain in a class, particularly if they include in their number graduates (or specialists) in social history, sociology, psychology, geography, and history – or any other richly informative discipline showing how other people and cultures contribute to our understanding of man as a whole. Thus it is not proper for an introductory writer or speaker on Comparative Education to talk pedantically in terms of the detail of his subject; yet he can often assume (and elicit) a very mature level of personal approach on the part of his students. After all, they are forward-looking young men and women of proved intelligence, even if they are still factually weak in his special field.

Therefore, partly by presentation (in books or lectures or in other ways) and partly by evocation from the very important background of the students themselves, a sympathetic appreciation can be obtained of the *whole way of life* exemplified in some 'area study'. Thus, if a school system is being studied, it can and must be seen in context – not inertly or statically, but with a dramatic conviction of its dynamic ecology. Like people preparing for the diplomatic service or for a sales campaign, we shall be most successful if for the time being we can sink ourselves in sympathy and insight into the thing we are studying. We must have the *feel* of it.

For this reason, dispassionate and objective surveys may possibly be too clinical and remote, at any rate if taken alone. It is far better to begin with a vivid 'inside story'; or, if that cannot be achieved, there may be dramatic or 'situation' films or plays or novels, specially prepared or chosen to communicate the essence of a culture to outsiders like ourselves. Sometimes, of course, the use of a native for this purpose is admirable; but here there may be as great a problem of communication (verbal or ideological) as we ourselves encounter when tackling the survey alone. Well-prepared study tours are useful. From the average students' point of view no less than from that of the harassed lecturer, however, such auxiliary methods of communication must come second to a good, sympathetic account in a book. Yet not many books set themselves to 'get it all over'; and those that do are sometimes criticized for too facile characterization. Be that as it may, the first stage in any effective Comparative Education approach must be a genuine acquaintance with the total ecological or cultural situation in a country. Other comparisons or problem-studies are unreal without that.

This point can be illustrated easily. Let us take any of the topics dealt with in this book, like language or religion in relation to schools. It is quite clear that multilingualism in India is not really comparable with multilingualism in Switzerland. Nor is the position of the Gaelic language in Scotland altogether like that of the almost identical language in Ireland, though both countries retain it after being overrun or dominated by an English-speaking majority in the same small kingdom. The religious problems of schools in France are like those of Belgium in many respects; but though the nations are in immediate proximity their history and circumstances make the problems different. As we have already seen, the Roman Catholic Church (with a world-wide uniformity of doctrine and moral teaching) is in a different position in Spain, Italy, France, Holland, England, and the United States. We therefore expect and find that the faithful behave and react differently in each of these places. It is not really true to say that we are studying 'a problem' in many contexts; we are really studying *many contexts* in which a most important constituent factor keeps recurring, to different effect.

With this caveat, then, we can come to our second level of study in Comparative Education – that of 'problems'. The present book is partly an illustration of this approach, but not typically so; for here we have constantly come back to the living context in which problems present themselves and are solved. Problems seldom appear in isolation, of course. A problem or factor may seem recognizable (like a comprehensive school, or segregation, for example); but it practically never occurs neatly or alone. In each new context it seems to attract to itself a new configuration of concomitant problems or factors. Therefore we must be ever on guard against such deceptive words as 'examination system', 'selection', 'single-track' or 'multiple-track' secondary schooling, 'democracy in education', 'child-centred' versus 'subject-centred' curriculum, and the like.

All words tend to take on different shades of meaning according to their context; but the difference here is not one of meaning only. It is a matter of differently constructed *institutions* in differently structured *environments*. We may therefore be effectively talking about different things. Of course, it is the careful evaluation of contextual differences that enables us to get down to the essence of a recurring problem – and problems do repay penetrating examination. For example, the *Year*

Book of Education (Evans Bros, London, and World Book Company, Yonkers-on-Hudson) annually deals with a particular educational problem or factor from the points of view of contributors in many different countries. There have been surveys of economics, philosophy, higher education, the role of teachers, and many similar factors in education. Yet we must never forget that such reviews are useful only in enabling us to size up the practical problems of men and women when we are back at our fundamental task of studying living people in their daily contexts.

A third level of study in Comparative Education is one normally beyond the purview of the student or the ordinary teacher; yet he may well come to it in the further study of any item of education that particularly interests him. This is the level at which specialists such as economists, psychologists, philosophers, and students of comparative religion or social anthropology bring varied expertise to bear on a particular area study. This third level is in several ways different from our first. On the first level we had students or other readers *dramatically informing themselves* about cultural systems as novices; here we have much more senior scholars *bringing the insights of their discipline* and the analytical powers of their techniques into the study of an 'area' – either regional or notional. Thus a corporate and concerted inquiry in depth can be made into the features of a particular culture, much as United Nations technical advisers go in to lend their skills to a newly developing country. However, in exactly the same way as those visiting experts, the specialists invited to probe into our study with us must be well oriented in terms of the total picture there before they can offer any *significant* contribution. So though the third level is much higher than the first, academically speaking, it does not rule out the first. It presupposes it.

Who are these third-level people? They must of course include university and other specialists whose familiar factual knowledge, hypotheses, and methods can be matched against other scholars' facts, hypotheses, and methods in attempting to understand a local culture more deeply. They must also include any other person whose specialist insight enables him to make a similar contribution. In this last category we must often number the local teacher and administrator, be he a subject specialist or simply the local man with his ear closest to the ground. The teacher undertaking some in-service training, or seeking to acquire some higher qualification, may contribute much at this level if he is genuinely original and mature in his observations. Though interdisciplinary comparisons and cross-checking are indeed of great value in building up research information about a particular area or problem, they are not by themselves examples of Comparative Education. They are just building up inter-departmental communication. In the present fragmentation of knowledge, intercommunication in itself is highly valuable not only for the participating scholars themselves but for the rest of mankind. It is too seldom done, though some Americans (notably in the departments at Harvard University for Near Eastern and Far Eastern studies) and some similar British research teams have been outstandingly successful.

The full value of Comparative Education as a discipline in its own right is appreciated when we realize the three-fold role it can play in this partnership of communication. Firstly, it can contribute the very important, basic concept of a 'culture' as the nucleus of any area study – not just in the narrower anthropological sense but with proper attention paid to consciously formative institutions like any instruction, schools, or 'ways of life'. This is a research tool of as great importance as economics or political studies, which it overlaps though remaining quite distinct. Secondly, it can adduce relevant evidence from comparable situations in other cultures, to be measured against the phenomena being studied in the area under review; for cultural factors may differ from situation to situation though the economic or political factors may seem identical. Thirdly (and without claiming hegemony), it can act as a kind of ghostly direction-finder or pointer for some of the specialized academic disciplines themselves, which it can compare and evaluate in an inter-cultural perspective. It can thus help to assess their fluctuating contribution to the totality of human understanding.

The contribution of theology to man's understanding has varied with time and place; so have those of psychological schools, economic theory, and political experimentation. In all these varying analyses man has been trying to study himself, to study his own making of himself, and to devise better ways of constructing his future. This re-making of the future for human betterment is substantially an educator's exercise. Thus it is surely relevant to know and consider what educators and other specialists have done or thought in comparable circumstances elsewhere. That is to say, Comparative Education, without in any way presuming to tell other disciplines what they *should* do, can show what has been done and is done. It can also introduce comparisons which may acquaint scholars with factors possibly overlooked in their *own* environment or perception. This it can most effectively do, not by aspiring to overlordship (which would be ridiculous), but by being acknowledged as a contributory partner in the whole endeavour of science to build up a complete understanding of the phenomenon of man.

These then are the three levels at which Comparative Education may be said to work: (*a*) the communicative level; (*b*) the level of factorizing or analytical inquiry; and (*c*) the holistic or interpretative level on which the various endeavours of man to shape his own development are marshalled and assessed to provide an appropriate perspective for study. In every case we must always have our feet on the ground, with our observations rooted in the various cultures. These are the trial-grounds of philosophies and of all man's creative endeavours. Thus, though we find a different body of students, teachers, and researchers working at the various levels of our comparative study (with books, methods, and concerns appropriate to each aspect), we must never forget that our real interest is in people – not in an academic exercise.

When all is said and done, our aim is not simply to undertake an academic research, essential though that is to the process. It is to look beyond the process to our end objective – a truer perspective on mankind. Philosophy suggests certain theoretical objectives. Theology looks altogether beyond the human plane. Our own study is one which, within the limits of earthly pattern-making, can enable any culture to see more clearly certain short-term directives – to suit itself, but with the benefit of other people's experiences. By looking through their eyes at ourselves, sometimes, we can recognize not what we imagine we are but what we really are. If we do not get so far, we shall undoubtedly recognize our common humanity. The first step to sympathy must be through our commonly experienced problems. It awakens a sense of commitment to all the uplifting aspirations of humanity.

The essence of civilization is to see that everyone matters to me, as my every act matters to them. This is the basic communication the teacher has to make. In making it, he civilizes not only others but himself.

APPENDIX

'The Gentleman': the Evolution of an Ideal[1]

Like Hinduism and the established Church of England, the idea of the gentleman is so elastic that it has something in it for everybody, though a diminishing number seem able to accept the whole prescription. Indeed, now that social evolution has made it possible for hitherto remote classes of person to claim consideration as 'gentlemanly' in some respect, it seems profitable to clarify the whole concept by appraising it in its social and historical setting.

No matter whether we are thinking of the original article or its latter-day derivatives, the 'gentleman' ideal combines at least the following ingredients: the feudal knight, a servant (*Knecht*) as he himself is served; the Christian knight-errant, constrained by personal honour in subjection to a divine master, and giving aid to the unfortunate; the troubadour, with his romantic and unconsummated love-ideal;[2] the pilgrim, especially in Bunyan's[3] sense, but not excluding the self-righteous self-sufficiency of Robinson Crusoe;[4] the post-Renaissance humanist; and the 'civilized and civilizing' Conquistador. Formidable though this composite picture is, it still omits the most important feature of corporate loyalty to one's peer group.

The amalgamation of these ingredients has been the work of centuries, and emphasis has changed markedly from time to time. The educator most responsible for the present vigour of the gentleman ideal as a cultural force was Thomas Arnold, headmaster of Rugby from 1828 to 1842. He is often named as a great originator; but here we must be careful. Genius may show itself in a new constellation of insights (as in

---

[1] The following essay, reprinted from the *Year Book of Education* for 1961 by kind permission of Messrs Evans Bros, Ltd, London, shows how even within one country a characteristic educational ideal evolves to take on a different complexion and to serve a different public.

[2] See, especially, H. H. Gert and C. Wright Mills, *From Max Weber: Essays in Sociology* (London, Kegan Paul, 1948), p. 346.

[3] The reference is to *Pilgrim's Progress*, of course.

[4] For penetrating insights into Crusoe as an educational ideal, see Professor H. C. Barnard's brilliant essay, 'The Educational Influence of Robinson Crusoe', in *Researches and Studies* (University of Leeds, January 1959).

Comenius), or in a new statement of viable ideas (as in Locke); the genius of Arnold revealed itself only partly in these respects, and much more in that aspect of genius most appropriate to an industrializing society – the establishment of a production line. Under Arnold's influence, not only Rugby but other Public Schools were cleansed, Christianized, better administered, partly modernized – and *widely copied*.

The dreadful state of the Public Schools during the preceding forty years is indicated by riots, violence, and irreligion in several of them – especially Eton and Winchester, but not excluding Rugby itself.[1] When Arnold began as headmaster, the famous Public Schools of Charterhouse, Harrow, Shrewsbury, Westminster, and Winchester had fewer than 500 boys between them. Not only residential schools, but the ancient day grammar (Latin) schools were in low water, remaining so in some cases until the impetus started by Arnold overtook them by mid-century. Some of these, like newly founded Public Schools (of which the majority now date from the period immediately after Arnold), began to cater for a nation-wide clientèle instead of restricting themselves to teaching the Classics to local boys. Arnold helped to set a fashion, and provided the machinery to satisfy it.

In this he was undoubtedly helped by several social and economic events, which must be mentioned not only for their historical importance but also because they contributed substantially to the evolution of the gentleman ideal in the ensuing period. These included the amassing of wealth by industrial entrepreneurs (who became ambitious for their children), the improved status and prospects of merchants in an expanding economy, the growth of the railway system which made nation-wide travel to boarding schools so much easier, and the development of an empire calling for rulers. All these events prompted a demand for gentility in their sons by many people who could not have aspired to it themselves, and facilitated the acceptance by generations of lonely boys of Arnold's new corporate dedication to the 'Christian gentleman' ideal in the school chapel, in the unrelenting discipline of the classroom, and in the arduous exercises of the playing field. The English upper middle class had long been characterized by its absorptive capacity; now absorption became easier because the neophytes had been processed for assimilation. Thus they became isolated from the godless upper class, of which Montesquieu had complained, and from both the bourgeois domesticity of their parents and the sordid preoccupations of the

[1] H. C. Barnard, *A Short History of English Education* (London, U.L.P., 1947), p. 21.

manufacturing towns which had paid for their schooling. The isolation and specialized production of a new type of 'gentleman' as a standardized constituent part of the new industrialization served to make that type more widely acceptable than it otherwise could have been. It undoubtedly broke some threads of continuity with previous ideas about localized gentility, though it maintained others. It is extremely doubtful, however, if Arnold ever saw his work in this light.

Arnold's perhaps unconscious indebtedness to predecessors and contemporaries is usually overlooked. Most people recollect that Locke's recommendations in *Some Thoughts concerning Education* (1689) anticipate much of Arnold's practice, not least in his insistence on gentlemanly behaviour, religion, 'hardening', and 'respect and good will to all people' fostered by 'reiterated actions fashioned beforehand into the practice of what is fit and becoming'. Arnold's 'character' looks like Locke's 'self-development'. So we can go on; but Professor Ulich has pointed out[1] that J. Gailhard's *The Compleat Gentleman* anticipated Locke by some ten years, and compares many previous or contemporary prescriptions of the kind. Both Lord Chesterfield's *Letters to his Son* and Lord Shaftesbury's *Characteristics of Men, Manners, Opinions, Times* coincide to a large extent with the new Public School mould; and Cardinal Newman's splendid definition of a gentleman in *The Idea of a University* must undoubtedly have reflected ideals current long before the 1850s, when he wrote it. Integrity, confidence, co-operation combined with strength to act alone, respect for order, and a willingness to recognize goodness wherever found (though perhaps condescendingly) – these are the characteristics of the gentleman as discerned far beyond the confines of Arnold's *Sermons* or Rugby School. Indeed, one remarkable feature of Newman's writing is his acknowledgement that gentlemanliness can be found without religion:

> Not that he may not hold a religion too, in his own way, even when he is not a Christian. In that case his religion is one of imagination and sentiment; it is the embodiment of those ideas of the sublime, majestic, and beautiful without which there can be no large philosophy.[2]

Such comments could hardly be surprising to circles all too well aware that the eighteenth century not merely produced rationalist

[1] R. Ulich, *The Education of Nations* (Harvard University Press, 1961), p. 96.
[2] J. H. Newman, *The Idea of a University* (London, Longmans, 1923), p. 208; quoted by R. Ulich, op. cit., p. 102.

philosophers and saints but inspired humane manifestoes that seemed likely at one time to surpass in charity and responsibility the views currently held in religious circles; yet they are surprising, coming from such a devout churchman who identified, as Arnold did, the essence of goodness with the practice of religious observance. It was the example of these humanists, and the tolerance of people like Newman, that made possible at a later stage the wide diffusion of the gentleman idea through the extension of Public School opportunities to those who shared neither the Christian faith nor the social assumptions upon which Arnold's sensibilities were based.

In passing we should also note that many 'innovations' of a practical kind attributed to Arnold were also used long before him in other types of school. The prefect system was anticipated by Bishop Butler's 'preposters', and by the *decuriones* of all the Jesuit schools in Europe for two centuries and more. The inclusion of other subjects than the Classics had been begun in Continental colleges almost as long ago; and both the Central Schools of Revolutionary France and the 'dissenting academies' of England had curricula much more modern than anything envisaged in Public Schools until long after Arnold. The practice of ascribing every modernity or ingredient of gentility to him is now discountenanced as the 'Arnold myth'. What then was his contribution? As already stated, it lay largely in his systematization of school government and purpose. His idea of control included the treating of his sixth form as gentlemen, and the devolution of responsibility downwards through the supervision of dormitories and studies. Thus, personal responsibility was coached in a social setting – the small group and the school – the whole endeavour being permeated with a sense of salvation through a great unfolding of the Christian purpose.

The flaws of this concept are obvious. At the worst, the moral formula for virtue becomes simply 'good form' – as in the current jargon; goodness consists of approved behaviour in obedience to a group code; sensibility and taste can displace sensitivity and charity; love for order can become mere 'discipline', as in the army and the colonies of the day; character can become obtuse narrow-mindedness and inflexibility; loyalty to the group can become an unacknowledged conspiracy against others; 'leadership' may not acknowledge the complementariness of all endeavours, but may think of compatriots and foreigners alike as people to be ordered about for their own good because of the leader's special insight, derived from a schooling which is tacitly identified with 'breeding'.

Thus this expanding aristocracy is conceptually restricted. Admission is not by birth only, as in the olden days, but by passing through approved training closely identified with particular studies in particular types of institution and revealed by particular talismans, such as ways of speech and characteristic punctilio. Dedication to the corporate ethos and aesthetic value-system is promptly assessable along a whole profile of tokens which quasi-automatically reveal whether a man is a gentleman or otherwise. The strange feature is that this making a man of the world is so other-worldly – a circumstance in part attributable to the isolation of small boys from home in preparatory schools from the age of seven until thirteen or fourteen, when they go to the Public School for another five years. Home contact is confined to the artificial experiences of the holidays. There is little place for real acquaintance with mothers, no place for companionship with girls or women, and no real partnership with other types of boys or men beyond the condescension implicit in the feudal slogan *noblesse oblige*. When Shackleton was enduring the utmost rigours of the Arctic in desperate isolation from the rest of the world, his team's quarters and prerogatives were neatly divided into those of the gentlemen and the others; and that was in the twentieth century!

This other-worldliness has been cumulatively enhanced by an unexpected factor: the elevation of youths to the status of gentlemen by recruitment from the lower orders. On top of the isolation and 'weaning' already referred to, we have thus to reckon with the conscious or unconscious snobbery of the parvenu glad to have made the grade towards a promising future; for that was entailed. Until the late 1920s and early 1930s a surprisingly small number of the alumni of the Public Schools (themselves less than 2 per cent. of the population) went on to university; their school experiences were enough to get them a heavy preponderance of the most responsible jobs in the country and the empire. That is to say, they sufficed socially rather than academically or functionally. Still, the function of the gentleman is clearly to rule others and be exemplary, and the Public Schools were until very recently preoccupied with the production of ruling-class gentlemen (and latterly, ladies too).

One specially remarkable feature of the gentleman is that in the discharge of his functions he is very often surrounded by a sort of penumbra or limbo, much as the knight in pursuit of the Holy Grail penetrated forests filled with monsters and mysteries, or with people needing his protection. To take the latter group first, it seldom made much difference whether they were Indians, Africans, or fellow-citizens – provided they kept to 'their stations' and were tractable. Indeed, within the paternalistic ideology of the gentleman each plane or 'station' is treated with great respect; for there may be some semblance of gentility even down there. At any rate, there may be a responsiveness to gentility which could reflect it further. A little further on we shall consider the important consequences of this view; but just now it is important to consider those who definitely are not gentleman, even by reflection.

The opposite of the gentleman is the cad. The word 'cad' is defined by the *Concise Oxford Dictionary* in terms which repay quoting: 'Person of low manners; person guilty or capable of ungentlemanly conduct, blackguard . . .; member of lower classes; hanger-on employed about (esp. school and college) games; . . . started at Eton and Oxford as name for townsmen.' In other words, 'cad' was once simply a social category, i.e. all outsiders. It very soon took on a pejorative meaning, ascribing grossness to them; and finally it acquired the moral connotation of villainy. By the end of the nineteenth century a man who was not a gentleman might indeed be an honest workman, or perhaps a rising lad aspiring towards the example of his betters; but for most 'gentlemen' it must still have remained very dubious whether he could ever be one of them. Transgression of the social bounds was a trespass against order and good taste. This we see abundantly in the writings of Galsworthy (from 1906 onwards), who for that reason is a popular author in the U.S.S.R.; but the rot had already set in, as the writings of Shaw and other outsiders were beginning to show.

Quite apart from the spread of popular education and the expanded opportunities for advancement which industrial development had created, at least three factors in the gentleman's penumbra itself had challenged his monopoly of the decencies. These were women, his own servants, and games. Galsworthy's female characters seem unreal fantasies to many modern readers, yet long before his time the gentlemen who had refused their womenfolk a proper education had begun to recognize their complementariness to men, not only sexually but socially and intellectually (still an astonishing recognition in the England of the 1870s!). Women's behaviour could not be judged by the norms set for men, yet it could be adequate and sometimes meritorious. Moreover, as passion is not class conscious, even servants and chorus girls and others of the lower classes, who were no longer so easily obtainable extra-maritally, began to climb by marriage into the preserves of the gentry and acquit themselves creditably there. Furthermore, a growing desire among the upper classes both to limit family responsibilities and to enjoy the society (as distinct from the possession) of women led to the adoption of contraceptive practices and other 'licence' that would once have been appropriate only to 'bounders' and outsiders. Stranger still, a recognition grew that even good girls were often fascinated by cads and foreigners, and no man easily tolerates this sort of disadvantage. Therefore, in the telling intimacy of the home it became obvious that 'women' could be transformed into ladies by no more than marriage, while ladies themselves were real women after all. Thus the feminine interests of the gentlemanly penumbra, studiously ignored in public by Victorian respectability and Arnold's monastic prescription for gentlemanly virtue, crept back into elegant society, no longer as a *demi-monde* but as a partnership between man and woman. To acknowledge partnership as arising out of basic but complementary differences was nearly without precedent in the gentlemanly scheme of things; and, in so far as it denied the unique perfection of that prescription, it helped to weaken its power in other respects.

To make matters worse, the occupational opportunities made available by the systematization of public education in 1870, and by the growing opportunities for secondary and higher education (particularly following a nation-wide tax-supported provision in 1902), made it clear that a larger number of the population were potential gentlemen than had ever been suspected. Distinguished scholars from the ancient universities admitted to having found their match in working men under the university extension scheme since 1872. A future Archbishop of Canterbury, William Temple, had actually combined with radicals in 1903 in the Workers' Educational Association, with the eventual purpose of opening up even Oxford to working-class students. Brains and gentlemanliness were far from being synonymous, of course, but there might be some connexion. Indeed, before such subversive goings-on had disturbed the social system long hallowed in hymns and catechism, many kindly employers had recognized honourable qualities in their servants. 'A gentleman's gentleman' was no empty phrase, though it did preserve time-honoured etiquette. However, the growing intimacy with ordinary men as genuine men that began in the Boer War and developed with a rush during the 1914–18 war opened many eyes to the fallacy of gentlemanly monopolies. Leaving aside all such radical nonsense as Barrie's *The Admirable Crichton* in 1902 (which showed a butler as the true leader and hero when his employers were shipwrecked on a desert island), 'nature's gentlemen' were becoming almost commonplace instead of the rarity they were once assumed to be.

Though there was some closing of ranks against possible encroachments from below, these were, in fact, facilitated by three gentlemanly characteristics: Christian charity, paternalism based upon the idea that *noblesse oblige*, and a keen consciousness of the need for 'fair play' in an unequal contest. A combination of the first two caused Sir Robert Morant, architect of the 1902 Education Act, to shape the new tax-supported secondary schools, not according to the civic and technological trends of the times, but according to a more 'honourable' concept – that of the Public Schools and their 'liberal' education. Dignified philanthropy above met and tamed radical demands from below by showing the way to become a gentleman as well as educated (the two ideas must be kept quite distinct in England). Robert Baden-Powell sought and fostered the ideal of gentlemanly chivalry and honour in the Boy Scout movement, particularly in its culmination in the Rover Scouts. An honest concern for the underdog has caused selectors of many kinds to overlook imperfections in an interview and to patronize struggling merit. This is not social justice; but it has opened the way for many, and the graciousness of manner often encountered has charmed away the hostility of many potential destroyers. Huge social absorption of a whole hierarchy of gentlemen of varying degree has thus taken place.

Tolerance and the sense of justice formalized in the notion of 'fair play', and strongly associated with the young gentleman's Public School games, have welcomed latter-day newcomers to society or career success just as the squire of old played cricket with the villagers; but they must still heed the rules of the game, and the game rather than mere victory must win paramount regard. This aloof sense of amateur honour (reflected in the words 'Gentlemen v. Players') has undoubtedly inhibited purposefulness and businesslike activity in a great many fields – from war, through business, to the full exploitation of technological discoveries. In the past generation, however, the growing challenge from (tax-supported) grammar school boys has undoubtedly modified this outmoded aloofness. In the Public Schools the young gentleman now works extremely hard and with notable success, as competitive university awards show; and when he leaves school he goes as adventurously into a working life as the conventions of 'the Establishment' will let him – sometimes more so. The stiff upper lip and the 'stuffed shirt' are giving way to something more flexible, though the inner sense of gentlemanly integrity is cherished as strongly as ever.

The public grammar schools (selective secondary schools) and the less privileged schools of other kinds, for girls as well as boys, show abundant evidence of the abiding force of the gentleman ideal. Most parents and teachers, even if they wish for better opportunities in academic or social prospects, would like the influence of this ideal to be enhanced rather than diminished. Not only in the richly varied extra-curricular activities of the schools, but throughout the scholastic occasions of the day, the words or implications of Locke, Arnold, Newman, and many others are detectable as a leaven, though they are almost never referred to openly. Moreover, though the caricature of the inflexible and priggish Briton dressing for solitary dinner in the remotest jungle is either pathetic or ridiculous according to your fancy, there lives behind those trappings an honourable educational ideal – that of unwavering honour and responsibility, softened by humanity. Therefore, not only to produce an élite in the usual sense but to universalize these qualities, other school innovations (from emancipated India to the boarding schools of the U.S.S.R.) are now seeking to perpetuate some gentlemanly virtues without the academic paraphernalia and the social injustices which marred their cultivation in England.

Bibliography

Note: Reference is made throughout the text to books particularly useful for the points under discussion. At the end of most chapters a short list of books covers the special problems reviewed in them. The following bibliography is for general use, and is limited to works in English.

1. Standard works in Comparative Education:

   CRAMER, J. F., and BROWNE, G. S. *Contemporary Education*. New York, 1956.

   HANS, N. *Comparative Education*, London and New York, 1950.

   KANDEL, I. L. *The New Era in Education*, Boston, 1955.

   KING, E. J. *Other Schools and Ours*, New York and London, 1959 and 1960.

   MALLINSON, V. *An Introduction to the Study of Comparative Education*, London and New York, 1957.

   ULICH, R. *The Education of Nations*, Cambridge (Mass.), 1961.

2. For world-wide factors affecting education, there is no better guide than the *Year Book of Education* published by Evans Bros in London and the World Book Company at Yonkers-on-Hudson (New York) for the University of London Institute of Education and Teachers College, Columbia University. Each year's volume deals with a particular topic, illustrated with contributions having special relevance to individual countries. The issues from 1954 onwards are most valuable.

3. The *International Year Book of Education* (UNESCO) lists educational events and reforms throughout the world, and gives useful statistics.

4. The *Compulsory Education* series of publications by UNESCO is very informative about the somewhat restricted range of schooling required by law in various countries.

5. The *Studies in Compulsory Education* issued by the United States Department of Health, Education and Welfare give first-class information about particular regions and problems.

6. The UNESCO series on *Problems in Education* is an authoritative source of information and comment on many of the recurring issues, and on developments specially worthy of note.

7. The *International Review of Education* (UNESCO, Hamburg) and the *Comparative Education Review* (ed. G. Z. F. Bereday, Teachers College, Columbia University) provide topical information and comment on educational problems and methodology.

8. For particular countries, UNESCO reprints from the *World Survey of Education* a brief descriptive outline based upon the information and statistics supplied to it by the Ministries or education offices of member countries; e.g. *Education in Austria*, 1955. It should be borne in mind that not all governments are equally objective or self-critical in the publications thus produced.

For countries specially referred to in this book, the following general publications are suggested:

DENMARK

DIXON, W. *Education in Denmark*, London and Copenhagen, 1959.

ENGLAND AND WALES

ALEXANDER, W. P. *The Educational System in England and Wales*, London, 1959.
BARNARD, H. C. *A Short History of English Education*, London, 1947.
FLOUD, HALSEY and MARTIN. *Social Class and Educational Opportunity*, London, 1956.
LOWNDES, G. A. N. *The British Educational System*, London, 1955.

FRANCE

KOHN, H. *The Making of the Modern French Mind*, New York, 1955.
MILES, D. W. *Recent Reforms in French Secondary Education*, New York, 1953 (very good, but restricted in value by its date).

GERMANY

LINDGREN, A. *Germany revisited*, Washington, D.C., 1960.

INDIA

KABIR, H. *Education in the New India*, London, 1956.
PANIKKAR, K. M. *Hindu Society at the Crossroads*, Bombay, 1955.

JAPAN

ENWRIGHT, D. J. *The World of Dew*, London, 1961.

STOETZEL, J. *Without the Chrysanthemum and the Sword*, London and Paris, 1955.

PUERTO RICO

BRAMELD, T. *The Remaking of a Culture*, New York, 1959.

SWEDEN

Occasional publications of the Ministry of Education.

UNITED STATES OF AMERICA

BEREDAY, G. Z. F., and VOLPICELLI, L. (edd.). *Public Education in America*, New York, 1959.

KANDEL, I. L. *American Education in the Twentieth Century*, Cambridge (Mass.), 1957.

LERNER, M. *America as a Civilization*, New York, 1957.

THISTLETHWAITE, F. *The Great Experiment*, Cambridge, 1955.

WHYTE, W. H. *The Organization Man*, New York, 1957.

U.S.S.R.

BEREDAY, BRICKMAN and READ (edd.). *The Changing Soviet School*, Cambridge (Mass.), 1960.

BEREDAY, G. Z. F., and PENNAR, J. (edd.). *The Politics of Soviet Education*, New York, 1960.

COUNTS, G. S. *The Challenge of Soviet Education*, New York, 1957.

KOROL, A. G. *Soviet Education for Science and Technology*, New York and London, 1957.

SIMON, B. *Soviet Psychology*, London, 1960.

9. For the relationship of education to social and political change throughout the world, the following books may be referred to:

COTGROVE, S. F. *Technical Education and Social Change*, London, 1958.

EMERSON, R. *From Empire to Nation*, Cambridge (Mass.), 1960.

HOGGART, R. *The Uses of Literacy*, London, 1957.

MACRAE, D. G. *Ideology and Society*, London, 1961.

MANNHEIM, K. *Ideology and Utopia*, London, 1936.

MEAD, M. *Cultural Patterns and Technical Change*, Paris, 1955.

O.E.E.C. *Forecasting Manpower Needs for the Age of Science*, Paris, 1960.

ULICH, R. (ed.). *Education and Mankind*, Cambridge (Mass.), 1962.
VAIZEY, J. *The Economics of Education*, London, 1961.
WARD, B. *India and the West*, London, 1960.
WILLIAMS, R. *The Long Revolution*, London, 1961.
WILSON, B. *Sects and Society*, London, 1961.

Index

The outline on pages 5 ff. should also be used to locate topics broadly treated

ability, 59, 63
Abitur, 342–5
absolutes, 143, 192
accent, 69, 282–3
activity methods, 277
Admirable Crichton, 366
adult education, 198–9
advertising, 296
Africa, 12
agnostics, 206
Alexander the Great, 308
Algeria, 214
American revolutionaries, 267
American universities, 38, 95, 153, 173–5, 182–3, 195, 212–13
Americanization, 91
Amish, 253, 265
année propédeutique, 192, 193
apartheid, 332
apprentices, 176
Aquinas, 264, 267
Aristotle, 137, 138, 167, 262, 273
Arnold, Matthew, 349
Arnold, Thomas, 66, 360 ff.
Asia, 77–8, 89
Atatürk, 111
Australia, 81, 178, 219, 244, 250, 331
Austria, 44, 62, 68, 130
authorities, 37, 39
authority, 37
automation, 14
automatism, 100
Aztecs, 57

baccalauréat, 177, 192, 209
Bacon, 231
Barnard, H. C., 361, 362
Barrie, J. M., 366
beatniks, 103
Belgium, 130, 236, 245–6, 319
Beloe Committee, 128
Bentham, 65, 70, 185, 276
Berufsschule, 170
boredom, 131
Bourguiba, 111
bowdlerizing, 237
Brackenbury, R. L., 261
brainwashing, 113
Brazil, 122
'breeding', 363
Britain, 53, 55, 65, 70, 98, 109, 137, 140, 144, 153, 175–87, 196, 210–12, 221, 244–5, 271 ff., 275 ff., 288, 298–300, 312, 324, 342–3
Buddha, 204
Buddhism, 248, 265
Burma, 92
business administration, 181

cad, 365
Cambridge University, 66, 68, 177, 180
Canada, 217, 244, 250–1, 312, 313
careers, 80, 84, 129
Caribbean, 77
Cartesianism, 98, 268
catharsis, 113, 114
Catullus, 97

Central Schools (French), 363
centralization, 99, 248 ff.
certificates, 128, 300 (see also separate names)
Ceylon, 78, 92, 111, 248
character, 67, 134, 271, 274
China, 12, 14, 71, 85–7, 105, 258, 293 ff., 307, 347–8
Chinese (language), 315, 323–4
Christ, 204 ff.
Christianity, 106, 204, 234, 264 ff., 272, 361
church schools, 243 ff.
civilization, 56 ff., 72, 359
Clarke, K., 94
class distinctions, 137 ff., 215–16, 299, 311, 344
Classics, 62, 120, 188, 271, 274, 361
Cobbett, 139
college (U.S.), 153–4, 173 ff.
College Entrance Examination Board, 94, 196
college of advanced technology (U.K.), 175, 180, 192
college of commerce, 175
collège (see lycée)
collège d'enseignement technique, 124
colour discrimination, 328 ff.
Comenius, 361
commitment, 203, 239, 359
Common Market (European), 352
common school, 145 ff., 159
Commonwealth (British), 68
communism, 99, 103, 106, 165, 167, 247, 302 (see Marxism, U.S.S.R.)
Comparative Education, 15, 47, 173, 347, 354–9
comparison, 28, 68, 173
complementariness, 32 ff., 49, 140, 345
comprehensive school, 145 ff.
Conant, J. B., 143, 149
Condorcet, 134, 268
Congo, 106, 273, 320

continuation education, 172
contraception, 90
correspondence courses, 178
costs of education, 75, 84
counselling, 303
county colleges (U.K.), 172
cours complémentaires, 216
cours complémentaries industriels, 124
creativity, 311 ff.
Crowther, Sir G., 188
Crowther Report, 132, 150, 172, 196, 302, 305
Cuba, 108
culture, 53, 56, 64, 70, 72, 234, 358–9
culture conflicts, 97 ff., 107, 110–13
culture générale, 117
curriculum, 40
cynicism, 343
Cyprus, 297
Czechoslovakia, 161, 247

Darwinism, 238
dating, 296
decentralization, 99
delinquency, 131, 294 ff.
democracy, 69
Denmark, 71, 80, 132, 142, 192, 193, 243, 318
Descartes, 268 ff.
determinism, 235
Dewey, 102, 276–7
Diderot, 134, 268
differentials in pay, 216 ff.
Dioscurus, 38
Diploma in Technology (Dip. Tech.), 180
discipline, 363
'dissenting academies', 121, 363
doctorate, 193, 225
dormitories, 194 (see 'student hostels')
Drucker, P., 305
dual system, 244
Durham University, 185
Durkheim, 98

école normale, 220
ecology, 29
economic change, 39, 82
economic 'laws', 280
educability, 59
'eighteen-plus' pressure, 178
Einstein, 308
Eire, 243, 313
Eisenhower, President, 149
Eliot, T. S., 65
emotions, 262
empiricism, 274 ff.
employment of children, 76
English language, 58, 313, 316, 318
enhetsskola, 145
escape, 113, 114
Eton, 361
eugenics, 327
Europeanization, 106
examinations, 128, 137 ff., 153, 166, 178
excellence, 138
existentialism, 279
'external degrees', 183

family change, 89-91
films, 90, 355
Flemish, 319-20
Floud, J., 94
France, 44, 53, 62, 68, 81, 98, 117,
        126-8, 130, 142, 177, 178, 192,
        204-5, 209, 220-1, 237, 246,
        249-50, 268 ff., 272, 363
Franklin, 126
French Revolution, 188, 267
Freud, 232, 283
further education, 169 ff.
Further Education Staff College, 181
fusion of schools, 145, 227

Gaelic, 313
Gailhard, 362
Gal, R., 62, 127
Galsworthy, 365
games, 367

Gandhi, 92, 112, 314, 316
'gap between the generations', 135, 295
Garfield, J. A., 74
General Certificate of Education, 153,
        192
genius, 158, 303, 308
'gentleman' ideal, 66, 68, 117, 360 ff.
Germany, 72, 125, 130, 132, 142, 192,
        221, 242, 275, 324
Gewerbeschule, 172
Ghana, 106, 273, 318
ginnasio-liceo, 151
girls *passim*, and see 'women'
grading teachers, 219
graduate schools, 123
grammar school, 65, 129, 144, 155, 368
grandes écoles, 192, 195
'grass roots', 252-3
Greek liturgy, 313
Grundschule, 142
gymnasie, 146
Gymnasium, 63 ff., 70, 143

Hammarskjöld, D., 108
handvaerkerskole, 172
Hans, N., 241
Harding, D. W., 104
Harvard University, 177, 195, 222,
        241, 358
Hauka sect, 113
Hauptschule, 142
Hebrew, 313
Hegel, 97, 235, 280
high school (U.K.), 146; (U.S.),
        147 ff.
higher education, 169 ff.
Higher National Certificate, 181
Hindi, 314
Hinduism, 90-1, 112, 360 (see India)
Hindustani, 314
Hitler, 236, 280
Höhere Schule, 143, 193
Holland, 130, 132, 193, 243-4, 245, 318
Hong Kong, 293

Hopkins, Mark, 74
human relations, 64, 72, 125
humanism, 278 ff., 362-3
Husén, T., 93, 146

ideology, 123, 231 ff., 281 ff.
illiteracy, 170
'immediacy', 37, 68, 201
independence of schools, 98, 244 ff.,
    320 ff., 360 ff.
Index (of Holy Office), 238
India, 71, 76, 78, 82-84, 100, 139,
    158, 247, 307, 314-17
Indonesia, 92
Industrial Revolution, 11
industrialization passim, esp. 14, 36,
    70, 82, 85, 89, 91, 104, 117 ff.,
    133, 242, 282, 307, 336, 361-2
insecurity, 103
in-service training, 225-6
institutes (U.S.S.R.), 159
Institutes of Education (U.K.), 183-5,
    221
institutions, force of, 233 ff., 262
international university, 352
internationalism, 340, 350 ff.
interviews, 138
involvement, 23, 47-8, 125, 258, 263
    (see 'ideology')
Islam, 91, 112, 203, 265
Israel, 352
istituti professionali, 130, 151, 174
Italy, 44, 117, 130, 139, 150-2, 310,
    325

Jamaica, 80, 106-7
Japan, 71, 82, 87, 105, 139, 157, 242,
    293-5, 323-4, 348
Jefferson, 268, 270
Jeffreys, M. V. C., 263
Jesuits, 98, 204-6, 237 ff., 363
Johannesburg, 113
Jonesmanship, 288
Judges, A. V., 262

Juliet, 308
Jullien, M.-A., 349
junior high school, 143

Kandidat Nauk, 224-5
Kelsall, R. K., 54
Kennedy, President, 149
Kerschensteiner, 126
Khrushchev, N. S., 100, 160
King's College (London), 185
knightly ideal, 360
Komsomol, 165, 301, 302
Koran, 32, 91
Krupskaya, 161

labour, 133
'Labour Reserve' schools, 162
ladies, 39, 366
laisser-faire, 91
Langevin-Wallon reforms, 142
language problems, 312 ff.
Lapie Commission, 246
Latin America, 107, 122
Lauwerys, J. A., 358
'laws' of behaviour, &c., 280
leadership, 363, 364
Leeds University, 183
Leicestershire Plan, 143
length of schooling, 289 ff.
Lenin, 239
Leninism, 88 (see 'Marxism' and
    'U.S.S.R.')
Lernfreiheit, 189
liberal education, 117, 119, 132, 157, 367
licence, 193
liceo scientifico, 151
Lincoln, 74
Lister, 207
Livingstone, 32
Locke, 361-2
logical positivism, 279
London County Council, 146, 184, 252
London University, 175, 180, 183,
    185, 186

loneliness, 113–14
Lutherans, 313
Luxembourg, 352
lycée, 62 ff., 134
lycée technique, 174

Macaulay, 100
Maintenon, Mme de, 202
management, 180–1, 213–14
'managers', 255
Malaysia, 106
Manchester College of Technology, 182
Mannheim, K., 231 ff.
Maori, 335
marriage and education, 303–5
Marx, 123, 126, 232–4, 235, 257 ff.
Marxism, 88, 99, 159, 280–1, 341
    (see also 'communism' and 'U.S.S.R.')
Massachusetts Institute of Technology, 179
materialism, 91
mathematics, 62, 157, 166
measurement, 59
Mechanics' Institutes, 70
Meiji Restoration, 348
Meno (Plato's), 208, 267
mental health, 113–4
Mexico, 44, 214
'middle rank' occupations, 70, 125, 129–30
middle school, 130, 141 ff., 220
Mississippi, 239, 332
Mitford, N., 54
Mittelschule, 70
Montesquieu, 361
Morant, 367
Morris, Sir C., 266
Mozart, 308
multilingualism, 314, 321–2, 356
music, 62
Muslims, 314 (see 'Islam')
Mussolini, 236, 280

Mutesa, 32

Napoleon, 134, 187
nation, 325
national character, 326 ff.
National Association for the Advancement of Colored People, 334
National Defense Education Act (U.S.), 149
Natural Law, 267, 278, 283
Nehru, J., 314
New York, University of, 187
New Zealand, 219, 241, 242, 244, 335
Newman, Cardinal, 362
Nigeria, 106, 273, 274, 317
normal schools, 183
Norway, 72, 142, 319–20

Occam (William of Ockham), 274
Octobrists, 165
Olympiads, 165
orientation period, 142 ff.
orthodoxy, 240
Orwell, G., 139
out-groups, 310
Owen, Robert, 126
Oxford University, 66, 68, 138, 177, 180, 183

Pädagogische Akademie, 221
Paine, Thomas, 267
Pakistan, 89, 90, 92
Pali, 317
parental choice, 63, 216
parochialism, 338–9
partiality, 349–50
paternalism, 270 ff., 298, 311, 364–6
Paul, St, 204
Pavlov, 283
'pecking order', 55, 288, 297
pedagogical institutes (U.S.S.R.), 223
Pedley, R., 143
Persian, 314, 317
personality, 266

philanthropy, 273
Philippines, 106
philosophy, 206, 231 ff., 257 ff.
physics, 157
Pilgrims, 101–2
Pioneers, 165
Plato, 208, 237, 266 ff., 272, 280
Poland, 247
Polo, Marco, 57
polygamy, 111
polytechnicization, 161
'polyvalent' training, 152–3
Popper, K., 235
population problems, 214
Potter, S., 54
pragmatism, 276 ff.
prefects, 274, 363
press 14, 135, 338–9
Princeton University, 195
private schools, 215 (see also 'church schools', 'independence of schools', and 'Public School (U.K.)')
problem-study, 356
programmes, 257
Protestantism, 205–8, 241 ff.
psychologists, 140, 283
psychology, 257 ff.
Public School (U.K.), 65, 129, 134, 144, 155, 213, 270 ff., 274, 345, 360 ff.
Puerto Rico, 77, 79, 106
Puritanism, 266

Rabelais, 203
race theories, 311, 325 ff., 328 ff.
radio, 14, 135
Rahmenplan, 142
Ramadhan, 111
Ramus, 139
rationalism, 266, 362–3
Ray, S., 90
reality, sense of, 130
Realschule, 142

recognition, need for, 59, 113
refinement, 40
religion, 111, 310 (see 'Christianity', &c.)
Renaissance, 204–6
renunciation, 265
Republic (Plato's), 272
research, failure to exploit, 299, 367
resources, 69, 84 ff.
revelation, 263
Robinson Crusoe, 360
roles, 34, 36
Roman Catholicism, 205, 237–41, 246–7, 269 ff., 282, 356
Rouch, J., 113
Rugby, 360 ff.
Russell (Lord), B., 257–8, 262

Sadler, M., 349
St Andrews University, 184
sandwich courses, 123
Sanskrit, 317
Sargant, W., 295
Sargent, Sir J., 316
scholarships, 195–7, 298
scholiasm, 38
school and society, 41, 67, 79, 135, 292 ff., 347
school and university, 155–6
school boards, 252–4
school districts, 148, 215
schooling, 55
schooling as a problem, 289
Schreiber, D., 94
Scotland, 80, 85, 184, 243, 313
scripts, 315, 323–4
scuola d'avviamento, 151
scuola media, 151
secular schools, 247
selection, 137 ff., 161
self-exclusion, 61, 127, 310 ff., 343
S.E.N.A.I., 122
sexuality, 103, 289 ff., 305
Shaftesbury, Lord, 362

Sheffield University, 182
Singapore, 214, 323
sixth form, 153
slavery, 33, 329 ff.
social change, 39, 41, 74–5, 80, 87, 88–91, 93, 97, 107, 110–3, 171, 213, 216, 254–5, 287 ff.
socialization, 102, 145, 303
Socrates, 204, 208
South Africa, 76, 239, 265, 273, 330, 332 ff.
Spain, 139
'special relationship', 186
specialization, 153, 157
Staatsexamen, 193
Stalin, 158, 187, 188
standards, 54, 120, 345–6
state colleges, 182
status, 137, 288, 297 (see 'class distinctions' and 'pecking order')
student hostels (dormitories), 194
studentereksamen, 192
students, 79, 85, 193 ff.
Studienschule, 143
subcultures, 26, 104–5
subjects, 67, 68
supernaturalism, 263–6, 289
Sweden, 93, 142, 145, 146, 318
Switzerland, 306, 320–1
symbolic value of education, 288
system, 278

teacher shortage, 212–18
teacher-grading, 219
teachers, 42, 80, 83, 110, 135, 200 ff., 259 ff., 344, 349, 353
teachers' colleges, 182–3, 220–7, 259 ff., 354
teachers' registration, 249
teachers (unqualified), 209–10
teaching machines, 217
technical college (U.K.), 175 ff., 179 ff.
technicians, 124, 172

Technische Hochschule, 192
technological change, 70, 117 ff., 133 (see also 'industrialization')
tekhnikum, 158 ff., 172, 174, 197
television, 14, 135, 339
Temple, William, 366
ten-year school, 158
Tennessee, 238
Terence, 336
tests, 138, 140
Texas, 338
'Third Way', the, 236
'three-tier analysis', 48, 258
troubadour, 360
Tunisia, 111
Turkey, 72, 111
Turkish, 315
tutorial system, 67, 274

Ulich, R., 39, 77, 354
underdeveloped countries, 45, 254
understanding, 21 ff., 227, 233, 311, 337 ff., 342, 347 (see also 'ideology' and 'involvement')
unemployment of graduates, 139
UNESCO, 75, 77, 289, 303, 305, 340
Union of Soviet Socialist Republics (U.S.S.R.), 12, 14, 44, 53, 71, 72, 91, 100, 120, 124, 130, 131, 132–3, 134, 144, 158 ff., 189, 194–5, 197, 222 ff., 239–40, 247, 306, 321, 340, 351, 365, 368
United States of America (U.S.A.), 12, 38, 44, 71, 72, 91, 95, 101–5, 107, 109, 110, 120, 122, 130, 131, 132, 140, 144, 146–9, 153, 157, 173–5, 182, 185, 189, 195, 197, 212, 216, 242, 245, 252–3, 273, 275 ff., 288–9, 290, 303, 305–7, 311, 313, 330–5, 337 ff., 339–40, 351
United States Supreme Court, 62, 330
universals, 273

universities, 67, 71–2, 120, 122, 153 ff., 173 ff., 175, 181 ff., 274

universities, new, 175, 184, 186 ff.

university college, 175

University College (London), 185

university development, 183–7, 188–90, 196

University Extension Movement, 198

university graduates, 196, 210–11, 217

University Grants Committee (U.K.), 181, 188–9

University, International, 352

University of Friendship, 351

Urdu, 314

utilitarianism, 276, 278, 280

Vaizey, J., 75

value judgment, 23, 37

value of education, 288

villages, 80, 83

vocational linkage, 117 ff., 157–8, 170

Wales, 82, 85, 222, 313

Webb, Sidney, 186

Welsh language, 313

Wesley, 266

West Indies, 107

Winchester, 361

Wolsey, 139

women, 90, 303, 306, 335–6, 365–6

work experience, 132, 161 ff.

Workers' Educational Association, 198, 366

Yale University, 195, 222, 241

youth organizations, 300 ff., 343

youth problem, 131, 289 ff.

Yugoslavia, 72, 301

Zen Buddhism, 113, 294